The Rough

First-Time Africa

written and researched by

Jens Finke

with additional contributions by

Daniel Jacobs, Justina Hart and Yorick Brown

ROUGH
GUIDES

NEW YORK • LONDON • DELHI

www.roughguides.com

Contents

◄◄ Samburu dancers, Kenya ◄ On safari

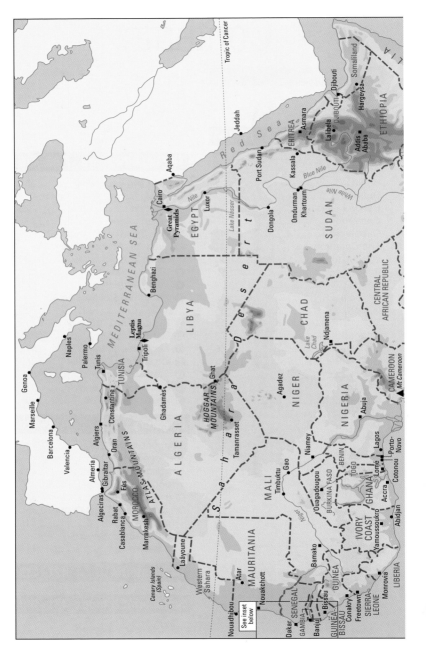

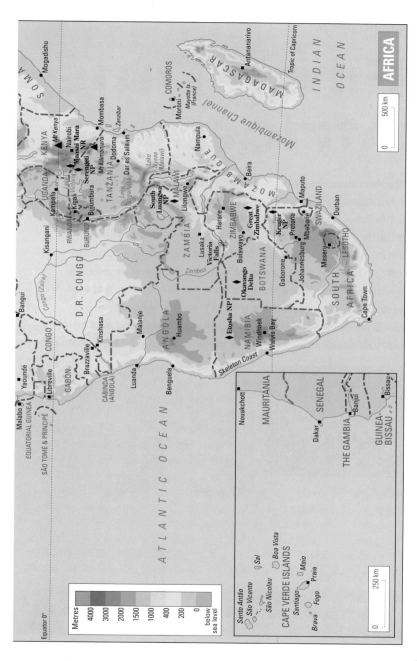

AFRICA

Equator 0°

Metres
4000
3000
2000
1500
1000
400
200
0
below
sea level

0 250 km

Santo Antão
São Vicente
São Nicolau
Sal
Boa Vista
Maio
Santiago
Praia
Brava
Fogo
CAPE VERDE ISLANDS

ATLANTIC OCEAN

Nouakchott
MAURITANIA
SENEGAL
Dakar
THE GAMBIA
Banjul
GUINEA-BISSAU
Bissau

SÃO TOMÉ & PRÍNCIPE
EQUATORIAL GUINEA
Malabo
Yaoundé
Libreville
Brazzaville
Kinshasa
GABON
CONGO
CABINDA (ANGOLA)
Luanda
Benguela
ANGOLA
Huambo
Malanje
D.R. CONGO
Kisangani
Bangui
Congo (Zaire)

Mogadishu
SOMALIA
Mt Kenya
Nairobi
KENYA
Mombasa
UGANDA
Kampala
RWANDA
Kigali
BURUNDI
Bujumbura
Lake Victoria
Serengeti NP
Maasai Mara NR
Mt Kilimanjaro
Zanzibar
Dar es Salaam
TANZANIA
Dodoma
Lake Tanganyika
Lake Nyasa (Malawi)
MALAWI
Lilongwe
South Luangwa NP
ZAMBIA
Lusaka
Zambezi
Victoria Falls
Okavango Delta
Etosha NP
NAMIBIA
Windhoek
Walvis Bay
Skeleton Coast
BOTSWANA
Gaborone
ZIMBABWE
Harare
Bulawayo
Great Zimbabwe
Kruger NP
Pretoria
Johannesburg
Mbabane
SWAZILAND
Maseru
LESOTHO
SOUTH AFRICA
Durban
Cape Town
Maputo
MOZAMBIQUE
Beira
Nampula
COMOROS
Moroni
Mayotte Is. (France)
Mozambique Channel
MADAGASCAR
Antananarivo
Tropic of Capricorn
INDIAN OCEAN

0 500 km

5

Introduction to

First-Time Africa

Mysterious, vast and blessed with an ineffable aura of adventure, Africa is the setting for many a holiday of a lifetime. In this most naturally diverse of continents, wildlife figures at the top of many tourists' agendas. You'll never forget your first heart-stopping encounter with a herd of elephants or a pride of lions, or seeing a glowering leopard up in a tree on the dusty, acacia-studded savannas south of the Sahara. Africa's other headliners are its often paradisiacal beaches, and the marvellously colourful coral worlds off many a coastline.

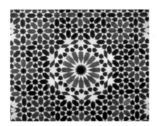

You could easily spend your entire holiday on a combination of beach and bush, but Africa's diversity stretches far beyond that. Scenically, you can look forward to lush equatorial rainforests harbouring mammals as yet unknown to science; alpine tundra and ice fields atop the continent's highest peaks, even on the equator; endless savannas and plains; swampy river deltas alive with birds; the world's hottest and largest desert. For a continent that's infamous for its lack of water, journeys along rivers and lakes provide some of Africa's most memorable experiences. A Nile cruise will transport you back in time to the realm of the Pharaohs; less glamorous, but no less rewarding, is a ferry ride along the River Niger into the heart of the desert – the most memorable (though not the most

All it really takes to get the most out of this fascinating continent is an open mind, and a free-ranging spirit

comfortable) way of reaching fabled Timbuktu.

Whether you'll be travelling in the lap of luxury, or muddling your way along using buses and local guesthouses, adventure will likely never be far away. You can go paddling among crocodiles and hippos, barrel down river rapids on an inflatable raft, or get your kicks on the end of a bungee rope over the Nile. In Togo, you'll get a kick of a different kind by sharing millet beer with the formidable market madames. For more challenging treats, tuck into deep-fried beetles in Zimbabwe, or brave the crunchy goo of Namibia's millipedes. In Central Africa, explore the Congo Basin's lush rainforests in the company of a Pygmy guide, and perhaps come face to face with gorillas or chimpanzees. In North Africa, history is a major attraction, whether you're an amateur Egyptologist anxious to explore pyramids for yourself, are crazy about Roman ruins, or are simply content to wander the labyrinthine souks and bazaars of millennial medinas in search of souvenirs or exquisitely decorated mosques. Whatever turns you on, Africa is likely to have it in plenty.

Although centuries of colonization – and ongoing globalization – have put paid to many traditional cultures, tribes remain an important factor in peoples' identities across Africa. The continent has literally thousands of different tribes or ethnic groups, each with their distinct cultures, musical traditions, oral heritage, and languages – some spoken by millions, others by only a

The cradle of mankind

An abundance of fossils, and recent genetic research, support the "Out of Africa" theory of human evolution, which postulates that our species arose in Africa. Much of what we know about mankind's evolutionary journey – from the first faltering steps of *Australopithecus* ("southern ape") some four and a half million years ago, to the first tools shaped by *Homo habilis* ("handy man") three million

▲ Paleontological dig, Ethiopia

years ago, through *Homo erectus* ("upright man") and *Homo sapiens* ("knowledgeable man") to ourselves, *Homo sapiens sapiens* – comes from the study of fossilized bones and skulls unearthed in Africa's Great Rift Valley. New finds continue to be announced, each one throwing previously cherished theories into disarray. The only thing that's certain is that paleontologists have only begun to uncover this epic story.

Of course, paleontological sites can be as dry as the bones they reveal, but that's not something that should put you off visiting: even if there's nothing much to see *in situ* (the most celebrated finds are safely housed in museums), the fittingly prehistoric aura of many fossil-rich sites such as Kenya's Lake Turkana and Ethiopia's Omo River valley (both exceedingly remote, and featuring volcanoes, crocodile-infested waters and impenetrable swamps as decoration) are well worth the rigours of a journey.

▷ Bab Boujeloud, Fes, Morocco

handful of elders. The most famous tribes have become tourist attractions: the Sahara's nomadic Tuareg (better known as "the Blue Men"), the cliff-dwelling Dogon of Mali, the red-robed Maasai and Samburu of East Africa, the Pygmies of Central Africa, and the San (or Bushmen) and the Zulu, both in Southern Africa.

In spite of the hassle you're likely to face from hustlers and touts in the more popular tourist destinations, by and large you'll find Africans are an amazingly welcoming, hospitable and generous bunch. It's all the more amazing when you consider that almost half of Africa's population lives on less than a dollar a day – the UN's laughably derisory "poverty line". A good way of getting on down with the locals is during festivals, some of which have roots stretching way back into the mists of time. Tribal encounters feature in many a tour operators' offerings, too, and if well managed can be a major boon to local economies, even a source of pride.

Giant groundsel

A first trip to Africa can be a daunting prospect, but there's little to be worried about. Every year thousands of travellers set off to explore Africa independently, and return with wonderful memories and often a desire to go back for more. All it really takes to get the most out of this fascinating continent is an open mind, and a free-ranging spirit. With common sense, safety is a non-issue, as is – barring the occasional upset stomach – health, as long as you've had any recommended jabs and started your anti-malarials, where needed. The business of travelling around on public transport is also simple enough, albeit often slow and perhaps uncomfortable. Food and accommodation are easy to sort out, too, and in the more popular destinations, whether on the beach, in the bush or in venerable old towns, you can find estab-

Felucca on the Nile

lishments to rival the world's classiest. If you're concerned about travelling with children, don't be. Package tours are an obvious choice for families, but independent travel is perfectly feasible: just be a little less

Mancala games

Mancala, a board game also known as *bao*, *awalé*, *oware* and by a host of other local names, can be seen being played in many parts of sub-Saharan Africa, often by market traders passing the time. The game features in many African fables as a test of which of the animals in the story is

▲ Playing *bao*, Zanzibar

the cleverest (you can bank on the hare for this role – whether or not he ends up cheating).

At its simplest, the board has two rows of six holes, and you can play without even having a board: a series of holes scratched into the earth and a handful of stones, beans or seeds are all that's needed. The rules vary widely, but the basic idea is that players take turns in distributing seeds from one of the holes on the row closest to them into adjacent holes, clockwise or anticlockwise, one seed per hole. The objective is always to clear the opponent's inner row by capturing his seeds. The element of skill lies in deciding which of your seeds to move to achieve this most effectively. The permutations involved are mind-boggling, and as with chess, the best players ruminate over many of lines of play at each move.

Like chess, mancala has ancient roots: wooden mancala boards survive from the sixth century, and there are much older "boards" etched into rocks at various Stone Age archeological sites. Modern game boards can be works of art, and make great souvenirs.

ambitious in the number of things you want to see and do, keep travelling times short, and ensure that children are adequately protected against bugs and sunshine. Besides, kids make friends easily, and as they'll frequently be the focus of attention, you'll find that you make friends more easily, too.

We can't guarantee that this book will help you avoid every potential problem as you travel around Africa, but it should certainly encourage and perhaps even inspire you. In any case, it's worth remembering that sometimes the best things in life are completely unexpected.

Whatever turns you on, Africa is likely to have it in plenty

25

reasons to go

It's not possible to see everything that Africa has to offer in one visit, or even in a lifetime. What follows, in no particular order, is a selective sample of the continent's highlights, from outstanding scenery and classic adventures to wildlife and cultural encounters, arranged in five colour-coded categories.

01 **Festivals and celebrations** Get initiated into voodoo in Benin, join a Tuareg get-together on the Sahara's fringes, admire a regal regatta in Zambia ... it's always worth coinciding with local shindigs.

02 Mountain climbing
Kilimanjaro's ice cap, rising almost 6000m above sea level, can be scaled in a week without specialist mountaineering skills. Other towering challenges include mounts Kenya, Cameroon and Toubkal (the last in Morocco), and Ethiopia's Ras Deshen.

04 The Atlas Mountains
North Africa's mighty Atlas – where the Greek god bore the heavens on his shoulders – is full of surprises, from medieval fortified villages to Africa's best skiing.

03 The Sahara An elemental land, eternal and magical; visiting can be a life-changing experience, whether you're in an air-conditioned four-wheel drive, or camel trekking in the company of Tuareg.

06 The great migration
The Serengeti's grasslands are the theatre for a never-ending cyclical migration of millions of wildebeests, zebras and antelopes. The event is most spectacular at Kenya's River Mara, where lions and crocodiles bring down the unwary amid gruesome scenes of carnage.

05 Africa's Great Lakes
Lakes Victoria, Nyasa (Malawi), Albert and Tanganyika were targets for many a nineteenth-century explorer eager to discover the source of the Nile. Visit today for ferry rides and some fascinating cultures.

07 The Great Rift Valley
The world's longest tectonic fault, stretching from Lebanon to Mozambique, is at its most dizzying and spectacular in Ethiopia.

09 Chimps and gorillas Come face to face with your distant cousins in Rwanda, Uganda, Tanzania, Gabon or Cameroon.

11 West Africa's mosques
In medieval times, the West African terminuses of the trans-Saharan caravan routes were a string of towns along the River Niger. Entrancing reminders from that time are dozens of wonderful earthen mosques, especially in Mali, which are lovingly replastered year upon year.

08 Scuba-diving and snorkelling Grab some snorkelling gear or take a scuba-diving course, and explore the immaculate coral reefs and atolls of the Red Sea, the Indian Ocean, or the Atlantic off West Africa.

10 The legacy of slavery
The slave trade existed for thousands of years in Africa, most profitably across the Sahara, but it was Europeans and Arabs who raised the trade to new heights – and depths. Zanzibar is full of relics of the East African slave trade; in West Africa, Senegal's Gorée Island and Ghana's coastal forts are incongruously attractive reminders.

12 The Namib Southwestern Africa's Atlantic coastline is flanked by the Namib desert, where you can poke around shipwrecks, visit a seal colony or gawp at towering dunes.

13 Ethiopia's churches

Ethiopia boasts some amazing churches and monasteries carved out of the rock, most famously at Lalibela, which serve as focal points for pilgrims and tourists alike.

14 Music Africa's arts are booming, none more so than music. Whether it's traditional genres or the latest in urban rap, you're sure to find something to shake those hips to.

15 Empires of the monsoon

The Swahili people grew wealthy on the back of the dhow trade across the Indian Ocean, as is clear from the ruined towns and palaces along the coastline between Somalia and Mozambique, and from Zanzibar's enchanting capital, Stone Town.

16 The land of the Pharaohs Cutting through the sterile deserts of northeastern African is the Nile, whose fertility breathed life into the ancient empires of Egypt and Sudan. Egypt's Pharaonic treasures need no introduction; Sudan's remains are almost as impressive.

ACTIVITIES | CONSUME | EVENTS | NATURE | SIGHTS

17 The River Niger The contrast between West Africa's longest river, which loops through the Sahara before ducking back down into the tropics, and the desert is an extraordinary one, as is travelling the river in winter by ferry or wooden *pinasse*.

18 Going on safari For most visitors to sub-Saharan Africa, wildlife safaris in search of elephants and lions, giraffes, crocodiles and hippos, and great dusty herds of antelopes, are de rigueur. There are hundreds of national parks and wildlife reserves to choose from.

19 Rock art Among mankind's earliest works of art are the enigmatic paintings and engravings adorning rock shelters right across Africa. Particularly rewarding areas are the Sahara's Tassili N'Ajjer Plateau, Tanzania's Irangi Hills, and parts of Namibia, Lesotho and South Africa.

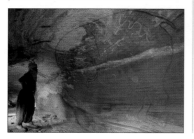

20 Victoria Falls The sheer power of the crashing Victoria Falls, on the Zambezi between Zambia and Zimbabwe, will leave you awestruck. There's a wealth of adventure sports to indulge in, too, from rafting to bungee jumping.

21 **Beaches** There's nothing like a bit of sand, a few swaying palm trees and a shimmering expanse of turquoise to help you unwind – you'll find blissful beaches all around the continent.

22 **Dogon country** Among West Africa's most traditional people are Mali's Dogon, who managed to protect their culture, and themselves, from armies and empires by building their villages halfway up cliffs. Explore the region on foot, and don't miss a traditional masked dance.

23 **Pony-trekking in Lesotho** Saddle up and ride off into them thar hills the way the locals do; the spectacular mountain scenery in this tiny southern African kingdom is reward in itself.

25 **People and cultures** For all its natural riches and historical and architectural wonders, the best thing about Africa is its people; the warmth of the welcome you'll be accorded speaks volumes about what the "developed" world has lost en route to prosperity.

24 **Bird-watching** Twitchers will get into a happy flap about Africa's birds: most countries have hundreds of species, many unique to particular mountains or forests.

| ACTIVITIES | CONSUME | EVENTS | NATURE | SIGHTS

First-Time Africa

Where to go

Algeria

Area 2,381,741 square kilometres
Capital Algiers
Population 34 million; mostly mixed Berber/Arab; Kabylie Berbers east of Algiers; Tuareg in the Sahara
Language Arabic or Berber dialects; urban Algerians often fluent in French

Religion Islam
Climate Mediterranean in the north, desert elsewhere; hot and dusty Simoom wind Feb–April
Best time to go April–Sept for the north; Oct–April for the Sahara
Currency Algerian dinar
Minimum costs $35/£19 per day

The history of Africa's second-largest country is one scarred by violence. Independence from France was only gained after a brutal war that claimed over a million lives. A fundamentalist insurgency in the 1990s killed another 150,000 people. The insurgency has now ended, but sporadic attacks on vehicles still occur in the north. Standard advice is to steer clear of the Kabylie Mountains and parts of Algiers; consult official travel advisories (p.418) for the latest. Travelling independently is possible but you may not be allowed access to certain regions without joining a group or convoy, and indeed most visitors come on organized tours.

In northern Algeria, the main attractions tend to blend a heady dose of history with verdant mountain scenery. The Sahara, untouched by the insurgency, provides more compelling reasons to visit, not the least of them being the adventure of travelling in such a vast and forbidding wilderness.

Main attractions

● **El-Oued and the Grand Erg Oriental** If it's dunes you're after, look no further than the Grand Erg Oriental – the Sahara's second largest dune field. On its northern fringes is the picturesque and bustling oasis town of El-Oued ("the

Average temperature ranges and rainfall

	Jan	Feb	Mar	Apr	May	Jun	Jul	Aug	Sep	Oct	Nov	Dec
Algiers												
Max °C	17	17	19	20	24	27	31	31	29	25	21	17
Min °C	6	6	7	9	12	16	19	19	17	14	10	7
Rainfall mm	80	82	73	61	40	17	5	7	34	76	96	115
Tamanrasset												
Max °C	19	21	25	30	33	35	35	34	32	29	25	21
Min °C	3	5	8	13	17	21	21	21	18	15	10	6
Rainfall mm	1	1	3	2	6	4	5	6	8	3	2	2

River"), well placed for travellers coming in from Tunisia. Almost as big a draw as the dunes is El-Oued's distinctive domed architecture – beautifully soft and rounded adobe forms.

● **The Hoggar Mountains** The Hoggar is an ancient and dramatic volcanic range deep in the heart of the Sahara. Peaking at almost 3000m, the mountains are home to Tuareg and the descendants of West African slaves, and enjoy a pleasantly mild climate by Saharan standards. The mountains are singularly photogenic, too: jagged brown and yellow peaks, eroded cliffs, and pink, blue or black basalt plugs. Scattered around are beautiful oasis villages, waterfalls, and prehistoric rock paintings. The starting point for explorations is Tamanrasset.

● **Tassili N'Ajjer** The Sahara's wild "Plateau of Chasms" harbours the world's finest and most extensive array of prehistoric rock art, scattered in and around a maze of gorges and ravines. The oldest paintings and engravings date back over 8000 years. Motifs cover all aspects of daily life: hunting, dancing, even horse-drawn chariots, and together with numerous depictions of animals long since gone, serve as reminders of the green land that Sahara once was – as indeed do the plateau's isolated cypress trees, some of them 2000 years old.

● **Numidian mausoleums** Algeria's most impressive monuments are a couple of conical pyramids: Kbour-er-Roumia near Algiers, and Medracen close to Constantine. Pre-dating Christianity, they consist of enormous stone mounds girdled by Ionic columns. Legend has it that Kbour-er-Roumia was the resting place of Queen Cleopatra, daughter of Egypt's Cleopatra.

Also recommended

● **Algiers** Much of Algeria's capital was destroyed during the conquest by the French, who replaced it with a broad European-style city. What remains of the old medina is a no-go area for tourists, so apart from lovely Mediterranean views (especially from the sixteenth-century kasbah crowning the hill behind the city), the attractions boil down to some well-conceived museums.

● **Constantine** Algeria's oldest continuously-inhabited city is capital of a pretty agricultural region in the east. The main sights are the picturesque streets of the Kasbah, the thirteenth-century Djemaa el-Kebir mosque, and the beautiful Ahmed Bey Palace, but it's as a base for exploring the region's historical attractions that the city is ideal.

● **The dolmens of Roknia** Close to Constantine, the fields of Roknia are home to several thousand Neolithic dolmens (burial chambers), one of archeology's biggest enigmas. The mystery is that they're identical in every respect to dolmens found in western Europe, raising questions about prehistoric ties between the continents.

● **Djemila** Exceptionally well-preserved ruins of a hillside Roman town, complete with a lovable little museum stuffed with mosaics, statues and other treasures.

● **Hippo Regius** The ancient Numidian city of Hippo Regius in the northeast was an early centre of Christianity under St Augustine. Its baths and forum are in good condition, and there are mosaics in a small museum.

● **Oran** Birthplace of Albert Camus and of Algeria's catchy raï pop music, this Mediterranean port has long been a bastion of liberalism. The Andalusian connection is evident in the fine arabesques that adorn many a building. There's also an oppressive Spanish castle, a good museum, and fine beaches away from the centre.

Routes in and out

The main airport is Algiers. There are passenger ferries from Spain (Almería to Ghazaouet, Alicante to Oran, Barcelona to Algeria and Oran), and France (Marseille to Algiers and Oran). The Moroccan border is closed to travellers, and crossing from Ghat in Libya may be impossible thanks to bureaucracy. There's road transport from Tunisia. For information on the safest trans-Saharan routes, see Ⓦ www.sahara-overland.com.

Algeria online

Algerian National Tourism Office
Ⓦ www.algeriantourism.com
Adventures of Algeria
Ⓦ www.lexicorient.com/algeria
Useful site-by-site coverage of the main attractions.
Tassili N'Ajjer
Ⓦ www.fjexpeditions.com/tassili.html
Intelligent accounts of the region and its rock art, with photos, travel advice, and virtual tours.

Raï – Rebel Music from Algeria
Ⓦ www.jeddy.org/borderless/rai An introduction to the music genre that conquered North Africa. Has audio clips.

Books

Mohammed Dib *Simorgh*. The last of the Algerian writer-in-exile's works, this is a pleasing jumble of styles and themes, anecdotes, essays and poems, and provides an entertaining introduction to the author's prolific output. There are also good English translations of *Savage Night* and *Who Remembers the Sea* – a harrowing description of the war of independence.
Jeremy Keenan *The Tuareg: People of Ahaggar*. Written in the 1960s, this book – part travelogue, part ethnography – remains the definitive English-language work on the Tuareg.
Ahlam Mosteghanemi *Memory in the Flesh*. Published in 1993, this was the first Arabic novel written by an Algerian woman. Mosteghanemi's works – which include the sequels *Chaos of the Senses* and *Passer by a Bed* – are ostensively love affairs, but in reality are dominated by the bitterness of contemporary Algeria's unrealized dreams.

Angola

Area 1,246,700 square kilometres
Capital Luanda
Population 17 million; over forty
ethnic groups, main ones being
Ovimbundu, Kimbundu and
Bakongo
Language Portuguese (official)
spoken by ninety percent; many
Bantu languages also spoken
Religion Christianity 70 percent,
traditional beliefs 30 percent
Climate Tropical in the north, semi-
arid and cooler in the south; rains in
the north Nov–April, scattered rains
in south March–July & Oct–Nov
Best time to go May–Oct for the
north; Dec–Feb south
Currency New Kwanza
Minimum costs $40/£22 per day

History has toyed cruelly with Angola, a land rich in oil, diamonds and other natural resources. Its war for independence lasted from 1960 until 1974, and the subsequent departure of 700,000 Portuguese colonists crippled the economy, which ended up being completely trashed by twenty-five years of civil war, in which UNITA rebels, backed by the United States, fought the left-wing government who had the support of the Eastern Bloc and – on the ground – Cuban troops. The death of UNITA's leader, Jonas Savimbi, in 2002 brought the war to an instant end. It had claimed almost 1.5 million lives. The war's devastating impact is visible wherever you go: walls riddled with bullet holes, amputees, rusty tanks, and wildlife parks emptied by the bellies of hungry soldiers and rebels. The majority of Angolans remain desperately poor, but the mood is definitely upbeat, as is the nightlife, and the reappearance of tourists – rare as they are – is confirmation that things are finally returning to normal.

The terrain ranges from tropical rainforest in the north (part of the Congo Basin) and desert dunes in the south to plunging mountains laced with waterfalls rising up behind some wonderful beaches. The main attractions are in the western half of the country, which is also the most populated region. Travelling around is safe so long as you don't stray off roads without a guide, as there are land mines all over the place. The main

Average temperature ranges and rainfall

	Jan	Feb	Mar	Apr	May	Jun	Jul	Aug	Sep	Oct	Nov	Dec
Luanda												
Max °C	30	31	31	30	29	26	24	24	25	27	28	29
Min °C	24	25	25	24	23	20	19	19	20	22	23	23
Rainfall mm	25	36	76	117	13	0	0	0	3	5	28	20

downside in fact is the scarcity of decent accommodation: even the most basic fleapit hotel can be painfully expensive, so consider bringing a tent.

Main attractions

● **Luanda** Angola's bayside capital is a seductive city. Founded in 1575, it became a major slaving port, and later the colony's cosmopolitan heart. Nowadays, its multicultural nature is best experienced through its excellent nightlife. There are good beaches on all sides, with watersports too, and plenty to please more genteel tastes: a museum for anthropology and traditional art, another – south of the city – on slavery, and military displays in the fortress of São Miguel. There are also innumerable Renaissance churches, and a hugely elegant two-storey building dubbed the "Iron Palace", designed by Eiffel.

● **Giant sable antelopes** Malanje town gives access to Cangandala National Park and the vast Luando Special Reserve, both home to the unique, and endangered, Palanca Negra – otherwise known as the Angolan giant sable antelope.

● **Kissama (Quiçama) National Park** Easily reached from Luanda, this park is the best prepared for tourism. A variety of habitats, from floodplains and savanna to baobab-studded shores, make it ideal for wildlife, and though animal densities are still low, the park has been partially restocked with elephants. Other inhabitants include roan antelopes, eland, bushbuck and waterbuck, and turtles on the beach.

● **Namibe** A pleasant coastal town little touched by the war, Namibe has colonial churches, two fortresses and surprisingly good nightlife. The beaches are good, too, although the Atlantic this far south is cold. Climb the hill behind for a spot of whale watching (in winter), or venture into the adjacent Reserva de Namibe for terrestrial wildlife.

● **Iona National Park** On the Namibian border, this vast wilderness has been targeted for tourist development. The current status of its wildlife populations is uncertain – before the war, it contained Angola's biggest variety of antelopes, together with mountain zebra, lions, elephants and leopards. The area is quite beautiful, too, ranging from coastal dunes to rugged mountains in the east.

Also recommended

● **Benguela** Angola's second biggest city boasts the ornate Baroque church of Nossa Senhora do Pópulo, and nice beaches nearby.

● **The Benguela Railway** Work is underway to rehabilitate the full length of this classic railway, from Zambia to the Angolan coastline. Once work is completed, trains will probably be diesel-powered; for now, you can catch the steam train from Benguela to Huambo.

● **Pungo Andongo** This village west of Malanje has two strange sights: black boulders scattered across an otherwise bare plain, and a stone "footprint" said to have been left by the warrior Queen Gingo, who allied with the Dutch to resist Portuguese occupation in the 1630s.

● **Bibala** Whether or not the waters of this spa really do possess therapeutic powers, the views of the Tundavala Gorge will both soothe and stimulate.

Festivals

The war destroyed many things, culture among them, although a few festivities have survived.

Carnaval Luanda; see p.243 for dates
A three-day riot of gaudy costumes, infectious music, drumming and *semba* dancers.

Festival of Kianda Bengo Province; July 26–27 The coastal people either side of Luanda traditionally believed in an ocean spirit or mermaid called Kianda. Through *semba* dancing and offerings of food and clothes, Kianda is asked to provide them with abundant catches of fish.

Routes in and out

The main airport is at Luanda. Coming by bus or taxi, you'll have to change at the border. Access is easiest from Namibia; the border with Congo is prone to closure depending on the political situation in that country. The Benguela Railway from Zambia may soon reopen.

Angola online

Angola Tourist Guide
Ⓦ**www.eltangola.com/turismo** The best visitor's guide.

Casa de Angola
Ⓦ**www.casadeangola.org**
Comprehensive showcase for contemporary arts. The text is in Portuguese, but there's plenty of stuff to look at.

Kissama Foundation
Ⓦ**www.kissama.org** Information about various national parks, and efforts to restock them.

Books

José Eduardo Agualusa *The Book of Chameleons*. In this wonderful novel – firmly in the country's magical-realist tradition – a gecko narrates the life of an albino businessman who sells personalized genealogies to his clients.

Pedro Rosa Mendes *Bay of Tigers: An Odyssey Through War-Torn Angola*. Ostensibly a travelogue, this is in fact dreamy suffusion of anecdotes, real or imagined, in which the Bay of Tigers remains forever a chimera, out of bounds thanks to the war.

Adebayo O. Oyebade *Culture and Customs of Angola*. A sweep across over one hundred ethic groups, in whose contemporary culture the war inevitably figures prominently.

Mayombe Pepetela *The Return of the Water Spirit*. A magical-realist novel tracing the decay of the elite's socialist ideals after independence, interwoven with the tale of a slave beheaded three hundred years earlier.

Benin

Area 112,622 square kilometres
Capital Porto Novo (official),
Cotonou (administrative)
Population 8.8 million; 42 ethnic
groups, the main ones being Fon,
Adja and Yoruba (south), Bariba and
Somba (north)
Language French spoken by most;
the most important local languages
are Fon and Yoruba

Religion Vodun 60 percent,
Christianity 25 percent, Islam 15
percent
Climate Tropical in the south, semi-
arid in the north; harmattan wind in
north from Dec–March
Best time to go Nov–Feb; Dec–
May for the Pendjari National Park
Currency CFA franc
Minimum costs $15/£8 per day

Shoehorned into a narrow corridor between Togo and Nigeria, Benin is among West Africa's most evocative destinations. While it has good beaches and a wildlife park worth visiting, the real attractions are cultural. As the heart of the "Slave Coast", Benin – or Dahomey as it was known – was an integral part of the trans-atlantic slave trade. The trade, which began in earnest in the seventeenth century, coincided with the birth of the kingdom of Abomey (later Dahomey), whose ceaseless expansion provided plentiful prisoners to sell into slavery in exchange for firearms. The turmoil of those times sped the expansion of a remarkable syncretic religion, Vodun, which on the other side of the Atlantic became Voodoo.

After French rule, Benin endured a succession of military regimes to become the democracy it is now. For travellers, it's an easy place to get to know quickly, and most enjoyable it is too. Apart from slave-related sights and Vodun fetishes, temples, priests and celebrations, the country has unforgettable markets and, if you're so inclined, you could even fix up an audience with a traditional king. In terms of landscapes, Benin has most of what the region has to offer, from swampy lagoons and golden beaches to forested hills and dusty savanna. Mix it up with a famously welcoming bunch of people, and it's difficult to understand how the country has managed to evade the touristic big time.

Main attractions

- **Abomey** As capital of the Dahomey kingdom, Abomey was where successive kings built their palaces. Some are partially ruined, but most have been restored, one now serving as the Royal History Museum, whose shocking highlight is a throne made of skulls. Other attractions include Vodun temples and brilliant crafts shopping.

- **Ganvié** A bewitching fishing village, Ganvié is built on stilts on the far side of Lake Nokoué, near Cotonou. Get around by pirogue.

- **Grand Popo** Grand Popo, most of whose architectural heritage was claimed long ago by the ocean, has

Average temperature ranges and rainfall

	Jan	Feb	Mar	Apr	May	Jun	Jul	Aug	Sep	Oct	Nov	Dec
Cotonou												
Max °C	31	32	32	32	31	29	28	28	28	30	31	31
Min °C	24	25	26	26	25	24	24	23	24	24	24	24
Rainfall mm	9	37	74	137	197	356	147	65	99	127	41	20

the country's finest stretch of sand, and good resorts.

● **Pendjari National Park** Benin may only have two national parks, but this one is worth the effort, with tons of animals, whether hippos and crocs in the Pendjari River, or elephants, buffaloes, lions and antelopes in the surrounding savanna. There's also an outside chance of cheetahs. Bird-watchers have two hundred species to tick off.

● **Ouidah** The port of Ouidah was Dahomey's dark heart, from where countless captives were sold to European merchants and shipped off to bondage in the Americas. You can follow their steps along the Route des Esclaves, from the centre of town to a monumental "door of no return" on the beach. Ouidah's other claim to fame is Vodun, centred around the Temple of the Sacred Python. There's also a sacred forest adorned with statues of deities. Both Vodun and slavery are covered by a museum in an old Portuguese fortress.

● **The Atakora Range** The northwestern hills are home to the Somba, most famous for multistorey Tata-Sombas – thick-walled, windowless fortress-like homes that enabled them to survive the rapacious attentions of Dahomey's slave-trading kings. A good base is the pretty valley town of Natitingou, which enjoys a refreshing climate by Benin's sweltering standards. It has a cultural museum and, within reach, the beautiful Kota

waterfalls. The region as a whole has the enduring liquid attraction of millet beer, tchouk, to which entire markets are dedicated (the drinking is done there too; pork is the traditional stomach padding).

Also recommended

● **Porto Novo** In between the flaking colonial houses of Benin's rather provincial capital are several great markets (including one for herbal remedies) and a trio of good museums, one of them in a nineteenth-century palace.

● **Cotonou** The country's largest city is predictably chaotic if friendly, with good seafood restaurants and nightlife, and the electrifying Marché Dantokpa, one of West Africa's largest, with a whole section set aside for Vodun fetishes.

● **Dassa-Zoumé** Even if you're not on pilgrimage (see "Festivals"), the verdant, boulder-strewn landscape around Dassa is worth the trip – great for walking and biking, and hippo-spotting on the Ouémé River.

● **Savalou** Close to Dassa-Zoumé and enjoying similarly intoxicating scenery, Savalou and the villages around it have the distinction of being a major Vodun centre.

● **Parakou** Its name meaning "everyone's town", Parakou is an ethnically mixed affair, its diversity best sampled in its restaurants and kaleido-scopic markets. There's also a museum of Bariba and Peul history, and a Bariba palace whose incumbent may entertain visitors.

• **Parc National du "W" du Niger**
The Béninois section of this transfrontier wildlife park is where – with your own transport and guide – you get to see the River Niger and, hopefully, a good many of its denizens: elephants and big buffalo herds are common, as are all kinds of antelopes.

Festivals

Traditional celebrations are held year-round, with the bulk of Vodun rituals taking place in December and January. Christian and Muslim festivals are also observed; see p.243 & p.245 for dates.
Assumption Day Dassa-Zoumé and Savalou; Aug 15 Following an apparition of the Virgin Mary, a small cave at Arigbo near Dassa-Zoumé has become the focus for a mass pilgrimage. Not wishing to be outdone, neighbouring Savalou has merged the pilgrimage with its traditional Festival of Yams – lots of singing and dancing, and chewing mealy tubers.
Donkonrou Baribaland; two months before Gaani Its name meaning "fire launching", the Bariba and Tèbo new year's eve sees a fire lit in front of the king's palace while, simultaneously, all other fires in his kingdom are extinguished. Each family then rekindles their flames from the royal one.
Gaani Baribaland; coincides with Maulidi (see p.245 for dates) Nikki, close to Nigeria, is the cradle of the Bariba and centrestage for a big bash that celebrates deliverance from Muslim invaders on the occasion of the Prophet Muhammad's birthday. Royal drums and trumpets are played throughout the eve, and continue during the big day's ritual

parade to various sacred sites, during which the king is on horseback.
Quintessence International Film Festival Ouidah; Jan One for celluloid-heads.
Vodun Day Nationwide; Jan 10 Forget about pin-cushion dolls and zombies. Apart from the serious business of worshipping, Vodun offers plenty of chances to stretch your legs and party. Best in Cotonou, Porto Novo or Savalou.

Routes in and out

The international airport is at Cotonou. There are buses from Mali and Niger and shared taxis from Togo. Public transport from Nigeria stops at the border.

Benin online

Benin Tourist Board
Ⓦ**www.benintourism.com**
Beninzik
Ⓦ**www.beninzik.com/**discotheque
Béninois rap and hip-hop.
Vodoun Culture and Lore of the Gods
Ⓦ**www.mamiwata.com/culture.html**
One of the less batty voodoo sites out there, dealing with the Béninois original.

Books

Paula Girshick Ben-Amos *The Art of Benin*. Amply illustrated and with in-depth text, this does justice to Benin's sophisticated artistic tradition.
Olympe Bhêly-Quénum *Snares Without End*. The only Béninois novel in English translation, a pessimistic tale of a man felled by unfair accusations of adultery.
Annie Caulfield *Show Me the Magic: Travels Round Benin by Taxi*. Who needs

gung-ho self-aggrandizement when you can have funny, charming, engaging, incisive and sensitive all in one? A great travelogue.

Bruce Chatwin *The Viceroy of Ouidah*. A painterly fictional account of the life of a Brazilian slave-trader.

Henning Christoph and Hans Oberlander *Voodoo: Secret Power in Africa*. Excellent photographs beauti-fully reproduced, and with intelligent text; a superior breed of coffee-table book.

Francesca Pique and Leslie H. Rainer *Palace Sculptures of Abomey: History Told on Walls*. Fon history and culture, the emphasis being on the bas-reliefs of Dahomey's palaces.

Botswana

Area 600,370 square kilometres
Capital Gaborone
Population 1.5 million; majority are "Batswana" (a term covering eight Tswana tribes plus Tswana-ized groups); others include Bakgalagadi, Bakalanga, and former hunter-gatherers called Basarwa (Bushmen)
Language English (official); Setswana is more widely spoken
Religion Christianity 70 percent, traditional beliefs 25 percent

Climate Semi-arid with desert extremes (hot days and cool or cold nights); summer rains Nov–March, dusty winds Aug
Best time to go June–Oct best for most wildlife parks; July & Aug for the Okavango Delta; Dec–March for Nxai Pan
Currency Pula
Minimum costs $30/£17 per day

Botswana owes much of its tourist charm to wildlife. Although eighty percent of the country is Kalahari, water, where it exists (most fabulously in the Okavango Delta), attracts animals in mind-boggling quantities. And as one-fifth of the country comprises wildlife sanctuaries, safaris are obviously a major thrill, whether you're driving, walking, or riding a horse or an elephant.

Water is not the Kalahari's only treasure. Diamonds have made the country one of Africa's richest. Unfortunately, development has come

at a terrible price for some: indigenous Basarwa communities, traditionally hunter-gatherers, have been systematically harassed by the government since the 1980s, persecution that recently intensified with the forcible eviction of communities from the Central Kalahari Game Reserve. The government says it wants to help them develop; the NGO Survival International points the finger at less altruistic motives such as the desire to mine for rumoured diamond deposits, and has called for a tourism boycott. If you decide to come, don't

Average temperature ranges and rainfall

	Jan	Feb	Mar	Apr	May	Jun	Jul	Aug	Sep	Oct	Nov	Dec
Gaborone												
Max °C	30	30	28	26	23	20	20	24	27	28	30	30
Min °C	22	21	19	16	11	7	7	10	15	18	20	21
Rainfall mm	95	84	71	41	13	6	3	5	16	43	66	90
Maun (Okavango Delta)												
Max °C	32	31	31	30	27	25	25	28	32	35	34	32
Min °C	18	18	17	14	9	5	5	8	12	17	18	18
Rainfall mm	109	97	89	28	5	3	0	0	3	13	48	71

do so expecting to meet "traditional" hunter-gatherers: these days the Basarwa only dress up for the benefit of visitors.

Main attractions

● **The Okavango Delta** On entering Botswana, the river Okavango slows down to spread across the Kalahari, creating the world's largest inland delta – a hot, humid and pristine alluvial wetland that quadruples in size to over 100,000 square kilometres when the river's floods peak in July and August.

The meandering streams and channels, swamps and oxbow lakes lend the delta a unique and primeval beauty, and attract great numbers of animals, including elephants and cheetahs, hippos and crocs, and many antelopes and birds. Part of the delta is fenced in as Moremi Game Reserve, the place for African hunting dogs. There are tons of lodges to choose from, and all manner of safaris, even some from hot-air balloons.

● **Chobe National Park** The semi-desert plains of northern Botswana are among Africa's greatest wildlife areas, celebrated for vast numbers

△ Impalas and an elephant at Chobe National Park

of elephants along the Chobe River and its waterholes. The summer rains turn Chobe's glistening salt pans into grasslands and swamps, attracting enormous zebra herds and a retinue of gluttonous lions. Spend a few days here and you're likely to see most of Africa's emblematic species.

● **Tsodilo Hills** The Tsodilo Hills, in the western Kalahari, have immense spiritual significance for the Ju/hoansi. The hills, they say, are the abode of their ancestral spirits and divinities, and one hill contains the imprint of the first spirit's knees as he prayed after creating the world. Taken together, the hills rank among Africa's greatest rock art galleries. Many paintings depict elands, an antelope associated with rain. Also common are images of men with erect penises, related to shamanistic trance rituals.

● **Nxai Pan National Park** In the rainy season Nxai is the country's best wildlife park, when its salt pans turn into lakes and grasslands, attracting a myriad of animals and birds, including raptors and

plenty of terrestrial predators. Among the more unusual species are blue wildebeest, red hartebeest, The bat-eared fox and brown hyena.

● **Gemsbok National Park** Now part of Kgalagadi Transfrontier Park (shared with South Africa), this is a desert land of salt pans, denuded vegetation and classic red Kalahari sand dunes. Inspiring landscapes aside, one reason to visit is the desert's ever-inventive inhabitants: black-maned lions and a host of other predators prey on a good variety of antelopes, including calving blue wildebeests before the rains, and large herds of eland after the rains. Birdlife is best during the rains, when they're attracted by temporary lakes left by thunderstorms.

Also recommended

● **Tuli and Mashatu Game Reserves** Close to the Limpopo River in the east, these two private sanctuaries are best seen on horseback, though night game drives are possible. Elephants are abundant, together with antelopes and their predators.

● **Makgadikgadi Pans National Park** Makgadikgadi's total inaccessibility during the rains, when temporary lakes and grasslands attract incredible numbers of birds, means that the park is primarily promoted for its stark salt-pan scenery in the dry season.

● **Mokolodi Nature Reserve** Ten kilometres from Gaborone, this small, privately-owned sanctuary is stocked with all the biggies, including white rhinos, elephants, cheetahs, leopards, and many different antelopes. The inmates are used to humans, so walkers (or elephant riders) can enjoy close encounters in relative safety.

● **Xai-Xai** Community-based tourism among Bushmen and Herero herders and farmers, completely off the beaten track in the desert close to Namibia. Accompany them on hunting and gathering trips, take horseback safaris, visit caves, or shake your legs in the evening with a traditional dance.

● **Khama Rhino Sanctuary** A community-run project in the Kalahari to preserve Botswana's rhinos, poached close to extinction in the 1980s. Among other wildlife here are lynxes and leopards.

● **D'Kar** This Kalahari village has become a cultural centre for the Basarwa Bushmen, with a flourishing artists' community, a cultural museum, and hunter-gatherer-style activities for visitors.

Festivals

Botswana's traditional celebrations have largely been replaced by contemporary festivals.

Kuru Traditional Dance and Music Festival D'Kar; Aug One of few opportunities for Bushmen communities to get together and celebrate what remains of their musical culture.

Maitisong Festival Gaborone; March/ April Nine days of music, dance and theatre covering most genres, from traditional to church choirs and hip-hop.

Maun Carnival Maun; see p.243 for Carnival dates Floats, music (everything from marimba bands to heavy metal) and an enjoyable country fair atmosphere.

Routes in and out

International flights land at Gaborone. There are buses from all neighbouring countries.

Botswana online

Botswana Department of Tourism
Ⓦ www.botswana-tourism.gov.bw and
Ⓦ www.botswanatourism.org.uk
African First Peoples
Ⓦ www.khoisanpeoples.org Militant organization supporting Botswana's embattled Bushman communities; winner of the Alternative Nobel Prize of 2005.
The Okavango Delta Peoples of Botswana
Ⓦ www.mindspring.com/~okavango
A few scholarly papers about the hunter-gatherer peoples of the northern Kalahari, plus useful pointers to books and websites.

Books

Anthony Bannister and David Lewis-Williams Bushmen: *A Changing Way of Life.* Published in 1994, a full-colour record of a lifestyle that didn't so much change as disappear. Includes a good section on rock art.

Peter Joyce and Daryl and Sharna Balfour *This is Botswana*. A lavish pictorial journey through the country's wilderness areas.

Alexander McCall Smith *The No. 1 Ladies' Detective Agency*. The first of a humorous series of fictional tales concerning Mama Precious Ramotswe, sassy head of Botswana's only spook agency.

Laurens van der Post *The Lost World of the Kalahari*. One of many works by the author about the Bushmen, this one describes an expedition for the BBC in the 1950s. Often criticized for romanticizing his experiences, van der Post has a genuine fascination and respect for the Bushmen, which comes across clearly here.

Burkina Faso

Area 274,200 square kilometres
Capital Ouagadougou
Population 14 million, half of whom
are Mossi; of the other sixty-plus
ethnic groups, major ones include
Fulani, Gourmantché, Bobo,
Bisa-Samo, Gourounsi, Dagari-Lobi
and Bwa
Language French (official) spoken
in towns; major ethnic languages are
Moré, Dioula and Fula

Religion Islam 50 percent,
traditional beliefs 30 percent,
Christianity 15 percent; Islam and
Christianity include traditional beliefs
Climate Semi-arid; dry and relatively
cool Nov–Feb, dry and hot March–
May, hot and rainy June–Oct
Best time to go Nov–Feb; Jan–April
for wildlife
Currency CFA franc
Minimum costs $17/£9 per day

A poor country even by West African
standards, landlocked and resource-
starved Burkina Faso has had a rough
time of it since independence. The
central grasslands where the majority
of the people reside are under constant
threat from the ever-expanding Sahara,
while the more fertile south, watered by
the Mouhoun, Nazinon and Nakambé
rivers (the Black, Red and White Voltas
respectively), is only sparsely inhabited
thanks to insect-borne diseases. A
succession of droughts has left most
Burkinabes well below the UN's poverty
line, while an equally insidious litany of

military coups and dictatorships (including the present regime) has impeded
economic and political development.

Despite all this, and a history of
conquests and forced migrations, the
country's numerous ethnic groups
have kept their identities remarkably
intact, together with a healthy dose of
traditions. The country's name means
"Land of the Upright People", a fair
description of its inhabitants. Culture is
easily Burkina Faso's richest resource,
and can be experienced via a packed
calendar of festivals. Other attractions
include a handful of wildlife reserves,

Average temperature ranges and rainfall

	Jan	Feb	Mar	Apr	May	Jun	Jul	Aug	Sep	Oct	Nov	Dec
Bobo-Dioulasso												
Max °C	31	33	35	35	33	30	28	28	29	32	32	31
Min °C	20	22	25	26	25	22	22	21	21	22	21	20
Rainfall mm	1	3	17	47	109	131	214	297	191	67	11	2
Ouagadougou												
Max °C	36	39	41	42	39	36	34	32	34	38	39	36
Min °C	14	16	21	24	25	23	22	21	21	22	19	15
Rainfall mm	0	1	5	22	74	106	176	240	136	33	2	0

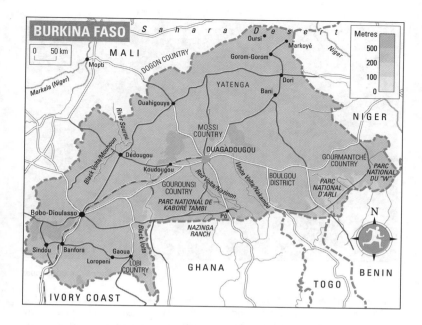

and various sites related to traditional kingdoms that have persisted to the present-day, albeit in ceremonial capacities.

Main attractions

● **Ouagadougou** The country's modern capital was the seat of an ancient Mossi kingdom, a fact of which you're reminded on Friday mornings by the curious Nabayius Gou ceremony, when the king re-enacts the hesitant decision of his eighteenth-century forebear to put duty before personal concerns (the suspected philandering of his favourite wife) at a time when war was in the offing. There's more on history and culture in the national museum, and in two specialist museums, one for ethnography, the other music. There's also a characterful market and vibrant nightlife.

● **Bobo-Dioulasso** The economic and cultural heart of the country was founded in the fourteenth century. Apart from excellent festivals, lively street life and cafés, there are pretty medieval quarters, a fine ethnographical museum, bronze-makers using the ancient "lost wax" technique, a kaleidoscopic market, and the 1880 Grande Mosquée, its studded minaret rather more phallic than most. Around town are even more attractions, namely a sacred pond filled with giant mudfish, a lake whose hippos you get to see in their lugubrious glory from a pirogue, and a pool in a forest that's popular with bathers.

● **Parc National du "W"** Named after the double bend in the River Niger on the border with Niger and Benin, this magnificent transnational park is probably the best place in West Africa to see big wild animals. Burkina's share, encompassing expansive wetlands,

△ Bobo-Dioulasso's Grande Mosquée

is best for birds and hippos, though you'll also see buffaloes, antelopes and monkeys, and possibly elephants, lions or leopards.

● **Lobi country** The forested hills close to Ghana and Ivory Coast have remained very traditional, partly on account of their distance from asphalt. The polygamous Gan and Lobi are the main ethnic groups here, both with superb musical traditions, of which you might hear impromptu bursts in the region's many cabarets or bars. The main town, Gaoua, has a good ethnological museum and magnificent Sunday market, and is the jumping off point for visiting stone ruins at Loropeni – enigmatic rectangular structures about which precisely nothing is known.

● **The Sahara** The ragged settlements in the north serve primarily as market centres for nomads such as Tuareg, Fulani, Bela and Songhaï. The main town is Dori, with an enjoyable daily market (etched calabashes are the speciality) and a fascinating artisan's district. For

day-trips, see the earthen mosques of Bani town, or head for one of the weekly markets at Markoye and Gorom-Gorom. Also in the area is Oursi, a desert lake flanked by pink and white sand dunes that's as popular with herders as it is with birds.

Also recommended

● **Around Ouahigouya** The capital of the northwestern kingdom of Yatenga, which broke away from Ouagadougou in the fifteenth century, is a good base for visiting earthen palaces and mosques. There's also a sacred hill where Yatenga kings are invested, plus former royal capitals and cemeteries.

● **Gourounsi country** The area around Pô on the Ghanaian border is dominated by the Gourounsi ethnic group, whose hand is instantly recognizable in their distinctive clay architecture – smooth and rounded mudcakes that are rebuilt every few years, giving older compounds a distinctly organic appearance. The architecture is at its finest in the traditional capital of Tiébélé.

● **Banfora** A small, sleepy town in a lovely area of cliffs and forests, Banfora has a good crafts market and several targets for excursions. Particularly unusual is a three-kilometre chain of naturally sculpted sandstone towers and needles at Sindou, that lend themselves well to rock climbing.

● **Kaboré Tembi National Park and Nazinga Ranch** Good wildlife areas on the fringes of Gourounsi country, at either of which you might see elephants, baboons, warthogs, monkeys and antelopes. The ranch is currently more favoured by animals, and guided game walks are possible. Cycling is possible in the national park.

● **Parc National d'Arli** Flanking Benin is the country's main wildlife refuge (and hunting area), where you stand good odds of seeing lions and elephants as well as antelopes, monkeys and hippos, and plenty of birds.

Festivals

Burkina Faso's diverse musical traditions are among the continent's most inspired, and inspiring, often featuring masquerades in which dancers wear carved masks embodying ancestral spirits. These art forms are most easily experienced at a plethora of modern festivals. Despite their staged nature, the performances are quite real, stemming as they do from living traditions. Islamic festivals (see p.245) are also celebrated, albeit on a smaller scale than in neighbouring countries.

Festival International de la Culture Hip Hop Ouagadougou & Bobo-Dioulasso; Oct Performances over two weeks.

Festival Jazz Ouagadougou & Bobo-Dioulasso; April/May Big names from around the continent.

Festival des Masques et des Arts (FESTIMA) Dédougou; March of even-numbered years Several hundred mask dances from Burkina Faso and neighbouring countries.

Festival Panafricain du Cinéma (FESPACO) Ouagadougou; Feb/March in odd-numbered years Africa's biggest, most star-studded film festival, concentrating on African cinema but not averse to featuring the best of worldwide cinema, too.

Nuits Atypiques Koudougou; Nov/Dec Burkina's third-largest town gets into party mode for four "atypical nights", when the crowds lap up performances of music, theatre and dance by traditional and contemporary groups.

Semaine Nationale de la Culture Bobo-Dioulasso; March/April in even-numbered years National Culture Week features music and dance, theatre and masquerades.

Routes in and out

International flights land at Ouagadougou. There's overland transport from neighbouring countries except Ivory Coast (because of the civil war there).

Burkina Faso online

Ministry of Culture, Arts and Tourism Ⓦ www.culture.gov.bf
An anarchist account of Burkina Faso Ⓦ www.struggle.ws/africa/accounts /chekov/bukina.html Irreverent travelogue touching all bases, from the "Big Man" complex and pointless NGOs to culture and insights on the reality of travel.
Art and Life in Africa Ⓦ www.uiowa.edu/~africart Brilliant

cultural resource from the University of Iowa, with dozens of essays, over a thousand photographs (including portraits and masks), music clips and video trailers, even entire books.

OuagaNet

ⓦ**www.ouaganet.com** Community-style portal with helpful forums.

Books

Malidoma Patrice Some *Of Water and the Spirit: Ritual, Magic and Initiation in the Life of an African Shaman*. A deeply spiritual introduction to the reality of traditional African religion in Burkina Faso, this magical book is a revelation. Describing the author's abduction by Jesuit missionaries during the French era, his escape and subsequent initiation as a shaman on his return, it delivers a powerful broadside against the Christian dogma of proselytizing evangelism (and its destruction of cultures) without resorting to militancy or melodrama.

Thomas Wheelock *Land of the Flying Masks: Art and Culture in Burkina Faso*. A lavish tome presenting the author's important collection of Burkinabe art.

Cameroon

Area 475,440 square kilometres
Capital Yaoundé
Population 17.3 million; around 200 ethnic groups, including Bantu and "semi-Bantu", Fulani (north), and Baka Pygmies (southeast)
Language French, and many African languages, most importantly Fula (north), and Douala and Bassa (south); English is spoken in the west and southwest

Religion Christianity 40 percent, traditional beliefs 40 percent, Islam 20 percent
Climate Tropical and often very wet in the south, with main rains July–Oct; drier in the north, rains May–Oct
Best time to go Dec–Feb
Currency CFA franc
Minimum costs $25/£14 per day

Cameroon, they say, is all of Africa in one country – an expression of its geographical and cultural diversity. It's so diverse, in fact, that it's hard to see what (apart from football) holds the place together. After a brief spell under German rule, Cameroon – the probable original home of the Bantu – was split between Britain and France, a division that still causes tension today. Still,

there's no denying that Cameroon has the lot: plains and mountains, desert and jungle, cities and seasides. The scenery is exceptional, the music wonderful, and the people hail from a vast array of very different ethnic backgrounds, including a Pygmy people, the Baka, in the southeast. All in all, Cameroon is a beautiful and fabulous land that amply rewards longer stays.

Average temperature ranges and rainfall

	Jan	Feb	Mar	Apr	May	Jun	Jul	Aug	Sep	Oct	Nov	Dec
Yaoundé												
Max °C	29	29	30	29	28	28	26	26	27	28	28	29
Min °C	19	19	19	19	19	19	19	18	19	18	19	19
Rainfall mm	23	66	147	170	220	152	74	79	213	295	117	23
Douala												
Max °C	31	32	32	32	31	29	27	27	29	30	30	31
Min °C	23	23	23	23	23	23	22	22	23	22	23	23
Rainfall mm	46	94	203	231	300	539	742	693	531	429	155	64
Kousséri												
Max °C	34	37	40	42	40	38	33	31	33	36	36	33
Min °C	14	16	21	23	25	24	22	22	22	21	17	14
Rainfall mm	0	0	0	3	31	66	170	320	119	36	0	0

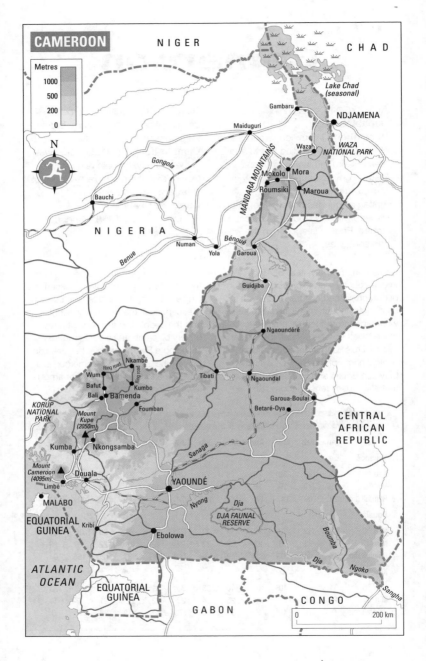

CAMEROON

Metres
1000
500
200
0

N

NIGER

CHAD

Lake Chad
(seasonal)

Gambaru

NDJAMENA

Maiduguri

Waza

WAZA
NATIONAL PARK

MANDARA MOUNTAINS

Mokolo

Mora

Roumsiki

Maroua

Gongola

Bauchi

NIGERIA

Numan

Bénoué

Benue

Yola

Garoua

Guidjiba

Ngaoundéré

Nkambé

Ring road

Wum

Bafut

Ring road

Kumbo

Tibati

Ngaoundal

Bali

Bamenda

Garoua-Boulai

KORUP
NATIONAL
PARK

Foumban

Betaré-Oya

CENTRAL
AFRICAN
REPUBLIC

Mount
Kupe
(2050m)

Kumba

Nkongsamba

Sanaga

Mount
Cameroon
(4095m)

Douala

YAOUNDÉ

Limbé

MALABO

Nyong

Dja

Boumba

EQUATORIAL
GUINEA

Kribi

DJA FAUNAL
RESERVE

ATLANTIC
OCEAN

Ebolowa

Dja

Ngoko

Sangha

EQUATORIAL
GUINEA

GABON

CONGO

0   200 km

First-Time Africa | WHERE TO GO

Main attractions

- **Mount Cameroon** Rising 4095m directly from the sea, Mount Cameroon offers hikers the formidable and hopefully uplifting challenge of scaling West Africa's highest peak. Despite being close to the Equator, the summit is bitterly cold – it can even snow up here. This is an active volcano (it last erupted in 2000), so in addition to forest, you'll be crossing lava flows. Should the prospect make you sweat, think of the masochists who sign up for the annual "Race of Hope" to the top, which is surely one of the most arduous marathons on earth.

- **Dja Faunal Reserve** The country's largest tract of virgin rainforest supports all kinds of wildlife, including lowland gorillas, forest elephants, sitatunga antelopes, mandrills and exotic birdlife. Human residents include Baka Pygmies, with whom it's possible to arrange treks into the forest.

- **Limbé** Picturesque and relaxed amid beautiful scenery, this lovely little beach resort was founded by the London Baptist Missionary Society and was originally populated by freed slaves from as far away as Jamaica. It's home to one of Africa's most important botanical gardens, and a zoo involved in serious primate conservation work.

- **Korup National Park** Comprising over 1000 square kilometres of Africa's oldest and most biologically diverse rainforest, Korup offers fantastic hiking terrain. The possibilities are virtually endless: aim for any number of waterfalls, take a botanical tour, winkle out some of the park's impressive haul of primates, or go birding: there are more bird species here than in any other site on the continent.

- **The Ring Road** A 360-kilometre loop through some of the finest scenery in Africa, traversing volcanoes, lakes and the Mencham Falls. Towns en route include Bafut, with its Fon's (local king's) palace, and Wum, close to a beautiful crater lake. In the dry season, the route can be covered by bicycle.

- **Douala** Cameroon's biggest city has a few colonial relics, notably the pagoda-style Manga Bell Palace, plus a run-down museum and a couple of good markets, but the city's big draw is its vibrant nightlife, featuring everything from traditional sounds to disco hits.

Also recommended

- **Yaoundé** Cooler and less hectic than Douala, but also more formal and less exuberant, Cameroon's administrative capital boasts three good museums featuring some wonderful works of art, and, on the outskirts, the tiny Mfou National Park where orphaned primates are rehabilitated.

- **Bamenda** The unofficial capital of Anglophone Cameroon, Bamenda is a lovely, fresh town set among pines and banana trees, great for buying local crafts and a handy base for excursions to Bali, with its crafts centre and royal palace; Batibo, the region's palm-wine centre; and the marvellous Awing crater lake for fishing or swimming.

- **Foumban** The capital of the Bamoun people is chock-a-block with culture and history, not to mention two excellent museums (one in a former palace), and an artisans' village producing bronze casts and wood carvings.

- **Kribi** Cameroon's second-biggest port is also a quiet colonial town, with gorgeous beaches and excellent seafood.

- **Maroua** One of the few cities in Cameroon that pre-dates colonial times,

△ The Mandara Mountains, near Roumsiki

retaining much of its traditional flavour, with old residential quarters, shaded boulevards, a small museum, a large market, and a stinky but very photogenic leather tannery.

● **Mandara Mountains** On the border with Nigeria, these eerily beautiful volcanic peaks offer the prospect of treks to mountain villages, from centres such as Roumsiki. Local culture is the other attraction – the multitribal heritage remains strong.

● **Mount Kupe** Mount Kupe's unique cloud forest has been preserved thanks to a local belief that it's home to ancestral spirits. The forest is certainly home to an amazing 320 bird species,

and chimpanzees, bushbabies and loris. Locals offer homestays and guided walks.

● **Waza National Park** Cameroon's most popular game park, offering the best savanna game-viewing in West Africa, with a good likelihood of seeing giraffes, elephants, lions and antelopes.

Festivals

Major Christian and Muslim festivals (see p.243 & p.245) are public holidays; of greater interest to visitors are traditional festivals.

End-of-year festivals Bafut and Bali; end Dec Public celebration of the rites of local secret societies, presided over by the Fon, and marked by dancing, flute-playing and the firing of guns. It's also known as Abin Lela or the Dance of the Flutes.

Grass-cutting ceremony Bafut; end April Everyone troops off into the grasslands to gather bundles for thatching important public buildings, parading their offerings in front of the Fon, before joining in a massive beanfeast washed down with lashings of palm wine.

Routes in and out

The major international airport is at Douala; Yaoundé and Garoua also have airports. Infrequent boats depart Calabar (Nigeria) for Limbé. Land border crossings are open (except for the one to Congo Brazzaville); you'll need to change buses or bush taxis at the border.

Cameroon online

Ministry of Tourism
Ⓦ**www.tourisme.cm**
Baka Pygmies
Ⓦ**www.pygmies.info** Text and photos, but sadly no recordings, by a young Italian ethnomusicologist.
Bakwerirama
Ⓦ**www.bakweri.org** Website dedicated to the Bakweri people, who live around Mount Cameroon. It features various

aspects of their culture, including myths, legends, music and food.
Mandara Mountains Homepage
Ⓦ**www.mandaras.info** This looks a bit dry from the outside, but dig in and you'll find a mass of information about the peoples and cultures of northern Cameroon. Similar is Ⓦwww.sukur.info.

Books

Mongo Beti *The Poor Christ of Bomba*. A French priest tries to convert a village to Christianity, with disastrous consequences, in this satirical parable from Cameroon's most distinguished novelist.

Gerald Durrell *The Overloaded Ark and A Zoo in My Luggage*. Durrell recounts his animal-collecting adventures in British Cameroon with much humour, though his patronizing attitude becomes tiresome.

Dervla Murphy *In Cameroon with Egbert*. Indefatigable Irish travel writer Dervla Murphy trades in her bicycle for a packhorse to jaunt around Cameroon with her teenage daughter.

Ndeley Mokoso *Man Pass Man!* A collection of thirteen darkly funny short stories, including the tale which gives the book its title, about an attempt to fix a football match with magic.

Ferdinand Oyono *Houseboy*. Caustic but humorous account of a domestic servant's life under colonialism. The follow-up, *The Old Man and the Medal*, is equally scathing.

Cape Verde

Area 4033 square kilometres
Capital Praia
Population 450,000; mainly Mestizo (Portuguese/African mulatto)
Language Portuguese (official), Crioulo or Kriolu (Creole)
Religion Roman Catholism blended with traditional beliefs

Climate Warm and temperate, with very low, erratic rainfall (mainly in storms from Aug–Oct)
Best time to go Any time is good, but marginally cooler Aug–Oct
Currency Cape Verdean escudo
Minimum costs $55/£31 per day

Cape Verde – the green cape (Cabo Verde in Portuguese) – consists of fifteen volcanic islands 600km off the West African coast. More in tune with the Canaries and Azores than with West Africa's savanna, bushland and tropical forests, the islands comprise two groups: Barlavento ("windward") in the north, which are hot and dry as they catch the tail end of the Sahara's tradewinds, and the greener Sotavento ("leeward") to the south. Most of the islands have rugged interiors with stunning views, perfect for hiking.

The islands were uninhabited prior to their discovery by Portuguese navigators in 1460. They proved less fertile than hoped, but their importance within the Portuguese empire was sealed during the booming trans-atlantic slave trade (most Cabo Verdeanos are descended from slaves). For visitors,

the charm of the place and its people is a big attraction, as is the combination of beach lounging and nightlife with activities such as scuba-diving, hiking and even horse-riding. Music fans are also well catered for: Cape Verde's honey-voiced cultural ambassador, singer Cesaria Evora, has put Cape Verde's melancholic yet vibrant music on the world-music map.

In political terms, the archipelago distinguishes itself from West Africa in being truly democratic and peaceful, despite widespread poverty and a string of droughts that have crippled the meagre economy. Cabo Verdeanos keep true to their cherished feeling of *morabeza*, meaning gentleness. Blend in good seafood, colourful markets and pretty pastel-coloured colonial towns, and there you have it: a subtle and infectiously charming destination.

Average temperature ranges and rainfall

	Jan	Feb	Mar	Apr	May	Jun	Jul	Aug	Sep	Oct	Nov	Dec
Praia												
Max °C	25	25	25	26	27	27	28	28	28	29	27	26
Min °C	20	19	20	20	21	21	23	24	25	24	23	21
Rainfall mm	0	0	0	0	0	0	8	16	96	20	43	0

Main attractions

• **Santiago** The archipelago's largest and most populous island, Santiago was the first to be settled by the Portuguese, for whom it served as a major entrepôt on the slave route to Brazil. The trade explains the island's distinctively African feeling, and wonderful music and festivals. The main town, Praia, is the national capital, politically as well as musically, and visitors looking for nightlife won't be disappointed. Historical interest is provided by a maritime museum (of treasures from shipwrecks), and by the former capital, Cidade Velha. Its magnificent sixteenth-century fortress of São Filipe, dominating the cobbled streets, once played host to Captain Cook, Charles Darwin and the pirate Francis Drake (as attacker).

• **Fogo** Its name meaning "fire", Fogo is an archetypal island-volcano, best explored on foot or on horseback. It's an island of contrasting landscapes, from the pastel-painted colonial town of São Filipe, set on a clifftop overlooking a beach of black volcanic sand, to the interior where bizarre lava formations jostle for room with verdant plantations, the latter producing surprisingly good wine. At the island's heart is the Pico de Fogo, which last erupted in 1995.

• **Sal** With plenty of sun and seemingly endless beaches, the barren island of Sal is Cape Verde's main tourist destination, with plenty of hotels and water sports (including scuba-diving), and a good selection of restaurants and nightlife in the pretty town of Santa Maria. Day-trips to the Pedro Lume salt mines and their salt lake, inside the caldera of an extinct volcano, for a Dead Sea-style float are always fun, as are short cruises along the coast or to neighbouring Boavista Island.

• **Santo Antão** An hour's sail from São Vicente, verdant Santo Antão has Cape Verde's most inspiring hiking scenery: several broken-backed volcanic peaks over 1500m, a rugged and equally broken coastline, tropical forests, and a heart-stopping hairpin road in from the ferry port. There are no beaches, but the island's celebrated *grogue* (rum) should provide solace.

• **São Nicolau** A rugged and lush volcanic land scattered with farming villages, all perfect for hiking. A peculiar attraction is the indigenous dragoeiro or "dragon tree", the national symbol that, legend has it, sprouted from the blood of the dragon slain by Hercules when he stole the golden apples of Hesperides. Activities include fishing trips with locals, bird-watching on the isle of Raso in search of the rare Cape Verdean lark, and lounging on black-sand beaches.

• **São Vicente** A good alternative to Sal is São Vicente, home to songbird Cesaria Evora and a host of other no-less-talented singers and musicians. As you might expect, Mindelo – the island's lively and cosmopolitan capital – enjoys an enviable nightlife. Its carnival is the archipelago's best, and the town is also a cultural and artistic centre. Ocean currents, tides and winds make for very good windsurfing.

Also recommended

• **Boavista** Home to Cape Verde's finest beach (Santa Monica), and with a barren but strikingly beautiful volcanic interior.

• **Brava** Cape Verde's smallest island is the place for amateur botanists, its many indigenous plants surviving on the mists that shroud Brava's peaks for much of the year. It's an attractive place, but don't come expecting beaches, or much in the way of facilities.

△ Volcanic terrain on Boavista Island

● **Maio** Flat, isolated and very sleepy, Maio island is home to just six thousand people. Tourists rarely visit, so you'll be sharing the dune-backed beaches with birds and perhaps a few fishermen.

Festivals

Every island has contributed to the archipelago's impressive musical traditions, but none more so than São Vicente.

Carnaval Mindelo São Vicente; Feb or March (see p.243 for dates) What Rio's carnival used to be like before glitter, heels and thongs took over the show.

Festival Internacional de Jazz (Festijazz) Baia das Gatas São Vicente; Aug All the big names are here: Cesaria Evora, Sara Tavares, and up-and-coming names in hip-hop.

Routes in and out

Flights from Europe, West Africa and the Canary Islands land at Praia on Santiago island, or at Sal. There are infrequent ferries from the Canaries and Dakar. Transport between the islands is by ferry or light aircraft.

Cape Verde online

Caboverde.com
Ⓦ **www.caboverde.com** Gloriously jumbled if very messy portal by an Italian inamorato of Cape Verde, with masses of practical and contextual information. The music pages are a particular delight, with hundreds of tracks taken from dozens of albums and performers. Plenty of photos, too, and it's all frequently updated.

Books

Basil Davidson *The Fortunate Isles: A Study in African Transformation*. A positive and not unduly critical survey mixing impression with historical accounts, up to the 1980s.

Richard A. Lobban *Cape Verde: Crioulo Colony to Independent Nation*. Thorough treatment of the country's history, politics and culture.

The Comoros

Area 2238 square kilometres
Capitals Moroni (Union of the
Comoros), Mamoudzou (Mayotte)
Population 850,000; Comorans are
a mix of Swahili immigrants, African
slaves, Malagasy and Arabs
Language French and Arabic are
the official languages; Shikomoro
(similar to Kiswahili) is the main
spoken tongue, with island-specific
dialects

Religion Islam 90 percent,
Christianity 10 percent
Climate Tropical; rainfall varies
considerably even on the same
island; cyclones possible Dec–April
Best time to go May–Sept in
general, but March–May & Oct–Nov
for scuba- diving
Currency Comoran franc [Union];
euro [Mayotte]
Minimum costs $20/£11 per day

The volcanic archipelago of the
Comoros, in the Indian Ocean between
northern Madagascar and Mozambique
(see map, p.97), comprises two
countries. The islands of Ngazidja,
Mwali and Nzwani form the Union of the
Comoros, while Mayotte remains under
French control. The Union in particular
is desperately poor, and experienced
severe political turmoil after independence in 1975, marked by over twenty
coups or attempted coups, and the
short-lived secession of Mwali and
Nzwani islands. Things stabilized in 2001,
and in 2006 a moderate Muslim cleric,
nicknamed "the Ayatollah" on account of
having studied in Iran, was elected to the
Presidency in the country's first peaceful
transition of power.

With the exception of French package
tours, the Comoros have yet to hit the
touristic big time. There's a lot going for
it though. Beautiful beaches and lush
volcanic interiors are to be expected,
and the scuba-diving is second to
none. There are also reminders of the
medieval Indian Ocean trading routes:
ruined palaces and trading towns,
eclectic cuisine, fanciful tales of sultans
and errant princesses, pirates and
magicians, and of course the Comorans
themselves.

Main attractions

● **Ngazidja (Grande Comore)** The
archipelago's largest island has many

Average temperature ranges and rainfall

	Jan	Feb	Mar	Apr	May	Jun	Jul	Aug	Sep	Oct	Nov	Dec
Moroni												
Max °C	30	30	31	30	30	28	28	28	28	29	30	31
Min °C	23	23	23	23	21	20	19	18	19	20	22	23
Rainfall mm	361	290	287	297	242	210	221	139	77	104	103	201

upmarket beach resorts and great diving. Moroni, the capital, is peaceful and charming, with a fortress, a fifteenth-century town and royal tombs nearby. The island's towering feature is the 2361-metre Mount Karthala, an active volcano with a kilometre-wide crater, which can be climbed.

● **Mwali (Mohéli) island** Thinly populated, Mwali is largely covered by lush forest. Attractions include a sulphur-ous crater lake, waterfalls, giant flying foxes (fruit bats with wing spans over a metre), traditional dhow-builders, and sailing trips in search of dolphins and turtles.

● **Nzwani (Anjouan) island** An island famed for making essential oils, jasmine, basil, ylang-ylang among them. The production and use of perfumes is a legacy of the Swahili, who arrived in the fifteenth century and also left a mark in Mutsamudu and Domoni, whose intricately carved doors and maze-like streets are a delight. Inland are forests and waterfalls, and the 1595-metre Mount Ntingui volcano.

● **Mayotte** Close ties with Madagascar give Mayotte a distinctly African (rather than Islamic) feel. The big attraction is the fringing coral reef, enclosing what's arguably the world's largest lagoon. Snorkelling and diving are a major thrill. Messing about in a dugout or on a dhow is fun, too, and the beaches are fantas-tic. Other attractions include the Arabic town of Sada (famed for its fine gold filigree jewellery), the fortified island-town of Dzaoudzi, and lemurs.

Festivals

Islamic holidays are celebrated through-out; see pp.243–245. Festivities of the nuptial variety take place especially between July and September, at which time you may well witness a traditional wedding take place. The proceedings, to which you'll certainly be invited to in rural areas, last over a week and feature dancing, Arab/Indian-inspired taarab music, and the showing-off of gold jewellery presented to the bride by the groom's family.

Médina Festival Mutsamudu (Nzwani); May, June or July Contemporary and traditional music from around the southern Indian Ocean.

Routes in and out

The international airports are Mayotte (with long-haul flights), and Moroni (on Ngazidja, linked to Mayotte, Tanzania, Madagascar and Mozambique). There are currently no ferries between Mayotte and the Union.

Comoros online

Ⓦ **www.mayotte-tourisme.com** The Mayotte tourist board.

Comores-online
Ⓦ **www.comores-online.com** An excellent all-round resource and the only really useful site for visitors.

Comité du Tourisme de Mayotte Malango-Mayotte
Ⓦ **www.malango-mayotte.com** Lots of good cultural and tourist information about Mayotte, in French.

Books

Franco Prosperi *Vanished Continent: An expedition to the Comoro Islands*. High adventure, mating sharks, primeval coelacanths, rafts of deadly jellyfish and other natural wonders described with engaging humour by a young Italian naturalist in the 1950s.

Samantha Weinberg *Last of the Pirates: The Search for Bob Denard*. Weinberg got it into her mind to track down the infamous French mercenary and instigator of many African coups, including four in the Comoros. She found him in South Africa, shortly before he launched yet another coup on the islands.

Michael Lambeck *Human Spirit: A Cultural Account of Trance in Mayotte*. An extensively researched work concerning spirit possession, mostly among women, and its meaning.

Djibouti

Area 22,980 square kilometres	**Climate** Mostly extreme desert, hottest June–Aug; seasonal rains Nov–April
Capital Djibouti (city)	
Population 650,000; main ethnic groups are Issa (Somali) and Afar; influential Yemeni (Arab) minority	**Best time to go** Nov–April in general, and for scuba-diving; Oct–Jan to spot whale sharks
Language French and Arabic (both official) widely spoken; other languages are Somali and Afar	**Currency** Djibouti franc
Religion Islam	**Minimum costs** $30/£17

Guarding the entrance to the Red Sea, with Yemen on the opposite shore, tiny Djibouti is mostly desert. But what a desert: bone-meltingly hot and danced over by dust devils, its craters, volcanoes, salt flats and fissures are part of the ever-expanding Rift Valley, which will one day make eastern Africa an island. There's life there, too: squirrels, diminutive dikdik antelopes and equally dainty gazelles are frequently seen, as are salt-carrying camel caravans – an unforgettable image.

Other than salt, and amazing marine life, Djibouti is poor in natural resources, and the majority scrape by on well under a dollar a day. The country's biggest earner is its French and US military bases, whose presence partly explains why the country is expensive to travel in. Outside the capital, the woesome infrastructure also impacts on costs: four-wheel-drives and organized tours are the usual way around.

Main attractions

● **Djibouti city** Like it or loathe it, Djibouti's capital is unavoidable. Its French Orientalist architecture is doubtlessly beautiful, but so decayed that it barely masks the town's squalor. Most tourists head for the "camel market", which lacks camels but does have Yemeni daggers, Arabic jewellery and Ethiopian amber carvings. The town's seafood restaurants display a distinct and delicious Yemeni influence, and there are nice beaches around.

● **Lac Abhé (Abbé)** On the Ethiopian border, this steaming lake is as

Average temperature ranges and rainfall

	Jan	Feb	Mar	Apr	May	Jun	Jul	Aug	Sep	Oct	Nov	Dec
Djibouti city												
Max °C	29	29	30	32	35	39	42	41	37	33	31	29
Max °C	22	23	24	25	27	29	31	31	29	26	23	22
Rainfall mm	10	19	20	29	17	0	6	6	3	20	22	11

△ Salt pan at Lac Assal

amazing as the lunar landscape you travel through to get there – an area so desolate it featured as the post-apocalyptic "Forbidden Zone" in the classic 1968 film, Planet of the Apes. Only flamingoes, ibis and pelicans are really at home, though nomads occasionally come to graze their herds on spring-watered grasslands scattered between hundreds of weird limestone chimneys, some up to 30m high – the handiwork of decidedly smelly fumaroles.

● **Lac Assal and Ardoukoba volcano** Continuing the theme of tormented beauty is this briny, salt-rimmed lake 157m below sea level in the swelter-ing Danakil Depression. Africa's lowest place, it holds high excitement for geologists: the road there passes the world's youngest volcano, Ardoukoba, which appeared in 1978. The volcano, its lava flows, and a very visible crack stretching for many kilometres are products of the ever-widening Rift Valley.

● **Ali-Sabieh and around** The market town of Ali-Sabieh, southwest of Djibouti city, enjoys an agreeably "cool" climate by national standards. The striking red mountains around it can be climbed in the company of border guards. The

desert plains and escarpments are prone to mirages, but their antelopes, jackals, goats and camel trains are real.

● **Scuba-diving and snorkelling** In contrast to the country's blistered landscapes, Djibouti underwater is a teeming soup of life, stupendously colourful too. Particularly prized by scuba-divers are the reefs of Tadjourah Gulf, where you might see eagle rays or swim with immense whale sharks. There are also dugongs, all sorts of sharks and turtles, and dolphins.

● **Red Sea cruises** Whether it's just for a few hours, or a week of luxury aboard a converted dhow or Turkish ketch, do mess about on the water. All trips take in the Tadjourah Gulf, and more adventur-ous ones sail north towards the straits that separate Africa from Arabia. Some offer scuba-diving, and all run day-trips to the other attractions mentioned above.

Festivals

Apart from Islamic holidays (see pp.243–245), the main event is Fest'Horn, a festival of music from eastern Africa every December in Djibouti city.

Routes in and out

The airport is at Djibouti city. There are buses, shared taxis and an unpredictable train in from Ethiopia. Overnight taxis arrive from Hargeysa in Somaliland. Flying is the easiest way to and from Eritrea; overlanding may mean hitchhiking. There's no regular sea transport from Yemen, but cargo dhows will take passengers.

Djibouti online

Office National du Tourisme de Djibouti
Ⓦ **www.office-tourisme.dj**

Djiboutian Sightings
Ⓦ **www.djiboutian.happyhost.org** A handful of historically-themed photo galleries.
Le Pays des Braves
Ⓦ **www.djiboutiweb.net** The best site for visitors, which isn't saying all that much. In French.
Radiodiffusion Télévision de Djibouti
Ⓦ **www.rtd.dj** Has a reasonable selection of music clips.

Books

Marie Christine Aubry *Djibouti l'Ignoré.* The best introduction to Djibouti's history and culture, but it's in French.

Egypt

Area 1,001,450 square kilometres
Capital Cairo
Population 78 million; most Egyptians are of mixed descent, blending Arab, Bedouin and Nubian
Language Arabic (official); English and French also spoken by the better educated
Religion Islam 90 percent, Coptic Christianity 5 percent

Climate Almost entirely desert, with extremely hot summers and warm winters (but cold nights); the dusty Khamsin blows Feb–April
Best time to go March, April, Oct & Nov in general, though the Red Sea coast is good all year-round
Currency Egyptian pound
Minimum costs $17/£9 per day

Thomas Cook knew what he was doing when, in 1869, he escorted his first tour to Egypt and the Holy Land, thereby inventing long-haul package tourism. No other country is more stuffed with monuments and antiquities; all the more astonishing when you realize that 96 percent of Egypt is desert, relieved only by the Nile valley and its delta.

As one of the world's oldest continuous civilizations, Egypt presents an astonishing sweep through five millennia of history: three thousand years of Pharaonic rule peppered by Assyrian, Persian and Greek invasions, and followed by Roman, Byzantine and Arab conquests, and colonization by Turkey, France and Britain. The most famous Pharaonic sights – the Pyramids and Sphinx, Valley of the Kings and Karnak – are just a tiny fraction of what can be seen. Among the country's later wonders

Average temperature ranges and rainfall

	Jan	Feb	Mar	Apr	May	Jun	Jul	Aug	Sep	Oct	Nov	Dec
Cairo												
Max °C	19	20	24	28	32	34	35	34	33	29	25	20
Min °C	9	10	12	15	18	20	22	22	21	17	14	10
Rainfall mm	5	4	4	1	1	0	0	0	0	1	4	6
Sharm El-Sheikh												
Max °C	22	22	25	30	34	37	38	38	35	32	27	23
Min °C	13	14	16	20	24	27	28	28	27	23	19	15
Rainfall mm	1	0	1	0	1	0	0	0	0	1	3	1
Luxor												
Max °C	23	25	29	35	39	41	41	41	39	35	30	24
Min °C	6	7	11	16	20	23	24	24	22	18	12	8
Rainfall mm	0	0	0	0	0	0	0	0	0	1	0	0

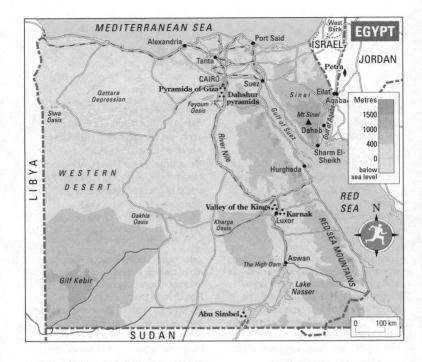

are some of the world's oldest churches, its oldest university, and an embarrassment of Islamic riches. It's a measure of Egypt's historical wealth that the list of attractions below only scratches the surface.

Antiquities aside, there are other treasures to lure travellers, too – luxurious Nile cruises, camelback desert adventures, oases, Red Sea beaches and coral reefs, isolated monasteries … Egypt really is an unforgettable experience.

Main attractions

● **The Pyramids and Sphinx** Just outside downtown Cairo at Giza, the Great Pyramid of Khufu is the only survivor of the Seven Wonders of the

World, flanked by two other pyramids and the Sphinx. The sheer size and geometric precision of the monuments (including many an astronomical alignment) have long fed crackpot theories about their hidden meaning and powers.

● **Cairo** Even had the Pyramids and Sphinx not been constructed on Cairo's doorstep, Africa's biggest metropolis would still be worth spending time in. Despite a population of over 14 million, Cairo has a surprisingly gentle (if predictably chaotic) feel. Apart from Giza, the indisputable highlight is the Egyptian Antiquities Museum. Even if you're prone to museum fatigue, don't miss this one – among its 130,000 exhibits are some of mankind's most beautiful creations, most famously the golden funerary mask of

Pharaoh Tutankhamen. The heart of the city itself is also a museum, especially of Islamic times – there are architectural masterpieces at every turn, including visitable mosques. Close at hand, too, are the ever-entertaining souks of Khan el-Khalili.

● **Dakhla oasis** A cluster of oases, gardens and lakes, Dakhla is life for fourteen settlements. The oldest and most memorable, with well-preserved traditional architecture, is the village of Al-Qasr, deliciously positioned amid pink dune-draped mountains. Despite having been largely abandoned, Al-Qasr's old town – dominated by a cylindrical twelfth-century minaret – remains intact, and conceals many a photogenic nook and cranny. Dakhla's other attractions include romantic Qalamoun village and its improbable desert lakes, the Muzawaka Tombs dug out of a table-top mountain, and the diminutive Egyptian– Roman temple of Deir el-Hagar, which became a Coptic monastery.

● **The Valley of the Kings** Halfway down the Egyptian Nile, Luxor (meaning "the Palaces") was ancient Thebes, capital of Egypt's New Kingdom in the second millennium BC. An obscene profusion of Pharaonic temples and tombs are found within a few kilometres of town, mostly famously at Karnak and in the Valley of the Kings. The latter was where generations of pharaohs excavat- ed their tombs; the most famous is that of Tutankhamen, which was opened in 1922 after 3274 years in darkness. Most of its treasures are housed in Cairo's national museum, though the pharaoh's mummy and innermost gold coffin are still in situ. Dozens of other tombs can also be visited, many lavishly decorated with hieroglyphs and cosmological scenes.

● **Karnak** While the Valley of the Kings is all about decoration, in Karnak it was size that mattered – its temples, arranged into three precincts, were built to gargantuan scales to house the gods. The most impressive is the colossal Temple of Amun, with its bulging columns and even more portly statues, but there are plenty more temples besides, less visited but no less imposing, including those of Khonsu and Ramses III, and an impressive avenue of ram-headed sphinxes.

● **Gilf Kebir** A day-trip to an oasis is probably enough desert for most, but for dedicated desert rats, longer excursions and expeditions are possible, both in the Sinai and west of the Nile. Especially recommended is the Gilf Kebir plateau in the Uwaynat Desert, with its evocative World War II wrecks and prehistoric rock art. The most famous paintings are in the Cave of the Swimmers, discovered by László Ede Almássy – who became the main character in *The English Patient*.

● **Red Sea holidays** Hot and dry all year round, the Sinai Peninsula has Egypt's best beaches and superlative snorkelling and diving. Sharm El-Sheikh and adjacent Na'ama Bay are brashest and plushest. Dahab is gradually moving upscale, but for now remains the backpackers' destination. Viable targets for day-trips include ancient Christian churches and Mount Sinai.

Also recommended

● **Alexandria** This venerable Mediterranean port has long been a crossroads of civilizations, and it was only natural that its library – long since destroyed – was the classical world's greatest. Until the 1952 Revolution, Alexandria was a cosmopolitan town, with sizeable communities from all around the Mediterranean. While it has lost the glitter and sparkle, it's still charming in the way that dignified old ladies can be, and in many ways its easy-going nature makes it a mirror for Egyptian society in general. Attractions include an excellent Greco-Roman museum, the ruins of Cleopatra's palace, nice beaches, and an architecturally dazzling new library, which contains several more museums and a planetarium.

● **Aswan and Abu Simbel** Egypt's "Gateway to Nubia", Aswan has a laid-back and distinctly African feeling, and its beautiful river islands, classic sailing excursions by felucca, attractive bazaars and good restaurants may entice you to stay longer than you intended. Though its monuments may pale in comparison to, say, Luxor's, they're still worth visiting – and it would be a shame to miss out on Ramses II's spectacular Sun Temples at Abu Simbel, which were shifted to higher ground in the 1960s to avoid inundation after the construction of the Aswan High Dam.

● **Dahshur pyramids** Less famous than Giza's but no less fascinating, and far less crowded, are the pyramids of Pharaoh Snefru. The Bent Pyramid, in which the pharaoh lies, has a distinctive angled top, a last-minute change after the pyramid's sides proved too steep to hold their weight.

● **Nile cruises** They may no longer be as opulent as when Thomas Cook started it all off, but a Nile cruise is still de rigueur if you have the money, offering an easy and comfortable way to see many of the Nile Valley's most famous sights.

● **Fayoum oasis** Supporting over two million inhabitants, this impressively green expanse is Egypt's largest oasis, and would be recommended unreservedly were it not for the lack of desert to cross to get there, as access is via the Nile. In addition to fabulous oasis gardens and surreal lakes, attractions include Pharaonic temples and monuments galore.

● **Siwa oasis** A series of gardens, lakes and settlements, each with its individual charm, Siwa has a history dating back to Palaeolithic times. Its oracle was consulted by Alexander the Great, and there are plenty of ruins from Pharaonic times. More recent remains include the mud-brick town of Shali, destroyed by rain in 1926. Also worth seeing is the "Mountain of the Dead", whose soft rock is punctured by hundreds of tombs, many richly painted.

Festivals

In addition to the standard Islamic festivals (see pp.243–245), dozens of localized Islamic and Coptic Christian religious dates are celebrated. Many are *moulid* pilgrimages, associated with particular saints and places. They're good times to hear traditional music, sample culinary delicacies, and simply blend in with the crowds. The Nile Delta town of Tanta is the scene for Egypt's biggest pilgrimage, the Festival of Sayid Ahmad al-Badawi in October. The event is an eight-day affair around the tomb of a thirteenth-century founder of the Sufi Badawiyya order, attracting more than two million people each year.

Routes in and out

The main international airports are Cairo and Alexandria; there are also charter flights from Europe to the Sinai Peninsula. Overland transport connects with Israel and Libya; Sudan is linked with Egypt by Nile steamer.

Egypt online

Tour Egypt
Ⓦ **www.touregypt.net**
Adventures of Egypt
Ⓦ www.lexicorient.com/egypt Norwegian Tore Kjeilen's insanely comprehensive encyclopedia to North Africa and the Middle East reaches its apogee in its treatment of Egypt: hundreds of informative and often amusing pages, and excellent photographs.
Egyptian Museum
Ⓦ **www.egyptianmuseum.gov.eg** A selection of the famous museum's vast collection.
Egyptology Online
Ⓦ **www.egyptologyonline.com** An attractive introduction to the subject.
Guardian's Egypt
Ⓦ **www.guardians.net** Info on Egyptian archeology and the latest finds. Good links, too.

Books

Mark Collier and Bill Manley *How to Read Egyptian Hieroglyphs: A step-by-step guide to teach yourself.* Does what it says on the cover – clear and understandable, even when you're trying to decipher stuff in the midday heat.

Christine Hobson *The World of the Pharaohs: A Complete Guide to Ancient Egypt.* Among the best of the many illustrated books on Egyptian antiquities.
Naguib Mahfouz *Palace of Desires; Palace Walk; and Sugar Street.* These books, comprising a trilogy, are among the best work of the late Mahfouz, who won the Nobel Prize for literature in 1999 for his impressive corpus of fiction, strongly influenced by Balzac and Victor Hugo.
Deborah Manley *The Nile: A Traveller's Anthology.* An admirably eclectic selection from over a hundred non-Egyptian writers, from classical texts to colonial ramblings from the likes of Lawrence Durrell and Evelyn Waugh.
Nawal el-Saadawi *Point Zero* and *The Hidden Face of Eve.* The best English translations of works by this outspoken feminist writer and novelist. *Point Zero* is a poignant and embittered tale of the life and tribulations of an everyday Egyptian woman. The non-fiction *The Hidden Face of Eve* is a major polemic concerning sexual aggression, female circumcision, prostitution, divorce and sexual relationships, all of which are taboo in Egypt.
Anthony Sattin *The Pharaoh's Shadow.* Fascinating discourse on lingering ancient Egyptian beliefs among the minority Copts.

Eritrea

Area 121,320 square kilometres
Capital Asmara
Population 4.6 million; main ethnic groups are Tigrinya, Tigre and Kunama
Language Tigray and Arabic (both official) are widely spoken; Italian and English are limited to more educated people
Religion Christianity 50 percent, Islam 50 percent
Climate Three climatic zones: coastal desert (hottest June–Aug, rains in north Dec–Feb); cooler and wetter central highlands (coolest Dec–Feb, rains March–April & June–Sept); and semi-arid western lowlands (very hot April–June, coolest Dec)
Best time to go Sept–Feb for the highlands; Nov–March for the lowlands and coast
Currency Nakfa
Minimum costs $12/£7

Known as Punt and Ta Netjeru ("the Land of the Gods") to the ancient Egyptians, Eritrea takes its modern name from the ancient Greek term for the Red Sea. History has not been kind, however: Eritrea fell under Ottoman dominion in the sixteenth century, and was subsequently ruled by Egypt, Italy and Ethiopia. Only in 1993, after a bitter struggle, did the country finally regain its independence, only to plunge into a brief war with Yemen, and a devastating conflict with Ethiopia which ended in 2000.

War has levelled much of this ancient country, but even so, it's not without its charms, among them many Orthodox churches and monasteries. Rugged and often spectacular landscapes are another big draw, ranging from the hellishly hot Danakil desert below sea level to green (and chilly) three-thousand-metre mountains. There's also the Red Sea, of course, its scuba-diving and snorkelling opportunities matching the best anywhere.

While independent travel is possible, a permit system restricts the movements of tourists beyond the main sights. The attractions mentioned below should be accessible.

Main attractions

● **Asmara** Perched on the edge of the highland plateau, Asmara is an attractive capital, much of it erected by the Italians in Art Deco style. Many a cosy café survives, and the National Museum has good displays on archeology, ethnography and natural history. There's also great bird-watching on the escarpment.

● **The Eritrean Railway** Get from Asmara to Massawa on one of Africa's last steam trains.

● **Massawa (Mitsiwa)** This delightful port town has its historical heart on two islands connected by causeways. Despite having been severely damaged in the war of independence, both contain gorgeous Ottoman, Italianate and Egyptian-style buildings well suited for aimless wanders. Escape the heat in one of many bars, and sample the

Average temperature ranges and rainfall

	Jan	Feb	Mar	Apr	May	Jun	Jul	Aug	Sep	Oct	Nov	Dec
Asmara												
Max °C	22	24	25	25	25	25	22	22	23	22	22	22
Min °C	4	5	8	9	10	11	11	11	9	8	7	5
Rainfall mm	4	2	15	33	41	39	175	156	16	15	20	3
Massawa												
Max °C	29	29	32	34	37	40	41	40	39	36	33	31
Min °C	19	19	20	22	24	26	28	28	26	23	21	20
Rainfall mm	35	22	10	4	8	0	8	8	3	22	24	40

fruits of the Red Sea in fine seafood restaurants. There are lovely beaches to the north (good for scuba-diving and snorkelling), and picturesque dhows bobbing in the port.

● **Dankalia** The blisteringly hot Danakil Depression or "Afar Triangle" stretches 600km between Massawa and Djibouti, much of it consisting of volcanic desert. Inhospitable is the word, not that the local Afar would agree – hard as nails, they're Eritrea's most traditionalist people.

● **Dahlak Archipelago** The Red Sea's largest archipelago, accessed from Massawa, comprises more than half of Eritrea's 350 islands, of which just four are inhabited. The largest, Dahlak Kebir, contains Afar fishing villages and ruins from slave-trading times. Reminders of Eritrea's recent history remain on Nacura Island, which was a prison during Italian and Ethiopian rule. When the Ethiopians left, they dropped a heap of military hardware into the sea – which has added to the

△ Restored Art Deco: the Impero cinema in Asmara

archipelago's reputation as a wonder-
land for scuba-divers.

● **Debre Bizen** This hilltop Orthodox
monastery, founded in 1361, became
famous for having devised its own
calendar. The problem was that
doomsday (due in 1500 AD) came and
went without incident, consigning the
calendar to history. The monastery is
home to sixty monks; women (indeed,
females of any species) cannot visit, to
shield the monks from temptation. For
men, the hike to the top is rewarded
by sweeping views and glimpses
of ancient works in the monastery's
library.

Also recommended

● **Nacfa** Now rebuilt, Nacfa was home
to the resistance against Ethiopia, and
as such was levelled by the Ethiopian
Air Force in 1983, leaving only the
minaret of the Grand Mosque (which
was used a landmark by pilots). The
town's sights are all war-related,
including bunkers and trenches that
gave access to what was virtually an
underground city.

● **Keren (Cheren)** This agricultural
town, overshadowed by peaks and an
imposing Egyptian fortress, contains
fine examples of Italian and Ethiopian
architecture, and the ruins of an imperial
palace destroyed in 1977. The lively daily
market is good for silverware, but try to
come on a Monday for the fascinating
livestock market.

● **Matara** The country's most interesting ruins, Matara dates from the early
days of the Abyssinian Empire of Aksum.
The highlight is a large stele called the
Hawulti, which was deliberately toppled
by Ethiopian troops in the latest war.

Festivals

Public expressions of traditional Eritrean
culture were greatly curtailed during the
Italian and Ethiopian occupation. As
such, the best times to be around are
Orthodox Christian holidays: January
7 for Leddet (Christmas), January 19
for Timket (Epiphany), August 11 for an
annual celebration at Debre Bizen, and
September 27 for Meskel (Finding of the
True Cross).

Routes in and out

The airport is at Asmara. Shared taxis
operate to and from Djibouti, which is
the only way to Ethiopia as the land
border is closed. The Sudanese border
is also prone to closure, and both border
areas are prone to rebel or bandit
activity, even bomb attacks.

Eritrea online

Ministry of Tourism
Ⓦ www.shaebia.org/mot.html
Dehai
Ⓦ www.dehai.org News, loads of links,
and informative forums.
Eritrea – adventure and hospitality
Ⓦ www.eritrea.be Comprehensive and
attractive country guide with plenty of
photos.
**Matara: Aksumite and Pre-Aksumite
City Site**
Ⓦ hometown.aol.com/_ht_a/atobrukh
/archaeology/matara/matara.html
A jumbled but informative site about
Eritrea's archeological heritage.
Revisiting Eritrea
Ⓦ worksandwords.com/ethtrav.htm
Entire book recounting a journey in
the late 1960s, mostly in what's now
Eritrea.

Books

Anne Alders *Eritrean Beauty*. Gorgeous people, gorgeous photos, and intelligent text. For a taster, see ⓦwww .eritreanbeauty.com.
Roy Pateman *Eritrea: Even the Stones are Burning*. A definitive survey of Eritrea's struggle for independence.
Sami Sallinen and Haile Bizen *Asmara Beloved*. A lovely coffee-table book about Eritrea's ever-charming capital.

Abeba Tesfagiorgis *A Painful Season & A Stubborn Hope*. The remarkable autobiography of an Eritrean-American woman in the 1970s: her time as a political prisoner, and the experiences of her children as freedom fighters.
Michela Wrong *I Didn't Do It For You*. Subtitled "How the world used and abused a small African nation", this intelligent and well-written travelogue tells the troubled story of both Eritrea and colonialism in general, through a series of often deliberately absurd and frequently jarring vignettes.

Ethiopia

Area 1,133,380 square kilometres
Capital Addis Ababa
Population 81 million; the main ethno-linguistic groups are Oromo (centre and south), Amhara and Tigrean (centre), Nilotic (west) and Cushitic (mainly Somali; east and southeast)
Language Amharic is the official language, with its own alphabet too; other languages include Oromo, Tigrinya and Somali; English is widely used, and Arabic, Italian and French may also be understood
Religion Islam 50 percent, Ethiopian Orthodox Christianity 40 percent
Climate Hot and humid in the lowlands, hot and dry in the south, temperate in the highlands; rains June–Sept
Best time to go Oct–March
Currency Birr
Minimum costs $12/£7 per day

Ethiopia has recently emerged from decades of military dictatorship, but political instability, famine, droughts, floods, rebel activity in the south, and on-off conflict with Eritrea still beset the country. Look beyond these problems, though, you'll find that Ethiopia is one of Africa's most fascinating places to visit. With its own calendar, one of the world's oldest brands of Christianity, and over seventy tribes and langu-ages, Ethiopia is a nation of immense complexity, and mystery. A sense of timelessness pervades the land: three thousand years of empires, dynasties, wars, revolutions and struggles can be explored through a bounty of monuments and sights.

Physically, Ethiopia is a land of contrasts. The hot, barren deserts of the country's extremities give way to the stunning central highlands, where the Blue Nile has its source amid a region of lush mountains, vertiginous canyons and gorges, rivers, waterfalls and lakes.

Average temperature ranges and rainfall

	Jan	Feb	Mar	Apr	May	Jun	Jul	Aug	Sep	Oct	Nov	Dec
Addis Ababa												
Max °C	24	24	25	25	25	23	21	21	22	24	23	23
Min °C	6	8	9	10	10	9	10	10	9	7	9	9
Rainfall mm	13	38	66	86	86	137	279	300	191	20	15	5
Lalibela												
Max °C	22	23	24	23	22	19	17	17	19	20	21	22
Min °C	7	8	9	10	10	9	9	9	8	8	7	6
Rainfall mm	7	13	50	53	35	43	245	232	43	17	13	6

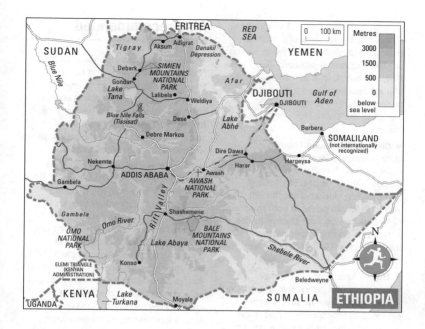

Main attractions

• **Addis Ababa** As third-highest capital in the world, at 2440m, Addis Ababa has a temperate climate – a good thing too, as there's plenty to see on foot in this cosmopolitan city of four million. Attractions include the National Museum (housing the fossilized skeleton of the early hominid known affectionately as Lucy), the informative Ethnology Museum, St George's Cathedral (built in 1896 to commemorate a victory over Italy), the Holy Trinity Cathedral (the final resting place of Ethiopia's last emperor, Haile Selassie) and the Mercato, reputedly Africa's largest market.

• **Aksum** Established over 3000 years ago, Aksum became the centre of the extensive Abyssinian Empire, which held sway over the region for many centuries.

Biblical myths and legends of the Queen of Sheba permeate this living museum: impressive stelae and tombs, ruined palaces and gigantic baths, and possibly even the original Ark of the Covenant, said to be kept inside the Church of Mary of Zion. There's also a 24-metre obelisk, looted by Mussolini in 1937 to stand guard in Rome, which was returned in 2005.

• **Lalibela** This otherwise quiet mountain village is famous for its wondrous rock-hewn churches, the focus of annual pilgrimages for Ethiopian Orthodox Christians. Fashioned in the twelfth century, the monolithic structures are connected by bewildering tunnels and passageways.

• **Gondar** Founded by Emperor Fasilidas in 1635, Gondar served as Ethiopia's capital for over two centuries, and its Royal Enclosure – sometimes referred to as the Camelot of Ethiopia – encircles the remains of churches, palaces and castles. Also worth seeing are the remarkable palace of Ras Beit, the oversized bath of Fasilidas (the masses flock here to be baptized during Timket), and the elaborate murals of the Debre Berhane Selassie church.

● **Simien Mountains** These spectacular mountains include Ethiopia's highest peak, Ras Dashen (4500m), gorges with drops of up to 1500m, and stunning views across the Rift Valley. Treks are possible from the town of Debark, offering the chance to see indigenous and rare species such as the Walia ibex, Gelada baboon and Simien fox.

● **Harar** Harar is an atmospheric walled affair, and getting lost among the labyrinth of narrow streets while exploring its mosques is all part of the fun. Harar is also an agricultural centre – its region is the birthplace of coffee. Apart from those pungent beans, you'll find mildly narcotic *qat* (*miraa*) sprigs on sale, together with superb handicrafts including baskets, silver jewellery and woven textiles. Also popular with tourists is the intricate house where French poet Rimbaud resided while he earned a small fortune as a gun-runner.

● **Lake Tana and the Blue Nile Falls** Lake Tana, Ethiopia's largest lake, has over thirty islands to explore, many with ancient churches and monasteries. The most famous of these, Dek Stephanous, is decorated with glorious frescoes and contains a priceless collection of icons and the remains of several medieval emperors. Just to the south of the lake are the 400-metre Blue Nile Falls, which, in the wet season, create a spectacle of "smoking water" while sheltering hippos, crocodiles and flocks of pelicans.

Also recommended

● **Cuisine** Ethiopian food is a delight, both on the taste buds and as a social event. The staple is injera, a large spongy pancake. Everybody is encouraged to share, tearing off pieces of injera to scoop up mouthfuls of exquisitely spiced meat, vegetables and stews, all washed down with honey beer.

● **Omo Valley** One of Ethiopia's more remote regions is home to staunchly traditional Omotic-speaking peoples, including the Dassanech, Hamar and Nyangaton. The various groups may welcome visitors, but floods and droughts have caused extreme hardship (and occasional armed conflict over pastures and water sources), so seek advice before you go. Other attractions in the region include the relatively undeveloped Omo and Mago National Parks, and one of Africa's top rivers for white-water rafting.

● **Bale Mountains National Park** Volcanic peaks, rocky gorges, redwood and juniper forests, heather moorlands, and an abundance of endemic birdlife and wildlife: the continent's largest Afro-alpine habitat rises to a height of over 4000m and offers unsurpassed opportunities for hiking, horse-riding and scenic drives.

● **Rift Valley lakes** The seven lakes south of Addis Ababa are a popular weekend getaway for the capital's residents. There are luxury resorts and watersports at Lake Langano, and fantastic bird-watching at lakes Abiyata and Shala.

Festivals

In keeping with the country's strong historical foundations, Ethiopia's festivals tend to honour its religious past. The Ethiopian Orthodox Church uses the Julian calendar, consisting of twelve thirty-day months and a thirteenth of five or six days. It's several years behind our own, Gregorian, calendar: the Millennium will be celebrated in September 2008. Traditional Muslim holidays are also observed; see p.245 for dates.

Enkutatash (New Year) Highlands, particularly Gaynt near Gondar, and Ragual Church near Addis Ababa; around Sept 11 Coinciding with the end of the rains, New Year marks the day when Makeda, Queen of Sheba, returned to Ethiopia to be welcomed with gifts of jewels. Expect bonfires, excited kids, processions and music.

Meskel (Finding of the True Cross) Best in Addis Ababa; around Sept 27 The discovery of the cross (meskel) on which Jesus is said to have died is marked by processions of flaming torches and crosses, brass bands and an army parade. They converge on a big bonfire surrounding a tree, which burns throughout the night. Strangers are welcomed into homes and likely to be offered honey beer.

Timket (Epiphany) Highlands, especially Lalibela; around Jan 19 Highlight of the Orthodox calendar, celebrated with three days of dramatic and colourful processions of replicas of the tablets of the laws received by Moses, culminating on the third day with mass baptisms.

Victory of Adowa Nationwide; March 2 Public holiday marking the Italian army's defeat in 1896, which confirmed Ethiopia's independence.

Routes in and out

Addis Ababa's airport is a major African hub. Buses, shared taxis and an unpredictable train connect with Djibouti, which is the only way to get to Eritrea. There's no public transport on either side of the Sudanese and Kenyan borders.

Ethiopia online

Ethiopian Tourist Commission
Ⓦ www.tourismethiopia.org
Addis Live!
Ⓦ www.addislive.com Online radio station, in English, offering wide choice of channels, music streams and videos covering all genres, plus live radio.
Dear Ethiopia
Ⓦ www.dear-ethiopia.com An endearing and well-illustrated overview of the main attractions, by a French tourist who fell in love with the country.
Ethiopia Icons: Faith and Science
Ⓦ www.nmafa.si.edu/exhibits/icons/index.html A short but beauteous introduction to these works of art.
Ethiopian Millennium
Ⓦ www.ethiopianmillennium.com Information on 2008's Y2K.

Books

Samuel Baker *The Nile Tributaries of Abyssinia*. One of several classic journey accounts by the nineteenth-century explorer. Free at Ⓦ www.gutenberg.org.
Neville Garrick *A Rasta's Pilgrimage: Ethiopian Faces and Places*. Powerful collection of well-composed photography and thoughts on Ethiopia from a Rastafarian perspective.
Ryszard Kapuscuski *The Emperor: The Downfall of an Autocrat*. Incisive portrayal of the last days of Emperor Haile Selassie.
Nega Mazlekia *Notes From the Hyena's Belly: An Ethiopian Boyhood*. Unforgettable account of Ethiopia in the 1970s and 1980s, a period of civil war, famine and mass executions.
Dervla Murphy *In Ethiopia with a Mule*. Fun and refreshing travel writing about a perilous solo trek through Ethiopia.

Gabon

Area 267,667 square kilometres	**Religion** Christianity 60 percent,
Capital Libreville	traditional beliefs 30 percent
Population 1.4 million; over forty	**Climate** Equatorial, with rains year-
tribes, most belonging to the Fang,	round (heaviest Oct–May)
Pounou, Nzeiby or Téké ethnic	**Best time to go** June–Aug
groups	(fractionally cooler and less rain)
Language French; the main ethnic	**Currency** CFA franc
language is Fang	**Minimum costs** $25/£14 per day

By African standards, oil-producing Gabon is rich, and after four decades under autocratic President Omar Bongo, it's also among the more stable countries. Straddling the Equator, the country boasts palm-fringed beaches, backed by estuaries and lagoons, equalling any other. But the real treasure lies in the hilly and lushly forested interior, along whose rivers most Gabonese live. The forests possess extraordinary zoological wealth, of which gorillas, chimpanzees and forest elephants are the most famous representatives.

It wasn't until 2000 that Gabon switched on to eco-tourism, finally goaded into action by the *National Geographic's* much-publicized "Megatransect" of the Congo Basin. Thirteen national parks were created, transforming the country from environmental nonentity to conservation darling. Although the country now touts itself exclusively as a wildlife destination, it's also – if you've a little perseverance – a great place for culture. The forests are the traditional home to Bibayak Pygmies, purveyors of the most complex, virtuoso and spine-tinglingly entrancing music you'll ever hear (micropolyphonic and multi-rhythmic, if you

must know). Gabon is also a major player in contemporary music, with innumerable rap and hip-hop crews drawing admirers. So, for a holiday well off the beaten track, get to Gabon before the masses cotton on.

Main attractions

● **Libreville** Gabon's small but lively oceanside capital holds most of the country's nightlife, and is the place to pick up Fang masks, an antique example of which recently chalked up a record €5.9 million at a Paris auction house. There are great beaches nearby, complete with resorts offering waterskiing, scuba-diving and birding around mangroves.

● **Lopé National Park** Accessible by train from Libreville, Lopé is a patchwork of savanna and dense forest around the Ogooué River, where gorilla tracking is the thing, accompanied by a Pygmy guide. You can also explore the river by pirogue, explore 2000-year-old rock engravings, go looking for troops of mandrill monkeys up to a thousand strong, or busy yourself with the park's 350 bird species.

Average temperature ranges and rainfall

Libreville	Jan	Feb	Mar	Apr	May	Jun	Jul	Aug	Sep	Oct	Nov	Dec
Max °C	30	30	30	30	29	28	26	27	28	28	28	29
Min °C	24	24	24	23	24	23	22	22	23	23	23	23
Rainfall mm	250	243	363	339	247	54	7	14	104	427	490	303

● **Loango National Park** A gem of a place on the south coast, protecting a one-hundred-kilometre stretch of uninhabited beaches, lagoons and swamps, and a belt of thick equatorial forest behind. Raw beauty aside, there's a chance of spotting wildlife on the beach, from gorillas and elephants to leopards and buffaloes, and whales are often seen offshore.

● **Crystal Mountains National Park** A botanical paradise, its mist-shrouded forests especially rich in orchids and begonias.

Also recommended

● **Akanda National Park** The mangroves and tidal mud flats of the northwest are home to the country's largest concentration of migratory birds, and turtles. Visitors get around by boat.

● **Ivindo National Park** This land of rivers and forests boasts two of Central Africa's most impressive waterfalls, plus gorillas and chimpanzees, and waterhole clearings where elephants are easily seen.

● **Mayumba National Park** Most easily reached by plane, this sandy, coast-hugging peninsula starts at the Congolese border and is home to the world's largest population of nesting leatherback turtles.

● **Minkébé National Park** A huge expanse of highland forest broken only by dome-like sandstone outcrops, rivers and marshy clearings, which you can get around by pirogue. The park is home to elephants, giant forest hogs and the rare Bongo antelope.

● **Bateke Plateau National Park** A magnificent area of forest-edged savanna, with liana bridges slung across its rivers. Residents include forest elephants, buffaloes and water-loving sitatunga antelopes. Gorillas are set to be reintroduced.

● **Lambaréné** Albert Schweitzer's hospital on the Ogooué River here can be visited, and you can also drift along the river in search of birds and hippos.

Festivals

Christian and Muslim festivals are observed; see p.243 & p.245 for dates. The main musical event is Festival Gabao Hip-Hop (in Libreville in June), which headlines crews from Francophone West Africa.

Routes in and out

The international airport is at Libreville. There's (slow) overland transport from neighbouring countries. Erratic ferries connect with São Tomé.

Gabon online

Gabon National Parks
ⓦ www.gabonnationalparks.com
News, profiles and practical info.
LBVGroove.com
ⓦ music.lbvgroove.com Contemporary
Gabonese music, with some full-length
soundclips including especially good
hip-hop. In French.
National Geographic – Congo Trek
ⓦ www.nationalgeographic.com
/congotrek Slick presentation of the
Megatransect expedition.
Rock Art in Gabon
ⓦ www.bradshawfoundation.com
/congo/gabon.html An attractive
introduction to the subject.

Books

Jan Brokken *The Rainbird: A Central
African Journey*. A tempting invitation to
visit, this travelogue includes a wealth of
stories and anecdotes from European
explorers, and an impressive amount of
cultural detail.
Louis Perrois *Fang*. A visual feast
concerning the Fang's emblematic art.
Albert Schweitzer *The Primeval Forest*.
The devout physician gained worldwide
admiration for humanitarian work in
Gabon. This volume comprises his first
two autobiographies.

The Gambia

Area 11,295 square kilometres
Capital Banjul
Population 1.5 million; ethnic
groups include Mandinka (largest),
Fulani, Wolof, Jola and Serahuli
Language Many Gambians are
trilingual, speaking English and one
or more tribal languages – Mandinka,
Wolof, Fula, etc
Religion Islam 85 percent,

Christianity 10 percent
Climate Tropical; rains Nov–May
Best time to go July–Oct for
beaches and wildlife; Nov–April for
birdlife
Currency Dalasi
Minimum costs $36/£20 per
day inland, double this for beach
holidays

A narrow, snaking finger of land poking into Senegal from the Atlantic, The Gambia is Africa's smallest country, and its lowest, topping out at little over 50m. The eponymous river that forms the country's spine was for centuries mistakenly believed to be a branch of the Niger, an easy route – so the Europeans thought – to the fabled riches of Timbuktu. Britain's lengthy occupation left many a mark, not the least of which being the country itself: in the nineteenth century, Britain and France had agreed that its borders be drawn according to the distance flown by a cannonball from the River Gambia, roughly 15km. The name, too, is a colonial throwback: it's from the Portuguese *câmbiar*, meaning to trade – which meant both gold and slaves.

Package beach holidays are how most visitors get to know The Gambia, but the country's small size also makes it easy to sample much of what the rest of West Africa has to offer: rusty termite-mound-dotted savanna scattered with colourful villages dominated by mango trees; mangrove-lined creeks, often accessible only by dugout; coconut groves and rice fields. There's even some wildlife – forest primates, hippos and crocodiles in the upper reaches of the river, and perhaps dolphins in tidal mangrove-lined creeks. But it's for birds that The Gambia comes into its own. The country's forests are a wintering ground for over 550 winter migrant species from Europe and the Arctic.

Average temperature ranges and rainfall

Banjul	Jan	Feb	Mar	Apr	May	Jun	Jul	Aug	Sep	Oct	Nov	Dec
Max °C	31	32	34	33	32	32	30	29	31	32	32	31
Min °C	15	16	17	18	19	23	23	23	23	22	22	16
Rainfall mm	1	0	0	0	1	63	232	347	255	76	2	1

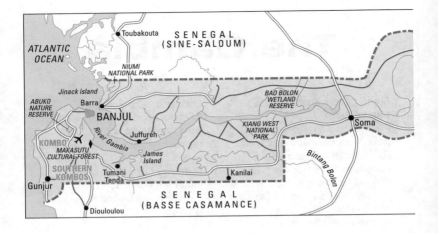

Main attractions

- **Beaches** The Gambia's beaches have long been a crowd-puller for wintering sun-starved Europeans, and there are plenty of hotels and resorts to choose from. The best beaches – wider, sandier, and with fewer visitors and hustlers than those just west of Banjul – are in the palm-fringed bays in the south, where you might share the shoreline with errant cows. Local wildlife includes turtles and aquatic birds.

- **Bao Bolon Wetland Reserve** On the north bank of the River Gambia, this 220-square-kilometre reserve is designated Wetland of International Importance, and The Gambia's largest protected area. Consisting of patches of thick forest, and freshwater swamps laced with mangrove creeks, it's home to dugongs, clawless otters, bush hogs, semi-aquatic sitatunga antelopes and hippos among others, but it's really for birds that the place is paradise – Egyptian plovers are the highlight.

- **Stone circles** Over a hundred prehistoric stone circles, some over 2000 years old, make pleasingly enigmatic targets for day-trips north of the river. Consisting of pillars, mostly shoulder height, the circles (and some rectangles) enclose burial mounds and may have had astrological significance. Whatever their purpose, the sheer size of some of the stones (the largest weighing ten tonnes) are a thought-provoking window onto an advanced civilization, of which few other traces remain. The main concentrations are at Kerr Batch and at Wassu.

- **River trips** Every hotel in The Gambia offers boat trips – anything from a few hours of messing about in pirogues to full-on adventures over several days. Almost everywhere has something worth seeing or doing, whether it's floating in and out of creeks and mangrove swamps in search of birds and critters, helping out with the oyster harvest, or heading down the coast for a taste of life in fishing villages.

- **Roots Pilgrimages** Inspired by Alex Haley's bestseller, *Roots*, and the TV series based on it, a Roots Pilgrimage traces the slave trade back to its origins, in Haley's case the village of Juffureh on

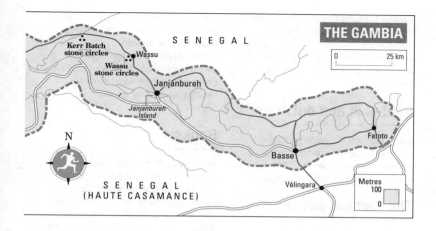

the north bank of the river, which now has a slavery museum. Trips include a boat ride to the former French trading post of Albreda, and the remains of the slave fort on James Island, from where captives were loaded on to their "floating coffins" (galleys) for transport to the Americas.

Also recommended

● **Abuko Nature Reserve** Within cycling distance of the beach resorts, tiny Abuko – covering just over a square kilometre – has fine patches of forest and savanna. Its meandering shady paths offer close encounters with monkeys, bushbucks, chameleons and crocodiles – from the safety of a viewpoint. In winter, Abuko's birdlife is extraordinarily rich.

● **Janjanbureh** Sitting midstream some 300km from Banjul, Janjanbureh is The Gambia's budding eco-tourism destination, its riverside camps sure to find favour with birders. The town itself is full of deliciously decrepit and photogenic colonial structures, and also serves as a

fine base for visiting Bao Bolon and the stone circles of Kerr Batch and Wassu.

● **Makasutu Cultural Forest** High-profile eco-tourism project with extensive local involvement, popular with day-trippers. Visits typically include a game drive, boat ride, guided forest walk and cultural performances. The associated Mandina Lodge is among the country's plushest.

● **Tumani Tenda** The Gambia's first cultural tourism project offers a welter of activities, whether plain old eco-tourism (there's a hide from where you can see bushbucks and porcupines), helping out with farming, oyster gathering and fishing, or paddling around in canoes and getting a sense of The Gambia's musical vibe.

Festivals

International Roots Festival May–June in even-numbered years The Gambia's big shindig, primarily aimed at African-Americans wishing to reaffirm their ties with the old continent, and – with luck – invest in the country.

Kanilai Cultural Festival May–June
Coinciding with the Roots Festival,
Kanilai is the showcase for Jola culture:
lots of music, wrestling bouts, fire-eating
and scaled-down initiation rites for
"homecomers".

Routes in and out

Banjul International Airport receives
plenty of European charters and
scheduled flights. There are several
overland crossings in from Senegal.

The Gambia online

Gambia Tourism Authority
Ⓦ**www.visitthegambia.gm**
Home Page of Momodou Camara
Ⓦ**www.gambia.dk** The best all-round
resource on The Gambia, with a bit of
everything and in quite some depth,
too. Includes a good intro to stone
circles, music, culture and wildlife, plus
a lively forum.
The Plymouth–Banjul Challenge
Ⓦ**www.plymouth-dakar.co.uk** The
Paris–Dakar is for wimps, as the
"Ultimate Banger Challenge" shows:
competing cars must cost no more
than £100, and vehicles surviving
the three-week, 4500km ordeal from
England are auctioned off for charity in
Banjul.
Raki Web Radio and Television
Ⓦ**goto.glocalnet.net/raki** Beautifully
polished site on Gambian music, with
musician profiles plus radio streams.
State House Online
Ⓦ**www.statehouse.gm** The official
take on what's going on; best read in
conjunction with Ⓦwww.freedom
newspaper.com, for an unofficial
riposte.

Books

Alex Haley *Roots*. Published in 1976,
the African-American author's fiction-
alized account of the search for his
ancestors became an instant bestseller.
The televised adaptation of the epic
quest became one of the most popular
shows in American television history.
Mark Hudson *Our Grandmothers'
Drums*. Wonderfully absorbing account
of the author's year-long stay in a
Gambian village, written with a genuine
love for the people and the place.
Richard Jobson *The Golden Trade*.
Entertaining account of an early
seventeenth-century expedition in search
of Timbuktu, a good part of which was
spent along the River Gambia. Digital
version at Ⓦpenelope.uchicago
.edu/jobson
Anna-Britt Sternfeldt *The Good Tourist
in The Gambia*. Thoughtful and honest
guide to responsible tourism, with
practical information on getting the
most out of the country while directly
supporting locals.

Ghana

Area 239,460 square kilometres
Capital Accra
Population 23 million; the main ethnic groups, each comprising several sub-groups, are Akan (Asante/Ashanti and Fante/Fanti), Ewe and Ga
Language English (official) is widespread; ethnic languages also spoken
Religion Christianity 60 percent, traditional beliefs 25 percent, Islam 15 percent
Climate Tropical, especially humid in the southwest, hot and dry in the north. Rain seasons are April–June and Sept–Nov in the centre and south, March–Sept in the north
Best time to go Dec–Feb
Currency Cedi
Minimum costs $12/£7 per day

The famously friendly country of Ghana, on the Gulf of Guinea, is – certainly for English-speakers – the best country in West Africa in which to begin an African experience. Visitors face only minimal hassle by regional standards (discounting the wilting humidity), and there's a heap of stuff to see and do. Ghana contains a broad spread of landscapes, from palm-backed tropical beaches and coastal lagoons, to rainforests, wooded hills and savanna, and – in the east – Lake Volta, one of the world's largest man-made reservoirs. Getting around is easy, even off the beaten track, and Ghana's ever-sliding currency makes it cheap for visitors.

An abundance of natural resources had made Ghana relatively well off compared to its neighbours. In the Middle Ages, the whiff of gold – first smelled via the trans-Saharan caravan trade – aroused the avaricious attentions of Europe's seafaring nations. Following the Portuguese, who arrived in 1471, were Dutch and Swedes, Danes, Prussians, French and English, all of whom left an impressive array of coastal castles and

Average temperature ranges and rainfall

	Jan	Feb	Mar	Apr	May	Jun	Jul	Aug	Sep	Oct	Nov	Dec
Accra												
Max °C	31	31	31	31	31	29	27	27	27	29	31	31
Min °C	23	24	24	24	24	23	23	22	23	23	24	24
Rainfall mm	15	33	56	81	142	178	46	15	36	64	36	23
Tamale												
Max °C	36	37	37	36	33	31	29	29	30	32	34	35
Min °C	21	23	24	24	24	22	22	22	22	22	22	20
Rainfall mm	3	3	53	69	104	142	135	196	226	99	10	5

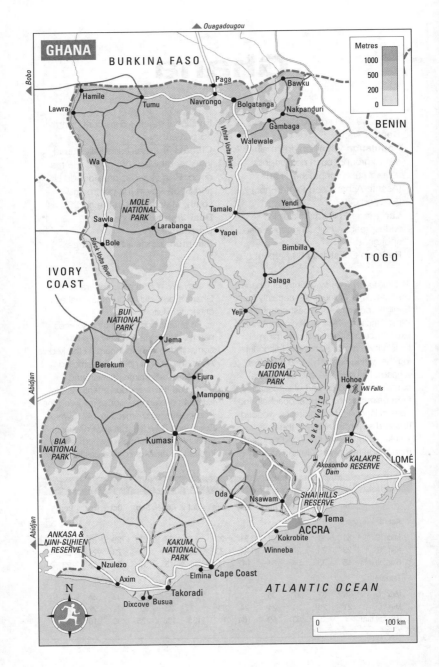

GHANA

BURKINA FASO

▲ *Ouagadougou*

◄ *Bobo*

◄ *Bobo*

Metres
1000
500
200
0

BENIN

Paga
Bawku
Hamile
Lawra
Tumu
Navrongo
Bolgatanga
Nakpanduri
Gambaga
Walewale
Wa

White Volta River

Mole National Park
Sawla
Larabanga
Bole
Tamale
Yapei
Yendi

Black Volta River

Bimbilla

TOGO

IVORY COAST

Bui National Park
Salaga
Yeji

Jema
Berekum
Ejura
Mampong

DIGYA NATIONAL PARK

Hohoe
Wli Falls

◄ *Abidjan*

Lake Volta

Bia National Park
Kumasi

Ho
KALAKPE RESERVE
LOMÉ
Akosombo Dam

◄ *Abidjan*

Oda
Nsawam
SHAI HILLS RESERVE
Tema
ACCRA
Kokrobite
Winneba

ANKASA & NINI-SUHIEN RESERVE
Nzulezo
Axim
KAKUM NATIONAL PARK
Elmina
Cape Coast
Takoradi
Dixcove
Busua

ATLANTIC OCEAN

N

0   100 km

fortresses. It wasn't just gold that aroused rivalries: ivory and slaves were major factors, too, and reminders of the slave trade abound. History and culture are best sampled at any one of an impressive roster of traditional festivals.

Main attractions

● **Cape Coast Castle** The most impressive of the castles and forts dotting the Ghanaian coastline, this was built by Swedes in the seventeenth century, and later housed the British government. In between, it served as a major slave-holding centre. Its disturbing history, and that of early African-Americans, is documented by an excellent museum, visits to which include guided tours of the castle's horrifying slave dungeons.

● **Elmina** Elmina was the first European base in Ghana, its huge Castle of St George founded by Portugal in 1482. After its capture by the Dutch, the castle saw its church become a slave market, and the hilltop fortress of St Jago was built to protect it. Tours of the castle include the small but distressing dungeons in which slaves were kept. The church-turned-slave market is now a cultural museum. Huddled around the whitewashed fortress is the town itself, with a colourful fishing harbour.

● **Kakum National Park** Within day-trip distance of Cape Coast Castle, Kakum's luscious rainforest is Ghana's premier natural attraction. You'll need both luck and patience to see many of its inhabitants, which include rare monkeys, bongo antelopes and even elephants. It's a good thing that someone came up with the idea of building an aerial walkway, a 350-metre-long cable-supported path giving an enchanting bird's-eye view of the forest.

● **Busua beach** The best of the country's tropical beaches, with safe swimming, golden sands backed by palm trees, bars, restaurants and hotels attuned to touristic tastes, and the British Fort Metal Cross in neighbouring Dixcove providing historical interest. Surfing's good here, too.

● **Nzulezo** Six hundred years ago, a group of people, unable to withstand attacks from their neighbours, abandoned Lake Chad in search of a more peaceful home. Their snail god led them to the dark and placid waters of the marshy Amansuri Lagoon. As there was no land on which to build, they drove raffia trunks into the silt and constructed their houses on top. Apart from TV antennas and painted walls, the village has changed little since then, and the attraction for visitors is the same as for locals – being in a peaceful refuge away from it all. Break your reverie with canoeing trips in search of monkeys and birds.

● **Mole National Park** Ghana's main wildlife refuge, in savanna country west of Tamale, is the place for walking and driving safaris, and ease of access makes up for low animal densities. Inhabitants include buffaloes and various species of monkey and antelope. With luck you might also see lions and elephants, both reintroduced. A special attraction is being able to pitch a tent where you fancy, so long as your accompanying guard deems it safe.

● **Kumasi** Likeable and hectic, Kumasi is the former capital of the Asante Kingdom. By the nineteenth century, the Asante had ejected Europeans from much of Ghana before being defeated by the British in 1874. Leading the onslaught was Lord Baden-Powell, whose brutal tactics (he blew up the entire capital after its capture) had little in common with the scout movement he was to found. Visitors have plenty to see, including an excellent Asante museum in the Ghana National Cultural Centre, a military museum, and another museum in the rebuilt Manhyia Palace, whose collections include wax effigies of kings and queens, made by Madame Tussauds. The town also houses the Okomfo Anokye Sword, which was struck into the ground by the city's founder and which, according to locals, cannot be pulled out, even by tractor.

Also recommended

● **Accra** The capital benefits from amiable vibes and virtually no hassle, which makes visiting the enormous and chaotic Makola Market a real treat. Most of the city is quite modern; if you miss "real" Africa, take a walk down to the packed and run-down James Town, on its own peninsula, where drum beats and excitable kids set the mood. Other attractions are the National Museum for traditional art, the impressive mausoleum (and museum) of Ghana's first president, Kwame Nkrumah, and nightlife well worth staying up for.

● **Lake Volta** Fed by the Black Volta and White Volta rivers, Lake Volta stretches along two-thirds of the country. Akosombo Dam is the place to head, both for water sports and catching the overnight Yapei Queen ferry to Yeji, halfway up the lake.

● **Shai Hills Reserve** A good place for wildlife close to Accra, with baboons, parrots and kob antelopes among others. You can get around on horseback.

● **Wli Falls** In the hilly region between Lake Volta and Togo, this narrow thirty-metre cascade drops straight out of the forest into a swimmable pool. Close by are bat colonies which local kids take pot-shots at with home-made flintlocks; the bats are a food source.

● **Larabanga Mosque** Beside Mole National Park is the country's most mysterious mosque, which believers say was built by Allah himself. The building is a take on the classic mud-and-stick temples of Mali and elsewhere in the Sahel.

● **Sacred crocodiles** The northern Ghanaian village of Paga has a special relationship with crocodiles, who are kept in several pools. They're apparently quite tame, so the only close-range snapping is that of cameras taking pics of visitors squatting on the crocs' tails.

● **Posuban shrines** The Fante, in the southeast, originally had defensive military regiments called Asafo ("war people"). Although their military purpose is no more, the companies survive as rival political forces, and act as advisors to local kings. Each keeps a small but brightly painted cement shrine, a posuban, of which a typical town has up to a dozen. Their motifs are rich in symbolism, and are generally a show of one-upmanship over rival companies.

● **Kokrobite** A funky alternative to Busua for a beach holiday, especially popular with backpackers, with several great shoreline hotels, even better bars, drumming lessons, good surf, and all-round Rasta vibes.

Festivals

Ghana is immensely rich for culture and celebrations. Most festivals feature a colourful durbar, in which local kings and chiefs dress up in all their finery and mount palanquins to receive homage from their subjects. Many events celebrate harvests, and often follow lengthy periods in which activities such as drumming, fishing or hunting are banned. Others commemorate historical events such as battles, pacts made with European powers, and migrations. Islamic dates (see p.245) are also celebrated, especially the Prophet Muhammad's birthday, which in Ghana is known as Damba. The following should give you a taste; the tourist board website has a full list.

Aboakye Winneba; May Groups of hunters compete to capture a live antelope and present it to their chief.

Edina Bronya Elmina; first Thurs of Jan Ancestors are paid homage through ritualized fish-catching by Asafo (military) companies, the firing of muskets, a chiefly procession, and much music and dance.

Hogbetsotso Anloga; Nov The Anlo-Ewe celebration of their ancestors' escape from a seventeenth-century tyrant. Similar is the Dodoleglime (Hohoe, also November), which means "coming out of the wall".

Homowo Festival Accra region; Aug or Sept The harvest festival for the Ga, Howowo – literally "hooting at hunger" – is celebrated with street processions of twins, offerings to the gods, dancing and drumming.

Jimbenti Tumu; Jan The one-day purification rituals of the Sissala people end with the ceremonial throwing of burning sticks to the eastern sky, to scare away demons.

Panafest (Pan-African Historical Theatre Festival) Various venues; July & Aug of odd-numbered years A modern take on the old festivals with slavery as the main theme, aimed in part at North American visitors. Features a grand durbar of chiefs, rites of passage, a re-enactment of a slave march, a midnight vigil at Cape Coast Castle and of course music and theatre.

Routes in and out

The international airport is at Accra. Buses and bush taxis arrive from Burkina Faso and Ivory Coast, bush taxis from Togo.

Ghana online

Ghana Tourist Board
Ⓦ www.ghanatourism.gov.gh
Akan Cultural Symbols Project
Ⓦ www.marshall.edu/akanart Nice site not just on Akan cloth patterns but their culture as a whole.
C.K. Ladzekpo: African Music and Dance
Ⓦ www.cnmat.berkeley.edu/~ladzekpo Put together by a renowned Ghanaian musician and musicologist, this features videos and articles on the culture, rituals and dances of the Ewe, plus tuition on their drumming techniques.

Books

Peter Adler and Nicholas Barnard *African Majesty: Textile Art of the Ashanti and Ewe*. A scholarly treatment of Ghana's most famous traditional art form.
Ayi Kwei Armah *The Beautiful Ones Are Not Yet Born*. The insidious reach of corruption, greed and other post-independence vices, explored through the disenchanted eyes of an incorruptible railway clerk.
John Chernoff *African Rhythm and African Sensibility*. Combining conversations with Ghanaian drum masters with musings on the philosophical and spiritual aspects of polyrhythms, this is a jumbled yet readable and enlightening guide.
Thierry Secretan *Going into Darkness: Fantastic Coffins from Africa*. Celebrating life in death, the carved and painted coffins of the Ga are tailored for the person inside: a giant sardine or boat for a fisherman, a Mercedes for an ambitious market woman.

Guinea

Despite considerable mineral wealth, Guinea – "Guinea Conakry" – has had a particularly rough time of it since independence in 1958. "We prefer freedom in poverty to wealth in slavery", declared Sekou Touré, the liberation hero-turned-tyrant whose brutal rule left the country economically reeling and internationally isolated. By the time he died in 1984, two million Guinéens had fled. The road to recovery has been hampered by instability in Sierra Leone and Liberia, whose problems (and refugees) have frequently spilled over the border, though with both of those countries now finally at peace, things are looking up.

For now, Guinea remains well off the tourist circuit, though that's bound to change as people switch on to the beauty of West Africa's most voluptuous land. Much of the country is mountainous, luxuriantly forested and extremely picturesque, its towns and villages little touched by European influence. The indisputable highlight is the central Fouta Djalon mountain range, in whose forests the Senegal and Gambia rivers are born. On the coast, there's an array of slavery-related sites, gorgeous beaches (the

Average temperature ranges and rainfall

	Jan	Feb	Mar	Apr	May	Jun	Jul	Aug	Sep	Oct	Nov	Dec
Conakry												
Max °C	31	31	32	32	32	30	28	28	29	31	31	31
Min °C	22	23	23	23	24	23	22	22	23	23	24	23
Rainfall mm	3	3	10	23	158	559	1298	1054	683	371	122	10
Mamou (Fouta Djalon)												
Max °C	33	34	35	34	31	29	27	25	28	29	30	31
Min °C	13	15	18	19	20	18	19	19	19	18	17	13
Rainfall mm	8	10	46	127	203	257	335	401	340	203	6	8

best on islands), and plenty for birders to twitch about.

Main attractions

- **Fouta Djalon** Hiking the tangled forests and cultivated valleys of the Fouta Djalon is the only excuse you need to visit the country. Its towns, charming places where you can immerse yourself in Fulani culture, make ideal bases for striking out in search of waterfalls or clambering peaks.

- **Îles de Los** This small archipelago southwest of Conakry was once a slaving base. The main island, the Île de Roume, its forested twin peaks separated by a sandy isthmus, attracts heaps of expats at weekends. There's upmarket beach accommodation there, and cheaper stays on the Île de Kassa. Another island has giant tortoises.

- **Boké** At the end of a long, mangrove-lined creek, the fortress from where many slaves were shipped to North America is now a museum, complete with harrowing holding cells and claustrophobic tunnels.

- **Parc National du Niokolo-Badiar** The savanna fringing the northern edge of the Fouta Djalon adjoins Senegal's Niokolo-Koba, and provides dry-season sightings of antelopes, monkeys, lions and leopards.

- **Conakry** For some, Guinea's capital is a filthy and enervating place from which to plan an escape. The good news is Conakry has several gorgeous beaches nearby, thumping nightlife and sense-tickling markets.

- **Parc National du Haut Niger** Drive or punt along the Niger in a pirogue in search of hippos and elephants, buffaloes, chimpanzees and waterbuck.

- **Guinée Forestière** Guinea's southeastern highlands could surpass Fouta Djalon for raw beauty, but their location beside Liberia (check the situation before leaving Conakry) has made them an obvious target for refugees, with nefarious consequences for some of the region's forests. Relatively untouched is Mont Nimba, at 1752m the region's highest peak. Its sacred forests contain the source of the River Niger, and troops of chimpanzees.

Routes in and out

Flights land at Conakry. Overlanding can be rough going, especially from Guinea-Bissau. Easier are bush taxis from Mali and taxis and buses from Sierra Leone.

Guinea online

Office National du Tourisme
Ⓦ www.mirinet.net.gn/ont
Foniké
Ⓦ www.fonike.info Nicely offbeat site showcasing Guinean rap videos.
webGuinée
Ⓦ www.guinee.net It's worth learning French for this one, an online library with several hundred books on all aspects of Guinea.

Books

Jean Barbot *Barbot on Guinea.* Masterful descriptions of life and culture, by a Huguenot slave trader who travelled twice to Guinea. An invaluable historical source, and a guiltily entertaining read.
Anthony Benezet *Some Historical Account of Guinea.* An early broadside (1772) against the Atlantic slave trade,

also providing a trove of cultural information. A free download from Ⓦ www.gutenberg.org.

Manthia Diawara *In Search of Africa*. Returning from exile, Diawara came to shoot a documentary about Sekou Touré. His search for a childhood friend became the thread of his book, a quest that mirrored recent Guinean history.

Camara Laye *The Dark Child: The Autobiography of an African Boy*. A graciously-written account of the tensions between old and new, in which the author describes his 1950s childhood, from a devoutly traditional village to the swirling modernity of Conakry.

Guinea-Bissau

Area 36,125 square kilometres
Capital Bissau
Population 1.6 million; main ethnic groups are Balante, Fulani, Manjak and Mandinga (Malinké)
Language Portuguese (official) spoken in towns, as is basic French; more common is Portuguese-influenced Creole

Religion Traditional beliefs 50 percent, Islam 45 percent, Christianity 5 percent
Climate Tropical, with heavy rains June–Oct; end of the dry season is stiflingly humid
Best time to go Dec–May
Currency CFA franc
Minimum costs $25/£14 per day

Tiny Guinea-Bissau, sandwiched between Senegal and Guinea Conakry, was Portuguese for five centuries until 1974, following an eleven-year armed struggle that only ended with the Portuguese Revolution. Since independence, the country has suffered inordinately from inept governments, a flatlining economy and, in 1998–99, a military uprising that somehow became a civil war. More recently it's entertained a series of failed, successful and rumoured coups d'état. Needless to say, impoverished Guinea-Bissau is well off the tourist radar, and there's not even a tourist board.

For adventurous souls, this is no bad thing, especially as – with the exception of the Senegalese border, where rebels are occasionally active (see p.143) – Guinea-Bissau is one of Africa's safest and friendliest destinations. Hassling tourists is unheard of, and the dearth of facilities is amply compensated for by traditional hospitality.

The country's main attractions are the wonderful beaches, and culture, of the Bijagós Archipelago, dozens of lushly forested Atlantic islands amid an ocean rich in marine life. The Bijagó islanders have long resisted external influences. Portugal's military might was unable to "pacify" them until the twentieth century, neither Islam nor Christianity left much of a mark, and the islands effortlessly side-stepped the country's last few decades of turmoil. Other attractions are more general: winsome Portuguese and African settlements, lively markets, mangrove-lined creeks, uncountable rivers (and ferry rides), a smattering of wildlife, and a wealth of music and culture.

Average temperature ranges and rainfall

Bissau	Jan	Feb	Mar	Apr	May	Jun	Jul	Aug	Sep	Oct	Nov	Dec
Max °C	32	33	34	34	33	31	30	29	30	31	32	30
Min °C	18	19	20	21	22	23	23	23	23	23	22	19
Rainfall mm	0	1	0	0	15	136	336	504	358	107	11	1

Main attractions

● **Bubaque** This Bijagós island is pretty much all there is of a tourist industry in Guinea-Bissau. Accessed by ferry, the rewards, besides being in picture-postcard beach heaven, are fascinating local culture, good facilities and boat trips around the archipelago.

● **Bolama** Also in the Bijagós is Bolama, whose town was first capital of Guinea-Bissau, and is now an atmospheric old place with crumbling colonial buildings. Mangroves flank most of the shoreline, giving way to gorgeous white beaches in the south.

● **Orango** The Bijagós Archipelago's largest, greenest and wildest island is arguably also its most charming. Apart from wonderful beaches, it's home to a marine park protecting rare salt-water hippopotamuses, turtles, sharks, dugongs and dolphins, and is also the setting for initiation ceremonies for inhabitants from around Bijagós.

● **Varela** Just inside the Senegalese border is the mainland's best beach, a truly paradisiacal stretch backed by palm trees and cashew-nut plantations. On the way there, look for locals equipped with bows and arrows – monkeys are the main kill.

● **Bafatá** Red laterite dust covers pretty much all of this pretty and laid-back town, birthplace of the independence movement hero, Amílcar Cabral. It's a good base for seeking out antelopes and monkeys along the Rio Gêba.

● **Bissau** The country's surprisingly prim Portuguese-styled capital is the continent's calmest, but there's little to detain you other than a pleasant market, and bands playing gumbe music deep into the night.

Festivals

Islamic and Christian holidays are observed; see p.243 & p.245 for dates. **Carnaval Bissau, weekend before Shrove Tuesday (see p.243 for dates)** Colourful and deliciously gaudy parades of giant papier-mâché floats, elaborate masks modelled on traditional lines, spangled dancers and thumping music from all over the country.

Routes in and out

Bissau has flights from Dakar and Lisbon. There are bush taxis from Guinea Conakry and Senegal (Ziguinchor), and taxi-hopping is possible from Banjul in the Gambia, but check the security situation in Casamance and the border area.

Guinea-Bissau online

Amílcar Cabral
Ⓦ www.vidaslusofonas.pt/amilcar _cabral_2.htm A short biography of the heroic freedom fighter, murdered by treacherous comrades in 1973.
World Routes in Guinea-Bissau
Ⓦ www.bbc.co.uk/radio3/worldmusic /onlocation/guinea-bissau.shtml Two-part radio documentary mainly dedicated to the country's music.
Guineé-Bissau.net
Ⓦ www.guinee-bissau.net The only decent resource for tourists, but in French.

Books

Amílcar Cabral *Unity and Struggle*. Calm and collected, rational, convincing and right, Cabral's own words make it obvious how he became a hero of the world's left-wing.

Toby Green *Meeting the Invisible Man*. Not just fine travel writing, this surreal book takes readers on a spiritual journey through Guinea-Bissau, in the company of a Senegalese photographer searching for the secret of invisibility.

Walter Rodney *A History of the Upper Guinea Coast, 1545–1800*. Written in 1970, Rodney's ground-breaking dissertation was an important step in breaking away from the hitherto Eurocentric treatment of African history.

Kenya

Area 582,000 square kilometres
Capital Nairobi
Population 36 million; ethnic groups
include Swahili, and Bantu, Nilotic
and Cushitic-speakers
Language English and Swahili, plus
tribal languages
Religion Christianity 70–80 percent,
Islam 6 percent

Climate Tropical along coast and
around Lake Victoria; temperate in
the highlands; desert north/northeast
Best time to go Jan–March & July–
Oct for beaches and wildlife; Feb &
Aug for Mount Kenya
Currency Kenya shilling
Minimum costs $20/£11 per day

Kenya is one of Africa's most exciting wildlife destinations. With Maasai Mara and Amboseli well known from wildlife documentaries, Kenya's wild side needs little introduction other than to say that even on a short trip, you can get to see many of Africa's most emblematic species – lions, elephants, zebras, buffaloes, and herds of wildebeest – with uncommon ease. A safari is of course de rigueur, whether it's a three-day spin in a shared minibus, a self-drive adventure, or being pampered in luxurious wildlife lodges. Kenya's sandy Indian Ocean beaches are another big draw.

If this smacks of mainstream tourism (and it is), escaping the crowds is simple. For a start, there's a string of ruined medieval trading towns along the coast to explore, and the Lamu archipelago – among the continent's most laid-back spots for indulging in *dolce far niente*, the sweet pleasure

Average temperature ranges and rainfall

	Jan	Feb	Mar	Apr	May	Jun	Jul	Aug	Sep	Oct	Nov	Dec
Nairobi												
Max °C	25	26	25	24	22	21	21	21	24	24	23	23
Min °C	12	13	14	14	13	12	11	11	11	13	13	13
Rainfall mm	38	64	125	211	158	46	15	23	31	53	109	86
Mombasa												
Max °C	31	31	31	30	28	28	27	27	28	29	29	30
Min °C	24	24	25	24	24	23	22	22	22	23	24	24
Rainfall mm	25	18	64	196	320	119	89	66	63	86	97	61
Kisumu												
Max °C	29	29	28	28	27	27	27	27	28	29	29	29
Min °C	18	19	19	18	18	17	17	17	17	18	18	18
Rainfall mm	48	81	140	191	155	84	58	76	64	56	86	102

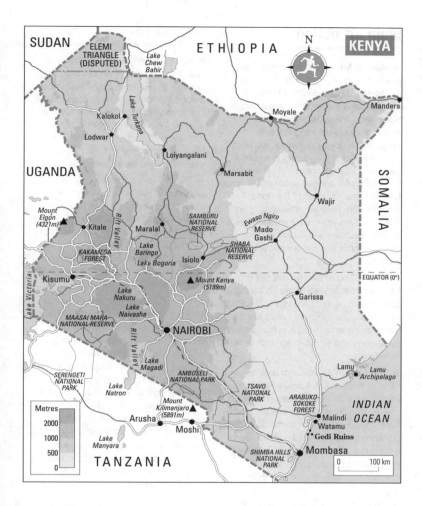

of doing nothing. Inland ("upcountry"), there's plenty to keep you busy, including a challenging hike up Mount Kenya (Africa's second-highest mountain), rainforest walks, and Lake Turkana in the northern desert – the reaching of which is an adventure in itself. The lake is one of several in the Great Rift Valley, which furrows clean through Kenya from north to south. The valley is the

domain of semi-nomadic cattle-herders such as the Maasai and Samburu, both of them favoured subjects for coffee-table books. You're likely to see their young warriors in tourist hotels as entertainers or purveyors of tourist trinkets, but to get to know them in more meaningful contexts requires plenty of time for travelling off the beaten track.

Main attractions

● **Maasai Mara** You can't have "been there, done that" without having seen the Mara – a great wedge of undulating grassland that receives the adjacent Serengeti's annual migration of 2.5 million animals, including immense herds of wildebeest. Whether you're on the ground or drifting along in a hot-air balloon, your best chance of witnessing the migration's perilous (and gory, thanks to crocodiles) crossing of the flood-swollen Mara River is between July and October. Even when the herds turn back to Tanzania, there's plenty of wildlife – but you'll spot many more fellow tourists than lions.

● **Indian Ocean beaches** A string of beaches from Malindi to the Tanzanian border have been extensively developed for tourism, though most hotels are low-rise, with accommodation in bungalows. Snorkelling and scuba-diving can easily be arranged.

● **The Lamu Archipelago** Just off Kenya's north coast, Lamu was a cradle of the Swahili civilization, and has preserved a timeless feel, despite having been "discovered" back in the Sixties by Nirvana-seeking hippies en route to Kathmandu. There are still no vehicles or sprawling beach resorts (actually, not many beaches either), but there are plenty of modest, often enchanting, hotels in traditional houses built of coral ragstone. If simply bumming around won't do, there's good snorkelling and diving on the surrounding reefs.

● **Lake Nakuru** If it's swashes of avian pink that tickle your fancy, Lake Nakuru is the place to be. It used to entertain flocks of flamingoes two million-strong, and though the spectacle has become unpredictable of late and the flocks have dwindled, you'd be unlucky to see less than tens of thousands, and there's plenty of other wildlife too.

● **Mount Kenya** An extinct volcano whose craggy peaks almost exactly straddle the Equator. You can clamber around the forested lower slopes at will, but to attempt its 5199-metre summit, a minor expedition is in order. Other than the feeling of accomplishment (or glorious failure), the mountain offers marvellous and often surreal views.

● **Tsavo** Tsavo's dramatic scenery and glimpses of Kilimanjaro have inspired many a novel, and even today, Tsavo – consisting of two national parks – has much to warm your romantic cockles. Big game is out in force, there are far fewer crowds than at Maasai Mara, and Tsavo's considerable size means you'll see few other people or cars.

● **Lake Turkana** This awe-inspiring lake is heaven on earth for adventurers and desert rats alike. The arid lands on either side are home to some of Africa's most traditional tribes, while the lake itself contains colonies of enormous (and mercifully rather lazy) Nile crocodiles. They're the decoration for what's really a Jurassic Park – an endless succession of finds of fossilized hominids continues to enlighten us about our origins. The best way of getting to see the lake, and the deserts, is on a "Turkana Bus" tour, in what are actually converted trucks.

Also recommended

● **Amboseli National Park** An environmentally-challenged dust bowl this may well be, but the sight of snow-capped Kilimanjaro filling the sky beyond Amboseli's elephants and acacias is the stuff of dreams, as are the flocks of flamingoes after the rains, when the plains become a lake.

- **Arabuko–Sokoke Forest** Kenya's last patch of indigenous coastal forest: come here if you're bananas about primates, cuckoo for birds, or hanker after reptiles and butterflies.

- **Gedi ruins** Serenaded by the constant chatter of cicadas, fourteenth-century Gedi – whose heyday coincided with the Shirazi civilization – is the most enigmatic of East Africa's abandoned coastal towns. The thick overgrowth makes it particularly photogenic.

- **Kakamega Rainforest** A few centuries ago, much of western Kenya was covered in rainforest. Today, Kakamega is virtually all that's left. With cheap accommodation and a wide choice of guided walks to choose from, it's a perfect hideaway for romantic nature-lovers on a shoestring.

- **Mombasa** Though dirty and chaotic, the island-city has a long and fascinating history, as evidenced by Fort Jesus – Portugal's last bastion in East Africa when they were evicted by Oman in 1698. Now a museum, it's a good place to get a grip on the great age and breadth of the Swahili civilization. Mombasa's "Old Town", mostly dating from the nineteenth century, has an agreeably Arabian feeling.

- **Nairobi National Park** The presence of so much big game on the city's doorstep never fails to amaze, though you'll need a dose of luck for that classic cheetahs-with-skyscrapers-in-the-background shot. The park's great if you've little time and want to see as much wildlife as possible.

- **Samburu and Shaba National Reserves** This duo marks the start of Kenya's northern deserts, and a frontier for wildlife, the existence of which would not be possible without the ewaso ngiro river. For visitors, the majestic palm trees lining the river lend the place an exotic feel quite unlike anywhere else in East Africa. Leopards are regularly seen, as are otherwise rare Grevy's zebras, reticulated giraffes and blue-legged Somali ostriches.

- **Shimba Hills National Park** Shimba's jungly forest and hilly grasslands make it a popular excursion from the coast, but staying overnight is preferable, whether you camp or splash out on a treehouse at Shimba Lodge, where you'll share your arboreal abode with monkeys, lizards and bushbabies.

Festivals

Given the demise of much traditional culture, Kenya's main get-togethers are agricultural shows, held throughout the year. Islamic holidays are celebrated on the coast (see pp.243–245).

International Camel Derby Maralal; Aug An enjoyable weekend up in the wilds of northern Kenya; spectate, or try your hand at an amateur race. For pros from the Emirates and even China, it's a serious 42-kilometre event with reputations at stake.

Maulidi Coastal towns, especially Lamu; see p.245 for dates The Prophet Muhammad's birthday is the big day (actually a week) for the Swahili, who celebrate with processions, performances of poetry, and wonderful music that well displays their Arabic, African and even Far Eastern roots.

Routes in and out

Kenya's main airports are Nairobi, with daily flights from all over, and Mombasa, mainly used by European holiday charters. There are international bus services from Tanzania and Uganda. Hitching is the only overland option into Ethiopia.

Kenya online

Kenya Tourist Board
Ⓦwww.magicalkenya.com
BZ's Kenya Travel Guide
Ⓦwww.bwanazulia.com/kenya
Practical stuff with good links, especially
for safaris.
Tim and Lara Beth's Kenya Pages
Ⓦwww.blissites.com/kenya Excellent
cultural site covering all bases.
**Traditional Music and Cultures of
Kenya** Ⓦwww.bluegecko.org/kenya
An enjoyable online encyclopedia put
together by the author of this book, with
hundreds of essays, photos, traditional
tales and fables, and hours of music.
Visit Kenya
Ⓦwww.visit-kenya.com Useful
information, listings and travel tips.

Books

Mohamed Amin *Portrait of Kenya and
Cradle of Mankind*. Two volumes of
ethnic photography thankfully bereft of
the shallow purple prose that commonly
afflicts coffee-table books. The photos
are also more genuine (not posed).
Cradle of Mankind specifically covers the
peoples of Lake Turkana.
Karen Blixen (Isak Dinesen) *Out
of Africa*. Thanks to the film, Blixen's
description of life on her coffee farm in
between the wars has become a cult
classic, notwithstanding the morally
repugnant colonial attitudes plainly in
evidence. To be fair, the book is honest
and never superficial (unlike the film),
and as such provides a welcome and

instructive read alongside one of Ngugi
wa Thiong'o's works (see below), from
the other side of the divide.
Caroline Elkins *Imperial Reckoning:
The Untold Story of Britain's Gulag in
Kenya*. A Pulitzer Prize-winning exposé
of Britain's murderous repression of the
1950s Mau Mau Uprising. Concentration
camps, rape, torture, murder and
wholesale theft are constant themes.
**Andrew Fedders and Cynthia
Salvadori** *People and Cultures of
Kenya*. A passionate work covering all
of Kenya's tribes in detail, written in
the 1970s. Though a lot of the traditions
described have since disappeared, it
remains the bible for those interested in
Kenyan culture.
Geoff Sayer *Kenya: Promised Land?*
Concise, readable essays and excellent
photographs by a long-standing Oxfam
collaborator. Gets straight to the point
concerning issues such as aliena-
tion, land dispossession and ethnic
conflict, and also illustrates how some
communities have overcome these
adversities.
Ngugi wa Thiong'o *The River Between;
A Grain of Wheat; Petals of Blood; and
Secret Lives*. Kenya's foremost writer,
Thiong'o has long opposed all abuses
of power. *The River Between* offers an
enlightening view on the British period
from the Kenyan perspective, while the
Mau Mau Rebellion – which hastened
the end of colonial rule – provides the
narrative for *A Grain of Wheat*. His most
famous work, *Petals of Blood*, is a bitter
tale of the betrayed dreams of independent Kenya. Rather lighter is *Secret Lives*,
an entertaining collection of short stories.

Lesotho

Area 30,355 square kilometres
Capital Maseru
Population 1.65 million; almost all
are Basotho
Language Sesotho; limited English
and Afrikaans spoken in towns
Religion Christianity 80 percent,
traditional beliefs 20 percent
Climate Temperate: cold winters
with snow in mountains, warm to hot
summers with heavy rainfall
Best time to go Aug–Oct & Feb–
April for the best weather; May–July
for skiing and snowy adventures
Currency Loti (plural maloti) and
South African rand
Minimum costs $25/£14 per day

Entirely surrounded by South Africa and sometimes mistaken for one of apartheid's ill-conceived semi-states, the mountainous Kingdom of Lesotho (pronounced Lee-su-tu) is in fact proudly independent and very different in character to its dominant neighbour. Whereas the "Rainbow Nation" next door is in many respects European, laid-back Lesotho prides itself on its African heritage. Few people in this fabulously beautiful and rugged land speak English or Afrikaans, though language isn't a barrier when the inhabitants, the Basotho, are among southern Africa's most hospitable.

An especially welcome contrast to South Africa is the almost total absence of fences, which means you can hike into upland regions at will. The sheer scale and raw beauty of the highlands – characterized by plunging valleys, improbable roads, inspiring vistas and remote villages – make Lesotho an exceptional hiking destination, whether you're happy just pottering around, or are tempted by southern Africa's highest peak, Thabana Ntlenyana (3482m). Ponies are the preferred mode of transport, particularly in the highlands, and you can do as the locals do: pony-trekking is the best way to see the

Average temperature ranges and rainfall

	Jan	Feb	Mar	Apr	May	Jun	Jul	Aug	Sep	Oct	Nov	Dec
Maseru												
Max °C	26	24	25	23	17	16	14	18	20	22	22	24
Min °C	19	18	17	13	7	5	4	7	10	15	16	17
Rainfall mm	127	106	105	56	26	13	12	20	30	74	99	105
Semonkong												
Max °C	23	22	21	18	14	11	12	14	17	19	20	22
Min °C	9	8	7	3	-2	-5	-5	-3	1	4	6	8
Rainfall mm	101	82	87	46	26	13	12	27	30	68	73	86

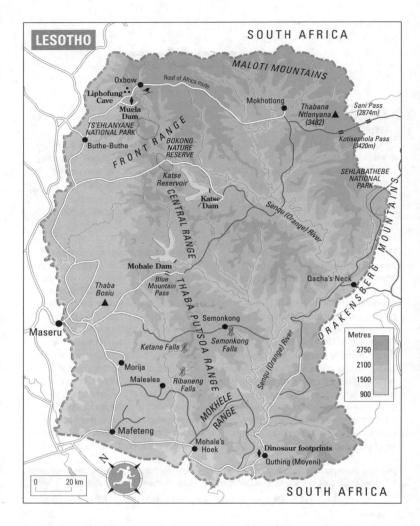

LESOTHO

SOUTH AFRICA

MALOTI MOUNTAINS

Oxbow
Roof of Africa route
Liphofung
Cave
Muela
Dam
TS'EHLANYANE
NATIONAL PARK
Buthe-Buthe

Mokhotlong
Thabana
Ntlenyana
(3482)
Sani Pass
(2874m)

Kotisephola Pass
(3420m)

FRONT RANGE
BOKONG
NATURE
RESERVE

Katse
Reservoir

Katse
Dam

SEHLABATHEBE
NATIONAL
PARK

CENTRAL RANGE

Senqu (Orange) River

Mohale Dam

Blue
Mountain
Pass

Qacha's Neck

Thaba
Bosiu

Semonkong

Maseru

THABA PUTSOA RANGE

Ketane Falls

Semonkong
Falls

DRAKENSBERG MOUNTAINS

Senqu (Orange) River

Metres
2750
2100
1500
900

Morija
Malealea

Ribaneng
Falls

MOKHELE RANGE

Mafeteng

Mohale's
Hoek

Dinosaur footprints

Quthing (Moyeni)

N

0   20 km

SOUTH AFRICA

country. Abseiling, rafting and birding are also on offer, plus activities such as consulting sangoma healers.

Main attractions

● **Pony trekking** The main centres are at Malealea and Semonkong, both

with access to the Thaba Putsoa range. Spectacular waterfalls and Bushman (San) rock paintings are common targets, though the trek itself is what you'll remember most fondly, sore buttocks notwithstanding.

● **Semonkong Falls** Plunging nearly 200m, these dramatic falls – their name meaning "smoking water" – are southern Africa's longest. In winter the plunge pool freezes over while the outside edge of the waterfall develops into an impressive ice cage. In summer, the pool is great for swimming in, in the company of bald ibises and bearded vultures soaring high above.

- **The "Roof of Africa" route** A narrow, winding road west of the Sani Pass and the South African border, this crosses a succession of ever higher passes (peaking at 3270m) as it twists through bleak, sparsely populated but nonetheless entrancing mountains. A popular route into the country, it's a journey that needs no justification other than the pleasure of travelling itself. The area is tremendous hiking country, though, and you'll find the hardy locals who eke out a living there among the most hospitable in the country.

- **Sehlabathebe National Park** An exceedingly remote mountain reserve with superb hiking in gloriously rugged terrain. Simply getting there is an adventure, especially if you attempt the forty-kilometre "Top-of-the-Berg" hike from Sani Pass in South Africa, which takes up to four days. The park is best known for prolific birdlife, including the rare bearded vulture (or lammergeier), and has impressive waterfalls, rock paintings, ancient Basotho stone dwellings, and chance encounters with antelopes, wild cats and jackals.

- **Bokong Nature Reserve** Another hikers' paradise, protecting extensive Afro-alpine wetlands, highland meadows and heathland boulder beds. Vaal rhebuck are commonly seen, as are bearded vultures, but the reserve's highlight is the Lepaqoa Waterfall, which freezes in winter to form a column of ice. For the energetic, guides and horses are available for an exciting two- or three-day trek across the alpine plateau to Ts'ehlanyane National Park.

- **Ts'ehlanyane National Park** Picturesque and rugged hiking and riding terrain that contains one of Lesotho's very few forested areas, together with thick bamboo jungle. Mammal inhabitants are mainly duikers, baboons and serval cats. There are also rare butterflies, bearded vultures and ground woodpeckers.

- **Rock art** Lesotho's original inhabitants, Bushman hunter-gatherers, were exterminated from Lesotho in 1873, following a series of incomprehensibly genocidal campaigns against them by the British. The Bushmen bequeathed a rich legacy of rock paintings and engravings, most easily seen at Liphofung Cave – a large sandstone overhang resembling a petrified wave.

Also recommended

- **Skiing** Between June and August there's a good chance of skiing in a wide basin near Oxbow. Extravagant plans for a large development with proper lifts and chalets are occasionally mooted, but for the time being the runs are short and the tows primitive.

- **Dinosaur footprints** Follow in the steps of the terrible lizards. The most accessible are at Quthing (Moyeni) and Morija.

- **Morija** A pleasant little nineteenth-century town containing Lesotho's oldest building, its first church, and a time-honoured printing press, Morija is also the nation's literary and arts capital, and has a good museum that organizes an annual festival.

- **Katse Reservoir** Lesotho's abundance of water and shortage of cash, and South Africa's monetary wealth and water shortages, are the hard facts behind the controversial Lesotho Highlands Water Project, the essential aim of which is to divert the flow of Lesotho's major rivers through tunnels into South Africa. The project's centrepiece is the massive 185-metre Katse Dam. You can take a guided tour through the tunnels inside the dam wall, and visit a botanical garden that acts as a refugee camp for critically endangered spiral aloes rescued from the construction sites.

Festivals

Horse races Semonkong; winter The Basotho have been riding since the mid-nineteenth century, and are well up there with the best. Semonkong's monthly races (usually on the last weekend) are wild spectacles in which aspiring young jockeys compete for prestige.
Morija Arts and Cultural Festival Morija; Oct A week-long celebration blending traditional music, dancing and horse-racing with crafts, theatre, cinema, sport and children's events.

Routes in and out

The only flights into Lesotho are from Johannesburg, landing at Maseru. There are nine overland crossings from South Africa. If arriving by public transport, you'll need to change vehicles at the border.

Lesotho online

Lesotho Tourism Development Corporation
Ⓦ www.ltdc.org.ls

Complete Guide to Lesotho
Ⓦ www.seelesotho.com A comprehensive spin around the country, compiled by a pony-trekking centre.
Lesotho Highlands Water Project
Ⓦ www.lhwp.org.ls Facts and figures on the billion-dollar dam-building project, plus information on Bokong Nature Reserve and Ts'ehlanyane National Park.
Sesotho Web
Ⓦ www.sesotho.web.za Good language site including riddles, proverbs and fables.

Books

David Coplan *In the Time of Cannibals: The Word Music of South Africa's Basotho Migrants*. Lesotho men have for decades sought work in South Africa's exploitative gold mines, where they developed "word music" – sung oral poetry. This book couples a deep love of all Basotho music with discussion of its social and cultural impact.
K. Limakatso Kendall (ed) *Basali! Stories by and about women in Lesotho*. Nicely translated traditional tales.
Mpho 'M'Atsepo Nthunya *Singing Away the Hunger*. The powerful and uplifting memoirs of a woman who lost her family to murderers, yet never strayed from the strictures of Basotho culture.
Gary N. Van Wyk *African Painted Houses: Basotho Dwellings of Southern Africa*. Protest murals among apartheid South Africa's Basotho.

Libya

Area 1,775,500 square kilometres
Capital Tripoli
Population 6 million; mostly mixed
Arab/Berber
Language Arabic (official); Italian
and English widely understood
Religion Islam
Climate Mediterranean along coast;
interior is extreme desert; the dusty

Ghibli blows Feb–April
Best time to go Nov–Feb for the
Sahara; May–Sept for the Jabal
Akhdar
Currency Libyan dinar
Minimum costs $50/£28 per day
travelling independently; at least
double that for organized tours

Ruled by the iron fist of Colonel Mu'ammar al-Qadhafi, Libya has been busily shedding its reputation as international pariah, and was taken off the US list of states sponsoring terrorism in 2006. Ninety percent of Africa's fourth-largest country is desert, one with summers so hot it pips Death Valley in the record books (57.8°C/136°F in the shade, recorded in 1922). Although the country is quite evidently paradise for desert-aficionados, of the trickle of tourists who make it here, most come for the country's well-preserved Greco-Roman ruins in and around the fertile mountains flanking the Mediterranean.

Libya's long and varied history has also left it with reminders of Phoenician, Byzantine, Arabic, Turkish, Italian, even Maltese and Spanish rule. Inland, deep in the Sahara, signs of human habitation are limited to ancient oases and caravanserais, and engravings and paintings left on rocks by Neolithic artists – witnesses to a time when the Sahara was fertile. The desert is the land of blue-robed Tuareg nomads, while its fringes are home to North Africa's original inhabitants, the Berbers. Both ethnic groups have kept their identities and cultures intact, and encounters with either are likely to provide many fond memories.

Average temperature ranges and rainfall

	Jan	Feb	Mar	Apr	May	Jun	Jul	Aug	Sep	Oct	Nov	Dec
Tripoli												
Max °C	16	17	19	22	24	27	29	30	30	27	23	18
Min °C	8	9	11	14	16	20	22	22	22	19	14	10
Rainfall mm	62	32	30	14	5	1	1	0	17	47	58	68
Ghadamès												
Max °C	17	20	25	28	35	39	41	40	37	30	24	18
Min °C	5	7	11	15	21	23	25	26	24	17	11	6
Rainfall mm	5	5	7	4	2	0	0	0	1	4	2	3

Tourist facilities beyond the coast are few and far between, and bureaucracy can be a hassle unless you're booked with a tour company. Independent travel is possible, albeit always escorted by a guide – you'll get a taste of the official passion for paperwork when applying for a visa.

Main attractions

● **Leptis Magna** North Africa's most extensive and complete Roman ruins, the remains of this originally Phoenician port include temples, an impressive amphitheatre, sea-front forums, opulent baths, plenty of marble-lined streets, and an extravagant arch honouring local boy made good, Emperor Septimius Severus.

● **Ghadamès** The "Pearl of the Desert" is among the Sahara's best preserved and most attractive oasis towns. Once an outpost of the Roman Empire, the old and now abandoned part of town was perfectly adapted to the desert: built of mud-brick and whitewash, the vaulted roofs over its narrow alleyways still protect against the pitiless sun.

● **Ghat and the Akakus Mountains** The evocative town of Ghat, close to Algeria, has been a trading centre since antiquity, thanks to its oasis which was a vital stopover for trans-Saharan caravans. Set on a hilltop is the old and now abandoned part of town, a mud-brick medina with an especially attractive mosque. Ghat is also the starting point for trips into the Akakus Mountains, a dramatic world of craggy rock formations and plunging escarpments in which you'll find Neolithic paintings and carvings from greener times past. Trips in the mountains can last several days, whether by four-wheel-drive, on foot, or by camel in the company of Tuareg guides.

● **Cyrenaica** Cyrenaica, in the northeast, was settled by Greeks in the seventh century BC, and enjoyed lengthy spells of independence, which gave its inhabitants an identity distinct from other Libyans. The region's fertile heartland, the Jabal Akhdar, well deserves its name, which means "Green Mountains". Specific attractions include exceptionally well-preserved Greek ruins at Cyrene, in an arcadian setting; splendid mosaics at Qsar Libya; and wonderful beaches at Derna.

● **Sabratha** Founded in the first century, Sabratha was a major city in Roman Tripolitania. Its colonnaded fifth-century amphitheatre is in surprisingly dapper condition, still used for events today. Accompanying it is an array of temples, fountains, public baths and mosaics, a good museum, and nice beaches.

● **Jabal Nafusah** These wild and scenic mountains in the northwest are a Berber stronghold replete with fortified medieval villages, some atop rocky escarpments. Spectacular desert scenery aside, there's plenty to keep you occupied, including mind-bogglingly clever multistorey honeycomb-like mud granaries called *ghorfas* (superb examples of which are at Nalut and Kabaw), and underground dwellings, especially at Gharyan, where one has been converted into a posh hotel.

● **Tripoli** Libya's cosmopolitan Mediterranean capital has a wonderfully vibrant medina, its jumbled cobweb of whitewashed alleyways and colourful souks peppered with Ottoman mosques and stately Italian mansions. The Jamahiriya Museum is also worth a look for its trove of classical art, including mosaics.

△ Remains of the market at Leptis Magna

Routes in and out

International flights touch down at Tripoli and Benghazi; there are onward flights into the Sahara. Ferries link Tripoli and Benghazi with various Italian ports, Malta, and sometimes Egypt. Buses and shared taxis connect Libya with Tunisia and Egypt; overland routes from other countries are generally closed to tourists.

Libya online

Adventures of Libya
Ⓦ **www.lexicorient.com/libya** A superlative resource, both practical and contextual, with good photos too.
Libya Rock Art
Ⓦ **www.libyarockart.com** Handy introduction to Libya's rock art, specifically the engravings of the Fezzan.

Books

Antonio Di Vita et al. *Libya: The Lost Cities of the Roman Empire*. Hundreds of seductive photographs accompanied by intelligent text that places the many sites into historical perspective.
Mansour O. El-Kikhia *Libya's Qaddafi: The Politics of Contradiction*. A perspicacious, even-handed and enjoyable analysis of the Colonel's radical ideology and policies, their impact on ordinary Libyans, and detailed background on the country's ethnic groups.
Hisham Matar *In the Country of Men*. A lyrical and evocative novel that explores a Libyan family's ultimately futile struggle against the dictatorship as their traditional values fall away, as seen through the eyes of their youngest son.

Madagascar

Area 587,040 square kilometres
Capital Antananarivo
Population 19.4 million; eighteen ethnic groups, mostly of mixed descent
Language French and Malagasy
Religion Traditional beliefs 50 percent, Christianity 40 percent

Climate Temperate inland, hot and humid along the coast, arid in the south, cyclonic rain storms Dec–March
Best time to go April–Oct
Currency Ariary
Minimum costs $10/£6 per day

Madagascar split off from the African continent some 165 million years ago. Isolation has meant that nine out of every ten plant and animal species on the island are found nowhere else on earth. Madagascar's national parks creep, crawl and buzz with uncounted insects, amphibians and other animals, most famously several dozen species of tree-dwelling, saucer-eyed lemurs. Your eyes might go saucer-like, too, once you take in the amazing landscape – cloud forests, wind-eroded rocks, waterfalls and crater lakes, and red, red earth everywhere. Add in a cluster of desert islands and protected coral reefs, and you have the world's most remarkable eco-tourist destination.

The country's history and people are also diverse. The original inhabitants were Malay-Polynesians who arrived some 2000 years ago, but as with many Indian Ocean islands, the population also descends from African slaves, Arab, Indian and Portuguese traders, and a spattering of pirates and French. The

Average temperature ranges and rainfall

	Jan	Feb	Mar	Apr	May	Jun	Jul	Aug	Sep	Oct	Nov	Dec
Antananarivo												
Max °C	26	27	26	25	23	21	20	21	24	26	27	26
Min °C	17	17	16	15	12	10	10	10	11	13	15	16
Rainfall mm	274	279	204	65	23	8	11	10	11	77	188	310
Antsiranana												
Max °C	30	30	31	31	30	29	29	29	30	31	32	31
Min °C	23	23	23	23	22	20	20	19	20	21	23	23
Rainfall mm	338	306	179	52	13	19	19	19	9	17	55	171
Toliara												
Max °C	32	32	32	31	29	27	27	28	29	29	30	31
Min °C	23	23	22	20	17	15	14	15	16	19	20	22
Rainfall mm	95	89	36	18	16	15	6	6	8	12	22	97

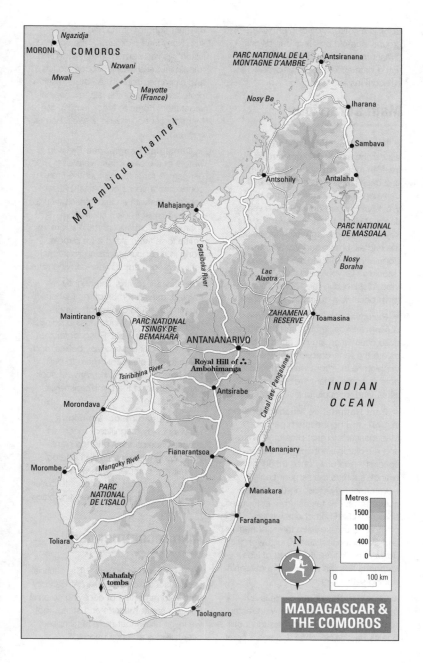

Ngazidja
MORONI   COMOROS

*PARC NATIONAL DE LA
MONTAGNE D'AMBRE*   Antsiranana

Nzwani

Mwali

Mayotte
(France)

Nosy Be   Iharana

Mozambique Channel   Sambava

Antsohily   Antalaha

Mahajanga

Betsiboka River   *PARC NATIONAL
DE MASOALA*

*Nosy
Boraha*

*Lac
Alaotra*

Maintirano   *PARC NATIONAL
TSINGY DE
BEMAHARA*   *ZAHAMENA
RESERVE*   Toamasina

ANTANANARIVO

Royal Hill of ∴
Ambohimanga

Tsiribihina River

*INDIAN
OCEAN*

Antsirabe

Canal des Pangalanes

Morondava

Fianarantsoa   Mananjary

Morombe   *Mangoky River*

Manakara

*PARC
NATIONAL
DE L'ISALO*

Metres	
	1500
	1000
	400
	0

Farafangana

N

Toliara

Mahafaly
tombs

0   100 km

Taolagnaro

**MADAGASCAR &
THE COMOROS**

result is a hotchpotch of interlinking ethnic groups, age-old beliefs and traditions, brilliant music, colonial influences where you'd least expect them, enjoyable celebrations and great food.

Main attractions

● **Parc National de l'Isalo** This sandstone massif is characterized by freakish rock formations, deep canyons and oases, and feels somewhere in between Jurassic Park and the Wild West. Visitors are drawn by the vegetation and views rather than wildlife, but key lemur species to watch for include the ringtail, brown and Verreaux's sifaka. Popular hikes include the plunging "Monkey Canyon", and visits to the Bara tribe, displaced in the 1990s when their town became a quarry for sapphire.

● **Parc National de la Montagne d'Ambre** Birds, lemurs and the blue-nose chameleon are big attractions here, as are the liana-draped trees literally dripping resin – from which the mountain gets its name. There are also crater lakes, and a couple of lovely waterfalls.

● **Parc National de Masoala** Opened in 1997, this northeastern park is Madagascar's largest protected area, and a biological hot spot where new species – and ones once thought extinct, such as the serpent eagle – are constantly cropping up. There's something for all tastes, from octopuses, coral reefs and humpback whales offshore to unique palm trees, butterflies and chameleons. History buffs won't go wanting, either: the island of Nosy Mangabe has the remains of a millennial trading settlement.

● **Nosy Be** This northern isle is an upmarket beach destination with restaurants and nightlife aplenty, though it still boasts pristine beaches and has a coral reef just right for diving and snorkelling. Nosy Be's nickname, "the scented island", is well earned: ylang-ylang and frangipani trees, vanilla, cocoa, coffee and cinnamon flourish. A nature reserve protects the last of the island's original vegetation, home to black lemurs, the Madagascar hog-nosed snake, chameleons and boas.

● **Canal des Pangalanes** The wild waters of the east coast were so dangerous for shipping that the French connected a series of coastal lakes and lagoons with a canal, which wends its way almost 500km south from Toamasina. Tourists can take a romantic cruise (or a ferry) along it (or paddle along in a pirogue), passing traditional fishing villages and lumber-carrying rafts.

● **Mahafaly tombs** The brightly painted, carved tombs of the Mahafaly tribe in the south consist of clusters of highly decorated, windowless buildings enclosed by tall walls. Respect for the dead is crucial to Malagasy beliefs, and these tombs often cost more to build than houses for the living. Always seek permission from the tomb's owners before visiting.

● **The Fianarantsoa–Manakara railway** Enjoy magnificent mountain scenery, rice paddies and tea plantations along this wonderfully battered old railway, complete with wonky rails. Trains take at least eight hours to cover the 163km, stopping at every tiny place en route.

Also recommended

● **Antananarivo ("Tana")** The national capital is a typically bustling African city filled with majestic but decaying colonial houses, street markets and steep, foot-wearying alleys that provide glimpses over hillsides and rice paddies.

- **Fianarantsoa** Beautifully situated on eucalyptus-wooded slopes, Madagascar's intellectual heart is also the country's wine capital – you can sample the output at various vineyards, and imbibe the magnificent views from the site of an old hilltop palace.

- **Nosy Boraha (Île Sainte-Marie)** Classic desert-island material on the east coast: beautiful beaches, swaying coconut palms, and offshore coral reefs. Hotels offer all manner of water sports, including scuba-diving, plus whale-watching.

- **Parc National Tsingy de Bemaraha** What are tsingies? Weird limestone formations, that's what, populated by countless birds and thirteen species of lemur.

- **Royal Hill of Ambohimanga** Perched atop an eagle's nest of a hill 20km south of the capital is the former royal palace and burial site of the Merina tribe. It's now a place of pilgrimage for locals, who come to assuage the spirit of the bloodthirsty Queen Ranavalona (see the review of Keith Laidler's book, p.100).

Festivals

Rural Madagascans have found plenty of excuses to party. Many celebrations feature a Hira Gasy, a blend of work songs, dances, street theatre and colonial costumes that originated as a means for the powerful eighteenth-century king Andrianampoinimerina to promulgate his reforms: he sent out troubadours and performers to add spice to his decrees. Christian and Islamic festivals are also celebrated; see p.243 & p.245 for dates.

Alahamady Be Nationwide; March
The Malagasy New Year is marked by three days of ceremonies and rituals, which include purification rites, animal sacrifices, singing and dancing, and feasts.

Donia Festival Nosy Be; May or June
A five-day festival showcasing traditional music and dance, giving visitors a chance to hear (and play) zithers, fiddles and dulcimers.

Famadihana Antananarivo and Fianarantsoa provinces; June–Sept
Famadihana means "returning" – referring in this case to the bones of the ancestors of the Merina and Betsileo tribes. Their bodies are exhumed, wrapped in fresh shrouds and reburied. Festivities last a couple of days and include the sacrifice or a pig or cow, and inevitably a feast.

Madajazzcar Antananarivo; Oct
International jazz festival.

Routes in and out

International flights land at Antananarivo Ivato airport. There are no ferries from the African mainland.

Madagascar online

Ministère de la Culture et du Tourisme
Ⓦ www.tourisme.gov.mg
Links to Malagasy Music
Ⓦ homepage.univie.ac.at/august .schmidhofer/links A comprehensive portal which includes official artist websites and interviews, lyric banks and links to sound clips. Mostly in French or Malagasy.
Madagascar
Ⓦ www.wbur.org/special/madagascar A gorgeous and encyclopedic audio-visual presentation on all aspects of the country, from lemurs, frogs and chameleons to the people, their music and culture.
Parcs Nationaux Madagascar
Ⓦ www.parcs-madagascar.com Official

introduction to the national parks and reserves. In French.

Truly Madly Madagascar
Ⓦ wpni01.auroraquanta.com/pv/madagascar An uplifting photographic insight into the people, their culture and traditions.

Wild Madagascar
Ⓦ www.wildmadagascar.org An excellent educational resource with comprehensive information about, and hundreds of photos of, fauna and flora, people, and parks. Clearly laid out and with travel forums too.

Books

Alison Jolly *Lords and Lemurs: Mad Scientists, Kings with Spears, and the Survival of Diversity in Madagascar*. Well-written mix of science, history, development and travelogue by a biologist who has been visiting the island for decades. Particularly forthright in its political views.

Ron Emoff *Recollecting from the past: Musical Practice and Spirit Possession on the East Coast of Madagascar*. Academic treatment of the fascinating connections between music, sound, remembrance, spirit possession and colonialism.

Keith Laidler *Female Caligula: Ranavalona, the Mad Queen of Madagascar*. Grippingly bloodthirsty account of Ranavalona's reign. Seizing the throne in 1828, she reigned for 33 years, by the end of which at least a third of the population had perished through execution or forced labour or, in the case of Christians, being hurled off the hill by her palace.

Dervla Murphy *Muddling through in Madagascar*. Endearing as ever, Murphy, accompanied by her daughter, walked and hitched across much of Madagascar in the 1980s. This account remains fresh, and paints a lively picture of the land and its people.

Peter Tyson *The Eighth Continent: Life, Death and Discovery in the Lost World of Madagascar*. This engaging book explores Madagascar's rich fauna and flora and examines the race against time to catalogue life before it disappears due to deforestation.

Malawi

Area 118,480 square kilometres
Capital Lilongwe
Population 13.4 million; main ethnic groups are Chewa, Nyanja, Tumbuka, Yao, Lomwe, Sena, Tonga, Ngoni and Ngonde
Language English and Chichewa both widely spoken
Religion Christianity 80 percent, Islam 15 percent
Climate Tropical moderated by altitude: dry season May–Nov, rainy season (often short but heavy cloudbursts) Dec–April, very hot and humid Nov–December
Best time to go Feb–April for flowers, birds and landscapes; Aug–Dec for scuba-diving); Oct & Nov for wildlife
Currency Malawian kwacha
Minimum costs $12/£7 per day

Predominantly rural, Malawi is an ineffably beautiful land blessed with ever-changing landscapes. The country's most obvious feature is Lake Malawi, the product of tectonic forces that are still pulling at the Great Rift Valley. Backed by mountains whose slopes in many areas plunge straight into the water, the lake (Nyasa to Tanzanians, Niassa to Mozambicans) is Africa's third largest, filling a trough almost 600km long. It's the world's most ecologically diverse lake, containing over six hundred fish species, four hundred of which are colourful evolutionary marvels called cichlids. Scuba-diving and snorkelling are possible, but don't fret if getting wet isn't your thing: the waters are so clear that you'll see most of its denizens from the comfort of a boat or a canoe. There's plenty of accommodation along the shores, and the more popular resorts offer sail-boarding, parasailing, water-skiing, and cruises over several days.

Malawi is more than just its lake, however. Here you can go mountain biking across flower-bedecked

Average temperature ranges and rainfall

	Jan	Feb	Mar	Apr	May	Jun	Jul	Aug	Sep	Oct	Nov	Dec
Lilongwe												
Max °C	27	27	27	26	26	24	24	26	28	30	30	28
Min °C	18	18	18	15	12	10	9	11	14	16	18	19
Rainfall mm	208	218	125	43	3	1	0	2	5	8	53	125
Nyika Plateau												
Max °C	23	23	24	23	22	20	19	22	24	26	26	24
Min °C	14	14	14	12	10	8	8	10	12	13	15	15
Rainfall mm	269	216	212	91	18	1	1	0	8	38	59	174

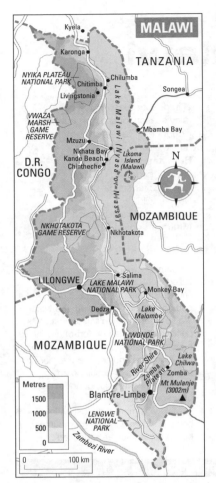

MALAWI

Kyela

Karonga

TANZANIA

NYIKA PLATEAU
NATIONAL PARK   Chitimba

Chilumba

Songea

Livingstonia

VWAZA
MARSH
GAME
RESERVE

Mzuzu

Mbamba Bay

Nkhata Bay
Kande Beach
Chintheche

Likoma
Island
(Malawi)

D.R.
CONGO

N

MOZAMBIQUE

NKHOTAKOTA
GAME RESERVE   Nkhotakota

LILONGWE   Salima

LAKE MALAWI
NATIONAL PARK   Monkey Bay

Dedza

Lake
Malombe

LIWONDE
NATIONAL PARK

MOZAMBIQUE

River Shire

Lake
Chilwa

Zomba
Plateau   Zomba

Mt Mulanje
(3002m)

Metres

1500

1000

500

0

Blantyre-Limbe

LENGWE
NATIONAL
PARK

Zambezi River

0   100 km

plateaus, or hike through lush primeval forest. And wildlife is a major draw, especially in the lowlands where drifting through swamps alive with birds, hippos and crocodiles is an exciting way to commune with nature. Add in a sprinkling of attractive colonial towns and wrap it all up with people renowned for their friendliness, and you'll understand Malawi's enduring popularity with tourists.

Main attractions

● **Lake Malawi National Park** Occupying Cape Maclear in the south, this park encloses a natural aquarium of astonishing clarity, where you can see zillions of colourful fish species, whether you're snorkelling, diving, or drifting around in a kayak. On land, there are antelopes, baboons and furry hyraxes (cute rodents that, incredibly, are most closely related to elephants). Birdlife is marvellous, too.

● **Northern Lake Malawi** Although the bulk of Lake Malawi's tourist facilities are in the south, the north isn't without its merits. Nkhata Bay, which has informal boat transport from Tanzania, is popular with backpackers and has the country's longest-established dive centre. Chitimba has great beaches, and gives access to the 1894 Livingstonia mission, still in use as a school, church and hospital. Slave trade-related artefacts are on display at Karonga museum, along with hominid and dinosaur remains, and backpacker-oriented Kande Beach is the place for cultural immersions.

● **Liwonde National Park** The wildlife in Malawi's best game park is attracted by the River Shire, which drains out of Lake Malawi along the park's western edge: elephants are often seen, as are thousands of hippos and crocs, plus antelopes and zebras. Lions are common enough, too, while the most memorable birds are Pel's fishing owl and elegant African fish eagles. Game walks are possible, but the best way to get around is by boat.

● **Nyika Plateau** Towering 2500m above sea level, the Nyika Plateau is a veritable garden of Eden. In the rains, its rolling grasslands are peppered with over two hundred species of orchids in flower. Forest-dwelling birds are another speciality, and include the endemic red-winged francolin. Leopards are Nyika's most famous mammals, though you're more likely to see antelopes and blue monkeys. Adding to the plateau's charms are inspiring vistas, waterfalls, and a small lake. Get around on foot, or explore on horseback or by bike.

● **Zomba Plateau** Southern Malawi's answer to Nyika, the crowning plateau atop this table mountain comes complete with lush flora and forests, cascades, lakes, fabulous views, and walking, riding and biking trails. Leopards are present (if rarely seen); giant butterflies are more likely to give you a flutter, as are augur buzzards and long-crested eagles. The town of Zomba, at the foot of the mountain, was Malawi's first colonial capital and has several attractive buildings from that period.

● **Mount Mulanje** Rising to 3000m, Malawi's highest mountain is all the more impressive for having its base – adorned with tea plantations – almost at sea level. Often graced with a misty necklace above which the craggy peaks extend, the mountain has a variety of summit routes for all levels of experience, and there are other trails lower down for seeing klipspringers, waterfalls and birds (big ones being black eagles and buzzards).

Also recommended

● **Lilongwe** Lilongwe is in fact two places: the bustling old town with its vibrant markets, and shiny new "capital city", complete with blue-glass high rises and spacious gardens. There's nothing much to delay you but it's a pleasant enough base.

● **MV Ilala** For getting around Lake Malawi, nothing beats this venerable ferry, which sails up and down the lake once a week, from Chilumba in the north to Monkey Bay in the south, dropping anchor at every two-bit fishing village along the way, for whom the ferry's arrival is a major event.

● **Nkhotakota Game Reserve** Viewing wildlife in this rugged land is challenging

△ Sunrise at Lake Malawi

on account of the thick woodland and tall grasses, but that's what makes seeing animals all the more memorable. Birdlife includes palm-nut vultures and giant kingfishers. The lakeshore village of Nkhotakota was a major slave-shipping centre.

● **Likoma Island** Sitting in Mozambican waters, Likoma remained Malawian on account of having served as the headquarters of Dr David Livingstone's Universities Mission to Central Africa. Heavily populated and cultivated, it has a lively market, plenty of bizarre baobabs and – equally bizarre – a huge cathedral, but serves mostly as a pleasant ferry stopover en-route to Mozambique's Niassa Province.

● **Lengwe National Park** A small park in the Lower Shire Valley with good odds on stripe-backed nyala antelopes.

● **Vwaza Marsh Game Reserve** Best visited as part of a Nyika Plateau trip, these lowland marshes and plains are good for seeing elephants, hippos and water birds.

● **Thyolo Tea Estates** One of several visitable tea plantations, this one close to Mount Mulanje.

Festivals

Muslim festivals are celebrated in the north and along the lake; see p.245 for dates.

Lake of Stars Festival Chintheche; Sept The best of UK club acts and DJs plus Malawi's finest (both traditional and contemporary) come together on the shores of Lake Malawi for a three-day charity bash; refreshingly eclectic and hugely enjoyable.

Traditional dances Lake Malawi; dry season Villagers all around Lake Malawi hold dances to mark the passing of the seasons, and rites of passage, for instance circumcision. The most popular dance is the ritualistic Gule Wankulu, in which dancers wear sacred masks.

Routes in and out

There are international airports at Lilongwe and Blantyre. Buses connect Malawi with Tanzania, Zambia and Mozambique, and ferries with Mozambique.

Malawi online

Malawi Tourism Association Ⓦ www.malawitourism.com
Axis Gallery – Nyau Masks Ⓦ www.axisgallery.com/exhibitions /maravi Short introduction to the masks used in the Gule Wankulu dance, from a commercial gallery.
Cichlid Fishes of Lake Malawi Ⓦ malawicichlids.com A fine example of ichthyophily – fish-loving – this has everything and more about the lake's multicoloured fish.
Friends of Malawi Ⓦ www.friendsofmalawi.org Compiled by returned volunteers, this contains short but useful introductions to Malawian culture and tourism.

Books

Benjamin Puertas Donoso *Across the Footsteps of Africa: The Experiences of an Ecuadorian Doctor in Malawi and Mozambique*. Fascinating, almost poetic descriptions of the physician's experiences with Médecins Sans Frontières in Malawian refugee camps towards the end of the Mozambican civil war.
Deborah Ellis *The Heaven Shop* A children's book that successfully elicits

sympathy and understanding for the plight of AIDS orphans, through the Cinderella-like tale of a 13-year-old girl.

Ad Konings *Malawi Cichlids in their Natural Habitat*. Lake Malawi's colourful fish feed a worldwide aquarium industry; this illustrated guide is one of few to go beyond cichlids as pets.

David Livingstone *The Zambesi Expedition*. Includes the doctor's (re)discovery of Lake Malawi (a Portuguese was the first European to get there, two centuries earlier), and his famous diatribes against the slave trade.

A free download from ⓦwww.gutenberg .org.

Jane Baker Lotter *To Africa with Spatula: A Peace Corps Mom in Malawi*. Engaging, good-natured and optimistic account of a Californian family's two years in Malawi in the 1960s, compiled from letters Lotter wrote to a neighbour back home.

Jack Mapanje *The Chattering Wagtails of Mikuyu Prison*. Deliciously lyrical vignettes of the poet's imprisonment under the dictatorial regime of President Hastings Banda.

Mali

Area 1,240,192 square kilometres	**Climate** Subtropical in south, arid in
Capital Bamako	north, swelteringly hot throughout;
Population 13 million; ethnic groups	rains (mainly in southwest) June–
include Bamana (or Bambara),	Sept
Malinké (Mandinka), Fulani, Soninké,	**Best time to go** Nov–Feb (dry
Songhaï, Dogon, Tuareg and Moors	season); Aug–Nov if travelling along
Language French (official); primary	the Niger
ethnic language is Bamanankan	**Currency** CFA franc
Religion Islam 90 percent	**Minimum costs** $25/£14 per day

In material terms, Mali is a desperately poor place. The marching dunes of the Sahara, and increasingly frequent droughts in the scrubby Sahel to its south, have seen to that. But culturally and historically, Mali is blessed with immense wealth. In medieval times, its cities were among Africa's most advanced, their riches stemming from the trans-Saharan caravan trade in salt and gold, and, later, in slaves. In such a dry land, however, neither the cities nor the empires to which they belonged – Ghana, Mali and Songhaï – could have existed without the River Niger, which appears to take a wrong turn in Mali, wending its way deep into the Sahara to breathe life to a vast inland delta. It's a compelling region, beautiful and sparse, and any trip down the great river, whether by ferry or by wooden *pinasse*, is the stuff of dreams and adventures.

Although the trans-Saharan trade is no more, Tuareg camel trains still carry precious slabs of rock salt from mines deep in the Sahara to the river, and the overall feel of Mali is still that of the "real" Africa: a timeless sort of place, whose charms transcend the hot and dusty plains that comprise it.

Average temperature ranges and rainfall

	Jan	Feb	Mar	Apr	May	Jun	Jul	Aug	Sep	Oct	Nov	Dec
Bamako												
Max °C	33	36	39	39	39	34	31	30	32	34	34	33
Min °C	16	19	22	24	24	23	22	22	22	22	18	17
Rainfall mm	0	0	3	15	74	137	279	348	206	43	15	0
Timbuktu												
Max °C	31	34	38	42	43	43	39	36	39	40	37	32
Min °C	13	14	19	22	26	27	25	24	24	23	18	13
Rainfall mm	0	0	3	0	5	23	79	81	38	3	0	0

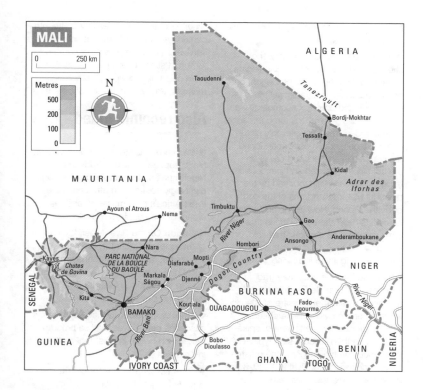

MALI	
0 — 250 km	A L G E R I A
Metres	
500	Taoudenni
200	Tanezrouft
100	Bordj-Mokhtar
0	Tessalit
	Kidal
M A U R I T A N I A	Adrar des Iforhas
Ayoun el Atrous	
Nema	Timbuktu
	River Niger
Nara	Gao
	Hombori · Ansongo
PARC NATIONAL DE LA BOUCLE DU BAOULÉ	Anderamboukane
Kayes	Mopti
Chutes de Govina	Diafarabé · Dogon Country
	Markala
Ségou · Djenné	N I G E R
Kita	BURKINA FASO
BAMAKO · Koutiala	Fado-Ngourma
	OUAGADOUGOU
GUINEA	River Niger
River Bani	Bobo-Dioulasso
IVORY COAST	GHANA · TOGO · BENIN · NIGERIA

Main attractions

● **Timbuktu** Timbuktu garnered fame from medieval reports of a fabulously wealthy town at the southern edge of the Sahara, a place whose houses were roofed with gold. It also gained infamy as the target for dozens of failed and often fatal European expeditions to find it. By the time the young French explorer René Caillie visited (and returned alive) in 1828, the gold trade was long gone. Today, the decline is complete, with just a few remaining camel caravans. Despite the poverty, and inevitable hustlers, the old mystique remains, and rubbing shoulders with Tuareg in the market

while haggling for swords and daggers is all part of the fun. Timbuktu's other attractions include beautiful earthen mosques and tombs, the houses of various explorers, and rather voyeuristic experiences in "genuine" Tuareg camps pitched around town.

● **The River Niger** The Niger is a natural artery for commerce and exchange, and – for the adventurous – a stage for one of the world's great river journeys, past bird-filled reed beds and lugubrious hippos. From August to November, you can catch a steamer along the 1300km that separate Bamako from Gao, a leisurely five or six days' sail. Be aware, though, that the reality can be uncomfortable, whether you're travelling by ferry or drifting downstream in a pirogue or a *pinasse*.

● **Trekking in Dogon country** The sheer sandstone cliffs of the Bandiagara Escarpment are home to the Dogon, one of the country's most traditional tribes, whose rich and complex cosmology was carried across generations through dance masquerades. Their unbelievably pictur-esque villages, now mostly abandoned, are perched in shelters and caves on the cliff sides – isolated and inaccessible refuges that were little touched by the powerful Muslim kingdoms of the north, or by the French. Nowadays, busloads of tourists have altered traditions that no army managed to change. That said, escaping the tourist circus is easy, and very rewarding if you like hiking.

● **Djenné** This ninth-century trading town on the River Bani, a tributary of the Niger, was a major centre of Islamic learning, and provided the architec-tural inspiration for the towering, spike-studded earthen mosques so typical of the Sahel. The main sight is the master-ful Grande Mosquée. Built in 1280, it has been ceremoniously replastered each February ever since. Running a close second is the town's market, a great place for gold jewellery, leatherware, pottery and bronzes.

● **Mopti** Easy access to Mopti, at the confluence of the Bani and Niger rivers, makes it the most visited of the Niger's port towns, but also the most hustley. Yet its charms do grow on you, especially in the bustling hive of activity that is the harbour, and at the incredible Thursday market, where you'll find bronze bracelets, golden-leaf Fulani earrings, and even flintlock pistols. You can also take a bird-watching trip by pirogue, or spend time fishing with the locals.

● **Gao** As the former capital of the Songhaï Empire, this ancient trans-Saharan trading town on the River

Niger reached its apogee in the fifteenth century. A mosque from that time survives, as do the pyramidal earthen tombs of sixteenth-century kings. The town also has a couple of excellent markets, and a wide choice of boat trips.

Also recommended

● **Bamako** Despite the modern veneer, Mali's capital – which straddles the Niger – has a distinctly African feel, and pleasingly so. Its main attractions are West Africa's best museum, and the cream of the country's nightlife.

● **Ségou** On the River Niger, the capital of the nineteenth-century Bamana Empire has a colourful Monday market, good bird-watching nearby, and pirogue trips to Kalabougou Island, home to celebrated potters.

● **Chutes de Gouina** Victoria Falls-style cascades near Kayes, whose breadth rather than height is what makes them impressive.

● **Parc National de la Boucle du Baoulé** Forget about wildlife (mostly hunted out), but do visit Baoulé for its rock paintings: there are two hundred sites in all, plus mysterious ancient tombs.

● **Kidal** A town in the heart of Tuareg country, surrounded by a desert of sun-blackened boulders, spiny acacia trees, sand dunes, and rock-strewn mountains enclosing small oases in their folds.

● **Hombori** The sheer, mesa-like outcrops and dramatic needle-like formations of Hombori comprise Mali's highest elevations, peaking at around 1200m.

Festivals

Mali is a musical powerhouse, having produced international stars such as

Salif Keita, Toumani Diabaté and the late Ali Farka Touré. All of these acknowledge their debt to the country's griot tradition, the griots being a caste of musicians who double as repositories for collective histories and genealogies. The tradition is most visible in masquerades, at which masked dancers represent ancestors or symbolic aspects of the universe. Muslim and Christian festivals are celebrated nationally; see p.243 & p.245 for dates. The tourist board's website has a full list of celebrations.

Dogon masquerades Dogon country The complex cosmological world of the Dogon was traditionally recreated via elaborate masked dances at funerals, at harvest celebrations (in June), and at the Dama ceremony every twelve years. Nowadays, the dances are performed whenever tourists come up with enough cash…

Festival of the Desert Essakane; Jan Three days of mainly Tuareg music and dance, poetry and camel races, a day's journey into the desert from Timbuktu.

Festival sur le Niger Ségou; early Feb An impressive programme boasting Mali's biggest musical stars, plus pirogue races, masquerades and other arts.

Sogo Bo marionettes Markala, Ségou region; March Before the rains arrive, the Bamana perform a series of puppet masquerades to put their moral universe to rights. Conflicts among a man's wives are a favourite theme.

Tamadacht Anderamboukane, Gao region; Jan A big desert get-together for the Tuareg: song and dance, camel and horse races, traditional bouts and acrobats, and loads of contests: best-dressed men and women, the prettiest tents, and the most fetching camels and goats.

Yaaral and Deegal: the Crossing of the Cattle Diafarabé and Dialloubé, near Mopti; usually Dec An annual swim across the River Niger by Peul pastoralists and their herds, returning from the Sahel's exhausted pastures to the evergreen lands of the Niger's inland delta. The cattle are garishly painted (there are beauty contests for them), and the whole shebang is one big excuse to party.

Routes in and out

Flights land at Bamako. Buses connect Mali with Senegal, Guinea, Burkina Faso and Niger, and there's a weekly train from Dakar in Senegal. Saharan border areas (Mauritania, Algeria and northern Niger) should be avoided unless you're informed and aware of the risks – currently the safest trans-Saharan road is the Tanezrouft route from southern Algeria.

Mali online

Mali Tourist Office
Ⓦ www.officetourisme-mali.com
Dogon Lobi
Ⓦ www.dogon-lobi.ch Over a thousand high-quality photos of the Dogon and their region – everything from portraits to festivals and funerals, together with extensive background.
Now That's What I Call Mali
Ⓦ www.bbc.co.uk/radio3/worldmusic /onlocation/mali1 .shtml Pioneering three-part radio documentary on Malian music by Andy Kershaw, recorded back in 1989 when the country was beginning its flight to world music celebrity.

Books

Amadou Hampaté Bâ *The Fortunes of Wangrin*. One of several humorous novels from Mali's foremost writer, whose output owes more than a touch to oral traditions. This one satirizes the impact of colonialism.

● **Banning Eyre** *In Griot Times: An American Guitarist in Mali*. Seven months of learning the kora gave rise to this great travelogue, in which vivid descriptions of Malian music rub shoulders with a colourful set of characters.

● **Jean-Marie Gibbal** *Genii of the River Niger*. A wonderful blend of ethnography and evocative travelogue, focusing on a healing cult based around river spirits.

● **Mamadou Kouyate** *Sundiata: An Epic of Old Mali*. An elegant transcription of one of Africa's most famous epics, the 700-year-old tale of a poorly young boy who become a great warrior and united the Mandinka people.

● **Jean-Marc Patras** *Seydou Keïta: A Retrospective*. An extraordinary collection of black-and-white studio photos of Bamako people taken either side of independence.

● **Bettina Selby** *Frail Dream of Timbuktu*. Lightly written account of a bicycle journey along the Niger, from Niamey to Timbuktu and beyond.

● **Walter E.A. van Beek and Stephnie Hollyman** *Dogon: Africa's People of the Cliffs*. An observant and detailed photographic study of traditional Dogon society and ritual.

Mauritania

Area 1,030,700 square kilometres **Capital** Nouakchott **Population** 3.2 million, mostly Moors; other peoples include Wolof, Soninké, Tukulor and Fulani, mostly living around the River Senegal **Language** Hassaniya Arabic (official); French widely spoken; Fula, Soninké or Wolof in south	**Religion** Islam **Climate** Mostly unremittingly dry, dusty, and hot, except in winter; the dusty harmattan blows Feb–April; July–Sept sees rains in the River Senegal area **Best time to go** Nov–March **Currency** Ouguiya **Minimum costs** $50/£28 per day

The western Saharan state of Mauritania is among the world's least known, most barren and poorest nations. In traditional tourist terms, this Islamic Republic has little to pull in the crowds other than desert, but for adventurous souls it's easily one of the most fascinating and enchanting places to visit – one where the journey, rather than the destination, is really what it's all about.

As the historical and cultural link between Morocco and Black Africa, Mauritania has a history and culture that are far from barren. Since antiquity, its oases were vital stops along trans-Saharan caravan routes, and the country was the heartland of the puritanical Almoravid Empire, which at its height even controlled Iberia. It's perhaps easy to see why the Almoravids were so keen to leave their homeland: with the exception of a handful of remote oases and a strip of irrigated land along the River Senegal, the entire place is desert, much of it covered by dunes.

For Mauritanians, survival has always been precarious, not helped in recent decades by increasingly frequent droughts, which have forced many to abandon their cherished nomadic ways for the squalor of Nouakchott's and Nouâdhibou's shanty towns. But many persist with nomadism, whether as

Average temperature ranges and rainfall

	Jan	Feb	Mar	Apr	May	Jun	Jul	Aug	Sep	Oct	Nov	Dec
Nouakchott												
Max °C	29	31	32	32	34	33	32	32	34	33	32	28
Min °C	14	15	17	18	21	23	23	24	24	22	18	13
Rainfall mm	0	3	0	0	0	3	13	104	23	10	3	0
Atâr												
Max °C	31	33	34	39	40	42	43	42	42	38	33	29
Min °C	12	13	17	19	22	27	25	26	26	23	17	13
Rainfall mm	3	0	0	0	0	3	8	30	28	3	3	0

herders or – now rare – long-distance caravaneers. Like all desert people, Mauritanians are extraordinarily welcoming. In such a tenuous land, hospitality has always been of paramount importance: you never know when you might need to call in favours. There's also a dark side to traditional Mauritania: slavery was only abolished in 1980.

Main attractions

● **The Adrar** The historical cradle of the Almoravid Empire was the Adrar massif, a land of sun-blackened rocks, sandy valleys and oases hidden amid canyons. Its capital, Atâr, is a surprisingly lively base for visits to the former Almoravid capital of Azoughui, and to prehistoric rock paintings. For many, the highlight is the fourteenth-century oasis town of Chinguetti, one of Islam's holy places – and one that risks being swallowed up by the Sahara's voracious sands.

● **Parc National du Banc d'Arguin** Covering a big chunk of Atlantic coastline between Nouakchott and Nouâdhibou, this is among the world's largest bird sanctuaries, a welcome refuge for over two million wintering migrants, herons, pelicans and flamingoes. The park is also home to the Imraguen, descendants of Mauritania's pre-Islamic inhabitants. At Nouâmghar, Imraguen fishermen have developed an amazing symbiotic relationship with dolphins. Responding to the sound of sticks beaten on water, the dolphins chase shoals of fish towards the shore, upon which the fishermen rush out with nets, to the benefit of both them and the dolphins.

● **Oualata** A tiny speck at the edge of eastern Mauritania's forbidding El Djouf (literally "the belly" – meaning a ravenously empty desert), this medieval city was one of the Sahara's great entrepôts, and is still a perfect refuge for travellers venturing this far. The fortified town boasts the country's most beautiful houses, with painted walls and doors and geometric stucco, and an ancient Qur'anic school that draws scholars from around the globe.

Also recommended

● **Ouadane** An important caravanserai founded over eight hundred years ago, this hillside town 200km east of Atâr contains an impressive collection of ruins, and an equally attractive new town. Together, they're strikingly beautiful, as much for their architecture as for their location beside extensive palm groves and sand dunes.

● **Aoudaghost** Hidden in the dunes, Aoudaghost was a stopover on the ancient caravan route from Morocco, and capital of a Berber empire that resisted Islam until the twelfth century. It was abandoned in the seventeenth, leaving a scatter of ruins, including a necropolis that's half-engulfed by sand.

● **Kumbi Saleh** In the dunes of eastern Mauritania are the ruins of the former capital of the Ghana empire (no relation to modern Ghana). Stone houses and one of twelve impressive mosques have been excavated.

● **The iron ore railway** Running from Nouâdhibou on the coast to the iron ore mines of the north is the world's longest train, its locomotives hauling several kilometres of rolling stock. The ride is free on board the open cargo wagons (face muffler essential to keep out the dust), though softies can pay for a seat in a carriage. The route is perfect for getting to Choum, for the overland journey down to the Adrar and beyond.

Festivals

Apart from the following, Islamic festivals are also celebrated; see p.245.

Festival International des Musiques Nomades **Nouakchott; April** A celebration of nomadic music; includes non-African groups.

The Guetna **Adrar mountains; July & Aug** Local festivities in honour of successful date harvests.

Routes in and out

Nouakchott and Nouâdhibou receive scheduled flights from Europe, including the Canary Islands. There are irregular winter-time charters from France to Atâr. Road access from Senegal is no problem. Bandits have been known to operate around the Malian border. Access from Morocco via the Western Sahara is possible for private vehicles but has been prone to closure; special permits may be required. The Algerian border is closed to tourists.

Mauritania online

République Islamique de Mauritanie
Ⓦ www.mauritania.mr/fr To Government site with useful links and short intros, plus the official pages of the Parc National du Banc d'Arguin. In French.

A Lovely World
Ⓦ www.alovelyworld.com/webmr Over six hundred photos covering the Adrar, Arguin and Nouakchott.

Adventures of Mauritania
Ⓦ www.lexicorient.com/mauritania The best all-round resource, with intelligent, up-to-date and beautifully illustrated articles covering every place you're likely to visit.

Musiques Nomades
Ⓦ www.musiquesnomades.com Home of the Nouakchott's annual music festival, with interviews and links to sound clips. In French.

Un Trek en Mauritanie
Ⓦ www.chinguetti.com Account of a trip to Chinguetti with great pictures. In French.

Books

Michael Asher *Impossible Journey.* Mauritania was the starting point for this former SAS officer's adventurous west-to-east crossing of the Sahara by camel. Kudos to Asher for not ignoring the culture and history of the countries he passed through.

Samuel Cotton *Silent Terror.* A militant call-to-arms against what the author sees as persisting slavery in post-abolition Mauritania. While Cotton makes many important points, his arguments are weakened by his simplistic view of Moorish society.

Jens Finke *Chasing the Lizard's Tail – Across the Sahara by Bicycle.* An unconventional travelogue that includes four chapters on Mauritania, blending pleasingly obscure research with personal adventure, which included a life-changing getting-lost-and-running-out-of-water experience. Also online at Ⓦ www.bluegecko.org/lizard.

James Riley *Sufferings in Africa.* Shipwrecked off the Western Sahara in 1815, the American Captain Riley and his companions sold themselves into slavery to survive. His painfully honest and enthralling account of the horrors of slavery, and of their journey to freedom, sold over a million copies, including one that influenced a young Abraham Lincoln. Don't forget that, at the time, millions of African–Americans were also enslaved.

Morocco and the Western Sahara

Area 446,550 square kilometres (710,850 square kilometres including the Western Sahara)
Capital Rabat
Population 32.3 million; majority are Berbers or Arabs, with Moors and Saharawi in the Western Sahara
Language Arabic and Berber; French is widely understood
Religion Islam
Climate Mediterranean in north (rains Nov–March); cold winters and hot summers in Atlas Mountains; hot and dry in the Sahara, with the dusty Sahat blowing Feb–April
Best time to go May–Oct for the beaches; April–Oct to hike in the mountains; Feb–April for skiing; Nov–April for the Sahara
Currency Moroccan dirham
Minimum costs $25/£14 per day

Bordered by the Sahara, the Atlantic and the Mediterranean, the Kingdom of Morocco lays on a suitably regal feast for the senses. Whether it's beaches or snow-capped mountains, deserts, history, culture or even shopping that excites you, you'll find it here in quantity.

Morocco's history has been more influenced by the Sahara – across millennial caravan routes – than by invasions from the east. The Ottoman Empire never got this far west, nor did Egypt's Caliphate. Instead, Morocco hosted a succession of Islamic dynasties

Average temperature ranges and rainfall

	Jan	Feb	Mar	Apr	May	Jun	Jul	Aug	Sep	Oct	Nov	Dec
Essaouira												
Max °C	18	18	19	19	20	21	21	22	22	22	20	19
Min °C	11	12	13	13	15	17	17	17	17	16	14	12
Rainfall mm	52	37	40	35	9	2	0	1	3	25	73	65
Fès												
Max °C	15	16	18	20	24	28	34	34	30	25	19	16
Min °C	4	5	6	8	10	13	17	17	15	11	8	5
Rainfall mm	63	66	72	62	35	15	2	3	12	46	68	75
Marrakesh												
Max °C	18	20	22	24	28	31	37	37	33	28	22	19
Min °C	6	8	9	11	14	16	20	20	18	15	10	7
Rainfall mm	32	38	38	39	24	5	1	3	6	24	41	31

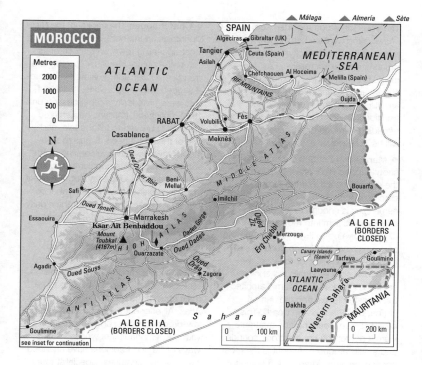

and empires, which at times also controlled the Iberian Peninsula and parts of West Africa. The country is rich in culture and folklore, whether in ancient coastal towns, the "Imperial Cities" of Rabat, Fès, Meknès and Marrakesh, or in the mountains and deserts inhabited by indigenous Berbers, whose proud heritage expresses itself through a rich and colourful cycle of pilgrimages, festivals and fairs.

Most of the beaches frequented by tourists are on the Atlantic, whose winter-time ocean temperatures are distinctly chilly. Ocean currents can also be dangerously strong, so choose carefully. Safer and warmer are the Mediterranean resorts, which get packed with Moroccans during holiday times.

Western Sahara, illegally occupied by Morocco since the 1970s, has little to detain you unless you're driving down to West Africa. Most of the indigenous Saharawis have spent the last three decades as refugees in western Algeria.

Main attractions

● **Fès (Fez)** Among the most fascinating and atmospheric cities on earth, Fès is the most ancient of Morocco's Imperial Cities, dating back to the ninth century. The larger, older part of town – Fès el-Bali – dates from this time. Fès el-Jedid, or "New Fès", is a nipper at just eight centuries old. Both are hugely enjoyable labyrinths stuffed to the rafters with monuments, many funded by Iberian Jews and Muslims expelled during the Spanish Inquisition.

The influx kicked off a golden age, when Fès was the western hemisphere's most advanced and refined city. Although the monuments are impressive, Fès' real magic is infused in its maze of narrow streets and bazaars, where goods are still transported by donkey, and traditional artisans have shown few signs of ceding to modernity. Souvenir hunters will be in heaven.

● **Marrakesh** Set at the foot of the snow-capped High Atlas, Marrakesh, the erstwhile capital of the Almoravid empire, is actually a desert town. The name itself is enough to set dreams of oriental exoticism into motion, and the city does live up to its allure. Though the caravans have long since gone (these days the camels are for tourists), the city's rose-coloured walls still enclose souks as good as any, Islamic architectural masterpieces, and the Jemaa el-Fna, the "Place of the Dead". This broad square would be unremarkable were it not for the riot of colour, sounds and smells around it. Twilight is the most enchanting time, when it's the stage for musicians, acrobats and jugglers, fire-eaters and snake charmers, fortune- and story-tellers, miracle-working quacks, beggars and hustlers, hashish sellers and smokers – and cooks conjuring up Morocco's best street food.

● **Essaouira** The prettiest, most relaxed and atmospheric of Morocco's Atlantic towns, Essaouira has been a port since Phoenician times. Huddled inside ramparts, the whitewashed town is full of narrow streets concealing dozens of traditional workshops (woodcarving is the speciality). The harbour is also attractive, and while the beach often offers better conditions for windsurfing than swimming, a growing number of excellent seafood restaurants will help you bide your time.

● **Chefchaouen** The capital of the Rif Mountains, in the north, is Morocco's most appealing town, with much of its sixteenth-century medina – clinging to a craggy mountainside – painted in ethereal shades of blue and white. Its inhabitants were historically a rebellious lot: until 1912, only two Christians had entered town and survived to tell the tale, and one of them had been disguised as a rabbi. Nowadays the welcome is warm, and Chefchaouen is popular with both day-trippers and long-stay pot-heads: kif (marijuana blended with black tobacco) is part of local culture, and for the elderly habitués of the town's cafés, a constant companion.

● **The Atlas Mountains** Extending over 2000km, the Atlas Mountains are at their highest and most spectacular in Morocco, where they're split into three main chains: the Middle, High and Anti-Atlas. All offer outstanding hiking terrain, jaw-dropping views, and encounters with Berber inhabitants whose villages, ways of life and traditions have changed little over the centuries. Specialist tour companies offer mule treks, white-water rafting, mountain biking and camping expeditions, and skiing is possible in winter. For the hardy, the highlight is an ascent of the snow-covered Mount Toubkal (4167m).

● **Ksar Aït Benhaddou** Typical of the more arid corners of the Atlas Mountains are the fortified mud-brick villages called *ksour* (singular *ksar*), which look every bit as medieval as anything Hollywood could dream up. In fact, Hollywood doesn't even need to try – an especially cinematic example, quite literally (it featured in *The Sheltering Sky* and *Lawrence of Arabia*) is the *ksar* of Aït Benhaddou, a towering, fairy-tale construction built by a Berber tribe notorious in the past for their raids.

Also recommended

- **Tangier** In the 1950s, Tangier, at the entrance to the Strait of Gibraltar, was an international free port with a reputation for hedonism. By the 1990s it had become the most disagreeable town in Morocco, thanks to the merciless attention of hustlers. Things have improved considerably, and the town retains a good deal of its cosmopolitan buzz. Apart from a beautiful beach, the market's always fun.

- **Asilah** On the Atlantic side of Tangier, this laid-back fishing village is a popular haunt for artists. The pretty whitewashed town has bags of charm, and its beach is as good as any.

- **Al Hoceima** A lively Mediterranean resort at the base of towering cliffs, especially popular with Moroccan families – which means crowded beaches in summer.

- **Volubilis** The Roman town of Volubilis remained inhabited – and virtually intact – until the seventeenth century, when the megalomaniacal sultan Moulay Ismaïl tore it down to provide building materials for the nearby city of Meknès. The surviving basilica is impressive, as are the mosaics.

- **The Sahara** Morocco's portion of the Sahara consists primarily of rocky hills interspersed with pebble-strewn plateaus. As such, the sand dunes of Erg Chebbi, accessed from Merzouga close to the Algerian border, have long entertained tourists as well as film crews. Camel rides are the best way to see why, whether for a few hours or a few days. Camel excursions can also be arranged in Zagora, otherwise famous for a quixotic road sign announcing Timbuktu as being 52 days away.

- **Dadès Gorge** The rugged land southeast of Marrakesh has one foot in the Sahara and the other in the Atlas mountains. The ever-changing but always dramatic scenery makes the Dadès Gorge one of Morocco's most popular excursions. Upstream, rusty cliffs draw in to enclose a succession of fortified villages and turreted kasbahs, some cute, some imposing, all ineffably medieval.

Festivals

There's no shortage of popular celebrations (moussems), many of them honouring Sufi saints, and timed to coincide with important harvests, or with Mouloud – the Prophet Muhammad's birthday. Other Islamic festivals (see p.245) are also celebrated, while tourism supports a good number of art and music festivals.

Fès Festival Fès; June Rare and beautiful sacred sounds from around the globe; Morocco's own output is completely bewitching.

Gnawa and World Music Festival Essaouira; June Morocco's eclectic gnawa music, a blend of Sufi and West African trance rhythms.

International Arts Festival Asilah; Aug A major showcase for contemporary Moroccan artists.

Wedding Festival Imilchil, Middle Atlas; Sept A traditional moussem combining lively fairs with something unheard of in the rest of the Islamic world: dressed up in their most colourful finery, Berber women from around the Atlas come here to find a husband, getting hitched at the end in a series of boisterous celebrations.

Routes in and out

Casablanca, Marrakesh, Tangier and Rabat are the main airports. Ferries connect Tangier and the Spanish enclave of Ceuta (Sebta) with Gibraltar and Spain. There are also ferries from Spain to the Spanish enclave of Melilla, and irregular ferries from Sète (France) and Genoa (Italy). The land border with Algeria is usually closed. The Mauritanian border with the Western Sahara is open to private vehicles, providing an asphalt ribbon right across the Sahara, but get the paperwork sorted before entering the region.

Morocco online

Moroccan National Tourist Office
Ⓦ **www.visitmorocco.com**
Adventures in Morocco
Ⓦ **www.lexicorient.com/morocco**
Exhaustive coverage of all the attractions, with plenty of photos.
Jewish Morocco
Ⓦ **rickgold.home.mindspring.com**
Often overlooked these days are the historically close ties between North African Muslims and Jews. This site offers an extensive and illustrated history, and coverage of the main Jewish sites.
Ministry of Communication: Moroccan Music
Ⓦ **www.mincom.gov.ma/english /gallery/music/music.html** A representative selection of traditional music (in MP3 format), from Andalusian-style string orchestras and Sufi chants to gnawa.

Morocco.com
Ⓦ **www.morocco.com** Nicely designed and comprehensive travel showcase with well-written city and destination guides, plus related articles covering everything from cuisine to art and culture.

Books

Izza Genini, Jacques Bravo and Xavier Richer *Splendours of Morocco*. Beautiful photographic portrait.
Walter Harris *Morocco That Was*. For thirty-five years, Harris was *The Times*' man in Morocco. His meticulous attention to detail, good nose for a story and agreeably eccentric persona keep this book fresh and fascinating.
William Lithgow *Rare Adventures and Painful Peregrinations*. In this masterpiece of Scottish wit, first published in 1632, Lithgow recounts nineteen years of traipsing around Europe and North Africa, mostly on foot. Full of comic irreverence, Lithgow had a healthy respect for the people he met and the countries he travelled through. Easily one of the most entertaining travel books ever written.
Barnaby Rogerson and Stephen Lavington (eds) *Marrakesh, The Red City*. Enjoyable anthology, including insightful pieces by Elias Canetti and Juan Goytisolo.

Mozambique

Area 801,590 square kilometres
Capital Maputo
Population 20.5 million; sixteen ethnic groups, the main ones being Makua, Lomwe, Makonde, Tsonga, Shona and Yao
Language Portuguese spoken by a third of the population; major tribal languages are Emakhuwa and Xichangana
Religion Traditional beliefs 40 percent, Christianity 40 percent, Islam (in the north) 20 percent
Climate Generally tropical and humid; north influenced by Indian Ocean monsoons; dry season May–Sept, rains Oct–April, risk of flooding Jan–March
Best time to go June–Aug for the best climate, but Sept for wildlife
Currency Metical (plural meticais)
Minimum costs $20/£11 per day

Almost five centuries of Portuguese domination over Mozambique ended in 1975, following a brutal war of independence. Just as brutal was the civil war that wracked the country until the early 1990s. Before all this, Mozambique had been among the most visited countries on the continent, and is now looking to reclaim something of its former status. Certainly, should paradisiacal beaches feature in your plans, you'd be hard put to find better: with over 2500km of coastline, the country is blessed with hundreds of great spots for sun-worshipping, or dipping beneath the translucent waters for glimpses of the western Indian Ocean's extraordinarily rich coral reefs.

Aquatic delights aside, Mozambique boasts historical sites related to the Portuguese conquest, and to the earlier, monsoon-driven dhow trade that had been dominated by Arabs, Persians and Swahilis. Indonesians and Chinese were also visitors, all of them contributing to a funky multicultural mix that left a very tasty mark in Mozambican cuisine.

Average temperature ranges and rainfall

	Jan	Feb	Mar	Apr	May	Jun	Jul	Aug	Sep	Oct	Nov	Dec
Maputo												
Max °C	30	30	29	28	26	25	24	25	26	27	27	29
Min °C	22	22	22	19	17	14	14	15	17	18	20	21
Rainfall mm	171	131	106	57	32	18	20	15	44	55	82	85
Ilha de Moçambique (near Nampula)												
Max °C	31	30	30	29	27	26	25	27	30	32	32	31
Min °C	22	22	21	20	18	16	16	16	17	19	21	21
Rainfall mm	228	216	181	81	23	16	22	8	6	24	83	184

The country's wildlife areas were decimated during the wars and are still recovering, though a handful are already worth visiting. War also disrupted social and cultural structures, but the country hasn't lost touch with its origins: traditional music and sculpture have influenced modern forms and genres, and the arts as a whole are blossoming.

Main attractions

● **Ilha de Moçambique** This small but unutterably beautiful fortified town was capital of Portuguese East Africa until 1898. Inevitably, the town was a blend of ideas and cultures, as shown by its picturesque coral ragstone buildings. Notable among them is a chapel built in 1522, a fact which makes it the southern hemisphere's oldest Christian temple. Two museums, an imposing fortress from 1507, boat rides, diving and snorkelling, and fishing expeditions with locals are other attractions.

● **Bazaruto Archipelago** Four islands and several tidal islets, at the place where the Limpopo once emptied into the ocean, make up this Indian Ocean paradise. Its perfect for swimming and beach bumming, snorkelling or diving off colourful reefs, and starlight dhow cruises. Marine life includes turtles, dolphins and dugongs, and the birdlife isn't bad either.

● **Pemba** Northern Mozambique's largest town, Pemba was a major trading centre for the Portuguese and Arabs, whose influences can be seen in the architecture and in Pemba's celebrated silver jewellery. The town is especially popular with backpackers, attracted by wonderful beaches and reefs.

● **Quirimbas Archipelago** The 200km between Pemba and Tanzania are flanked by 32 islands, each peppered with idyllic beaches and unspoiled reefs. Marine life is there in all its glory, from turtles (and their nesting beaches), whales and dolphins to the endangered dugong, and – on the mainland, protected as part of Quirimbas National Park – elephants and leopards. The Ilha da Quilálea is particularly good for wildlife (including mangrove-loving birds), while the Ilha de Ibo is home to a pretty colonial town, complete with three fortresses and a magnificent church.

● **Manica Province** The mountains marking the Zimbabwean border are a naturally diverse world of forest-clad peaks, highland plateaus, rivers, lakes and waterfalls. Chimoio is the base for hikers and mountain bikers: destinations include sacred rock paintings at Chinhamapere, a rock with an old man's profile called the Cabeça do Velho; Chicamba Real Dam for bird-watching; and the country's highest peak, Monte Binga (2436m).

● **Niassa Province** Bordered by Tanzania and Lake Niassa (also called Nyasa or Malawi), the province of Niassa has been bypassed by tourism, and indeed by any substantial development, thanks to often impassable road from the rest of the country (it's easier to get there from Malawi). Isolation has made the forests, tangled woodland and hill-studded savanna of the mammoth Reserva do Niassa one of the continent's best places for elephants – at least 12,000 at the last count.

Also recommended

● **Maputo** Mozambique's metropolitan capital has good restaurants and nightclubs, and a range of other attractions, too: colonial fortresses and churches, a glorious wrought-iron train station designed by Eiffel, museums, a pungently spectacular fish market, and beaches all around, including on the Ilha da Inhaca, which is favoured by snorkellers and divers. The city also serves as a base for safaris to Maputo Elephant Reserve.

● **Inhambane** A sleepy town, founded in 1534, that's capital of a province famed for its embarrassment of heavenly beaches, all soft white sand and limpid turquoise water backed by swaying palms and casuarinas. Best known is Praia do Tofo, popular with surfers and amply endowed with facilities for all tastes and pockets.

● **Great Limpopo Transfrontier Park** Newly inaugurated and eventually slated to become the world's largest protected wildlife area, Great Limpopo currently links Mozambique's Limpopo and Banhine national parks with South Africa's Kruger. Elephants are the main attraction, and tourist options include four-wheel-drive trails and game walks.

● **Parque Nacional de Gorongosa** Before the war, this was one of the best parks in Africa. It'll probably never recover its former glory, but has been well managed since peace returned, and now has sizeable populations of lions, elephants, crocs, hippos and antelopes.

● **Traditional music** If delicate, mind-bending music is your thing, ask around in the coastal town of Quissico for performances of Chopi timbila xylophones and marimba "thumb pianos".

Festivals

Many Mozambicans remain true to their origins, with neither Christianity nor Islam having made significant inroads beyond the coast. The result is quite extraordinary musical traditions often linked to sacred ceremonies little known outside the country. The end of the dry season is the best time to catch local festivities, when spirits are invoked to ask for rain.

Carnaval Quelimane; see p.243 for dates Zambézia Province is Mozambique's "little Brazil", complete with a samba-doused carnival.

Routes in and out

The international airports are Maputo, Beira and Nampula. Buses arrive from Malawi, Zambia, Zimbabwe and South Africa, and minibuses connect with Swaziland. Road access from Tanzania means catching a chain of local buses and shared taxis along the unsurfaced coastal road, which may be blocked during the rains. Niassa Province is most easily accessed by ferry from Malawi.

Mozambique online

Ministry of Tourism
Ⓦ www.moztourism.gov.mz In Portuguese.
Mozambique Tourist Guide
Ⓦ www.turismomocambique.co.mz
The best all-round resource, reliable and comprehensive.
Iluminando Vidas
Ⓦ www.iluminandovidas.org
Condensed version of an exhibition of Mozambican photography. Over 100 black-and-white photos, plus biographies.
World Routes in Mozambique
Ⓦ www.bbc.co.uk/radio3/worldmusic /onlocation/moza.shtml Two hour-long radio programmes from the BBC on Mozambican music.

Books

Mia Couto *Sleepwalking Land*. Couto's novels and stories are always worth seeking out. This one, set at the end of the civil war, is the tale of a dead passenger on a burned-out bus, whose notebooks are found and read by a young boy to an old man, both refugees.

Henning Mankell *Secrets in the Fire*. A young girl steps on a land mine, losing her legs and her sister. A tale of courage and resilience in post-war Mozambique. **Julio Navarro** *Malangatana*. Beautifully produced retrospective of the Mozambican painter Malangatana, widely considered one of Africa's best contemporary artists.

Namibia

Area 825,418 square kilometres
Capital Windhoek
Population 2.1 million; half are Ovambo; other ethnic groups include Kavango, Herero, Europeans, Damara, Nama and Bushmen (San)
Language Oshivambo, English and Afrikaans; German is spoken by thirty percent of Europeans; other languages include Herero and Nama

Religion Christianity 85 percent, traditional beliefs 15 percent
Climate Mostly desert or semi-arid, driest in the east, coolest on the coast; hottest Dec–March, scattered rains Oct–April
Best time to go May–Oct
Currency Namibian dollar and South African rand
Minimum costs $25/£14 per day

The former German colony of South West Africa was the last African country to gain independence, when in 1990 South Africa withdrew after seventy years of occupation. The country's name comes from desert flanking its coast, a word meaning "vast". True to its name, much of Namibia is wilderness: large and dry, sparsely populated and tremendously handsome.

Given the unforgiving landscape, Namibia's owes its comparative wealth to minerals, especially diamonds. Despite social inequalities inherited from apartheid, relations between the country's ethnic groups are peaceful. Furthermore, the indigenous Bushmen have been treated well by regional standards, making cultural tourism among them a real attraction. Namibia's other draws are primarily natural, not the least of which being its desolate yet devastatingly beautiful shoreline, though it's sadly too cold for swimming. Flanking

Average temperature ranges and rainfall

	Jan	Feb	Mar	Apr	May	Jun	Jul	Aug	Sep	Oct	Nov	Dec
Caprivi Strip												
Max °C	31	30	31	30	28	26	26	29	33	34	33	31
Min °C	19	19	17	14	8	5	4	6	11	17	19	19
Rainfall mm	177	166	97	27	2	2	0	0	5	35	80	165
Swakopmund												
Max °C	23	23	23	24	23	23	21	20	19	19	22	23
Min °C	15	16	15	13	11	9	8	8	9	11	12	14
Rainfall mm	0	5	8	3	3	0	0	3	0	0	0	0
Windhoek												
Max °C	28	27	26	25	22	20	20	22	26	27	29	30
Min °C	20	18	17	15	11	8	7	10	15	17	20	21
Rainfall mm	78	80	79	38	7	1	1	1	3	12	27	42

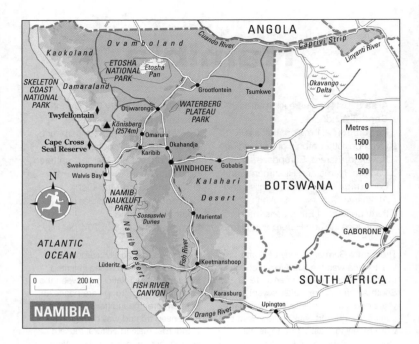

Map labels: ANGOLA, Cuando River, Caprivi Strip, Linyanti River, Ovamboland, Kaokoland, ETOSHA NATIONAL PARK, Etosha Pan, Grootfontein, Tsumkwe, Okavango Delta, SKELETON COAST NATIONAL PARK, Damaraland, Twyfelfontein, Otjiwarongo, WATERBERG PLATEAU PARK, Könisberg (2574m), Omaruru, Cape Cross Seal Reserve, Karibib, Okahandja, Swakopmund, Walvis Bay, WINDHOEK, Gobabis, Kalahari Desert, BOTSWANA, N, NAMIB-NAUKLUFT PARK, Sossusvlei Dunes, Namib Desert, ATLANTIC OCEAN, Mariental, GABORONE, Lüderitz, Fish River, Keetmanshoop, SOUTH AFRICA, FISH RIVER CANYON, Karasburg, Upington, Orange River, NAMIBIA, 0 200 km, Metres 1500 1000 500 0

the coast is the Namib Desert – which is Africa's coolest desert (thanks to Atlantic mists), the world's oldest, and which contains the world's highest sand dunes (up to an amazing 400m tall). Beyond the Namib is a highland plateau of savanna and ragged mountains, while the east of the country is swallowed up by the Kalahari. The only really lush corner is the northeastern Caprivi Strip, home to wildlife parks and reserves, and to most of the country's 630 bird species. There's more wildlife on the coast, most spectacularly a gigantic seal colony.

Given the size of the place, renting a car (or using organized tours) is recommended; if you want a challenge, the country's impressive network of four-wheel-drive trails is it.

Main attractions

● **The Skeleton Coast** Along the desolate and inhospitable northern coastline, sand dunes plunge straight into the ocean. The shifting sand banks they create, the Atlantic's frequent fogs and the desert inland were a deadly combination for mariners. The area is scarcely inhabited and infrequently visited (there are more elephants than tourists), yet its rusty shipwrecks, fogs and dunes possesses an almighty photographic beauty.

● **Cape Cross Seal Reserve** Between October and December the southern end of the Skeleton Coast is home to the world's largest breeding colony of Cape Fur seals; up to 100,000 of the blighters, a photogenic gathering as chaotic and cacophonous as it is malodorous.

● **Swakopmund** Namibia's main seaside resort is at its best in the morning and evening, when the Bavarian-style onion-shaped spires of its colonial buildings emerge from the Atlantic mists. Thoroughly charming it is too, as is the eclectic blend of inhabitants, from hippies and artists to hard-bitten fishermen and miners. A wide range of activities should detain you longer than anticipated: choose from, among others, dolphin- and seal-spotting boat trips, surfing, touring the Namib (which comes right up to town), quad-biking and sand-skiing, horse- and camelback safaris, even ballooning and skydiving, and spectacular birding at Walvis Bay.

● **Namib Naukluft Park** The desert's many wonders are most easily seen at Namib Naukluft Park. Wildlife is best in and around the short Sesriem Canyon, where springbok, zebras and ostriches are fairly common, as are soaring lappet-faced vultures and falcons; you'll need luck to see oryxes though. The canyon continues to a salt pan beside the flabbergastingly tall dunes of Sossusvlei. In the rains, the pan becomes a temporary lake attracting good numbers of water birds, including flamingoes, but the park's outstanding attraction is the extraordinary plant *Welwitschia mirabilis*. With just two leaves (which are permanent, too, so they're invariably torn into ribbons) and a potential lifespan of over two millennia, it well deserves the second part of its name.

● **Fish River Canyon** On the border with South Africa, the now mostly dry Fish River gouged a gigantic 161-kilometre cleft that plunges over half a kilometre in places. The views, including – otherworldly halfmens – succulent "trees", can be enjoyed over treks lasting several days. Tracks are probably all you'll see of leopards and mountain zebras; more common are baboons, ground squirrels, klipspringers and hyraxes. In the south, go canoeing on the Orange River.

● **Caprivi Strip** The narrow finger of land that heads eastward between Angola, Zambia and Botswana is Namibia's most verdant area by far, and

△ The fantastic dunes of Namib Naukluft Park

much of it is protected by national parks and nature reserves. The several rivers which cross it are great places for seeing crocodiles and hippos, while lions and elephants, giraffes, buffaloes and rare antelopes abound in the wetlands and plains around them. Birding, needless to say, is fantastic, with over four hundred species. The area is best seen on foot or by boat.

● **Waterberg Plateau Park** This plateau sits astride a flat-topped mountain, its red sandstone cliffs home to Namibia's only breeding colony of Cape vultures. Springs on the eastern side sustain subtropical woodland into which various rare animals were introduced a few decades ago, among them rhinos, leopards, sable and roan antelopes. A graveyard recalls the genocide perpetrated by the Germans against the Herero and Nama in 1908, in which 100,000 people died. At Okonjima nearby, the non-profit AfriCat Foundation funds the conservation of cheetahs and leopards with guided tours, homely overnight stays and great birding.

● **Etosha National Park** At the heart of Namibia's most famous park is a vast salt pan which gets painted pink with flamingoes during and shortly after the rains, when it becomes a lake. Permanent waterholes in the surrounding bush and grasslands attract the Big Five and many other species besides.

Also recommended

● **Cultural tourism** Over the last decade, some Bushman communities have been granted official title to ancestral lands, and have set up a series of cultural tourism projects around Tsumkwe town to supplement subsistence farming. In return, tourists get to share age-old hunter-gathering tips and

traditions. Upmarket travellers have the wonderful Nyae Nyae Conservancy to head for.

● **Windhoek** "Windy Corner", the country's multiethnic capital, has little to detain you other than cultural tours of Katutura township. With a little time, though, you could explore the surrounding mountains on horseback.

● **Brandberg Mountains** Enclosing Namibia's highest peak, the Königsberg (2574m), the rugged Brandberg range draws avid climbers from all around, but most people come to marvel at the Bushman rock art, including the woefully misnamed "White Lady" who is, in fact, a male shaman.

● **Twyfelfontein** Its name meaning "doubtful fountain", this eroded sandstone valley in Damaraland contains yet more rock art – 2500 engravings in all, the oldest 6000 years old.

● **Kaokoland** The northern Skeleton Coast is backed by the bleakly beautiful Kaokoland, its eroded desert mountains studded with huge baobabs and succulents. Life for the semi-nomadic Himba, who can be visited, would probably be untenable without seasonal rivers and the perennial Kunene along the Angolan border. The latter especially is also a magnet for wildlife, including desert elephants, rhinos, oryxes and Hartman's zebras.

● **Lüderitz** Southern Namibia's coast and hinterland is a strictly controlled diamond concession. The only access is to the coastal town of Lüderitz, its German Art Nouveau buildings providing a weird contrast to the barren solitude of its surroundings. The attractions are flamingo-filled bays, seals and jackass penguin colonies, an abandoned whaling station, and the nearby dune-swamped, diamond-mining ghost town of Kolmanskop.

- **Drinking** Round it all off with a drink. Northern Namibia's Ovambo regard the marula tree as quasi-sacred on account of its many uses, not the least of which is fermenting its fruit to make a head-pounding brew called omagongo. The stuff's at its best in March. For less adventurous quaffers, Namibia's lager has gathered aficionados around the world.

Festivals

The dates for most traditional festivities depend on rains and harvests. Fixed dates apply to various events commemorating episodes in the uprising against German rule in the early 1900s.

Day of the Red Flag Okahandja; Aug 26 A commemoration in honour of the Herero Paramount Chief, Samuel Maharero, who was one of the leaders of the uprising against Germany that culminated in genocide. The event features music and dance, a traditional beauty contest, and a procession with men dressed in military uniforms that winds uphill to the graves of their forebears.

Oktoberfest Nationwide; Oct Germany bequeathed Namibia a Bavarian-style beer-swilling, sausage-guzzling festival.

Routes in and out

International flights land at Hosea Kutako International Airport near Windhoek. Luxury bus services arrive from South Africa; there are also buses from Botswana and Zambia. Change buses at the border if you're coming from Angola. There's a train from Upington in South Africa to Windhoek.

Namibia online

Namibia Tourist Board
ⓦwww.namibiatourism.com.na

The Namibia Library of Dr. Klaus Dierks
ⓦwww.klausdierks.com Pleasing jumble of scholarly papers on Namibian history by the late doctor, including works on rock art and little-known pre-colonial sites. Also has a book-length illustrated chronology.

Namibia Community Based Tourism Association
ⓦwww.nacobta.com.na All about cultural tourism; also has good coverage of traditional celebrations.

Namibia Wildlife Resorts
ⓦwww.nwr.com.na The company running Namibia's national parks operates this website, providing full information on each of them.

Rock Art of Twyfelfontein
ⓦwww.bradshawfoundation.com /twyfelfontein An extensive survey of rock engravings.

Welwitschia mirabilis
ⓦwww.plantzafrica.com/plantwxyz /welwitschia.htm A good intro to one of the world's most amazing plants, with instructions for growing it.

Books

Henno Martin *The Sheltering Desert*. A classic tale of survival: the true story of two German geologists who avoided internment during World War II by hiding out in the Namib.

Jean du Plessis *Desertscapes of Namibia*. Dreamlike photos of the Namib, Kalahari and Skeleton Coast.

Mary Rice *Heat, Dust and Dreams: An Exploration of People and Environment in Kaokoland and Damaraland*. Documenting the Himba, Herero and Damara cultures on the verge of change, with photographs as beautiful as the people, body decorations and items they portray.

Niger

Area 1,266,700 square kilometres
Capital Niamey
Population 15 million; majority ethnic group is Hausa; other groups include Songhaï-Djerma, Tuareg and Fulani (including Wodaabé)
Language French (official), Hausa, Djerma, Fula, Tamachek (Tuareg) and Kanuri
Religion Islam 80 percent, traditional beliefs 15 percent
Climate Mostly desert; tropical savanna in extreme south; meagre rains July–Aug
Best time to go Nov–March for the best weather; Sept for the Cure Salée festival; Dec–June for Parc National du "W"; Feb–May for birdlife
Currency CFA franc
Minimum costs $35/£19 per day

A vast, arid state on the edge of the Sahara, Niger is a desperately poor place. Droughts are a frequent occurrence, and the country's recent history has lurched between military coups, dictators and uprisings. Despite all that, it's still a great place to visit, with a diverse cultural heritage stemming from its location at the crossroads of north and south, with many an important caravan route starting and ending there. Trade was centred on slaves, gold and salt, the profits of which funded a succession of empires. In many ways the country still feels medieval, as the world was reminded in 2003 when the government was forced to announce the abolition of slavery. In the winter months Saharan Tuareg can still be seen leading camel caravans carrying salt, and Fulani cattle-herders on the desert's fringes are among the region's proudest and most traditional people. Indeed, Nigériens as a whole are the best reason for visiting Niger.

Main attractions

● **Agadez** With the silhouetted Aïr Mountains on the skyline, the ancient Tuareg city of Agadez, a trans-Saharan trading centre since at least the eleventh

Average temperature ranges and rainfall

	Jan	Feb	Mar	Apr	May	Jun	Jul	Aug	Sep	Oct	Nov	Dec
Agadez												
Max °C	28	31	35	39	41	41	39	38	39	37	32	29
Min °C	12	14	18	23	26	26	25	24	25	22	16	13
Rainfall mm	0	0	0	2	6	10	35	50	8	0	0	0
Zinder												
Max °C	29	33	36	40	41	38	35	33	36	37	34	31
Min °C	15	17	21	25	27	26	24	23	24	23	19	15
Rainfall mm	0	0	1	1	15	39	129	168	54	5	0	0

△ A camel caravan, Niger

century, is a fascinating and beautiful place. Sitting astride caravan routes from Libya, Egypt and Lake Chad, Agadez changed hands several times over the centuries. Its architecture is typically Sahelian – brown mud-brick with finely-chiselled details, a prime example of which is the enchanting Grande Mosquée, built in 1515 when the city was part of the Songhaï Empire. Its towering 27-metre minaret – which can be climbed – is studded with hundreds of wooden stakes, providing structural support and handy scaffolding for the necessary annual repairs. Other attractions include the palace of the present Sultan of Agadez, and three markets where you'll find anything from camels, goats and decorated salt cakes, to spices, Tuareg clothing and exquisite handicrafts, including especially fine leatherwork and silver "Agadez crosses" – traditionally worn as amulets.

● **The Aïr Mountains** Stretching north from Agadez, this Saharan range shelters green valleys, spring-fed rivers and waterfalls that sustain improbable populations of gazelles and ostriches, antelopes, leopards, lions and even giraffes. The Aïr's importance to humans can be seen through the ruins of medieval caravanserais, and rock art from Neolithic times. On the edge of the Aïr, camping under the stars among the westernmost dunes of the Ténéré desert is every bit as romantic as it sounds, especially if you're travelling by camel.

● **The Ténéré desert** The western-most part of a vast sand sea that stretches well into Chad, the Ténéré is the classic dune-filled desert, and a more photogenic – or silent – spot on earth would be difficult to find. It's not all about dunes, though: hidden oases provide amazing contrasts, isolated outcrops turn up Neolithic rock carvings, and around the oases of Bilma and Fachi, you stand a good chance of seeing salt-carrying caravans in October and November. Along the way, don't miss the memorial to what was the world's loneliest tree – a millennial acacia sadly felled by a truck in 1973. Most visits are by four-wheel-drive, though longer expeditions by camel are possible from the Aïr.

● **Zinder** The former capital of the French colony and the Sultanate of

Damagaram has been politically eclipsed by Niamey, but retains its importance as a trading town. Travellers will find particularly fine examples of Hausa clay architecture, especially in the maze-like old quarter of Zengou. The present Sultan of Zinder resides in an impressive nineteenth-century palace. For many, the Thursday market is the highlight, whether for encounters with Tuareg and Fulani, or for leatherwork.

● **Parc National du "W"** This magnificent park, named for a series of bends in the River Niger, is probably the best place in West Africa to see big animals, include elephants and buffaloes, lions, hyenas and jackals, a profusion of antelopes and primates, and hippos. Twitchers are kept busy, with over 300 recorded bird species in the park (find them from a pirogue, if you wish), including vast quantities of winter migrants.

Also recommended

● **Niamey** The country's modern capital doesn't promise much, but is an enjoyable place to keep you busy, including the National Museum, one of West Africa's best markets, and camel races on Sundays. Out of town, Boubon Island is a popular day-trip, thanks to pirogue rides, abundant birdlife and a flourishing pottery industry.

● **Ayourou** Another day-trip from Niamey, the quiet river town of Ayourou is especially worth visiting on a Sunday, when the weekly market draws traders from far and wide. The livestock section (Nov–April) is especially interesting for seeing Tuareg trading camels.

● **Ingal** West of Agadez, Ingal is the easiest place to visit or stay with Tuareg and Fulani, and the locality has its share of Neolithic engravings and fossilized

dinosaurs, some in situ, others in a museum.

● **The Djado Plateau** North of the Ténéré, this is a wonderfully remote and dramatic land of weathered sandstone and hidden oases. Specific attractions include the semi-buried cities of Djado and Djaba, and rock paintings depicting animals long since gone.

Festivals

Music is an especially accessible door to Nigérien culture, best experienced at one of the country's many festivals. The most traditional are tied to the seasons, especially the end of the rains in August, September or October. Muslim festivals are also celebrated (see p.245), most spectacularly in Agadez.

Bianou Nationwide Celebrations in the run-up to the Islamic New Year are at their most exuberant in Agadez, where the Sultan's red-turbaned guards compete in potentially dangerous horseback cavalcades.

Cure Salée In-Gall; Sept Towards the end of the rains, Tuareg camel-breeders and Wodaabé (Bororo) cattle-herders converge with their herds on salt flats west of Agadez, whose brine provides their livestock with an annual "salt cure". For the nomads, it's their one big get-together before parting ways. The week-long festivities include camel races, plenty of music and dancing, and beauty contests – for men, women and beasts. The contest for men, called the *Gerewol*, involves young men of the Wodaabé tribe, who preen themselves with lots of ochre make-up, jewellery and distinctly feminine (at least to non-Wodaabé eyes) ceremonial garb – all just to please the girls, and perhaps plant a seed of romance.

Festival de l'Aïr Iferouâne; Dec A three-day bash organized by Tuareg, with beauty pageants, all-round camelmanship, music and dancing.

Routes in and out

Niamey airport receives flights from Europe and elsewhere in West Africa; Agadez has winter-time flights from France. There's road transport in from Benin, Burkina Faso, Mali and Nigeria. Banditry is a perennial problem in Saharan border regions; the safest and most feasible Saharan routes are via Tamanrasset (Algeria) and along the so-called "Marlboro route" from Libya. You're likely to be accompanied by officially-appointed guides or guards for part of the way.

Niger online

Africa Speaks

Ⓦ www.patstoll.org/afspeaknew A collection of essays and stories by Nigérien students about all aspects of life in Niger, from love and courtship to magic and traditional beliefs.

Agadez-Niger

Ⓦ www.agadez-niger.com Attractive introduction to the desert region of Agadez, with plenty of categorized photo sets (from arts and crafts to the Wodaabé's celebrated *Gerewol* celebration); in French.

Tuareg Fotogalerie Moula-Moula

Ⓦ www.moula-moula.de An excellent reason to learn German, this is one of those websites that surpass superlatives, containing hundreds of quality photos of Niger's desert regions and the Tuareg, and five CD-length recordings of Tuareg concerts.

Books

Carol Beckwith and Mario Van Offelen *Nomads of Niger*. Photographer Beckwith has been criticized for her romantic, stylized vision of Africans; in this book, the ineffably style-conscious Wodaabé provide her with irreproachable subjects.

Peter Chilson *Riding the Demon: On the Road in West Africa*. Chilson spent a year driving up and down Niger's car wreck-littered highways in the company of bush-taxi drivers, truckers, a holy man and others as they went about their lives. For Chilson, the road became a metaphor for Niger, and the journey touched upon the essence of what it is to be human. Definitely not just another travelogue.

Paul Stoller *Fusion of the Worlds* and *In Sorcery's Shadow* (with Cheryl Olkes). Two very readable ethnographies of Songhaï spirit possession cults in southern Niger, in which Stoller follows the ground-breaking tradition of film-maker Jean Rouch in being both enthusiastic about his subject, and personally involved – In *Sorcery's Shadow* recounts his apprenticeship to a sorcerer.

Nigeria

Area 923,768 square kilometres
Capital Abuja
Population 136 million; the main ethnic groups are Yoruba, Hausa, Fulani and Igbo (Ibo); important minorities include Ijaw, Tiv, Kanuri, Ibibio and Edo
Language Yoruba, Hausa, Igbo, Fula and some 250 others; English (and/or Pidgin) widely used, especially in urban areas

Religion Islam 50 percent, Christianity 40 percent, traditional beliefs 10 percent
Climate Tropical in the south, dry and arid in the north; rainy seasons are May–July in the south, Sept–Oct in the west, April–Oct in the east, July–Aug in the north
Best time to go Dec–Feb
Currency Naira
Minimum costs $20/£11 per day

The Niger and Benue rivers divide Nigeria, Africa's most populous country, into three ethno-linguistic zones: the Yoruba-dominated west, the Igbo-dominated east, and the Hausa- and Fulani-dominated north. Tensions between these are never far from the surface, and in 1967 erupted into a bitter civil war when the east tried to secede as the Republic of Biafra. Currently, tensions centre on the Niger Delta region, whose inhabitants have seen their land and livelihoods blighted by the oil industry, and on the largely Muslim north, where non-Muslim minorities have become the target for occasional violence.

Don't let this, or Nigeria's reputation for crime and scams, put you off. The fact that such a diverse nation exists at all – Nigeria contains over 250 tribes – speaks volumes for how the majority manage to get on with their neighbours. For visitors, Nigeria is a friendly and largely easy-going place to travel around in (certainly once you're out of Lagos), and its dynamism – and wealth of attractions – makes it an exhilarating and very enjoyable country to visit.

Average temperature ranges and rainfall

	Jan	Feb	Mar	Apr	May	Jun	Jul	Aug	Sep	Oct	Nov	Dec
Lagos												
Max °C	31	32	32	32	32	29	28	28	28	29	31	31
Min °C	23	25	26	25	24	23	23	23	23	23	24	24
Rainfall mm	28	46	102	150	269	460	279	64	140	206	60	25
Kano												
Max °C	30	33	37	38	37	34	31	29	31	34	33	31
Min °C	13	15	19	24	24	23	22	21	21	19	16	13
Rainfall mm	0	0	3	10	69	117	206	310	142	13	0	0

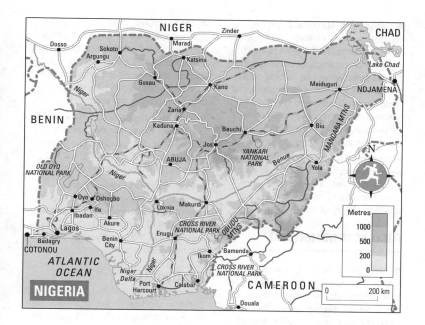

Main attractions

● **Lagos** Frenetic monster metropolis and commercial capital of West Africa, Lagos is an exciting if slightly edgy city. Downtown Lagos Island is home to a national museum and a handful of houses built in Brazilian style by returned former slaves, but it's everyday life that really brings the place alive. Street markets, all very different, are well worth checking out, as is the nightlife, and don't forgo a visit to the vibrant working-class district of Obalende for a bowl of its fiery pepper soup. Though the crime rate is high, elementary precautions should see you all right.

● **Kano** The main city of the north, Kano still features several of its original thirteenth-century gates, along with a number of homes decorated in tradition-al Hausa style. There's also an excellent museum, a busy market, and dye pits where cloth is coloured with real indigo. Having checked out all that, plus the emir's palace and the central mosque, climb Dala Hill for a panorama over the whole place.

● **Sokoto** The spiritual centre of Islam in Nigeria, this is also the main Fulani centre, and one of the north's most interesting cities, with an excellent museum, a huge market, handsome Sahelian mosques, and a pilgrimage site – the tomb of the Usman dan Fodio, founder of the Sokoto Caliphate (1807).

● **Yankari National Park** This vast reserve is home to elephants, hippos, buffaloes and the odd lion, but what most visitors come here for are the wonderful Wikki Warm Springs, where you can bathe in a pool of crystal-clear hot water.

• **Cross River National Park** Two separate areas of rainforest either side of the border town of Ikom. Elephants, monkeys and chimpanzees are among the residents, as well as its own gorilla sub-species (the Cross River gorilla, the world's most endangered primate). The region also boasts some three hundred curious carved monoliths dating from around the third century.

• **Badagry** The lovely beach here belies Badagry's brutal history as a slave station, commemorated today by the Black Heritage Museum, covering the appalling history of slavery in Nigeria.

Also recommended

• **Zaria** Best preserved of the seven Hausa cities: explore the old walled town, check out the Friday Mosque, the emir's palace, the market and the old mud houses, plus a museum devoted to the (patchy) history of Nigeria's army.

• **Benin City** This is home to the famous Benin bronzes, a few of which, having escaped looting by the British, can be found in the museum. The city still preserves big chunks of its original walls, and a few houses dating from before the 1897 British onslaught in which much of the old city was destroyed.

• **Oshogbo** A town full of artists, including an elderly Austrian lady who became a priestess of the Yoruba God of Creation, Obatala, in the 1960s. A sacred forest contains a shrine to a female water deity, and is at the centre of the Oshun Festival every August.

• **Calabar** A steamy and very laid-back town perched on the hilltops overlooking the Calabar River. Attractions include a scattering of colonial architecture, an old cemetery, and a rehabilitation centre for orphaned monkeys and chimpanzees.

• **Jos** Everybody loves Jos, a relaxed highland town with a number of attractions: a museum containing 2000-year-old Nok artefacts (including terracotta figures), another on traditional architecture, and a tiny wildlife park in which pygmy hippos are the stars.

• **Oyo** The main attraction in this small but ancient former Yoruba capital is its market, a great place to buy talking drums or carved calabashes, not to mention palm wine to drink out of them.

• **Port Harcourt** Sprawling and sweltering, with a chaotic market, a charming "Old Township" (complete with a street full of wood-fired kebab stalls), and ferries to the quaintly old-fashioned islands of Bonny and Brass.

Festivals

Christian and Muslim red-letter days are national holidays; see p.243 & p.245 for dates. Muslim festivals are especially important in the north, where Id al Fitr, Tabaski and the Prophet's birthday are celebrated with much ceremonial pomp, often including cavalry displays.

Argungu Fishing Festival Argungu, Feb or March The start of the fishing season is marked by three days of festivities including swimming and canoe races and bare-handed fishing, and culminates with fishermen armed with nets and calabashes plunging into the Sokoto River for a fishing contest.

Egungun Western Nigeria; usually April A Yoruba ancestor festival, with masquerades, sporting events, drumming and dancing. The biggest commemorations are at Ibadan, Badagry and Okene.

Igue Benin city; Dec Procession of the Oba (King) of Benin city, followed by several days of celebration, with traditional dancing and much drinking and eating.

Ogun **Western Nigeria; June–Aug**
A Yoruba festival in honour of the god
of iron, with singing, dancing and
drumming.
Pategi Regatta **Pategi (100km
downriver from Jebba); Feb–March** A
regatta on the Niger, with horse-racing,
swimming, dancing and music.
Sekiapu **River and Cross River states;
Oct** Masquerades, regattas and a great
deal of merriment.

Routes in and out

Lagos, Kano, Port Harcourt and Abuja
have international airports. Bush taxis
connect Lagos with Ghana, Togo and
Benin, and Kano with Niger. Land
journeys from Cameroon and Chad
involve changing vehicles at the border.
There are infrequent boats between
Limbé (Cameroon) and Calabar.

Nigeria online

**Nigeria Tourism Development
Corporation**
Ⓦ**www.nigeriatourism.net**
**G.I. Jones Photographic Archive
of Southeastern Nigerian Art and
Culture**
Ⓦ**mccoy.lib.siu.edu/jmccall/jones** A
unique archive of 1930s photographs,
primarily of the Igbo – the people, their
art and their ceremonies.
Ifa Link
Ⓦ**www.cultural-expressions.com/ifa
/ifadef.htm** All you ever wanted to know
about Yoruba religion.
Motherland Nigeria
Ⓦ**www.motherlandnigeria.com** Lots
of material on Nigerian art, culture and
society (check the "Contents" page),
including articles, pictures and music.

Pidgin English dictionary
Ⓦ**www.ngex.com/personalities
/babawilly/dictionary** All the essenco
you need to sabi Pidgin like a Naija (in
other words, all the essentials you need
to know West African English like a
native Nigerian).
Yoruba Art in Wood and Metal
Ⓦ**www.fa.indiana.edu/~conner
/yoruba/cut.html** Illustrated with ample
texts about all aspects of traditional
Yoruba culture.

Books

Chinua Achebe *Things Fall Apart*.
Colonialism undermines the traditional
ways of an Igbo village in this classic by
Nigeria's best-known novelist.
Elphinstone Dayrell *Folk Stories from
Southern Nigeria*. Why fish live in the sea
and other tall tales. Online at Ⓦwww
.sacred-texts.com/afr/fssn.
Olaudah Equiano *The Interesting
Narrative of the Life of Olaudah Equiano*.
Autobiography of a Nigerian sold into
slavery as a child. He eventually paid for
his freedom and became involved in the
abolitionist movement. Online at Ⓦwww
.gutenberg.org.
Helon Habila *Waiting for an Angel*. The
precarious life of a journalist under the
brutal military regime of the early 1990s,
bleak but not fatalistic.
Chukwuemeka Ike *Sunset at Dawn*.
A sometimes bitterly satirical but very
human account of the civil war, told
through the eyes of Biafrans living out
the tragedy of their ill-fated republic.
Ben Okri *The Famished Road*. Almost
a ghost story, this tale of a Yoruba
boy who lives partly in the spirit world
conjures up a hauntingly magical, but at
the same time highly evocative picture of
village life in rural western Nigeria.

Rwanda

Area 26,338 square kilometres
Capital Kigali
Population 8.5 million, most of whom are Hutu; the Tutsi are a large minority
Language Kinyarwanda and French; English and Swahili also spoken in urban areas
Religion Christianity 60 percent, traditional beliefs 30 percent, Islam 10 percent

Climate Mostly temperate due to altitude, but hot along Tanzanian border; rains Jan–May & mid-Oct to mid-Dec
Best time to go June–Sept for wildlife; Dec–Feb for migrant birds
Currency Rwanda franc
Minimum costs $25/£14 per day

It took precisely one hundred days, from April to July 1994, for eight hundred thousand Rwandans to lose their lives. The Rwandan genocide was the last in a litany of massacres, the product of a Belgian "divide and rule" policy that had exacerbated divisions between the ruling Tutsi ethnic group, traditionally cattle herders, and the predominantly agricultural Hutu majority, who had always been deprived of power. The killing spree was also the most shameful episode in the history of the United Nations, which had merely observed the killings without trying to stop them. In the end, it was only the invasion of Rwanda by Tutsi exiles that put an end to the bloodshed.

Over a decade later, reconciliation has been swifter to come than anyone dared imagine. The main *genocidaires* have been tried before an international tribunal in Tanzania, and the country's economy is recovering well. Tourism features prominently in the government's plans, and Rwanda is fast carving a niche for itself as one of Africa's finest eco-tourism destinations, with good reason. The country boasts some of Africa's most inspiring landscapes, from rainforest-cloaked volcanoes to beautiful lakes and waterfalls, and archetypal African savanna. Birdlife is astonishingly diverse, and there's ample wildlife besides, most famously mountain gorillas.

Main attractions

● **Parc National des Volcans** At the southern tip of the Virunga Mountains, Volcanoes National Park is the last stronghold of mountain gorillas (made

Average temperature ranges and rainfall												
	Jan	Feb	Mar	Apr	May	Jun	Jul	Aug	Sep	Oct	Nov	Dec
Kigali												
Max °C	23	23	23	22	23	23	24	25	25	23	22	23
Min °C	18	18	18	18	18	18	18	19	18	18	18	18
Rainfall mm	69	100	106	183	92	20	9	34	86	102	127	100

famous by primatologist Dian Fossey, whose life – and murder, in 1985 – were recounted in the film *Gorillas in the Mist*). Several hundred gorillas live on the steep rainforest-clad slopes; an hour spent tracking them can provide memories for a lifetime. Even without gentle giants, it's exhilarating to trek through Virunga's rainforest, populated by numerous if elusive elephants (their presence given away by droppings), and habituated troops of rare golden monkeys. Climbers have some of Africa's highest peaks to aim for, including the 4519-metre Karisimbi volcano.

● **Nyungwe Forest National Park**
Eastern Africa's largest tract of virgin rainforest is one for statisticians as well as nature lovers: there are over two hundred types of tree; hundreds of flowers ranging from exquisite orchids to bizarre giant lobelias; thirteen primates including chimpanzees and Hoest's monkeys; and over three hundred bird species, star of which is the Great Blue (actually multicoloured) Turaco. The steep terrain means much of the forest is unexplored (the uttermost source of the Nile, now believed to be in Nyungwe, was only pinpointed in 2006), so there's

△ Gorilla encounters, Volcanoes National Park

always a chance of finding something new. Add in plentiful walking trails, waterfalls and viewpoints, and this gets very close to Eden.

● **Lake Kivu** Straddling the Congolese border, Kivu is the largest of numerous freshwater lakes gracing the Albertine Rift Valley – the westernmost branch of the Great Rift. Of several lakeshore towns offering palm-backed beaches, watersports and excursions, the best are Gisenyi, with several enchanting colonial-era hotels, and diminutive Kibuye. The two towns are connected by a spectacular roller-coaster hillside road.

● **A'Kagera National Park** Flanking the eponymous river defining the Tanzanian border, A'Kagera's acacia savanna and network of lakes and marshes is unique in this otherwise mountainous country. Wildlife is here in force, and a plethora of picturesque campsites makes it a major draw for visitors. You can reasonably expect to see elephants, giraffes, zebras and over a dozen antelope species (including buffaloes), together with hippos and crocs. Birders have over five hundred species to go for; fish eagles, shoebill storks and papyrus gonoleks are the major thrills.

Also recommended

● **Kigali** Rwanda's capital is pleasant if nothing special, but does have good restaurants, crafts shops, a colourful market, and memorials to victims of the genocide (the city tour includes the former Radio Television Libre des Milles Collines which incited it all).

● **National Museum** In the small southern town of Huye (formerly Butare), the superb National Museum has one of the continent's finest ethnographic collections, and is the base for the Intore Dance Troupe, whose explosive

drumming displays were formerly reserved for Rwandan royalty.

● **The Royal Palace at Nyabisindu** Close to Huye, Nyabisindu (formerly Nyanza) was the feudal seat of the Tutsi monarchy. Their restored nineteenth-century palace is now a museum.

● **Burera, Karago and Ruhondo lakes** These small lakes in the shadow of the Virunga Mountains are amid Rwanda's most traditionalist areas, where you'll see fishermen braving the waters in dugout canoes, and respectable women smoking pipes (a widespread habit in East Africa's lake zones). The profuse birdlife includes crowned cranes and malachite kingfishers.

Festivals

Pan-African Festival of Dance (FESPAD) Kigali; Aug A major event featuring groups from around Africa. **Rwanda Film Festival Nationwide; March** Two weeks of screenings all over the country as part of "Hillywood", featuring inflatable screens.

Routes in and out

Kigali receives flights from Europe and Africa. Buses come in from Uganda, Burundi and Tanzania. Overlanding from Burundi or Congo carries a risk of rebel attacks and is ill-advised.

Rwanda online

Rwanda Tourism Board
Ⓦ www.rwandatourism.com
The Dian Fossey Gorilla Fund International
Ⓦ www.gorillafund.org Information on the primatologist's work and legacy, current research, and plenty of info on our distant cousins.

Leave None to Tell the Story: Genocide in Rwanda

Ⓦ www.hrw.org/reports/1999/rwanda

A sobering, reliable and non-sensationalist book-length account of the genocide, its causes and consequences, from Human Rights Watch.

Books

Romeo Dallaire *Shake Hands with the Devil*. As UN commander in Rwanda in 1994, Dallaire became the fall guy for that organization's abject failure to prevent or limit the genocide. Here, he rails against official manipulation, hypocrisy and incompetence to paint an unsettling picture of the real agendas of the UN, various NGOs and the world's most powerful nations.

Dian Fossey *Gorillas in the Mist*. When Fossey began her work in the 1960s, the public equated gorillas with King Kong; her study of four gorilla families revealed them to be (mostly) gentle giants. Her book, on which the film was based, is also an angry diatribe against poachers – who may have been responsible for her death.

Philip Gourevitch *We Wish To Inform You That Tomorrow We Will Be Killed With Our Families*. Interviewing victims and perpetrators, heroes and onlookers, Gourevitch gives an impartial, harrowing and humane understanding of the forces that led to genocide.

Paul Rusesabagina *An Ordinary Man: The True Story Behind 'Hotel Rwanda'*. Autobiography of the hotel manager who saved over a thousand people during the genocide by sheltering them in his hotel, at the same as he served, flattered and cajoled the killers downstairs.

São Tomé and Príncipe

Area 1001 square kilometres
Capital São Tomé
Population 180,000; most are African-European Creoles (Mestiços); others are Angolares (from Angolan slaves), Forros (from freed slaves), and Serviçais (African contract workers)
Language Portuguese; French is also common; Creole languages are Forro (around São Tomé city), Angolar, and Lingwa-iyé or Príncipense (Príncipe island)
Religion Christianity

Climate Equatorial, with temperate highlands; dry seasons – the Gravana (June–Sept), and the Gravanita (Jan–Feb) – can be cloudy; paradoxically, the rainy seasons have a better chance of clear skies, as rain tends to fall in short but heavy bursts
Best time to go Jan–Feb for trekking and birding; Feb–June for scuba-diving; Oct–Dec for the beaches
Currency Dobra
Minimum costs $20/£11 per day

These two rugged volcanic islands in the Gulf of Guinea, 200km off the coast of Gabon, are probably Africa's best-kept secret. A lack of conflict and isolation from the mainland has cast a spell of forgetfulness over the international media, and ensures that only a trickle of tourists come here each year. As yet, there's still little in the way of organized tourist facilities, though things are slowly changing. Oil wealth, which began to be drilled in 2005, promises more radical change, hopefully none too damaging.

When the Portuguese discovered the islands in 1471, they were uninhabited. Most Santomense descend from slaves shipped in from the continent to work on sugar plantations and, later, cocoa and coffee estates. The resulting blend of peoples and traditions has forged a vibrant and easy-going Creole culture similar to that of Cape Verde and the

Average temperature ranges and rainfall

	Jan	Feb	Mar	Apr	May	Jun	Jul	Aug	Sep	Oct	Nov	Dec
São Tomé												
Max °C	30	30	31	30	29	28	28	28	29	29	29	29
Min °C	23	23	23	23	23	22	21	21	21	22	22	22
Rainfall mm	81	107	150	127	135	28	0	0	23	109	117	89

Caribbean, one that expresses itself deliciously through local cuisine (in which seafood stars), and in some startlingly out-of-context celebrations inherited from Renaissance Europe.

The island's attractions – other than culture, charmingly dilapidated colonial towns and plantation houses propped up on stilts, in which you can stay – are summed up by "tropical luxuriance": rainforest, rare plants and birds, virtually deserted palm-fringed beaches, steaming mangroves, marine turtles, whales and dolphins.

Main attractions

● **Pico de São Tomé** The two-day ascent of this, the archipelago's highest point at 2024m, is strenuous and tricky, taking you through cloud-wrapped rainforest in which birds and orchids are an especial pleasure.

● **Plantation tours** Guided tours of the archipelago's centuries-old plantations, the Roças, offer insights into the production of high-grade coffee and cocoa, and a glimpse into a history steeped in the slave trade. The Roça de Água Izé has a train now used by visitors; others have had their old wooden buildings turned into affordable bases for rural and community-based tourism.

● **Whales and dolphins** July to October are the best months for clambering aboard a boat in search of dolphins and migrating humpback whales.

● **Scuba-diving and snorkelling** The big pulls include rays, turtles, a host of pelagic fish, and – for experienced divers – underwater caves. There are dive centres on both islands, and dive sites to suit all levels of experience.

● **São Tomé town** The national capital is an enjoyable if somnolent place. The colonial architecture is particularly attractive, from a cathedral founded in 1576 to the squat fortress of São Sebastião, now a museum of religious and colonial art.

● **Príncipe island** The country's tiny other half, 150km northeast of São Tomé island, offers one upmarket resort, the charmingly run-down town of Santo António, cocoa plantation tours, hiking, birding, snorkelling, and the 948-metre Pico de Príncipe, which can be climbed in a day.

● **Turtle-watching** The islands play host to five species of marine turtle, which used to feature in Santomean cuisine before the animals were declared endangered. They can be seen laying eggs between October and February, particularly at Praia de Micolo.

● **Lagoa Amélia** Trek through rainforest to reach this volcanic crater lake at the heart of Ôbo Natural Park. Monkeys and giant begonia are among the many wonders to be seen. The lake itself is covered by thick vegetation, so can be walked over in parts.

Festivals

This being a Catholic country, saints' days are widely celebrated, blending religious processions, feasting, music, dance and theatre; Ⓦwww.navetur -equatour.st/Culture.htm has the dates. Two theatrical traditions inherited from Portuguese celebrations are especially fascinating: the Auto de Floripes is a re-enactment of semi-mythical battles in France between the Christian Emperor Charlemagne and Moorish invaders, while Tchiloli is a play in which Charlemagne's son is accused of having murdered the nephew of the Marquis of Mantua. Both stories are wonderfully absurd in the context of São Tomé, especially given the contrast between often fanciful Roman or Renaissance costumes, and African dancing.

Bienal de Arte e Cultura São Tomé city; June/July of even-numbered years A growing event for contemporary artists; ⓦwww.bienal-stp.org has a lovely catalogue in PDF format.

Festa de São Lourenço Santo António, Príncipe; Aug 14–17 A great time to witness the Auto de Floripes.

Festa de San Zudon Ribeira Afonso, São Tomé; Jan 10–13 A holiday in honour of Isidro, patron saint of workers. A procession of his effigy kicks off three days of music, feasting and dance. It's a good time to witness the colourful and frenetic Dance Congo (an epic tale performed by fishermen that tells of a plantation owner's foolish descendants), and the Tchilolí.

Routes in and out

The international airport at São Tomé has flights from Angola, Cape Verde, Gabon and Portugal. There are irregular ferries from Douala (Cameroon) and Libreville (Gabon).

São Tomé and Príncipe online

Tourist Board of São Tomé e Príncipe
ⓦwww.turismo-stp.org

A Month in the Forest of Príncipe
ⓦwww.ggcg.st/jon_principe.htm
Nicely illustrated, with plenty of reptiles and birds.

Dispatches From African Islands
ⓦwww.calacademy.org/science_now /sao_tome** Informal field journals from the California Academy of Sciences, with plenty of pictures to give you an idea of São Tomé's wild side.

Navetur
ⓦwww.navetur-equatour.st The best all-round tourist site, from the isles' main tour operator.

Books

Donald Burness *Ossobo: Essays on the Literature of São Tomé and Príncipe*. Three wide-ranging essays concerning mythical birds, contemporary poetry and drama, and literature about a massacre in 1953. Also has a selection of poetry.

Françoise Gründ *Tchiloli: Charlemagne à São Tomé sur l'île du milieu du monde*. Beautiful photos and (French) text about one of Africa's strangest cultural celebrations.

Peter Jones and Alan Tye *The Birds of São Tomé and Príncipe with Annobon*. The most up-to-date birding book for the isles.

Senegal

Area 196,190 square kilometres
Capital Dakar
Population 12.1 million; main ethnic groups are Wolof, Fulani and Serer; others include Jola, Mandinka and Soninké
Language French (official), plus local languages, especially Wolof, Pulaar (Fula), Jola or Mandinka
Religion Islam 94 percent,

Christianity 5 percent
Climate Tropical, heavier rainfall in Casamance; dry season Dec–April in the north, Oct–June in Casamance
Best time to go Oct–April for the best weather; March–May for Niokolo-Koba
Currency CFA franc
Minimum costs $35/£19 per day

West Africa's most Francophile country is also its most stable. Lacking coups d'état or dictators, and boasting a well-developed tourist infrastructure and the French language as a common denominator between the country's tribes, Senegal is a particularly good choice for first-timers. Although there are few immediately overawing attractions, there is a little bit of everything that West Africa has to offer, making for pleasingly diverse holidays.

Most of Senegal is perfectly safe to travel around in on your own, but be sure to get the latest news on the southern Casamance region, which was scene of a low-key, on-off separatist guerilla conflict until a peace accord was signed in 2004. Since then fighting has occasionally flared between hardline rebels and the Guinea-Bissau army along the border.

Main attractions

● **Dakar** At first glance, Senegal's modern and overcrowded capital is no-one's idea of a favourite city, even if the annual Dakar Rally has infused it with a sprinkling of mystique, but linger a while and there's a good

Average temperature ranges and rainfall

	Jan	Feb	Mar	Apr	May	Jun	Jul	Aug	Sep	Oct	Nov	Dec
Dakar												
Max °C	26	27	27	27	29	31	31	31	32	32	30	27
Min °C	18	17	18	18	20	23	24	24	24	24	23	19
Rainfall mm	0	0	0	0	0	18	89	254	132	38	3	8
Ziguinchor												
Max °C	33	34	35	35	35	33	31	30	31	31	32	31
Min °C	17	17	19	20	22	24	23	23	23	23	21	18
Rainfall mm	0	3	0	0	12	142	406	559	338	160	8	0

chance you'll come to love it, especially if music's your thing. World music superstar Youssou N'Dour's stomping ground contains a welter of bands and clubs, with something to see most nights. Day-time pleasures include dozens of colourful markets, each with its own speciality. There's also a good cultural museum, scuba-diving (best Feb–April), and excursions to Gorée Island (see below) and another island, Madeleine, the latter a haven for sea birds.

● **Île de Gorée** Just 3km from Dakar, Gorée is a popular escape from metropolitan heat and confusion, and the island's harbour, cannon-studded fortress and gently dilapidated French colonial architecture are an utter delight. Gorée's quasi-paradisiacal incarnation today contrasts with its sordid history as West Africa's most notorious slave market. It was from here, over a period

of three centuries, that millions of slaves were loaded aboard ships bound for the Americas. Two buildings have been converted into museums, and serve as focal points for African-Americans seeking their roots.

● **Saint Louis** Founded during the rule of Louis XIV, the former capital of French West Africa bears comparison with old Havana. The town's location between desert and tropics, river and ocean made it the ideal place from which to begin the colonization of West Africa. With its pastel-painted townhouses, the place has an inescapable air of decaying aristocratic grandeur. If merely soaking up the mood isn't enough, there are good beaches along the nearby "Barbary Tongue" peninsula, two bird reserves within easy reach, and the endless coming and going of colourful fishing pirogues to admire.

△ The Maison des Esclaves museum, Île de Gorée

● **Parc National des Oiseaux de Djoudj** The River Senegal's marshy wetlands, on the border with Mauritania, provide a vital refuge for wintering birds and a ton of local species, too, amounting to some three million birds annually – making this one of Africa's most exciting birding areas.

● **The Siné-Saloum delta** The Siné-Saloum delta is Senegal's most beautiful natural area, a land of swampy lagoons, islets and sand dunes, mangroves and snaking shallow creeks, all of which are paradise for migratory birds, flamingoes, herons, storks and pelicans. The most pristine parts comprise a national park. The area is best explored by pirogue.

● **Parc National de Niokolo-Koba** In the southeast, the rich and varied mix of savanna, tropical riverine forest, lakes and marshes makes Niokolo-Koba one of West Africa's better places for spotting large mammals, most commonly antelopes, buffaloes and

hippos, plus crocodiles and a good selection of birds.

Also recommended

● **Parc National de Basse Casamance** A patch of jungly forest, mangroves and swamps, wildlife can be excellent towards the end of the dry season. Highlights include rare antelopes, buffaloes, crocodiles, many monkeys and sometimes leopards.

● **The Petite Côte** South of Dakar, the palm tree-lined "Little Coast" has some of Senegal's best beaches, luxury holiday resorts aplenty, and a ton of activities including horse-riding, water sports, and golf.

● **Wrestling** The Senegalese are suckers for traditional wrestling, called "Lamb", which resembles the Olympic sport of Greco-Roman wrestling but without the silly suits. Sunday is the big day, especially in Dakar.

- **Retba Lake** This pink salt lake (its colour derived from iron oxide-excreting algae) is a popular target for excursions from Dakar.

Festivals

Senegal isn't lacking in festivals, whether traditional or contemporary, and Islamic dates are also celebrated in style, especially Korité and Tabaski; see p.245 for dates.

DAK'ART Dakar; May in even-numbered years A major biennale of contemporary African art.

Kagran Casamance; May In this Malinké celebration, held towards the end of the dry season, the Kagran spirit – incarnated by a dancer wearing a carved mask – takes to the streets following a ritual animal sacrifice to ensure prosperity for the coming year.

Les Fanals Saint Louis; end Dec Magical night-time parades of decorated paper lanterns (*fanals*) relive the time of the Signares – envied half-caste women of colonial times whose elegance and refinement mirrored how the town still likes to see itself.

Saint Louis Jazz Festival Saint Louis; May A major international event attracting renowned musicians from the States, Africa and elsewhere.

Tabaski Saint Louis In addition to the religious aspect of Tabaski, furious races are held in specially-made pirogues (some accommodating up to a hundred rowers), for which the entire town descends on the shore to cheer on their favourites.

Routes in and out

Senegal's main airport is Dakar, with flights from Europe, Africa and America.

There's road access from all neighbouring countries, and a weekly train from Bamako in Mali to Dakar.

Senegal online

Senegal Tourist Office
Ⓦ www.senegal-tourism.com
Au Senegal
Ⓦ www.au-senegal.com
Comprehensive and amply illustrated travel and tourism guide, with detailed destination accounts, hotel reviews, sections on cuisine, music and the arts, and handy festival listings.
Mora Gallery
Ⓦ www.moragallery.com Attractive presentation of this New York gallery's collection of contemporary Senegalese art.

Books

Mariama Bâ *So Long A Letter*. Extraordinarily powerful and beautiful tale of a woman's life shattered when her husband takes a second wife.

Sembène Ousmane *God's Bits of Wood*. The most famous novel by this entertaining, committed and political writer concerns the 1947 rail strike.

Léopold Senghor *The Collected Poetry*. A good selection from Senegal's first President, whose works – originally in French – contributed significantly to the ideology of Négritude (the incorporation of the colonial experience into a sense of "Africanness"), later criticized for its reliance on European aesthetics.

South Africa

Area 1,221,037 square kilometres
Capital Pretoria (Tshwane)
Population 47 million; main African groups are Zulu and Xhosa; white minority (10 percent) are mainly Afrikaners, descended from Dutch settlers; "coloureds" account for 9 percent, and include Bushmen (San)
Language Eleven national languages, of which Zulu, Xhosa, English and Afrikaans have the most speakers

Religion Christianity 80 percent
Climate Mostly temperate; semi-arid in the north, wetter in the east
Best time to go May–Oct in the east; Nov–April in the west; May–Sept for wildlife; Aug–Oct for landscapes and flowers
Currency South African rand
Minimum costs $30/£17 per day

The "Rainbow Nation" has undergone one hell of a transformation since Nelson Mandela's release from prison in 1990. For much of the twentieth century, the country's African and coloured population suffered racist oppression under white minority rule, oppression that gained legal currency under apartheid. Of the country's white presidents, only F.W. De Klerk had the prescience to see the necessity of change, and it was he who directed the country towards true democracy. Multiracial elections in 1994 saw Mandela elected the country's first black President. Although Mandela's dream of a nation of all colours is still a generation or two away, the giant strides that South Africans have taken in forging a more equitable society have

Average temperature ranges and rainfall

	Jan	Feb	Mar	Apr	May	Jun	Jul	Aug	Sep	Oct	Nov	Dec
Cape Town												
Max °C	26	27	25	23	20	18	18	18	19	21	24	25
Min °C	16	16	14	12	9	8	7	8	9	11	13	15
Rainfall mm	15	17	20	41	69	93	82	77	40	30	14	17
Durban												
Max °C	28	28	28	26	25	23	23	23	23	24	25	27
Min °C	21	21	20	17	14	11	11	13	15	17	18	20
Rainfall mm	134	113	120	73	59	28	39	62	73	98	108	102
Kruger National Park												
Max °C	33	32	31	29	28	26	26	27	29	30	31	32
Min °C	21	20	19	15	10	6	6	9	13	16	18	20
Rainfall mm	94	96	66	38	14	11	11	8	28	40	63	92

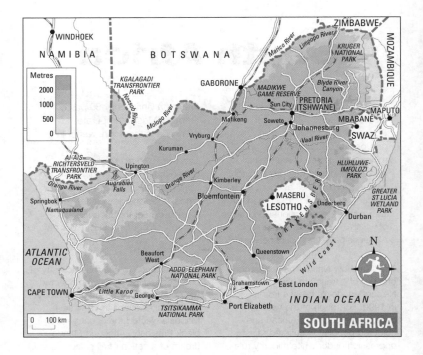

SOUTH AFRICA

been remarkable. Even so, the racial divide is still in evidence, especially economically.

South Africa can make for a gentle introduction to the continent. Most of the tourist facilities are run by whites, and slick highways, rural towns centred around identikit shopping malls, even the temperate climate, conspire to make the country the least African in Africa. While you may be disappointed if you're looking for the "real" Africa, at least culture shock is minimal.

For travellers, diversity is a constant theme. Beautiful landscapes are the country's stock-in-trade, and there's a mass of places worth visiting and things to do. Cape Town is the place for cosmopolitan pleasures and wine-tasting excursions, the south coast for whales and dolphins, the Kalahari

desert for pure wilderness, rock art all over the place, and a regal choice of game reserves and national parks. The country is also king of outdoor sports: mountain biking, surfing, snorkelling and diving, abseiling and bungee jumping, white-water rafting and canoeing, even microlight flights and skydiving.

Unless you have a month or two, it's best to concentrate on one or two regions. Note that you'll need to rent a vehicle or take an organized tour to make the most of things, as public transport is limited to getting between urban centres.

Main attractions

● **Cape Town** South Africa's safest and most compelling city sits at the foot of the continent in a magnificent bay overshadowed by the flat-topped Table Mountain. The city's Bo-Kaap quarter is especially attractive, full of luridly painted Cape Dutch and Georgian buildings. There's also a Dutch castle from 1666, a revolving cable car to the top of the mountain, and bustling cosmopolitan life whose vibrancy is aptly expressed through the country's best restaurants, lively street life and famously tuned-in nightclubs.

● **The Drakensberg** For sheer jaw-dropping beauty, nothing rivals the "dragon's mountains" hugging the border with Lesotho (where the highest peak is located). With waterfalls, plunging gorges, an incredible wealth of ancient Bushman rock paintings, and dawn and dusk colours that seep into the soul, these mountains are simply awesome.

● **Kruger National Park** One of Africa's greatest safari parks, Kruger is part of the Great Limpopo Transfrontier Park, and is contributing wildlife to repopulate Mozambique's portion of the park. Elephants are the big stars, though there are 145 other mammal species to

look out for. Some visitors visit Kruger on "beach and bush" trips: Kruger for big game, followed by Mozambique for birds and beaches.

● **The Wild Coast** At the southern limits of the Indian Ocean, this is a refreshing land of deserted beaches, jagged cliffs, subtropical forests and peaceful isolation. It's also the country's most "African" area, where getting a handle on local Xhosa culture is easy. Add in great hiking and diving, and a string of good backpackers' lodges, and it'll be hard to leave.

● **Storms River and Tsitsikamma** Tsitsikamma National Park contains one of the country's best preserved forests, its tall yellowwoods best seen while dangling from steel cables, part of a unique "canopy tour". Almost as heart-stopping is the wobbly suspension footbridge over the mouth of the nearby Storms River. Other activities include mountain biking and hiking, snorkelling and scuba-diving.

● **Kgalagadi Transfrontier Park** Covering both sides of the Botswanan

△ Table Mountain offers great vistas over Cape Town

border, Kgalagadi encloses a large part of South Africa's portion of the Kalahari. Actually semi-desert, it's particularly beautiful in spring when the sandy plains are dressed in grasses and wildflowers. You'll also enjoy the Kalahari's classic red dunes, and glimpses of its hardy denizens, gemsbok, lions and suricats among them.

● **Blyde River Canyon** A thirty-kilometre canyon that, in places, has gouged almost 800m out of the rock, leaving the visitor to marvel at vertiginous views and bizarre rock formations. Birders have the rare bald ibis to look forward to.

● **Namaqualand** In August and September this corner of the Northern Cape puts on nature's most spectacular floral display, when seemingly every inch of ground bears colourful wildflowers watered by dew captured from rolling Atlantic mists.

Also recommended

● **Johannesburg** Jo'burg's reputation for violent crime precedes it, sadly with reason. Still, a dollop of common sense should see you right, and the metropolis does have its attractions. Music is one, visiting gold mines another, but most memorable is a township tour – sprawling Soweto offers hands-on experiences of a side of life too often ignored.

● **Wine tours** You've probably already tasted South Africa's excellent wines back home, but that's only cheap plonk. A wine tour from Cape Town lets you sample rare and wonderful vintages at any one of two hundred estates.

● **Robben Island** Half an hour by boat from Cape Town is the green isle that housed apartheid's political prisoners. Mandela's cell, where he spent nearly two decades, is a must-see,

as is the lime quarry in which inmates laboured.

● **Hluhluwe-Imfolozi Park** KwaZulu-Natal's finest game reserve is the best place in Africa for white rhinos, of which there are over two thousand here. See them on foot or, better, from the back of a donkey.

● **Augrabies Falls** On the edge of the Kalahari is Africa's second-biggest waterfall, where the Orange River crashes through soft sandstone into an echoing gorge.

● **The Richtersveld** Straddling the Namibian border, this fiercely hot and rugged mountain desert is home to the Nama, formerly hunter-gatherers, nowadays herders who, post-apartheid, are gradually reclaiming their land and heritage. A number of settlements offer cultural tourism, while Ai-Ais Richtersveld Transnational Park is the place to search for "halfmens", bizarre succulents that, from afar, resemble humans.

● **Whale-watching** The southern Cape's "Whale Coast" is for communing with these gentle giants – either done from a boat or the shore – and with dolphins.

● **Greater St Lucia Wetland Park** Birds, birds and more birds, plus fishing, hiking, riding, kayaking and Zulu village tours.

● **Durban** A major Indian Ocean holiday destination for South Africans, where high-rise hotels jostle for space along a lively "Golden Mile". Surfing is the big thing. The city's Indian influence expresses itself everywhere, most memorably through its rickshaws, which are pulled by Zulus dressed in impressively feathered finery.

Festivals

Apartheid destroyed much of South Africa's indigenous culture, so festivals are contemporary affairs. In rural areas, they tend to have food and drink as themes. Ⓦwww.africinfo.org has a good list.

Arts Alive Festival Johannesburg; Sept–Oct Great music and cultural workshops, most eclectic on the fringe.

Cape Town Pride Cape Town; Shrove Tuesday (dates on p.243) Pink and proud of it, Cape Town's fabulous gay and lesbian carnival parades have engendered all sorts of spin offs, from beauty contests and a grand ball to pink tie dinners.

Durban International Film Festival Durban; June Hundreds of films, the spotlight being on South Africa's own output.

National Arts Festival Grahamstown; July Shostakovich to Soweto jazz, plus theatre, dance, arts and cinema.

Splashy Fen Music Festival Underberg; April This gets close to England's Glastonbury Festival in feel, if not as muddy. The music covers all bases, and there's a "rainbow zone" for the spiritual side of things.

Tweede Nuwe Jaar Cape Town; Jan 2 The city's "second new year" was the only day when slaves were given time off. Nowadays, dancing Cape Minstrels from the coloured community give the streets a carnival atmosphere.

Routes in and out

Johannesburg, Cape Town and Durban have international airports. There are bus services from neighbouring countries, and trains from Windhoek (Namibia) to Upington. Overland truck tours from Kenya are popular with some travellers; see p.203.

South Africa online

South African Tourism
Ⓦwww.southafrica.net

Coast to Coast
Ⓦwww.coastingafrica.com Online version of the eponymous backpackers' guide to the country.

Poetry International Web
Ⓦsouthafrica.poetryinternationalweb. org Gems from fifteen poets, including Antjie Krog.

Rage
Ⓦwww.rage.co.za Trendy coverage of street culture: music, fashion, media and events.

South African National Parks
Ⓦwww.sanparks.org All the info you need.

Zigzag
Ⓦwww.zigzag.co.za Where to surf, with beach cams and details of upcoming events.

Books

Adrian Bailey *Wild Kruger: A Visual Celebration of Africa's Premier National Park.* A voluptuous temptation.

W.H.I. Bleek and L.C. Lloyd *Specimens of Bushman Folklore.* A colonial-era collection of traditional tall stories to make you laugh and marvel – great for kids, too. Get it for free at Ⓦwww.sacred-texts.com/afr/sbf.

J.M. Coetzee *Disgrace.* Superficially the tale of a professor's downfall, this – like all of the Nobel prize-winner's books – is built on hidden foundations of suppressed violence, and hits hard against the habitual justifications given for the white presence in South Africa.

Antjie Krog *Country of My Skull.* Everyday stories of torture and abuse as told to the post-apartheid Truth and Reconciliation hearings, giving thought-provoking insights into the country's often paradoxical complexities, and ample material to meditate on truth, guilt and forgiveness.

David Lewis-Williams *Images of Mystery: Rock Art of the Drakensberg*. One of many excellent books by Lewis-Williams about southern Africa's rock art and the Bushmen, all of which concern the intricate connections between the act of painting and shamanism.

Nelson Mandela *Long Walk to Freedom*. The great man's autobiography.

Thomas Mofolo *Chaka Zulu*. Mofolo's classic fictional account of the (real) nineteenth-century founder of the Zulu empire. A magical blend of history and myth in the style of oral literature.

Alan Paton *Cry, The Beloved Country*. Fantastic novel from 1948 that reminds us that things were never really black and white. Here Paton, a long-time opponent of apartheid, describes a black priest's journey from rural Natal to Johannesburg to find his missing son, painting an angry picture of injustice and resilience along the way.

Sudan

Area 2,505,810 square kilometres
Capital Khartoum
Population 41 million; 40 percent
Arab, plus hundreds of African ethnic
groups
Language Arabic (official), and
many tribal languages
Religion Islam 70 percent,
traditional beliefs 25 percent,

Christianity 5 percent
Climate Mostly hot desert; south
of Khartoum the climate becomes
more tropical, with scattered rains
April–Nov
Best time to go Dec–March
Currency Sudanese dinar
Minimum costs $25/£14 per day

Sudan, Africa's largest country and among its poorest, has been devastated by almost five decades of civil war, genocide and famine. The primary cause of the country's woes is the Arab-Muslim government's criminal attitude towards the supposedly inferior, non-Muslim black African cultures in the south. Still, things finally seem to be changing for the better: the 2002 peace accord for the south remained in force at the time of writing, and the international community has finally began to concern itself with Darfur. For now, however, travelling in the south or west is not recommended.

Tourism is barely in its infancy, and given that much of the country is off-limits, classic attractions are limited to a string of antiquities along the Nile (which can be travelled on uncomfortable but hugely memorable ferries), the coral reefs of the Red Sea, and the everyday bustle, colour and sound of markets. Dedicated tourist facilities are limited, and the bureaucracy can be obstructive, so come armed with plenty of patience, and determination.

Main attractions

● **The Nile Valley** Northern Sudan's Nile valley was the cradle of the ancient Kingdom of Meroe, which briefly controlled Egypt. A wealth of temples, pyramids and ruins abound. Easiest to visit are the Temple of Amun near the port of Karima, which has good examples of Sudan's curiously pointed pyramids; Ramses II's Temple of Amara; and the ruined city of Meroe, whose temple complex was almost as large as Karnak's.

Average temperature ranges and rainfall

	Jan	Feb	Mar	Apr	May	Jun	Jul	Aug	Sep	Oct	Nov	Dec
Khartoum												
Max °C	31	33	37	40	42	41	38	37	39	39	35	32
Min °C	16	17	21	24	27	27	26	25	26	26	21	17
Rainfall mm	0	0	0	0	4	5	46	75	25	5	1	0

- **Khartoum and Omdurman** At
the dusty confluence of the Blue and
White Niles, Sudan's current and former
capitals inevitably feature on any itinerary. Khartoum's National Museum has a
wealth of material from Meroitic times,
while Omdurman has an enjoyable souk
and camel market, and – on Fridays
– the wonderful sight and sound of
whirling dervishes (Sufi adepts) in the
cemetery.

- **Dongola** A palm oasis along the Nile,
Dongola boasts a colourful souk and, on
the opposite shore, the Temple of Kawa,
swamped by orange sand. Before its
conquest by Egypt, Kawa was capital of
the Kingdom of Cush.

- **Kassala** On the Eritrean border,
highland Kassala has Sudan's best
climate and souks.

- **The Red Sea** Sudan's 650-kilometre
coastline is unspoiled, both on land
and under the waves. The main tourist
centres, where scuba-diving can be
arranged, are Port Sudan and Arous.

- **Dinder National Park** You'll need to
go with a tour company to see Sudan's
main wildlife sanctuary, on the Ethiopian
border. Lions and giraffes are among the
inhabitants.

Routes in and out

The main airport is Khartoum. Nile
ferries connect Egypt (Aswan) with
Wadi Halfa, from where there are more
ferries and a train. Other overland routes
into Sudan are potentially dangerous,
closed, or could require a Kafkaesque
paper chase.

Sudan online

Adventures of Sudan
Ⓦ **www.lexicorient.com/sudan** Bags of
info for tourists.
Melik Society
Ⓦ **www.melik.org.uk** Illustrated account
of Britain's nineteenth-century meddling
– General Gordon, Kitchener and the
Mahdi.
Michael's Sudan Page
Ⓦ **www.m-huether.de/sudan** Art and
music clips.
Nuba Mountains Homepage
Ⓦ **home.planet.nl/~ende0098** Accounts
and photos of travels through the
highland region southwest of Khartoum.
Sudan Artists Gallery
Ⓦ **www.sudanartists.org** Wonderful
eye-candy from contemporary artists.

Books

Michael Asher *A Desert Dies*.
Extraordinary tale of travels with the
Kababish nomads of western Sudan
during the 1980s.
George Rodger *Village of the Nubas*. A
classic photo journal from the 1950s on
Nuba culture, including great images of
traditional wrestling bouts.
Deborah Scroggins *Emma's War*.
The true story of an English aid worker
who married a Sudanese warlord, with
ultimately fatal consequences.

Swaziland

Area 17,363 square kilometres
Capital Mbabane (administrative);
Lobamba (royal and legislative)
Population 1 million; almost all are
Swazi
Language English and siSwati
Religion Christianity 50 percent,
Zionist (Christian/traditional blend)
40 percent
Climate Lowlands are tropical,
highlands more temperate; summer
(Nov–May) brings short heavy
downpours; winters are sunny and
usually dry
Best time to go May–Oct are best
in terms of climate and wildlife;
Nov–May for rafting
Currency Lilangeni (plural
emalangeni) and South African rand
Minimum costs $25/£14 per day

The tiny Kingdom of Swaziland, sandwiched between Mozambique and South Africa, has been autonomous since the nineteenth century and independent since 1968. The present ruler, King Mswati III, was forced to liberalize his country's political system in the 1990s, though it remains autocratic.

The biggest problem facing Swazis is HIV/AIDS. An infection rate of over forty percent has put population growth into reverse, and trashed the nation's economy. Increasingly frequent droughts haven't helped either.

For all that, Swazis are a welcoming bunch, and the feel of the place is refreshingly different to that of South Africa. Cultural traditions, many of them related to the monarchy, are a good reason to come. Wildlife parks are another; walking is the most exciting way to get around them, but you can also saddle up, mount a mountain bike, or ride around in an open-topped jeep. Tourists are also enticed with a series of thematic trails – subjects range from arts and crafts to history, birding and wildlife – which you can either travel under your own steam or as part of an organized tour.

Main attractions

● **Rock paintings** Throughout southern Africa, Bushman hunter-gatherers left their mark in outdoor rock art, depicting people, sacred animals, hunting and battle scenes, and dances. Swaziland's best sites are in the west, at Nsangwini and Sandlane.

Average temperature ranges and rainfall												
	Jan	Feb	Mar	Apr	May	Jun	Jul	Aug	Sep	Oct	Nov	Dec
Mbabane												
Max °C	25	25	24	23	21	19	20	21	23	23	23	24
Min °C	15	15	13	11	8	5	5	7	10	11	13	14
Rainfall mm	253	225	152	88	34	19	20	35	69	142	198	207

- **White-water rafting** Get your adrenaline kicks along the Great Usutu River. In winter, when water levels are low, combine a shorter rafting trip with hiking and abseiling.

- **Mkhaya Game Reserve** Take a hike in this scrubby acacia-studded reserve to come face-to-face with black and white rhinos, elephants, Nguni cattle and other endangered species.

- **Mlilwane Wildlife Sanctuary** A tranquil reserve whose pretty hills, waterfalls and inhabitants are best seen on horseback. Spend the night in a traditional "beehive" hut, or sip a beer within snorting range of wallowing hippos.

- **Hlane Royal National Park** Eastern Swaziland's hardwood bushland is the haunt of lions, elephants, white rhinos, many antelopes, and plentiful birdlife, including nesting white-backed vultures. Best in winter.

- **Cultural tourism** Though a little artificial, Swaziland's cultural tourism ventures are increasingly popular. The standard arrangement is for you to sleep in a specially-built traditional "village" a short distance from a real one, and spend the day with locals visiting artisans, healers and elders, and trying your hand (or feet) at various activities, including dancing.

- **Malolotja Nature Reserve** The beautiful rolling mountains in Swaziland's northwest enclose this wild reserve, perfect for hiking, with over 200km of trails and 300 species of birds. If you need places to aim for, any one of the myriad streams and waterfalls should fit the bill. Otherwise, the reserve also contains the world's oldest mine, begun 40,000 years ago by Stone Age painters searching for haematite, used as a pigment.

Festivals

Swaziland's best festivals have a royal flavour.

Incwala ("Kingship Ceremony") Lobamba; Dec Royal astrologers decide the exact dates for this series of harvest-cum-new year celebrations, which begin with November's full moon, when a specially chosen group of people visit Mozambique to collect foam from the ocean and water from rivers. The celebrations climax over six days in December, with the symbolic reconstruction of cattle kraals, the capture of a sacrificial bull by young boys, and the eating of the first fruits by the king, dressed in full battle regalia.

Umhlanga Lobamba; Aug/Sept Based on a fertility dance, this coincides with the annual ceremonial repairing of the queen's kraal. The ceremony peaks on its sixth and seventh days, when up to 25,000 elaborately dressed young women sing and dance before the king, who chooses one to add to his collection of wives.

Routes in and out

Flights land at Matsapha, close to Manzini. There is lots of overland transport fron South Africa, including buses from Mbabane, and the backpackers' Baz Bus from Durban and Johannesburg. There are also minibuses from Mozambique.

Swaziland online

Swaziland Tourism Authority Ⓦ www.welcometoswaziland.com
Swaziland National Trust Commission Ⓦ www.sntc.org.sz Loads of background information on culture,

wildlife and the environment, together with practical details.

Virtual Tour of Swaziland
Ⓦ **www.visitswazi.com/tour** Another great site, especially useful on culture.

Books

Philip Bonner *Kings, Commoners and Concessionaires*. This history of the nineteenth-century Swazi state is let down by its exclusion of oral sources but remains the definitive work.

James Hall *Sangoma: My Odyssey into the Spirit World of Africa*. Encouraged by the singer Miriam Makeba to explore his fascination with African women, this white American became apprenticed to a Swazi traditional healer. The resulting memoir is a candid account that provides an excellent overview of traditional Swazi beliefs.

Tanzania

Area 945,000 square kilometres
Capital Dodoma
Population 39 million; over 120
ethnic groups, mostly Bantu-
speakers; Nilotic-speakers include
Maasai
Language Swahili plus tribal
languages
Religion Christianity 45 percent,

Islam 35 percent
Climate Tropical along the
coast and lake zones; highlands
temperate; north semi-arid
Best time to go Jan–Feb &
July–Oct
Currency Tanzanian shilling
Minimum costs $17/£9 per day on
mainland, double this on Zanzibar

Lying just south of the Equator, Tanzania is East Africa's largest nation, and has a quartet of iconic attractions – Zanzibar, Kilimanjaro, the Serengeti and Ngorongoro Crater – to fill the brochures. It's an immensely reward-ing place to visit, whether you're turned on by culture, wildlife, beaches, or a physical challenge.

With terrain ranging from craggy volcanic peaks, forests and woodland to swamps, lakes and semi-desert scrub, Tanzania is one of the four most naturally diverse nations on earth. The country contains Africa's largest mammal population, over 1500 bird species, and three-quarters of East Africa's plant species (over ten thousand). And with over one third of its territory set aside for nature conservation, much of it adapted for eco-tourism, safari-goers will be in paradise. Safaris tend to cover one of three geographical areas: the Northern Safari Circuit, which includes Ngorongoro and the Serengeti; the Southern Safari Circuit, where Selous is

Average temperature ranges and rainfall

	Jan	Feb	Mar	Apr	May	Jun	Jul	Aug	Sep	Oct	Nov	Dec
Dar es Salaam												
Max °C	32	32	32	31	30	29	29	29	30	31	31	32
Min °C	23	23	23	22	21	19	18	18	18	20	21	23
Rainfall mm	78	52	131	269	176	42	31	27	28	66	132	116
Arusha												
Max °C	28	29	28	25	23	22	22	23	25	27	27	27
Min °C	14	14	15	16	15	13	12	13	12	14	15	14
Rainfall mm	66	77	138	223	83	17	8	7	8	24	119	103
Kigoma												
Max °C	28	28	28	28	29	29	29	30	30	29	28	28
Min °C	19	19	19	20	19	17	16	17	19	20	19	19
Rainfall mm	122	127	150	130	43	5	3	5	18	48	142	135

a favoured upmarket destination; and the remote west, which includes the chimpanzee refuges of Gombe Stream and Mahale Mountains, and untamed Katavi for muddy buffalo herds and giant pods of hippos.

Add to this Tanzania's rich ethnic diversity, superb hiking, some consummately romantic wildlife lodges and camps, wonderful coral reefs for snorkelling and diving, and a genuinely warm welcome, and you have a holiday of a lifetime.

Main attractions

● **The Serengeti** Star of countless wildlife documentaries, the Serengeti's plains are the stage for the annual eight-hundred-kilometre migration of 2.5 million mammals – including vast herds of wildebeest – to and from Kenya's Maasai Mara. Primeval it may be, but so is our fascination with it, whether the spectacle is that of lions picking off the weak or unwary, or the drama at river crossings, when crocodiles add to the carnage under the watchful gaze of vultures. While upmarket tourist lodges and luxury camps wax lyrical about the migration passing under your nose, in reality you'll probably be driven out to see the herds, so camping serves just as well.

● **Ngorongoro and the Crater Highlands** Adjacent to the Serengeti, the enormous caldera of a volcano that blew apart 2.5 million years ago provides the spectacular backdrop for a tapestry of game and predators. Close-up encounters with lions, buffaloes and black rhinos in Ngorongoro Crater are virtually guaranteed – as are sightings of fellow safari-goers. To escape the crowds, trek along the Crater Highlands to an active volcano, Ol Doinyo Lengai (the Maasai's "Mountain of God"), and then on to Lake Natron, an immense soda sump set amid unremittingly bleak terrain that appeals to flamingoes and desert fanatics alike.

● **Zanzibar** Forty kilometres off the mainland, Zanzibar has a dreamlike allure on par with Marrakesh and Timbuktu. Comprising the islands of Unguja and Pemba, it has beaches aplenty for indulging in toes-in-the-sand languor, plus multicoloured coral reefs perfect for diving or snorkelling. The capital, Stone Town, is an Arabian-style labyrinth of crooked alleyways, opulent nineteenth-century mansions, palaces and bazaars. Much of it was built on the back of slavery, of which there are reminders at every turn, including harrowing underground cells. The spices for which Zanzibar is famous can be sampled on spice tours as well as on your plate. Other popular excursions include dolphin-spotting, and forest walks in search of red colobus monkeys.

● **Chimpanzees** The forest-dwelling chimpanzees of remote Gombe and Mahale Mountains national parks, both on the eastern shore of Lake Tanganyika, have been studied since the 1960s, most famously by Jane Goodall. Some troops can be tracked on foot – every bit as exciting and romantic as it sounds.

● **Cultural tourism** Tanzania's pioneering community-run cultural tourism initiatives enable visitors to experience local life in intimate ways. Apart from offering the chance to rub shoulders with Maasai and other tribes, meet healers, elders and artisans, accompany honey collectors and farmers, and perhaps learn a few nifty dance moves, the programmes highlight natural attractions, and homestays are often possible, too. Profits fund local development projects.

● **Hiking in the Eastern Arc Mountains** Ancient rainforests filled with rare animals, plants and birds, and eyeballing monkeys are some of the things that make hiking in these isolated granite massifs one of Tanzania's foremost pleasures. The main ranges are the Pare, Usambara, Uluguru and Udzungwa Mountains.

● **Kilimanjaro** The roof of Africa at 5891m, Kilimanjaro draws hikers from the world over, although fewer than a third of them get to the snow-capped Uhuru Peak at the very top. The climb needs at least a week, taking you through thick rainforest to alpine meadows and barren, bitterly cold high-altitude tundra. But get there quick – 2014 is the date scientists have posited for the disappearance of the mountain's ice cap, thanks to global warming.

Also recommended

● **Mount Meru** A dormant volcano west of Kilimanjaro, Meru (4566m) is part of Arusha National Park and takes four days to climb and descend. Expect good hiking and exceptional views, especially of Kilimanjaro. On the lower slopes, crater lakes, meadows and forests provide a good sampler of northern Tanzania's varied habitats and wildlife.

● **The MV Liemba** Over on Lake Tanganyika, this pre-World War I steamer inspired the African Queen movie and offers an unforgettable ferry ride down to Mpulungu in Zambia, calling at a string of fascinating villages along the way.

● **Southern Highlands** The towns of Mbeya and Tukuyu are good bases for nature tourism: there are several crater lakes to choose from, plus forests, a bat cave, Mount Rungwe volcano, waterfalls, and Kitulo National Park – a botanical paradise known to locals as God's Garden.

● **Indian Ocean slaving ports** Several nineteenth-century slaving ports retain atmospheric ruins ripe for haunting, and also have beaches nearby. Particularly good are Pangani, Bagamoyo and Mikindani.

● **Rock paintings** The natural rock shelters of central Tanzania's Irangi Hills preserve some of the world's most ancient paintings. The oldest – and most skilful – date back over eighteen thousand years, and depict hunter-gatherer lifestyles not so different from that lived by the area's Sandawe and Hadzabe tribes until recently.

● **Lake Nyasa** Also called Lake Malawi, Nyasa is the Rift Valley's southernmost lake, home to hundreds of species of colourful cichlid fish that well repay lugging snorkelling gear along. The overnight ferry to Mbamba Bay is also blissful, especially for its views of the Livingstone Mountains.

● **Kilwa Kisiwani** More historical colour in Tanzania's wild south is provided by the ruins of the Swahili island-state of Kilwa Kisiwani, centuries ago East Africa's richest town thanks to its control of Mozambique's gold exports.

● **Mafia Archipelago** South of Zanzibar, the Mafia Archipelago has its own share of historical ruins and stunning reefs. Nights in one of Mafia's handful of upmarket beach hotels are often included in beach-and-bush holiday packages.

● **Selous Game Reserve** Africa's largest nature reserve is mainly used by trophy hunters, but the scenic northern sector – around the Rufiji River – is reserved for tourism. The luxurious lodges and camps along the river are a firm favourite with upmarket travellers.

● **Tarangire** A national park and conservation area that preserve a wonderfully wild and rough-around-the-edges feel. Big game is present year-round, especially elephants, their size more than matched by giant baobab trees.

● **Lake Manyara National Park** At the foot of a particularly steep section of the Rift Valley, Manyara lacks the wildlife numbers of other northern safari parks but makes amends with tree-climbing lions and ample birdlife, including pelicans and pink flamingoes.

Festivals

Apart from the traditional celebrations below, three contemporary events are worth coinciding with: Dar es Salaam's East Africa Art Biennale in December (odd-numbered years only) for contemporary art, and two music festivals on Zanzibar, namely Sauti za Busara in February, and the Festival of the Dhow Countries in July.

Bulabo dance contests Bujora, near Mwanza; June Tanzania's biggest tribe, the Sukuma, hold annual dance competitions in which rival dance societies compete in gladiatorial-style displays of crowd-pulling prowess; the bigger the crowd, the more powerful their *dawa* (medicine, meaning magic).

Bull fights Kengeja, Zanzibar; Sept–Feb Don't worry about the bulls (which aren't killed) in this throwback to Portuguese rule on Pemba Island; it's the hapless matadors you should be concerned about.

Mwaka Kogwa Makunduchi, Zanzibar; July Introduced to Zanzibar by Zoroastrian immigrants over a millennium ago, Mwaka Kogwa ("washing the year") is based on Persian New Year celebrations. The proceedings include mock fights and the ceremonial burning of a hut, from which elders make theatrical escapes.

Routes in and out

Tanzania's international airports are at Kilimanjaro in the north, Dar es Salaam and Zanzibar. A ferry on Lake Tanganyika sails weekly from Zambia; also connecting with Zambia is the TAZARA railway. There are buses from all neighbouring countries except Burundi and Mozambique. From the latter, you can reach Tanzania by catching a series of minibus taxis along the coastal road, which is likely to be blocked during the long rains.

Tanzania online

Tanzania Tourist Board
Ⓦ **www.tanzaniatouristboard.com**
BongoFlava
Ⓦ **www.bongoflava.com** All you

wanted to know about Tanzania's latest musical craze, a blend of rap, hip-hop and R&B.

Sukuma Museum
Ⓦ **www.photo.net/sukuma** Hundreds of jaw-droppingly gorgeous photographs and reams of text concerning the Bulabo dance contests.

Tanzania National Parks
Ⓦ **www.tanzaniaparks.com**
Encyclopedic coverage, with beguiling photos too. For information on Tanzania's marine parks and reserves, see Ⓦ www.marineparktz.com.

Books

Richard Francis Burton *Zanzibar and Two Months in East Africa*. Entertaining if extremely bigoted account of the explorer's adventures. Free at Ⓦ www.wollamshram.ca/1001/Blackwood/zanzibar.htm.

Javed Jafferji and Graham Mercer *Tanzania: African Eden*. A beautiful photographic sweep across the nation, with many aerial photos.

Mitsuaki Iwago *Serengeti*. Simply the best volume of wildlife photography ever assembled, this makes most coffee-table books look feeble.

Henry Morton Stanley *How I Found Livingstone*. Bombastic bestseller by the famous explorer; available for free at Ⓦ www.gutenburg.org.

Emily Ruete *Memoirs of an Arabian Princess*. The extraordinary memoirs of Zanzibar's Princess Salme, whose 1860s elopement with a German merchant caused a great kerfuffle.

Togo

Area 56,785 square kilometres	Christianity 30 percent, Islam 20
Capital Lomé	percent
Population 6.4 million; largest ethnic	**Climate** Tropical on the coast, drier
groups are Ewe, Mina and Kabyé	in the north; rains April–June
Language French (official) is	**Best time to go** Aug has the best
widely understood; over forty local	weather; Nov–March best for wildlife
languages	**Currency** CFA franc
Religion Vodun 50 percent,	**Minimum costs** $20/£11 per day

The business of government in the sliver-thin country of Togo is a family concern: the dictator Gnassingbé Eyadema ruled the country from 1967 to his death in 2005, when he was replaced by his son. Elections occur, but are not taken seriously; nor are human rights. That said, Togo is easier for first-timers to get to grips with than many other West African countries. Getting around and other practicalities are straightforward, and despite its compact size Togo manages to pack in a good range of scenery and things to see and do, and taste – Togolese food, especially, is excellent. Providing cultural interest is Vodun (voodoo), the country's biggest religion, one in which spirits loom large: the Ewe alone have over six hundred of them.

Main attractions

● **Lomé** Radiating outward from its central market, Togo's capital is a great place for shopping and eating, with several craft markets and a Vodun fetish market, though sightseeing is limited to a few old colonial buildings such as the German cathedral.

● **Togoville** This was the site of Germany's treaty with Mlapa III, on the basis of which the colonialists laid claim to the whole country and part of Ghana. Togoville is firmly on the tourist trail, and would-be guides lie in wait to collar foreigners and steer them round the royal palace, the 1910 cathedral, and a few of the local fetish shrines.

● **Aného** Once the colonial capital, Aného is now a laid-back town whose nineteenth-century German churches, cemetery and colonial villas make for a pleasant stroll. At Glidji, 4km north, you pay your respects to the chief before checking out the local voodoo shrines.

● **Dapaong** A great base for exploring the northern hills; major attractions are a series of photogenic cliffside cave dwellings that were originally used whenever other tribes invaded the area (they're now places of pilgrimage), and prehistoric rock paintings at Namoudjoga. The town is best on Wednesday and Saturday, when you'll be able to sample heady *tchakpalo* millet beer in the market.

● **Kpalimé** A centre for weaving, with a wonderful market, Kpalimé is also the ideal base for exploring the scenic evergreen mountains of Kloto and Agou.

● **Fazao-Malfakassa National Park** The gallery forests and fertile plains of

Average temperature ranges and rainfall

	Jan	Feb	Mar	Apr	May	Jun	Jul	Aug	Sep	Oct	Nov	Dec
Lomé												
Max °C	31	31	32	31	31	29	27	27	28	30	31	31
Min °C	23	24	25	24	24	23	23	22	23	23	23	23
Rainfall mm	15	24	52	118	145	224	71	8	35	61	28	10

Togo's best wildlife park are home to elephants and buffaloes, antelopes, monkeys and lots of birds.

Festivals

Christian and Muslim festivals are observed (see p.243 & p.245 for dates), including some of the lesser Christian feasts such as Ascension (forty days after Easter), Pentecost (aka Whitsun; fifty days after Easter), Assumption (Aug 15) and All Saints Day (Nov 1). For traditional festivals, August and September are the big months. The tourist board website has a good round-up.

Ayiza Ewe country, especially Tsévié region; second Sat of Aug Ewe harvest festival, celebrated with a bean-feast.

Epe Ekpe (or Yékéyéké) Glidji, near Aného; mid-Sept Dress up in a white toga to enjoy this week-long Vodun celebration, suffused with a sense of the sacred.

Evala Kabyé country, especially Kara; July A boys' peer-group initiation with traditional wrestling tournaments, followed by Akpema, which is the girls' initiation ceremony. Evala is the main Kabyé festival, and practically a public holiday.

Routes in and out

The international airport is at Lomé. Direct bush taxis or buses arrive from Accra (Ghana), and taxis and buses from Cotonou (Benin) and Ouagadougou (Burkina Faso). There are also direct bush taxis from Lagos (Nigeria).

Togo online

Togo National Tourist Office
ⓦ www.togo-tourisme.com
Voodoo and West Africa's Spiritual Life
ⓦ www.npr.org/programs/re /archivesdate/2004/feb/voodoo A great collection of videos, recordings, images and intelligent articles about Vodun, particularly in Togo.

Books

Fuziya Kassindja *Do They Hear You When You Cry?* Powerful autobiographical account of the author's flight from the country to escape a forced marriage and genital mutilation.

Tete-Michel Kpomassie *An African in Greenland*. At last, a travelogue written by an African about faraway climes. As a teenager, Togolese-born Kpomassie found a book on Greenland. Working his way north for ten years, he finally reached the land of his dreams, and fell in love with the Inuit and their culture. Brilliantly observed and hugely entertaining.

George Packer *The Village of Waiting*. A very honest account of two years spent as a Peace Corps volunteer in a rural Togolese community, who learned a lot more from the locals than they did from him.

Tunisia

Area 164,418 square kilometres
Capital Tunis
Population 10.3 million; mostly mixed Arab/Berber, with "pure" Berbers in the south and highlands
Language Arabic (official) plus minority Berber dialects; French widely understood
Religion Islam

Climate Mediterranean in north, with rains Oct–May; progressively drier and hotter in south, with desert extremes
Best time to go May–Oct; avoid the Sahara in summer
Currency Tunisian dinar
Minimum costs $25/£14 per day

Tunisia, hemmed in by the Mediterranean, Algeria's Atlas Mountains and the Sahara, has long found its identity being fashioned by powerful visitors: Phoenicians, Romans, Byzantines, Arabs, Ottoman Turks and the French. Ever since Tunisia's own Carthaginian Empire was defeated by Rome, tolerance and co-existence have become the surest way to survive invasions, and this is reflected in the welcome that's afforded to visitors today.

The country's many conquerors left it a rich legacy of monuments, especially Roman – often better preserved than their Italian counterparts. The Arabs and Turks bequeathed uncountable architectural gems and the maze-like medinas at the hearts of all the big cities, particularly enjoyable examples of which are Tunis, Sfax and Kairouan. Tunisia also has the best of the Maghreb's beaches, with warm shallow waters and well-developed tourist infrastructure. Mediterranean beaches are not the only sands on offer: the Sahara's northern fringe is a popular target for excursions, where it's not so much dunes and oases as Berber culture that's the attraction, especially their weird and wonderful multistorey *ghorfa* granaries, and underground dwellings that featured in *Star Wars*.

Average temperature ranges and rainfall

	Jan	Feb	Mar	Apr	May	Jun	Jul	Aug	Sep	Oct	Nov	Dec
Tunis												
Max °C	14	16	18	21	24	29	32	33	31	25	20	16
Min °C	6	7	8	11	13	17	20	21	19	15	11	7
Rainfall mm	64	51	41	36	18	8	3	8	33	51	48	61
Douz												
Max °C	17	19	22	25	30	34	37	37	34	28	23	18
Min °C	7	8	11	13	18	22	24	25	22	18	12	8
Rainfall mm	13	8	8	7	8	6	0	2	19	12	9	18

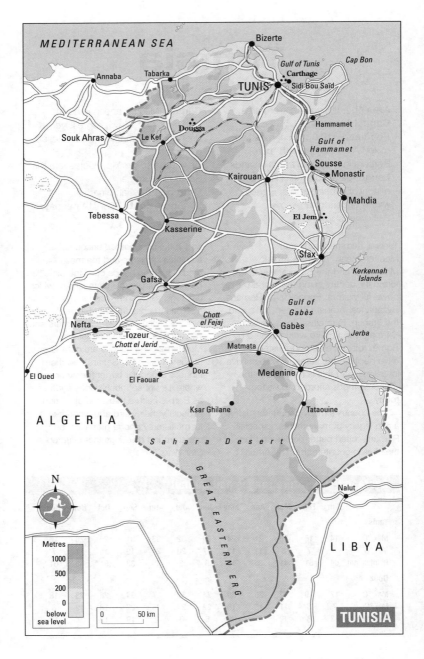

MEDITERRANEAN SEA

Bizerte

Gulf of Tunis   *Cap Bon*

Annaba   Tabarka   **Carthage**

TUNIS   Sidi Bou Saïd

Hammamet

Dougga

Souk Ahras   Le Kef   *Gulf of Hammamet*

Sousse
Monastir

Kairouan

Mahdia

Tebessa

El Jem

Kasserine

Sfax

Kerkennah Islands

Gafsa

Gulf of Gabès

Chott el Fejaj

Nefta   Gabès   *Jerba*

Tozeur
Chott el Jerid   Matmata

El Oued   Douz   Medenine

El Faouar

Ksar Ghilane   Tataouine

ALGERIA

Sahara   Desert

N

Nalut

LIBYA

Metres
1000
500
200
0
below
sea level

0   50 km

TUNISIA

Main attractions

● **Carthage** Rome's big rival was Carthage, epitomized by the story of Hannibal crossing the Alps with his army of elephants. According to legend, the city of Carthage was founded by Queen Dido in 814 BC, and became infamous for its practice of child sacrifice. After defeat by Rome in 146 BC, the city – close to present-day Tunis – was razed to the ground. A scattering of ruins remain, but the real treasures are housed in Tunis' magnificent Bardo Museum.

● **Chott el Jerid** An overwhelming silence prevails in this magically powerful, and elementally beautiful place, a vast salt pan in the northern Sahara. Once part of the Mediterranean, the chott was cut off when sea levels fell, and gradually dried up. The salt still retains moisture and the lake occasionally floods in winter, so any attempt at crossing it other than along the raised causeway will probably see your vehicle disappear into quicksand. Should the Zen thing not appeal, you could always go sand-yachting…

● **Jerba** Tunisia's most popular beach destination may have been the "Island of the Lotus-eaters" mentioned in Homer's Odyssey, in which the sweet lethargy induced by the mythical lotus fruit made it impossible for visitors to leave. Away from the beach, pay a visit to one of several mostly abandoned fortress-mosques whose thick ramparts served to protect locals against Mediterranean pirates, or visit the synagogues of the island's Jewish community, the first of whom arrived some two thousand years ago.

● **Ghorfas** Nowadays desert, south-eastern Tunisia was once Rome's granary. It's also where the indigenous Berbers developed amazing architectural prowess when building *ghorfas*, fortified multistorey grain stores made of mud and palm trunks, and resembling honeycombs. Some of them served as dwellings, but most are now abandoned. The best are around Medenine and Tataouine.

● **The Sahara** Stark and elemental, a Saharan experience is likely to stay with you forever. The desert's classic dunes are best seen at El Faouar, near Douz, which is also the starting point

△ One of Jerba's old mosques

for camping trips to the oasis of Ksar Ghilane. Dune surfing is also possible, as are camel rides, whether for an hour or over a week.

● **Sidi Bou Saïd** A visual serenade in blue and white, this exquisite Mediterranean village of elegant hillside villas has long been favoured by artists, aesthetes and the affluent, and is one of those places for which the word photogenic might well have been invented.

● **Tunis and Sfax medinas** The old quarters of these coastal towns are archetypal Arabian medinas of narrow crooked streets, hidden souks and feverish activity. Getting lost in the labyrinths is unavoidable, and very much part of the pleasure, especially with so many enchanting nooks and crannies to explore. The medinas have distinct commercial sectors: copper and brass workers in one place, hatters (for Turkish-styles fezzes) elsewhere, and shops selling perfumes in the alleyways around the main mosques.

Also recommended

● **Bathing in a hammam** A gift from Turkish occupation; there's a whole ritual involved, leaving you sweated, scrubbed, massaged and most definitely refreshed.

● **Dougga** The ruins of a small Roman town, complete with capitol, horseshoe-arranged latrines, and a brothel.

● **Matmata** The Berber inhabitants of Matmata found shelter from the desert, and their warlike neighbours, by burrowing their houses underground in the soft sandstone. From the surface, it looks like there's almost nothing there other than moonlike craters. These days the dwellings are famous for having provided the backdrops in the original *Star Wars*;

a handful have been converted into affordable hotels.

● **Kairouan** Tunisia's spiritual centre contains a wealth of historic mosques and mausoleums, and impressive open-air cisterns built over a thousand years ago that kept the city furnished with drinking water. Kairouan is also the place to buy carpets.

● **El Jem** The Roman world's best-preserved amphitheatre, scene of many an unequal fight between hapless captives and lions.

● **Hammamet** Arguably Tunisia's finest beach, with all the facilities you might desire (including horse-riding and golfing), though it's very much a tourist ghetto.

● **Tozeur and Nefta** Two medieval oases on the desert's fringes, both stuffed with date palms and ancient crumbling mosques and Sufi mausoleums.

● **Kerkennah Islands** This beach destination has, thankfully, yet to hit the big time; with its shallow warm water and friendly locals, it's a particularly good family destination away from it all.

● **Bizerte and Mahdia** Two very pretty Mediterranean port towns, especially worth visiting if photography's your thing – the light and colours can be fabulous.

Festivals

Much of Tunisia's impressive festival roster is aimed at tourists. Events invariably include music and some kind of folkloric pageant; email the tourist board for upcoming dates. Other events include the Carthage International Festival in July and August (for film and music), and a summer concert series including a Jazz festival in the northern resort of Tabarka. See pp.243–245 for information about Islamic festivals.

Festival of the Sahara Douz; Nov
A big celebration of desert arts and
folklore, featuring camel and greyhound
races, pageantry, poetry and music,
even sand hockey. Also in November is
a similar bash at Tozeur.

Lag B'Omer Jerba; May Major pilgrimage to La Ghriba synagogue, held on
the thirty-third day after the start of
Passover.

Routes in and out

Tunisia's main airports are Tunis, Jerba
and Monastir, the latter two mainly used
by European holiday charters. There are
ferries from several Italian ports, and
from Marseille in France. Overlanding
from Algeria is possible from the Sahara,
but not in the north. The Libyan border is
open, but you may not be able to get a
visa in Tunis.

Tunisia online

Tunisian National Tourism Office
Ⓦ www.tunisietourisme.com.tn and
Ⓦ www.tourismtunisia.com
The Star Wars Traveler
Ⓦ www.toysrgus.com/travel/tunisia
.html Set-by-set directions and photos
for Tunisia's many *Star Wars* locations.

Books

Alexander A. Boddy *To Kairwân
The Holy*. Nineteenth-century Tunisia

through the eyes of a bigoted, short-
sighted and remarkably stupid
Anglican reverend, thanks to which he
unwittingly provided us with a most
entertaining read.

Gustave Flaubert *Salammbô*.
Ingredients: sex, violence, intrigue,
human sacrifice, torture, disagree-
able characters and gallons of gore.
Cook in a loosely historical setting (the
Carthaginian Civil War), and serve hot.
Easily Flaubert's worst novel, but also his
most gripping.

Monia Hejaiej *Behind Closed Doors:
Women's Oral Narratives in Tunis*.
Challenging stereotypes about women
in Islam, this compilation of traditional
women's tales is told by three expert
story-tellers, each with very different
points of view.

Orr Kelly *Meeting the Fox*. Engrossing,
almost bullet-by-bullet account of the
US Army's painful progress through
North Africa during the Second World
War. The Allies' victory over Rommel's
troops in Tunisia was a major turning
point.

Mustapha Tlili *Lion Mountain*. The
inhabitants of an isolated mountain
village, epitomized by a stubborn old
heroine, struggle to resist the insidious advances of the modern State
in its guises of progress, tourism and
dictatorship. For all the heavy themes,
Tlili's prose is infused with a lightness
and gaiety that brings it close to poetry,
qualities that lose nothing in the skilful
translation.

Uganda

Area 241,038 square kilometres
Capital Kampala
Population 31 million; over 30 tribes, the main ones being Baganda, Ankole, Basoga, Iteso and Bakiga
Language English is the most widely spoken, Swahili less so; tribal languages are also spoken
Religion Christianity 65 percent, Islam 15 percent, traditional beliefs 15 percent

Climate Mostly tropical tempered by altitude, with rains generally March–May and Nov; semi-desert in the northeast, scattered showers April–Oct
Best time to go June–Aug & Dec–Feb
Currency Uganda shilling
Minimum costs $15/£8

Uganda, a place of breathtaking beauty and a wide range of habitats, sits in both central and eastern Africa, a happy coincidence that makes it one of the best places on earth for seeing animals. In the south and west you'll find typically central African species such as gorillas, chimpanzees and other primates, while in the north and east it's classic east African savanna fauna that dominates, including elephants, lions, leopards and countless antelopes. And overhead, the country has over a thousand bird species to its name.

By rights, Uganda should be right up there with Kenya and Tanzania as a major tourist destination, but conflict has for too long been its major theme for the international media. Two brutal dictators, Milton Obote and Idi Amin, between them liquidated 400,000 "opponents", and in the 1970s a civil war brought the country to its knees. Although those dark days are long gone, conflict remains a theme in the north and northeast, and along part of the Congolese border. That said, safety isn't a worry elsewhere, and the tourism infrastructure is well developed, too.

Average temperature ranges and rainfall

	Jan	Feb	Mar	Apr	May	Jun	Jul	Aug	Sep	Oct	Nov	Dec
Kampala												
Max °C	28	28	27	26	25	25	25	25	27	27	27	27
Min °C	18	18	18	18	17	17	17	16	17	17	17	17
Rainfall mm	46	61	130	175	147	74	46	86	91	97	122	99
Kabale												
Max °C	24	24	23	23	22	22	23	23	24	23	23	23
Min °C	9	11	11	11	11	9	8	9	10	11	11	10
Rainfall mm	58	97	130	125	91	28	20	58	97	99	109	86

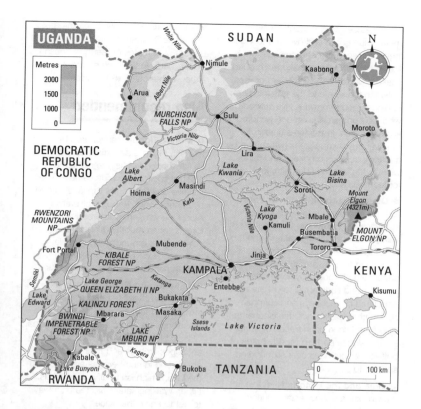

Main attractions

● **Rwenzori Mountains National Park** The jagged Rwenzoris, marking the western boundary of the Rift Valley and the border with Congo, were known to ancient Greeks as the "Mountains of the Moon". They're an area of phenomenal natural beauty, with mist-shrouded equatorial forests along the mountains' flanks, weird "Afro-Alpine" vegetation further up (lobelia, groundsel, bamboo and heather, all of them giant), and glaciers and ice-caps on top. The highest peak, which can be climbed in a week, is the 5109-metre Margherita. Animal lovers won't be disappointed: 560 bird species have been recorded, and both forest elephants and chimpanzees are present.

● **Bwindi Impenetrable Forest National Park** Bwindi is Uganda's star tourist attraction – or rather, its inhabitants are. The park is home to half the world's six hundred mountain gorillas, some of which can be tracked by tourists. Out of the limelight but if anything even more of a thrill are the park's chimpanzees. There are also elephants, rare giant forest hogs and a whole lot of birds. All in all, a superb place in which to hike in wild, untrammelled countryside.

● **Murchison Falls National Park** Approaching Lake Albert, the Victoria

Nile squeezes itself through a seven-metre-wide gorge and over the thundering Murchison Falls, the pressure of the water sufficient to make the ground shake. Popular with visitors are cruises between the lake and the falls in search of hippos and enormous Nile crocodiles, who feed on gargantuan one-hundred-kilo Nile perch. In the forests south of the river are chimpanzees (which can be tracked), colobus monkeys and rhinos, while in the Victoria Nile delta, look out for leopards and shoebill storks.

● **Queen Elizabeth National Park** QEII for short, this huge wilderness straddles the Equator in the Western Rift Valley and includes the eastern shore of Lake Edward. The park encompasses everything from swamps, channels and crater lakes favoured by flamingoes, to savanna and substantial forest areas populated by monkeys and chimpanzees. Other wildlife includes elephants, lions (often seen up in trees), Uganda kob antelopes and big muddy herds of buffalo. Birders have over six hundred species to aim for.

● **Jinja and the Victoria Nile** Jinja is a town with a distinct Asian influence, a legacy of coolies shipped in by the British to build the Kampala–Mombasa railway. The town lies close to the point where the White Nile empties from Lake Victoria and begins its three-month, four-thousand-kilometre trek to the Mediterranean. Apart from historical cachet (this particular "source of the Nile" was the holy grail for many a nineteenth-century explorer), the big draw is a range of adventurous thrills and spills: quad biking, bungee jumping over the Nile's Bujagali Falls and – best of all – some of the wildest white-water rafting on the continent.

● **Kibale Forest National Park** This ancient rainforest covers the lower slopes of the Rwenzoris and has chimpanzees as its main attraction, though there are plenty other primates too – in fact, Kibale contains the highest density of primates on earth. It doesn't do too badly in the butterfly stakes, either, with around 150 species.

Also recommended

● **Mount Elgon** Often ignored by tourists, Elgon is an extinct volcano, its flat-topped peaks (the highest at 4321m) encircling a wide caldera. The stiff five-day trek to the top is rewarded by springs warm enough for bathing. Along the way, enjoy impressive bamboo forests, open moorland inhabited by solitary giant groundsel and lobelia, and various caves and waterfalls. Rock climbing and abseiling are also possible.

● **Lake Mburo National Park** Yet another great wildlife park, containing a mixture of forests, papyrus swamps, grasslands and acacia-studded savanna. Classic big-game animals such as antelopes, zebras and their predators are around in numbers, as are hippos in the lake, which isn't half bad for birds, either. Walking safaris are the best way to get to know the place.

● **Ssese Islands** Lake Victoria's Ssese Islands are easily accessible by steamer from Entebbe or Bukakata, and by local outboard "taxis". The main attraction is really just chilling out on the beach, but if you must do something, take a bird book with you and track down some of the many species.

● **Kampala** Uganda's bustling, modern capital has developed rapidly over the last decade but still carries a pleasingly prim provincial air. Most visitors spend their time organizing gorilla tours, but don't miss hands-on displays of traditional Buganda musical instruments in the Uganda Museum, and the tombs of Buganda kings atop Kasubi Hill.

Also out of town, Mpanga Forest and Mabamba Swamp (for shoebill storks) are pleasant day-trips.

● **Entebbe** For most visitors Entebbe, south of Kampala on a peninsula in Lake Victoria, is just the international airport. But hang around and you'll find that planes aren't the only things in the sky; the marshy lagoons attract an abundance of birdlife, waders and raptors especially, and – an amazing sight after the rains – immense clouds of pinkish lake flies, on which the birds gorge themselves silly. Offshore, Ngamba Island's forests are home to several dozen orphaned chimpanzees. There's also a century-old botanical garden.

● **Kalinzu Forest** In the southwest close to Fort Portal, this is a simple way of getting close to nature, with a good selection of guided walks along the escarpment of the Rift Valley and in the valley itself. Expect spectacular views of Lake Edward and the Rwenzori Mountains.

● **Lake Bunyoni** Close to Kabale, this lake is set amid towering forest-draped mountains. It's great for bird-watching, and the adventurous can wobble across the lake in a dugout to visit some of its 29 islands. Unusually for Uganda, the lake is free of bilharzia, so swimming is safe.

Festivals

Decades of dictatorship ushered in the end of many traditional celebrations, and as yet there are few signs that the kings of Buganda and Busoga (see websites, below) are getting around to re-creating the former glory of their royal orchestras. Your best chance of catching a really traditional festival is in the northeast, which is sadly for the most part out of bounds.

Amakula Kampala; May International cinema festival with both African and non-African films screened at various locations in the city.

Imbalu Mbale and around; Aug of even-numbered years The circumcision of Bagisu boys marks their passage into adulthood, and is celebrated every two years in a series of colourful (and noisy) events in which dancing features prominently.

Kwetu Fest Ntinda, near Kampala; see Ⓦwww.ndere.com for dates A biannual celebration of the nation's traditional cultures, featuring over twenty groups of musicians and dancers.

Routes in and out

Flights land at Entebbe, near Kampala. There are buses in from Kenya, Rwanda and Tanzania, but passenger trains from Kenya are no more.

Uganda online

Tourism Uganda
Ⓦ**www.visituganda.com**
MusicUganda.com
Ⓦ**www.musicuganda.com** News, gossip, full-length tracks and videos, mainly of rap and reggae.
Uganda Community Tourism Association
Ⓦ**www.ucota.or.ug** Details of locally run eco-tourism and cultural-tourism projects.
Uganda's kingdoms
Ⓦ**www.buganda.com** and
Ⓦ**www.busoga.com** Abolished in 1966, the kingdoms of Buganda and Busoga were reinstated in 1993. Their websites carry info on culture and history, and royal news and upcoming events.
Uganda Travel Planner
Ⓦ**www.traveluganda.co.ug** An amazing resource stuffed with

information, including up-to-date entrance fees and all manner of practicalities.

World Routes in Uganda
ⓦ www.bbc.co.uk/radio3/worldmusic /onlocation/uganda.shtml Two superb radio programmes about traditional Ugandan music, with plenty of rare and beautiful sounds, from Buganda Royal Court music to some wicked xylophone playing.

Books

Giles Foden *The Last King of Scotland*. Idi Amin's bloody rule was at once terrible and absurd. It's the latter quality that provides the meat for this novel set in the 1970s, a darkly comical account of the dictator's (fictional) Scottish physician's admiration for the big man.

Moses Isegawa *Abyssinian Chronicles*. Narrated by the son of a man named Serenity and a woman named Padlock, this captivating novel, set during Amin's rule, follows a boy's education and his family's poignant struggle to survive. Isegawa deals masterfully with the universal themes of dreams and desires and their inevitable collision with reality.

David William Pluth *Uganda Rwenzori: A Range of Images*. It's easy to produce a beautiful coffee-table book when the subject is the Rwenzori Mountains.

Zambia

Area 752,614 square kilometres
Capital Lusaka
Population 12 million; over 70 ethnic groups, largest being Bemba, Nyanja, Lozi, Ngoni and Tonga
Language English, plus many tribal languages
Religion Christianity 65 percent, Islam 30 percent
Climate Tropical, mostly tempered by altitude (exceptions are the hot and humid Zambezi and Luangwa valleys); May–Sept is dry and relatively cool; Sept–Nov dry and hot; rains Nov–April
Best time to go March–May for the Victoria Falls); May–Aug for landscapes; July–Oct for wildlife; Nov–March for birds
Currency Zambian kwacha
Minimum costs $20/£11 per day

It's difficult to know where to start with Zambia: the Victoria Falls, a bamboozling array of adventure sports on the Zambezi River, or a regal choice of wildlife parks, which the more adventurous can sample on foot, on horseback, from a canoe, or even from the back of an elephant. The country is also home to 750 bird species, many of them found in extensive wetland areas painted all over Zambia's highland savanna.

Until the nineteenth century, Zambia contained a myriad of ethnic chiefdoms and kingdoms, which fell into disarray when southern Africa's Zulu Empire, under King Shaka, expanded militarily, pushing waves of invaders and migrants northwards. During colonial times, when the country was known as Northern Rhodesia, many tribes were urbanized, but remarkably each has kept its sense of identity and much of its culture intact.

As in neighbouring Tanzania, Zambians prize "joking relationships" – light-hearted inter-tribal rivalry – as a way of diffusing potentially serious tensions. The result is a calendar crammed with festivals, and a peaceful and hospitable nation where visitors are readily made to feel at home.

Average temperature ranges and rainfall

	Jan	Feb	Mar	Apr	May	Jun	Jul	Aug	Sep	Oct	Nov	Dec
Lusaka												
Max °C	27	27	28	27	26	24	24	27	30	32	30	28
Min °C	18	17	16	14	11	8	7	9	13	16	17	1
Rainfall mm	245	186	95	35	3	0	0	0	2	18	90	208
Victoria Falls												
Max °C	30	30	30	30	28	26	26	28	33	34	33	30
Min °C	19	19	18	15	10	7	6	9	14	18	19	19
Rainfall mm	174	141	80	24	6	1	0	1	2	25	70	169

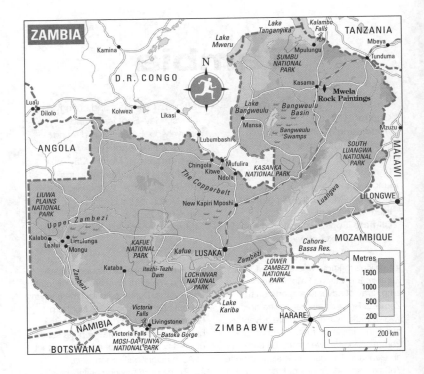

Main attractions

● **Victoria Falls** At the end of the rains, the Victoria Falls – on the border with Zimbabwe – are the world's largest cascades, where the Zambezi spreads out over 1700m to drop 108m into a tumultuous cloud of mist. The falls are best seen from the spray-filled path along the flanking forest edge, or from above in a microlight or helicopter. In the dry season, when first impressions might be disappointing, get your kicks with a walk along the lip of the falls.

● **Zambezi River activities** Together with Zimbabwe's Victoria Falls town, Zambia's pleasantly dilapidated Livingstone town is Africa's capital of adventure sports. On the river, take your pick from rafting or jet-boating down the raging rapids, kayaking or river-boarding (surfing). Upriver, you can enjoy a more sedate canoeing safari or a boat cruise, and there's also abseiling, bungee jumping and "gorge swinging" (a variant on the bungee theme).

● **Kafue National Park** Despite being one of the world's largest wildlife areas, Kafue has received little tourist development, so you're likely to feel as though you have the place to yourself. In the northwest, the Busanga Plains host herds of red lechwe, blue wildebeest and swamp-dwelling sitatunga antelope. Hippos, especially in the dry season, are also big attractions, together with lion prides, cheetahs and leopards. In

△ Hippos lurk at South Luangwa National Park

the south, Itezhi Tezhi reservoir and the rivers feeding it are prime birding habitats. You'll also see hippos, crocs and animals coming to drink. Canoeing safaris are a special attraction.

● **The Bangweulu basin** Girdled by papyrus swamps, seasonal floodplains, termite grassland and woodlands is Lake Bangweulu, whose name means "where water meets the sky". This hot and humid world is perfect for birds; among the four hundred species is the rare shoebill stork. The prima donnas of the mammalian world are two swamp-loving antelopes: the black lechwe (often in herds of thousands), and the shy sitatunga. Sizeable herds of puku antelope are also present, and crocodiles, hippos and buffaloes abound. In the dry season, elephants are occasionally sighted. Most of the basin is public land and has few tourist facilities; the exception is Kasanka National Park in the southwest.

● **South Luangwa National Park** The Luangwa valley ranks among the continent's richest wildlife sanctuaries, and is Zambia's best-equipped for tourism. There are many lodges which act as bases for walking safaris, night-time game drives and – during the rains – boating along the river and its oxbow lakes in search of birds.

● **Lower Zambezi National Park** Zambia's ultimate lazy wildlife experience is drifting down the Zambezi and its channels in a canoe, dodging hippos and crocodiles while looking for Africa's most emblematic species. Elephants are often seen at the water's edge, and buffaloes and waterbucks are common, as are other antelopes, small primates and fish eagles.

● **Liuwa Plains National Park** Remote and scenically dramatic wildlife area in the far west that's famous for vast herds of blue wildebeest, who migrate in from Angola during the rains. Predators include lions and African hunting dogs.

Also recommended

● **Lusaka** Zambia's energetic capital has enjoyable nightlife, bustling markets, a good museum and several privately-run game reserves nearby.

● **Mosi-Oa-Tunya National Park** A small riverside park upstream of Victoria Falls, home to Zambia's only rhinos. Get to see them by open-topped vehicle, on foot, or on the back of a horse or elephant.

● **Lake Kariba** Created by the damming of the Zambezi in the 1950s, the lake is a centre for fishing, canoeing and houseboat safaris, plus tours of an underground power station.

● **Lake Tanganyika** Occupying a deep trough in the Great Rift Valley, Tanganyika has the potential to be a major tourist attraction, but awkward access means it's little visited. Its attractions are many and varied: blue duikers and other wildlife at Sumbu National Park; sacred balancing boulders; slave-trade sights; Zambia's oldest church; the 221-metre Kalambo Falls and loads of birds.

● **Lochinvar National Park** A broad floodplain that's home to the unique Kafue lechwe antelope, and that is also great for birds, especially raptors. Another attraction is a rock gong – a natural outcrop that chimes when struck. Locals used it to greet passers-by.

● **The Copperbelt** Ore extracted from the craggy hills along the Congolese border has paid Zambia's way since the 1920s. In Zambia you can visit Africa's biggest open-cast mine, or take a tour underground.

● **Mwela rock paintings** The boulder-strewn landscape of northern Zambia's Kasama district offered plenty of natural shelters for Stone Age artists; the area contains almost a thousand paintings.

Festivals

Although much of the population is urbanized, national and tribal pride means that traditional festivals are very much alive, any of which are well worth coinciding with. The tourist board's website has a full list.

Ku'omboka Near Mongu town; Feb or March In Barotseland on the Upper Zambezi, the Lozi spend half the year farming the river's fertile valley. Towards the end of the rains the river's floods force them to higher ground. The ceremonial migration is by boat across the floodplain. Heading the flotilla is the Lozi king and his family, who are paddled in massive war-canoes from their winter palace at Lealui to the summer palace at Limulunga, whose inhabitants greet the king with a night of song and dance.

Lwiindi Ceremony Mukuninot, near Victoria Falls; July Every year before the rains, the Leya give sacrifices and prayers to their ancestral spirits dwelling in the gorges of the Victoria Falls. Expect much singing, dancing and feasting once the serious business of asking for rain is over.

Umotomboko Ceremony Kazembe village, Mansa (west of Lake Bangweulu); July 29 A two-day ceremony beside the Ng'ona River in honour of the nineteenth-century Lunda chief Kazembe; expect war dances, colourful costumes, hypnotic drumming and speeches.

Routes in and out

Most international flights land at Lusaka. All land borders are open, but there's no cross-border transport from Angola, and the Congolese border area is unsafe. The TAZARA railway links Zambia's rail network with Dar es Salaam (Tanzania), and work is underway to rehabilitate the Benguela Railway to Angola. A weekly ferry on Lake Tanganyika links Mpulungu with Kigoma (Tanzania).

Zambia online

Zambia National Tourist Board Ⓦ www.zambiatourism.com A wonderful site that renders many others redundant, covering as it does everything from traditional festivals to wildlife in magnificent detail.
Barotseland.com Ⓦ www.barotseland.com Everything about the Lozi, including photos of the Ku'omboka ceremony.

Books

Michael Main *Zambezi: Journey of a River*. Well-researched travelogue, especially strong on local myths and anecdotes.
David Rogers *Zambia Landscapes*. A full-colour once-over.
Benjamin Smith *Zambia's Ancient Rock Art: The Paintings of Kasama*. A handy introduction that also floats the intriguing theory that Zambia's mostly geometric rock art may have been painted by women.
Jan and Fiona Teede *The Zambezi, River of the Gods*. A lavishly illustrated guide to the great river.

Zimbabwe

Area 390,580 square kilometres
Capital Harare
Population 13.2 million; majority are Shona; the other sizeable ethnic group is Ndebele
Language English; major ethnic languages are Chishona and Sindebele
Religion Syncretic (mixture of Christianity and traditional) 50 percent, Christianity 25 percent, traditional beliefs 24 percent
Climate Subtropical; rains Nov–April
Best time to go March–May for the Victoria Falls; May–Oct for climate and wildlife; Nov–April for landscapes
Currency Zimbabwean dollar
Minimum costs $30/£17 per day

Few people these days consider Zimbabwe for a holiday. Copious media coverage of President Mugabe's misdeeds have put paid to a once promising tourist industry, though that's the least of the country's woes. Zimbabwe is virtually bankrupt. The forcible redistribution of the country's prime farmland away from the minority white population devastated the country's cash crop economy, and in 2006 the inflation rate topped 1000 percent. Food and fuel shortages have become part of life, together with poverty and political repression. Average life expectancy is the world's lowest: 37 years for men, 34 for women, and with famine now a very real threat, many Zimbabweans are emigrating in search of better prospects.

For all that, Zimbabweans are a remarkably considerate and welcoming lot, and so long as you keep political opinions under your beer glass, you're unlikely to come a cropper. Top of most visitors' agendas are the Victoria Falls, the world's largest when the Zambezi is in spate. For hiking and flowers, the verdant Eastern Highlands beckon, while for wildlife the whole country – much of it savanna – is scattered with beautiful parks and reserves. Culturally, you

Average temperature ranges and rainfall

	Jan	Feb	Mar	Apr	May	Jun	Jul	Aug	Sep	Oct	Nov	Dec
Harare												
Max °C	26	26	26	26	24	22	22	24	28	29	28	26
Min °C	16	16	15	13	9	7	7	9	12	15	16	16
Rainfall mm	191	177	99	37	7	2	2	3	7	40	93	183
Victoria Falls												
Max °C	30	29	30	29	27	25	25	28	32	33	32	30
Min °C	18	18	17	14	10	6	6	8	13	17	18	18
Rainfall mm	167	126	70	24	3	1	0	0	2	27	64	174

won't go wanting either. Prehistoric rock paintings abound, as do ruined medieval cities, the most famous being spectacular Great Zimbabwe.

Main attractions

● **Victoria Falls** Dwarfing the Niagara Falls are what locals call Mosi-oa-Tunya, "the Smoke that Thunders". Spanning 1700m, and plunging 108m at their highest, this vast curtain of water – and the frothing, mist-shrouded gorge below – is one of the world's natural wonders. "Vic Falls" is also the place for adventure sports: white-water rafting, canoeing, horse riding, bungee jumping, even parachuting or bodyboarding. You can also relax on a sundown cruise or take a hike through dense forest on the south side of the falls in search of rare birds, elephants and buffaloes, giraffes and antelopes.

● **Great Zimbabwe** Amid a granite landscape replete with ancient rock art is the ruined stone city of Great Zimbabwe, the largest and most impressive of over a hundred such sites. Inhabited between the eleventh and fifteenth centuries, the city was the capital of the Shona empire of Monomotapa, and at its peak housed twenty thousand people and controlled both Zimbabwe and Mozambique. The site consists of several complexes, the most famous being the Great Enclosure, its massive walls studded with conical towers. Inside were at least three hundred separate structures, all built without the use of mortar. Colonial-era historians refused to believe that Africans had built such an impressive place, an incredulity that became an outright lie in the 1970s when radio carbon dates were officially censored. Come independence in 1980, the city's name became that of the nation.

● **Chinhoyi caves** The limestone region north of Harare is pitted with caves and sinkholes, some filled with water. One of them, "the Sleeping Pool of Sinoia", is scuba paradise; the intense blue of its crystalline water offers a positively spiritual diving experience.

△ Rafting the Zambezi near Victoria Falls

- **Domboshowa rock paintings**
The easiest of several rock art sites to visit, Domboshowa is a granite outcrop whose overhangs were used as a natural canvas by hunter-gatherers as far back as 13,000 years ago. Common motifs are human figures, elephants, hunting scenes and elands (long associated with rain by hunter-gatherers).

- **The Matobo Hills** These "bald heads" emerge on the edge of the Kalahari desert, enclosing a beautifully surreal area dominated by huge granite outcrops and often precariously balanced boulders. The extraordinary landscape has long impressed humans: arch-colonial bad guy Cecil Rhodes chose to be buried atop a rock dubbed World's View, and the hills were sacred for Bushmen, who left fine rock paintings throughout the area. Many depict animals still present today. Among the species you're likely to see in real life are black and white rhinos, zebras and giraffes, large antelopes, and – a rarity elsewhere – leopards. Up above, black eagles are the main attraction among the area's 300-plus bird species.

- **Hwange National Park** Close to the Victoria Falls is the country's largest and most accessible wildlife park, its acacia-studded savanna positively bursting with animals. Elephant herds up to a hundred strong provide the most memorable sight, though there's plenty else, too: sizeable herds of buffaloes and zebras, many giraffes, substantial numbers of predators and prolific birdlife.

- **The Eastern Highlands** Half the eastern border with Mozambique is marked by cloud-draped mountains popular with hikers and horse-riders. Topping 2500m, the highlands hold plenty of botanical interest, and wildlife, not the least of which being birds. Add in waterfalls, rock paintings and elegant colonial-era towns, and you have a great place to explore over a week or more.

Also recommended

- **Harare** Formerly one of sub-Saharan Africa's most prosperous cities, Zimbabwe's capital has suffered badly from the recent economic and political turmoil. Despite this, its markets remain as vibrant as ever, as does its very musical nightlife. The Shona ethnic group dominate, and you'll find their trademark stone sculptures everywhere, including in the excellent National Art Gallery.

- **Chizarira National Park** A remote and magnificent land of dazzling escarpments and endless views. The odds on seeing lions, elephants and otherwise elusive leopards and black rhinos are good.

- **Mana Pools National Park** The changing course of the Zambezi left a series of waterholes that attract a rich variety of wildlife in the dry season. The stars are black rhinos, though you'll also see elephants, buffaloes, big hippo pods and crocodiles, and perhaps lions or a leopard. While game drives are possible, walking around is better, and you can also see the riverside proceedings from a canoe.

- **Lake Mutirikwe National Park** Saddle up a horse and ride off into the bush to see white rhinos.

- **Gonarezhou National Park** Flanking Mozambique in the southeast, this is a ruggedly handsome land of eroded red sandstone cliffs and outcrops, good for big-game viewing in the dry season. Elephants are recovering well from poaching and are easy to see, as are buffaloes, zebras, giraffes and antelopes, hippos and lots of birds.

- **Kwekwe** A gold-mining town between Harare and Bulawayo whose mines may, plausibly enough, have been those of King Solomon. The town has a mining museum, and serves as a base for visiting wildlife reserves where horseback or even elephant-back safaris provide the appeal.

- **Lake Kariba** Created by the damming of the Zambezi, this reservoir was – until pipped by Egypt's Lake Nasser – the world's largest, measuring 220km by 40km. Along its shore are several holiday resorts offering sailing, fishing, water-skiing and – at Matusadona National Park – game viewing by car, boat, canoe, on foot or even from a houseboat.

Festivals

Harare International Festival of the Arts (HIFA) Harare; April The best time to catch Zimbabwe's fast disappearing traditional music, plus groups from neighbouring countries.

INTWASA Bulawayo; Sept Showcase for contemporary art, drama, music and dance, cinema and fashion.

Zimbabwe International Film Festival (ZIFF) Harare, Bulawayo and Chitungwiza; Aug–Sept Workshops, discussions and plenty of screenings, with much Zimbabwean output.

Routes in and out

Zimbabwe's international airports are Harare, Bulawayo and Victoria Falls. There's road transport from all neighbouring countries, including comfortable buses from South Africa. International passenger trains are currently suspended. For hyper-luxurious rail trips from South Africa to Victoria Falls, see Ⓦwww.rovos.co.za.

Zimbabwe online

Zimbabwe Tourism Authority
Ⓦ**www.zimbabwetourism.co.zw**
Mbira: Constraint and Mobility in Shona Society
Ⓦ**www2.kenyon.edu/Projects /Ottenhoff/welcome.htm** An accessible introduction to the art of *mbira* ("thumb piano") playing (among Africa's most delicate sounds), with music clips.
Spirits in Stone
Ⓦ**www.spiritsinstone.com** A vast range of Shona sculptures and other arts, from this commercial gallery.

Books

Paul F. Berliner *The Soul of Mbira: Music and Traditions of the Shona People of Zimbabwe*. Berliner marvellously conveys the mellifluous beauty of *mbira* playing with the quasi-mystical relationship that its players have towards it, and its sound.

Peter Garlake *The Hunter's Vision: The Prehistoric Art of Zimbabwe*. Neolithic eye-candy, albeit mostly in black-and-white.

Martin Meredith *Our Votes, Our Guns: Robert Mugabe and the Tragedy of Zimbabwe*. No doubts where the author stands on this one, as he traces the slow and painful disintegration of post-independence Zimbabwe in the hands of the liberator-turned-kleptocrat.

Alexander McCall Smith *The Girl Who Married a Lion and Other Tales from Africa*. Funny collection of folk tales gathered in Zimbabwe and Botswana; meet clever Hare, stupid Hyena, and the man with a tree growing out of his head.

Anthony and Laura Ponter *Spirits in Stone*. Full-colour coffee-table tome primarily about Shona stone carvings, including substantial sections on Zimbabwean history and culture.

First-Time Africa

The big adventure

Planning your route

Swahili saying, meaning "Have a safe trip"

May the dhow be on top and the waves below

Deciding where to go and what to do in Africa is no easy matter – there's simply so much to choose from. Apart from considerations of climate (see chapter 3) and money (chapter 4), keep the following general advice in mind as you put your dreams into motion:

- **Be flexible** Obviously, the more detail you can pack into an itinerary, the better, but be aware that planning can only go so far. Roads get blocked, transport breaks down, guidebooks slip out of date, and you simply might not like the place that sounded just dandy on paper. In any case, it's always good to know that you can change tack once you're there; often, the best places aren't in the guidebooks at all.
- **Take your time** Don't cram too much into too short a holiday; Africa doesn't work well if rushed, and its myriad attractions are best savoured at your leisure. There's also Africa's "traditionally" slow concept of time to factor in, which – coupled with often dire roads (and transport) – means unexpected delays should, well, be expected. Working in some slack to get acclimatized and cover off-colour days (take a bow, travellers' diarrhoea) is also wise. For independent

chapter 1 | PLANNING YOUR ROUTE

187

travellers, a trip of least three weeks is recommended to begin to grasp the essence of any one country, with a month or more being ideal.

- **Vary your itinerary** Unless you're absolutely hooked on one theme for your trip, it's best to mix and match. Combine mountains and beaches with deserts or rainforests, wildlife with people and culture, cities with rural villages, and you'll come away with a richer and more rounded experience.

Africa in focus

Each of Africa's regions has its own distinctive flavour and mood. Culture, music and food differ enormously between them, as do scenery, wildlife and climate. Even within each region, countries distinguish themselves quite markedly one from another. Although visiting just one country is likely to provide you with far more attractions (and memories) than you could possibly hope to cover, exploring several countries in one go will give you a broader feeling for the land and its people.

Africa's trouble spots

At the time of writing, the following countries were no-go zones for tourists. Be aware that regions immediately bordering them may also be unsafe. For advice about specific areas to avoid in other countries, refer to the travel advisory websites listed on p.418.

Burundi More peaceful than it was, but still unpredictable and potentially dangerous.

Central African Republic Widespread rebel and bandit activity.

Chad Unpredictable; on-off conflict with rebels.

Congo, Democratic Republic Unpredictable; relatively safe in the centre and west, but most of the rest lies under rebel control or has been invaded by countries anxious to grab a share of Congo's bountiful natural resources.

Congo, Republic Unstable; rebel activity.

Ivory Coast Chaotic, unpredictable and partly controlled by rebels; risk of civil war flaring up again.

Somalia Murderous anarchy; no effective government since 1991. However, the internationally unrecognized Republic of Somaliland in the north is safe for travellers.

North Africa

Sandwiched between the Sahara and the Mediterranean, North Africa – which, for purposes of this discussion, includes Egypt, often considered part of the Middle East – boasts a serendipity of inspiring panoramas and is the continent's most visually impressive region. North Africa has it all: shimmering desert wastelands, sensuous sand dunes, gaunt volcanic ranges eroded to their cores, the craggy snow-capped peaks and sheer jaw-dropping grandeur of the Atlas Mountains, the wild Atlantic, the majestic River Nile, and blissful shores, from the wild Atlantic to the fabulous coral reefs of the Red Sea.

Adventurous souls have the Sahara to play with – the world's largest and hottest desert, which stretches right across the continent from the Atlantic to the Red Sea. Short desert escapades can be arranged in all countries, but the most accessible place for a serious desert adventure is Mauritania. Hardly visited by tourists and making virtually no impact on the international media, it's one of the world's least known yet most fascinating countries, one in which one in five of the population remain nomadic. If it's classic dunes you're after, though, Algeria and Libya are best, while for oases of the imagination (palm trees, small lakes, more palm trees), head to Egypt.

Egypt, of course, is unmatched for antiquities, although there are plenty elsewhere, too, including a wealth of well-preserved Roman ruins (particularly in Libya and Tunisia), and remains from the empires of Carthage, Phoenicia and Byzantium. Rock art is another ancient treasure well worth seeking out: the Algerian and Libyan Sahara are rich in Neolithic rock paintings and engravings left thousands of years ago when the desert was green.

North Africa's cities can be just as fascinating, especially when they contain a medina – a labyrinthine, medieval heart, in which getting lost is an unavoidable pleasure. The medinas in Cairo, Tunis, Kairouan and Fès date back over a thousand years, and visiting them can feel as though you've gone back in time. Among their narrow twisting streets, barely wide enough for laden donkeys (or mopeds – watch out), you'll find some of Islam's finest architectural flights of fancy, while the bazaars are sheer paradise for shopaholics, selling anything from Persian-style carpets and perfumes and equally aromatic sweets, to fine filigree jewellery, silver daggers and handmade lutes.

Islam is the main religion of North Africa, although small Jewish communities established long before the Islamic conquest remain to this day, and Egypt has its Copts, who follow an ancient brand of Christianity. In the Maghreb – the "western lands" of Libya, Tunisia, Algeria and Morocco – most people are a blend of Arab and indigenous Berber, but sizeable communities of "pure" Berbers survive, especially in remote and mountainous zones. Morocco's Atlas Mountains are particularly rewarding if you're interested in culture. There, the local Berbers defended themselves in towering fortress-like villages made of sun-baked clay.

North Africa's other indigenous peoples are Egypt's Bedouins, and the Sahara's various nomadic groups, most famously the Tuareg, for whom life would be untenable without their camels. For all of them, hospitality to strangers is deeply ingrained, necessarily so: surviving in such a hostile environment would be impossible without mutual help. The one thing you shouldn't expect to see, though, is the caravan trains of yore: although a handful of relatively short routes are still travelled by caravans, mostly carrying salt, the advent of motor vehicles and ocean-going freighters has put an end to the trans-Saharan trade routes on whose gold, and slaves, many a kingdom and empire was founded. For more on Berbers and Tuareg, see "Tribal Africa" on p.211.

West Africa

In the 1970s and 1980s, West Africa's public persona was – with few exceptions – a sorry one indeed, that of a region of brutal military dictators who raised corruption, and the imaginative use of Switzerland's banking laws, to an art form. Interminable coups d'état, civil wars, repression, crumbling infrastructure, and stark poverty were also the order of the day. Although many of the bad old ways (and kleptocrats) remain, together with an unfair share of roadblocks manned by bribe-seeking cops, things are looking rather better these days, certainly for those nations not directly threatened by the ever-expanding Sahara.

It's all a far cry from medieval times, when the region gave rise to a succession of glorious kingdoms and empires, which reached their (literally) golden age at a time when Europe had yet to stumble upon the Renaissance. Clustered around the Niger, Senegal, Gambia and Volta rivers, the empires' cities – most famously Timbuktu – grew rich on the profits of trans-Saharan trade in gold, slaves and salt. Magnificent earthen mosques are the most impressive reminders of those times, especially along the River Niger, a trip along which is one of the world's classic journeys (see p.199).

Traditional culture has survived well, having been able to adapt to new ways rather than be swept away, and it's this that by and large provides the best reason to visit. The Sahel – the disconsolately dry belt of savanna that flanks the Sahara's southern fringes – is home to the Fulani (or Peuhl) ethnic group, most of them cattle herders. The Fulani's Wodaabé tribe are famed for their celebrations, in which bachelors dress up and pull silly faces to woo the girls; see "Tribal Africa" on p.211. The Sahara, to the north, is the realm of the blue-robed Tuareg, masters of the desert and of the old camel caravans. South of the Sahel is the hot and muggy coastal belt, with its steaming tropical forests, traditional kingdoms surviving as part of modern states, and Vodun religion – which became Voodoo in Haiti, Candomblé in Brazil and Santería in Cuba. Far from featuring Hollywood style zombies and pincushion dolls, Vodun is an intimate and eclectic blend of Catholicism and religious beliefs inherited from the many different tribes that converged on Benin and Togo during slaving times. This part of West Africa has the continent's most vibrant arts-and-crafts traditions, its wooden masks, figures and bronzes – to name but a few – adorning the halls of many an international museum. Equally impressive is West Africa's musical output: the likes of Youssou Ndour, Salif Keita and Cesaria Evora are well known internationally, but it's the traditional genres that can really blow your mind, and a rich array of festivals make it well worthwhile keeping an eye on the calendar as you plan your trip.

Scenically, West Africa's most impressive areas are the Saharan regions of Mali, Niger and Chad, the Guinea highlands, and the laid-back volcanic archipelagos of Cape Verde, and São Tomé and Príncipe. Given the barren climate in the north and high human population densities elsewhere, wildlife interest is limited compared to eastern and southern Africa, but with a bit of patience there's always somewhere worth visiting, and bird-watching is wonderful throughout.

Other than in Cape Verde, Senegal, the Gambia, Ghana and to some extent Mali, tourism is in its infancy, so you can reasonably expect adventures along the way. This is by no means a bad thing, and intrepid travellers willing to escape the niceties (or otherwise) of organized tours will find West Africa an endlessly stimulating place to explore.

Central Africa

Central Africa is completely off the tourist radar. The reason is simple: most of its countries have either been in conflict or under particularly pernicious dictatorships since independence in the 1960s, and the preceding colonial regimes were exceptionally brutal. International news coverage of the region is limited to coup attempts (real or rumoured), civil wars, political assassinations, outbreaks of virulent Ebola fever, and precious little else. It's hardly a coincidence that Joseph Conrad's troubling book about the River Congo was named *The Heart of Darkness*, even though the real darkness – to paraphrase geographer George Kimble – has only ever been our ignorance of it.

In fact, Central Africa truly is the heart of the continent, being the cradle of the Bantu, the broad ethno–linguistic group of peoples that dominates almost all of sub–Saharan Africa. Having mastered the art of iron smelting many millennia ago, they were the first people in sub–Saharan Africa to rely primarily on agriculture. Their success at this led to increased human population which, three or four thousand years ago, prompted the first of many slow migrations that eventually fanned out across virtually the entire continent south of the Sahara.

Important though the Bantu heritage is, the region is even more remarkable for its other indigenous people, the Pygmies (see "Tribal Africa", p.211), whose small physical stature is a physiological adaptation to the rainforest habitat of the Congo River basin. Some Pygmy groups remain in the thickest forests, living lifestyles little changed over the millennia, but many have had to bow to pressure to confirm to modernity and settle down like everyone else. It's a real shame, as their culture is irreplaceable, and musically the Pygmies are giants – their mastery of multipart polyphony, whether in song or through xylophones, transcends any superlatives and is arguably the most beautiful human sound on earth.

At present, tourists are pretty much restricted to Gabon and Cameroon, in both of which you can – if you're dedicated and tactful – get to know Pygmy groups, and a wealth of other local cultures. For the trickle of tourists that come here, the main attractions are in the amazingly green, rainforest-clad highlands, which happen to be fantastic places for tracking gorillas and chimpanzees. The beaches aren't half bad either, so if you're looking for eco-tourism far away from the crowds, either country is seriously worth considering.

The region's other countries all feature in some way or another in the "don't go" lists of official travel advisories. The most accessible are Equatorial Guinea (a small, oil-rich nation suffering under a particularly nasty dictatorship) and the western parts of the Democratic Republic of Congo. In 2006, the latter finally acknowledged its name by holding its very first multiparty elections, but government control over much of this enormous country is non-existent, and war is a daily reality in the east and in many border regions. Other than Kinshasa's celebrated nightlife, the main attraction is the Congo Basin rainforest, second only to the Amazon in scope and species diversity.

East Africa

In some ways, East Africa doesn't fit the African archetype as snugly as West Africa does. For a start, getting around is far less daunting as there's more asphalt on the roads, tourist facilities are well developed, and the overall travelling experience is smoother. In fact, East Africa can feel disappointingly Westernized at first, but if you venture off the main circuits you'll find plenty that survived the predations of colonists and missionaries. You're also guaranteed to find the wild Africa of your dreams: entire animal encyclopedias thriving in dozens of national parks and game reserves. With world-famous wildlife areas such as the Serengeti and Maasai Mara, East Africa is a major eco-tourist destination. Wild beasts aside, fine beaches are another big draw, where the warm equatorial waters of the Indian Ocean lap a largely unspoiled coastline scattered with mangroves, palm-backed beaches and multicoloured coral reefs rated highly by divers and snorkellers.

Inland, landscapes vary from arid deserts in the north to lush equatorial cloud forests and even high-altitude alpine tundra. Cutting East Africa in two is the Great Rift Valley, an ever-expanding gash in the earth's crust that stretches between Lebanon and Mozambique, and which has created varied and often dramatic scenery. Millions of years ago, the Rift Valley saw the birth of a number of giant volcanoes, including Mount Kenya and Mount Kilimanjaro, both of which can be climbed. To the west, in Uganda and Rwanda, the savanna gives way to the forests of the Virunga and Rwenzori Mountains, home to Dian Fossey's celebrated mountain gorillas. Chimpanzees can most easily be seen in Uganda, and in western Tanzania, both part of Africa's "Great Lakes" region. The biggest lake is Lake Victoria, the main source of the White Nile.

Culturally, the region has plenty of interest, from central Tanzania's ancient rock paintings to a chain of ruined mercantile towns on the coast that recall the heyday of the Swahili civilization, which once traded as far afield as China. The coast also contains many a reminder of the Zanzibar-dominated slave trade, while the hinterland – "upcountry" in local parlance – is home to some of Africa's most famous (and certainly most photographed) tribes, including the Maasai, Samburu and Turkana. There are several hundred tribes in all, but the ghastly Rwanda Genocide, and smaller-scale but no less horrific massacres in neighbouring Burundi, took place in a region that only contains three. Rwanda has recovered remarkably well (although the scars will remain for many years to come), but Burundi has yet to fully emerge from the turmoil.

The Horn of Africa

The Horn of Africa is East Africa's poorer relation, better known for famine and war than for tourism. It's not helped by being difficult to access overland from elsewhere in Africa: crossing Sudan poses lively risks, southern Ethiopia is prone to banditry, too, and Somalia is an absolute disaster. Independent travel isn't a problem inside Ethiopia, but can be awkward in Eritrea and Djibouti, where most tourists come on speciality package tours. For all that, this is a fascinating corner of the continent to explore.

Barely 30km from Djibouti, at the entrance to the Red Sea, is Yemen and the Arabian Peninsula. The Arab influence can plainly be seen in the physical features of the people of the Horn of Africa, yet the region's inhabitants have long resisted outside domination. Culturally, the Horn remains quite diverse, especially in the southern parts of Ethiopia and Sudan, which are home to some of Africa's most traditional peoples, the Nuer and Dinka among them – see "Tribal Africa" on p.211. Ethiopia is the only African country never to have been colonized (though briefly occupied by Italy), and its own brand of Orthodox Christianity – established in the fourth century – survived repeated attempts at Islamic conquest.

The most popular destination for tourists is Ethiopia, offering a good range of sights and activities, from marvelling at the Blue Nile Falls to visiting ancient rock-hewn churches, lapping up views of the Great Rift Valley, and great cuisine. Eritrea is not without its charms either, including Orthodox churches and monasteries, chilly mountains, and the devilishly hot and harshly beautiful Danakil desert. Djibouti's landscapes are if anything even more elemental, having been formed by the ongoing rupture of the Great Rift Valley, that will eventually see the Horn of Africa and East Africa forming an island. All of this is in stark contrast to the multicoloured riches teeming beneath the surface of the Red Sea, most easily accessible from Djibouti and Eritrea.

Southern Africa

Southern Africa offers an amazing variety of attractions and land-scapes, from Lesotho's quasi-Siberian highlands (where you can even go skiing in winter) to the enormous dunes of the Kalahari and Namib deserts. There's excellent wildlife viewing, great beaches, and much historical interest too.

On the wildlife front, southern Africa's national parks and reserves rival those of East Africa, and have the advantage of being considerably cheaper to visit. Among the stars are South Africa's Kruger National Park, Botswana's Chobe National Park and the Okavango Delta, and Namibia's Etosha Pan. The lions, suricats and red dunes of the Kalahari are well known from documentaries, but an even more amazing desert is Namibia's Namib, home to the world's tallest sand dunes and the extraordinary *Welwitschia mirabilis*, a bizarre two-leafed aloe that can live for up to 2000 years. The River Zambezi is also a great place for animals, best seen from a boat, but the river is most famous for its thundering cataract – the Victoria Falls. The river either side of the falls, accessible from both Zambia and Zimbabwe, is the focus for a welter of adventure sports, from bungee jumping and white-water rafting to helicopter rides. Other activities in the region include stupendous hiking in South Africa's Drakensberg and in the mountainous kingdom of Lesotho, where pony-trekking is also a big deal.

For classic beach holidays, the Indian Ocean is the place, especially in Mozambique, and on the islands of Madagascar and the Comoros. The latter are completely different in feel to the mainland, with their inhabitants and cultures blending African with French, Arabian and East Asian elements. The Comoros also has a huge active volcano to explore, while Madagascar is one of the most biodiverse nations on earth – new species are discovered all the time, and eco-tourism is a major attraction.

Scuba-diving and snorkelling are popular attractions through-out the region, including on Lake Malawi. Historical interest is provided by remains from missionary and colonial times, and the slave trade. Unfortunately, the rugged Atlantic coast is too cold for swimming, but that doesn't mean it's without attraction, from gigantic seal colonies and the Namib's sand dunes tumbling into the ocean, to whale and dolphin spotting, and even diving with sharks.

Culturally, the region's most emblematic peoples are the Zulu – whose militaristic nineteenth-century empire spread havoc right across the region – and the Bushmen, or San. The latter are south-ern Africa's original inhabitants, and were hunter-gatherers until recently (see "Tribal Africa", p.211). The most easily seen aspect of Bushman culture, perfectly expressing their profound attachment to the land, is a wealth of shamanistic rock paintings and engravings found across the region. These days, however, few if any Bushman groups still engage in hunter-gathering, and indeed many have been evicted from their traditional lands.

Their tragedy can be explained in part by the search for diamonds, which has helpd assure the prosperity of South Africa, Namibia and Botswana. In consequence, those three countries are also Africa's most Westernized, and have well-developed infrastructures. This is great for minimizing culture shock, but can be disappointing. Zambia, on the other hand, has a healthy sense of tribalism and peaceful coexistence, making it one of Africa's most rewarding cultural destinations. To the east, Malawi is a gem of a place that combines wonderful wildlife viewing, great hiking and lakeside activities with a famously friendly welcome. West of Zambia, Angola is a good place for venturing where few other tourists have been: after decades of war, the country has made great strides towards regaining a semblance of normality.

North Africa to West Africa Crossing the Sahara can be a life-changing experience, but it's not a challenge to be treated lightly; see below.

North Africa to East Africa Conflict in Sudan has blocked this route for decades, but there are a handful of travellers – almost all in their own vehicles – who come this way each year. Ethiopia is the safest route, though there's a risk of banditry in zones bordering Sudan and Kenya, which you'd have to cross. With the peace accord in southern Sudan still holding, and some hope that the conflict with the Lord's Resistance Army in northern Uganda may soon also come to an end, it's worth keeping tabs on the Sudanese route, too.

Across the Maghreb Overlanding across North Africa is currently impossible thanks to frosty relations between Morocco and Algeria.

West Africa to East Africa Central Africa's various no-go zones have prevented east–west overland travel for years. For all but the most foolhardy, Cameroon or Gabon are the farthest east you can travel by land.

East Africa to Southern Africa Starting in Kenya or Uganda, it's easy and safe to travel overland to Southern Africa, whether by public transport, in your own vehicle, or as part of an overland truck tour (see p.203). The usual route passes though Malawi and Zambia via the Victoria Falls. Crossing Mozambique from Tanzania is possible in the dry season.

West Africa to Southern Africa Overlanding across the equatorial forests and swamps south of Gabon is extremely slow going and decidedly adventurous. The main impediment, other than patchy transport, is the situation in either of the Congos, whose borders may be closed. Once you're in Angola, you shouldn't have any trouble continuing down to South Africa.

Classic journeys

Exactly what makes a journey a classic is difficult to say. Sometimes, the destination makes it all worthwhile, even if it's just the name: "the road to Timbuktu" comes wrapped in a haze of exoticism, even though the place itself isn't all that special. Your mode of transport can do the trick, too: the train rides on pp.334–335 all make for memorable journeys. But if you're looking for that certain "wow" factor, any of the following should fit the bill.

Across the Sahara

Even though some of the romance (and danger) has been removed by the advent of GPS, crossing the Sahara – easiest from north to south – is a classic adventure. The usual way to get across these days is by four-wheel-drive, a mode of transport that purists scoff at. Motorbikes, for their part, are more manoeuvrable, easier to take off track, and give more miles to the gallon (bring an external fuel tank). But the problem with any kind of motorized transport is that high speed makes it easy to forgo encounters with people along way (there *are* people to be met in the Sahara, even in its remotest corners), and to miss all the little details that make desert travel so magical: the bugs in the middle of nowhere, tiny miraculous plants pushing up from the sand, the sight of sleeping snakes given away by coils of sand, even the smell of the place.

Along the western route from Morocco to Senegal via Mauritania, you might consider cycling – not as nutty as it sounds (it provided this author's introduction to Africa), especially now that the road is asphalt all the way. The days of vast camel trains are a thing of the past, though, and even the famously traditional Tuareg have taken to driving vehicles. While we don't recommend that first-timers try crossing the desert by camel, it is possible. Just be sure you don't fall for the old trick of buying a camel while it's seated (to discover, after paying, that it's a leg short), and don't expect to ride them all the way, either – your buttocks won't let you! One of the things the desert teaches is that anything is possible – even walking across the Sahara unaided by man, beast or machine other than a sail-powered skip (read Geoffrey Howard's *Wheelbarrow Across the Sahara*, out of print but not hard to find secondhand).

In spite of the vast open spaces and spindly "roads" marked on maps (which are likely to be dozens of tyre tracks spreading out over kilometres, and which disappear after sand storms), most trans-Saharan routes are closed to tourists, certainly if you're heeding official advice. Banditry and rebellions in border areas are the usual culprits, and currently affect all routes other than the Morocco–Senegal road. A chunk of that route passes close to the Atlantic, but the land itself remains hot, dry and desolate, and scenically rather monotonous once you're over the Atlas Mountains. If you're prepared to face a little more risk (tourists have been kidnapped in recent years), Algeria–Niger is the least dangerous of the other routes, and a most beautiful one it is too, taking you straight through the heart of the world's largest desert.

The security situation regarding all the routes connecting Algeria and Libya with Mali, Niger or Chad changes frequently, while the eastern routes that pass through western Sudan are both dangerous and likely to be bureaucratically impassible. In a region whose inhabitants are naturally nomadic, whether they travel by camel or in stolen cars, gauging the risks is not an exact science. The best source of up-to-date advice is Chris Scott's Sahara Overland website (Ⓦ www.sahara-overland .com); his book of the same name is invaluable on the ground. For more specialized queries, ask the members of the 153 Club (Ⓦwww .the153club.org), an informal Saharan travellers' group named after the number of Michelin's old northwestern Africa map. Lastly, heed common sense: don't go in summer, when temperatures top fifty degrees in the shade.

The River Niger

Following a river from start to end has an irresistible logic to it, one that has provided many a travel writer with the perfect narrative thread. For real adventure, there's nothing to beat the River Niger, whose 4200-kilometre journey takes it through all of West Africa's vegetational

The N'srani

Everyone in Africa has a special word for white folk. In North Africa it's N'srani, a word deriving from Nazareth, and denoting a Christian. N'srani, particularly crazy ones on bicycles, are much loved by officials, especially in the back of beyond.

I'd been stopped at one of many military roadblocks in the Western Sahara, and after an hour of idle questioning was escorted into town to repeat my story all over again in front of the Commissaire. To be fair, the motive I gave for being there – wanting to cycle across the Sahara – certainly gave them grounds for suspicion.

Once at the barracks, I was subjected to half an hour of interrogation by a fat and heavily bearded gentleman, who sat sweating behind a typewriter throughout. Using one finger, he laboriously thumped out my details on a waxed sheet of stencil paper, as I stood in front of his desk like a naughty schoolboy. At first, the questions were perfectly reasonable: things like where I was going, where I'd been, and why on earth I was cycling rather than driving. After a while, though, the questions took a more surreal turn. My mother's nationality (Lebanese) was fair game, and her maiden name might possibly have been an official requirement, too, but the colour of her eyes? And was she blonde?

"Do you love your mother?" he asked, all the time assiduously typing out my responses with his finger. "Ah, that is good. Very good."

At last, he stood up, shook my hand (very firmly and painfully), and said: "You may go now, N'srani." He even allowed himself a glimmer of a smile. Perhaps the Nazarene was not the devil after all? But the oddest thing was that, as I was leaving the office, I caught a glimpse of the sheet he had been typing on. What I had assumed to be my painstakingly transcribed answers was in fact gibberish – he'd just been going through the motions of typing without ever intending to file a report. Out in the middle of nowhere, I guess grilling a nutty N'srani is about as good as it gets for breaking the boredom.

–Jens Finke

△ Even trucks make it onto the Niger

zones, from rainforest and savanna to the dusty heart of the Sahara, then back out through increasingly tropical terrain to Nigeria's oil-rich but troubled Niger Delta.

You could theoretically follow the river all the way from its source in Guinea, but much easier – and more feasible if you don't have mounds of time, or money to spend having your own pirogue built – is to sample the great river in Mali. Here there are cargo-carrying pirogues and larger pinasses that are used as taxis by locals, and ferries that operate towards the end of the year when water levels are at their highest. Along the way, you can stop by at Timbuktu, admire the amazing medieval mosques at various intervals, dance with Tuareg at a local festival, and get to know local fishermen and their spirit cults. From Gao (the farthest point reachable by ferry in Mali), you can continue in a succession of pirogues across the border to Niamey in Niger, but sailing beyond there to the river's outlet in the Gulf of Benin is unlikely, as the road network is good.

The River Nile

At 6718km, the Nile is the world's longest river. In colonial times, controlling its source (and therefore its life-giving floods) was deemed essential for securing Egypt. The problem for the Europeans was that although they'd found the source of the Blue

Nile, Ethiopia's Lake Tana, in 1622, they remained utterly ignorant as to the source of the greater part of the river's flow, the White Nile. Their quest was not helped by the Greek "Father of History", Herodotus, having mistakenly stated that West Africa's Niger was a branch of the Nile. Pliny the Elder compounded the confusion by writing that the Nile gushed forth not far from the Atlantic Ocean. In the nineteenth century, the mystery of the Nile's source attracted dozens of competing expeditions, mostly travelling overland from East Africa. Only in 1863 was the question finally settled, when John Hanning Speke and James Grant sailed down the Nile from Lake Victoria to Khartoum.

The easiest way of getting to know the Egyptian Nile is to buy a place on a Nile cruise – not so much Agatha Christie in style these days as package-tour kitsch, but fun nonetheless, and a great way of seeing Upper Egypt's most celebrated treasures, including Karnak and the Valley of the Kings. Budget travellers wanting to travel on the river, rather than beside it on buses and trains, will need plenty of time for catching a string of feluccas, from the river's delta near Alexandria all the way to Aswan, from where there are packed local ferries into Sudan. Onward ferries, and a train, link up to Khartoum, at the confluence of the White and Blue Niles.

Khartoum is as far upriver as you can safely head, given that southern Sudan is still out of bounds (for following the White Nile) and the Ethiopian border region (for the Blue Nile) prone to banditry. Lake Tana can easily be visited once you're in Ethiopia, and Lake Victoria – the main body of water from which the White Nile flows – is accessible from Kenya, Tanzania and Uganda. To get to the uttermost source of the Nile, you'll have to venture into Rwanda's Nyungwe forest (a not unpleasant prospect, in fact – it's a wonderful place), but don't expect anything more than a plaque beside a trickle, if that.

Dhow-hopping

Cradled by the monsoon winds, East Africa and the Horn of Africa have been trading with the outside world for at least five millennia. It was the Persians who introduced the elegant lateen-rigged vessels that became the region's maritime emblem: the dhow.

Sadly, the use of dhows as marine packhorses is gradually coming to an end, but, ever-mindful of tourist tastes, local entrepreneurs in popular beach areas are likely to offer dhow trips. They're well worth doing: there's nothing quite like a floating sundowner, cocktail in hand, for sheer lazy relaxation. For more adventurous souls, consider long-distance dhow-hopping. It's theoretically possible to catch a succession of dhows all the way from Egypt to Madagascar or the Comoros, hugging the coastlines of Sudan, Eritrea and Djibouti, Somalia (probably not such a great idea given the risk of pirates), Kenya, Tanzania and northern Mozambique, passing by a succession of ruined medieval cities along the way, and the enchanting islands of Lamu and Zanzibar, once key ports of call for the dhow trade.

You'll need plenty of time for dhow-hopping (months rather than weeks), not so much for the sailing itself, but for arranging things. The authorities are rarely happy with the thought of tourists venturing out on dhows, primarily for reasons of safety (there are no real marine rescue services in the region), and they may well put up a series of bureaucratic hurdles, for which the fine art of negotiation, and knowing when to proffer a little baksheesh (treated as a present, rather than a bribe) is a definite advantage. And you'll have to repeat the shenanigans every time you switch boats.

Lastly, don't expect any kind of luxury. Toilet facilities, for example, are likely to be cantilevered contraptions slung over the vessel's side.

Crossing the continent overland

"Cairo to Cape Town": the phrase exerts a magnetic pull on romantic minds, recalling arch-colonialist Cecil Rhodes, whose dream of a trans-continental railway passing entirely through British territory was never realized. For travellers, the journey between these two great cities is generally tackled from north to south, but at present insecurity in southern Sudan puts paid to any such plans unless you're willing to cheat with a flight or two, or take a detour via Ethiopia into Kenya – though note the latter carries a risk of banditry in both the Sudan/Ethiopia and Ethiopia/Kenya border regions. Keep an eye on the situation in southern Sudan though: if the current peace accord holds, Cairo to Cape Town via Sudan and Kenya could once again become a tantalizing proposition.

For now, the good news is that there is another trans-African route. The Western Sahara and Angola, both of which were barred to visitors because of long-running conflicts, have reopened to transit, so a trans-African trip from Morocco to South Africa via West

Africa is possible, so long as the borders of either of the Congolese republics are open. For information on crossing the Sahara in its central regions, see p.198.

For travellers of a youthful disposition, the worry and bureaucratic tangles involved in planning epic overland trips can be avoided completely by buying a place on an overland tour. These – generally in converted army trucks – travel along all or part of the way from the UK to West Africa via Morocco and the Western Sahara, and between Nairobi and Cape Town. The connection between West and East Africa (generally Cameroon and either Kenya or Uganda) is by plane. Journeys last from a few weeks to several months, depending on the route, and while they're often superficial and rather hurried affairs, they do provide a handy means of getting an overall feel for the place, and crossing off the major attractions. Be aware that these truck tours can be dominated by petulant 20-something party animals in road-trip mentality, so expect booze to feature prominently among the activities.

Travel themes

Sizzling on the fine golden sands of a tropical beach while listening to the wind caress the fronds of the coconut palms is indubitably the stuff of dreams, as is slinking into the turquoise expanse as dhows glide by beyond the reef. But really, you're not coming all the way to Africa just to do that, are you? Africa has almost as many attractions as there are desires, and a good deal are just as hedonistic as lounging around on a beach, even if they require a little more effort to get to. The following themes should get the ball rolling.

Beaches

So, the minute I suggest you get off the beach, here's some advice about choosing one in the first place. In short, Africa's most popular beach areas are along the Mediterranean (especially Tunisia), on Egypt's Sinai Peninsula, all along the Indian Ocean from Kenya to Mozambique, and on the Indian Ocean islands of the Comoros and Madagascar. West Africa, including Morocco's Atlantic coastline, also has wonderful beaches, but a potential problem is strong ocean currents, so look for beaches in sheltered locations. Bearing that in mind, it's hard to find fault with Morocco, Senegal, Cape Verde or Guinea-Bissau, the latter two being especially blissful. Around Africa's bulge, Ghana is a budding tropical beach destination and benefits from plenty of cultural interest besides, including a string of European coastal fortresses from slaving days. South of central Angola, the Atlantic becomes too cold for swimming thanks to an Antarctic ocean current.

Just as important as geographic location is the style of holiday you have in mind. In some resorts you'll be sharing paradise with hundreds or even thousands of holiday-makers, together with noisy jet-skis, power boats, clingy "beach boys" selling trinkets (or romance), and all the rest. In others, you'll find "all-inclusive" resorts catering exclusively to nationals of one or another European country, with nary a whiff of Africa within their hermetically sealed confines. Other places are set up for overland truck tours: expect to meet plenty of dazed, dreadlocked and sunburnt ravers at those. But by and large, most "resorts" are both low-key and low-rise, with accommodation in thatched bungalows being particularly common.

Lastly, don't forget that when to go is also important. Although the prospect of a cut-price, off-season holiday can be alluring, you're riding your luck when it comes to the weather. For example, although the southern Mediterranean enjoys mild winters by European standards, it's perfectly possible to fall on an unlucky streak and have two weeks of cloud and drizzle, or even snow, as seems to happen with northern Tunisia's shores once every few decades. Equally, in tropical and equatorial regions the rainy seasons and months immediately around them are best avoided – not so much to stay dry, but because the combination of heat, extreme humidity and mosquitoes can easily turn a holiday into a trial.

Diving and snorkelling

Corals thrive in warm, shallow waters, and are a strange mix of animal and mineral: the coral we know as decoration is actually an external skeleton excreted by microscopic animals called polyps. Growing together in colonies of billions, the polyps eventually form reefs, providing a perfect habitat for all kinds of marine life, from sea cucumbers, sea stars and crustaceans, to a dazzling and colourful array of fish, dolphins, sea turtles and whales.

Caressed and nourished by the warm South Equatorial Current, the coral reefs fringing Africa's Indian Ocean coastline offer exhilarating scuba-diving and snorkelling, with an abundance of colourful and sometimes heart-stopping marine life to be seen within a short boat ride of the beaches. Scuba-diving is most spectacular off Pemba on Zanzibar, around Tanzania's Mafia Island, off northern Mozambique, and around the Comoros Islands. On the Atlantic side, Cape Verde also has a good reputation, particularly for wrecks, while for many the Red Sea reefs accessible from Egypt, Eritrea and Djibouti are among the world's best. For something different, Lake Malawi (Lake Nyasa) has both stunning scenery and hundreds of colourful species of fish, most of them unique, and Zimbabwe and South Africa both have diveable sink holes. Diving in the Mediterranean (specifically Tunisia) is possible but coral cover isn't a patch on the Indian Ocean or Red Sea.

All these places have dive centres that offer diving courses accredited by PADI – the Professional Association of Diving Instructors (Ⓦ www.padi.com). PADI accreditation doesn't guarantee safety or quality, but does set minimum standards for courses. The standard one for beginners is a four- or five-day Open Water course, which can be followed up with a three- to five-day Advanced Open Water course. If you're not sure whether diving is your thing, most centres offer single or double dive tasters. Full details of the courses, and a list of accredited dive schools, are given on PADI's website. The centres have all the equipment you need, but if you're already experienced, bring optional stuff like dive computers, as they're rarely found locally.

If the idea (or cost) of scuba-diving scares you, snorkelling is an excellent and cheap alternative. You also have more reefs to choose from, as the shallower corals unsuitable for diving are just perfect for snorkellers. They're often closer to shore, too, sometimes within wading distance. If you plan to do a lot of snorkelling, you'll save money by bringing your own mask, snorkel and flippers.

Useful websites include Ⓦ www.scubalinx.com, which keeps seemingly accurate tallies of user feedback on most of Africa's dive centres, ranked differently according to various criteria; and Ⓦ www .scuba-search.com, a handy search engine. Two recommended books for snorkellers as well as divers, despite being out of date (1993), are Anton Koornhof's *The Dive Sites of East Africa*, and the same author's *The Dive Sites of South Africa*. Both are beautifully illustrated, and contain thoughtful sections on environmental matters. The definitive guide to the Red Sea is Robert Myers' *Coral Reef Guide: Red Sea*, up to date and stuffed with wonderful photographs. Alternatively, pick up the *Globetrotter Dive Guide: The Red Sea* by Guy Buckles, which features over 125 diving and snorkelling sites, and has information on tourist practicalities.

Dolphin and whale spotting

If you're exceptionally lucky, migrating whales can be seen – or more often heard singing – when you're diving in the Indian Ocean towards the end of the year, but the best place to see them is in South Africa, either from the southern shoreline or from a boat. Dolphins can be seen throughout the year around much of the continent; organized dolphin tours are big business in South Africa and Zanzibar (Tanzania), but think twice about joining dolphins for a swim: the long-term effects of having tourists leap into their lives day after day remain unknown.

Wildlife safaris

For many visitors, Africa south of the Sahara *is* wildlife. Most countries here have at least a handful of parks and reserves worth visiting, and some – especially in eastern and southern Africa – will spoil you rotten. Chapter 12 gives an overview of what to expect in each region, and also describes the many different styles of safari that are available, from traditional game drives to seeing it all on horseback, or even from an elephant.

Primate tracking

Coming face to face with chimpanzees and gorillas can be an intensely moving experience. Except for Gambia and Gabon, an hour spent with the great apes doesn't come cheap, however reckon on several hundred dollars all counted. The best places for tracking these and other primates are mentioned on pp.362–363.

Dian Fossey's *Gorillas in the Mist*, and any of Jane Goodall's many books on chimpanzees, make good reading. The most authoritative websites are ⓦwww.janegoodall.org and ⓦwww.gorillafund.org.

Bird-watching

Any way you care to look at it, birding in Africa is a complete thrill, whether it's for sheer numbers, species counts, vast flocks of winter migrants, or catching glimpses of rare species. Almost two and a half thousand species have been recorded, more than half of which are found nowhere else, and a good proportion of those are locally endemic, too, meaning their range is limited to one particular forest or mountain range. At the best places, spotting four hundred species a week is actually nothing special.

The best time is from November to March, when resident species are joined by Eurasian migrants. Recommending regions or countries without being unfair to others is quite impossible, as virtually every African country has its own special highlights, so the following list is an unavoidably partial selection. The best all-round African bird-watching resource, with plenty of onward links and book recommendations, is ⓦ www.africanbirdclub.org. To find fellow bird freaks, point your browser to ⓦ www.birdingpal.com or join the discussions at the uk.rec.birdwatching newsgroup.

- **Parc National du Banc d'Arguin, Mauritania** Halfway down the western Sahara, Arguin Island and its sand banks form a huge sanctuary for birds crossing the desert; life is so good that over two million of them see no reason to fly further and spend the winter there.
- **Parc National des Oiseaux de Djoudj, Senegal** An extensive wetland paradise in the delta of the River Senegal, this is the first stop for wintering migrants after crossing the Sahara.
- **The Gambia** A favourite with British birders, this is waterfowl territory, and also a great place for birds of prey in winter.
- **Bale Mountain National Park, Ethiopia** Deep in the Ethiopian Highlands, Bale boasts a range of habitats, including high-altitude alpine plateaus whose denizens include the Abyssinian longclaw and endemic Roguet's rail.
- **Murchison Falls National Park, Uganda** Offers virtually guaranteed sightings of many a birder's favourite, the shoebill stork.
- **Great Rift Valley, East Africa** The Rift Valley lakes are home to the world's largest populations of flamingo, both greater and lesser. Lake Natron (Tanzania) and the adjacent Lake Magadi (Kenya), both caustic cauldrons of soda set amid blistering desert landscapes, are favoured nesting grounds, but the flocks are at their most impressive in the algae-rich waters of lakes Baringo, Bogoria and Nakuru in Kenya, and Manyara in Tanzania.
- **East African Arc** This chain of ancient granite mountains, for the most part cloaked in forest, stretches from southern Kenya's Taita Hills to Tanzania's Southern Highlands. The mountains' isolation from one another has fostered the evolution of dozens of unique bird species.

- **A'Kagera National Park, Rwanda** There are over five hundred species, including shoebills, to look out for here, plus profuse lake-loving birdlife and several hundred more species in the Nyungwe Forest National Park.
- **Caprivi Strip, Namibia** This narrow snaking patchwork of woodland, swamps, marshes and rivers is Namibia's only really green area, and home to most of the country's 630 bird species.
- **Great Limpopo Transfrontier Park** Comprising South Africa's Kruger National Park and several wildlife areas in Mozambique, the park has a species count topping five hundred, a third of which are rare or otherwise endangered.
- **South Africa** The muddy, marshy estuaries along South Africa's remote and windswept west coast are an avian magnet, attracting wintering migrants from as far away as the Arctic. The shoreline off Cape Town is hugely inspiring, too, with around four hundred species, including penguins, petrels and other hardy Antarctic survivors.

Trekking, hiking and mountaineering

Hiking gives you unparalleled contact with local people and nature. As this is Africa, nature could mean anything from orchid meadows and flower-strewn hills to buffaloes furious at being disturbed, or even lions. Still, rest assured that the chance of your number being called by a beast is very slim indeed, especially as the most dangerous animals tend to be tucked safely away in national parks and reserves. Regulations in those areas mean that you're generally accompanied by a guide or an armed ranger when hiking, assuming it's allowed at all. Some of the best places for seeing wildlife as you foot it around are on pp.368–369.

As to hiking outside protected areas, some countries are easier than others. Across much of South Africa, fences limit walkers to roadside verges, while the mountainous kingdom of Lesotho – entirely surrounded by South Africa – has virtually no fences at all, making for some of the finest hiking on the continent. There are other things to consider, too: while traipsing around the Congo Basin's equatorial rainforest can be a mud-caked endurance test complete with endless rounds of tsetse fly-swatting, fending off clouds of hungry mosquitoes and burning off blood-sucking leeches, you can forget it all if you choose a highland region instead, for cooler weather, better views, and much better odds on actually enjoying yourself.

While day-long treks are possible, extending walks over several days can give you an extraordinary sense of freedom, and is also an ideal way of breaking the ice with locals, many of whom (rightly) assume that most tourists are incapable of walking much further than from a hotel to a beach. Of course, what you might consider an impressive daily tally will probably be peanuts to the locals, but they'll be too polite to tell you. Particularly enjoyable areas for long-distance walks are Morocco's Atlas Mountains; the Drakensberg in Lesotho and South Africa; Tanzania's East African Arc mountains (Udzungwa and Kitulo national parks in particular); the Virunga Mountains and Nyungwe Forest in Rwanda; Dogon country in Mali; Malawi's Nyika Plateau; the Ethiopian Highlands; Cape Verde's volcanic peaks; and the cool Namib desert.

You don't need rock-climbing skills to scale Africa's highest peaks – Tanzania's Kilimanjaro (Africa's highest at 5891m) and Mount Meru (4566m), Mount Kenya (5199m), Rwanda's Virunga volcanoes (reaching 4519m), Mount Toubkal (4167m) in Morocco's Atlas Mountains, and Ras Deshen (4500m) in Ethiopia's Simien Mountains. But climbing any of these, with the exception of Ras Deshen, requires a heap of money to cover park fees, porters and guides, supplies and equipment; a six-day attempt on Kilimanjaro will cost no less than $1000 per person. The fact that scaling these mountains requires no real expertise other than a good level of fitness has also led to the dangerous misconception that they're somehow easy.

If you walk faster...

The longest distance I ever walked was in the desert west of Kenya's Lake Turkana, when, with money and supplies almost exhausted, and a broken promise from a minivan driver to pick us up from what had really been a lakeshore paradise, my friend and I hired a young man to guide us to back to the nearest town. We left after sunset, with no real idea of how far we'd have to walk. Inevitably, thighs, calves and feet soon began to complain, and gradually a monotonous refrain took hold. Every half hour or so, one of us would ask Alfred, our (drunken) guide, how far we still had to go. "Not far," he'd say, pointing just over the moonlit horizon.

Over low dunes, bushes and dried river beds we stumbled – again the same questions, again the same replies. Eventually, perhaps eight or nine hours into our hike and with his flask of *changaa* firewater long since emptied, Alfred began to tire of our constant complaints. Once again we asked our question, and this time he snapped, "It is less if you walk more quickly!" Einstein would have been proud. When we finally arrived, 55km and thirteen hours later, my friend and I were half dead, and even Alfred, we thought, looked a little the worse for wear. We paid him and bade farewell over a cup of sickly sweet tea. He turned around and promptly set off back home – walking more quickly.

– Jens Finke

They're not. Altitude sickness on Kilimanjaro alone claims the lives of about a dozen hikers each year. The golden rule is to take your time, even if it means shelling out more for additional days.

Adventure sports

No matter what kind of weird and wonderful activity tickles your fancy, chances are you'll be able to do it in South Africa. The other focus for adventure sports is the Victoria Falls area on the Zambezi River, accessible from both Zambia and Zimbabwe. The following are just a selection of what's on offer:

- **Abseiling (rappelling)** South Africa has loads of sites and companies, and Swaziland's not bad either, but the biggest thrills are in Lesotho (for the world's longest commercial abseil, at 204m) and at the Victoria Falls.
- **Bungee jumping** When it comes to bouncing up and down on the end of a rubbery tether, South Africa's Bloukrans Bridge jump is the world's longest, but the leap from Victoria Falls Bridge tops it for location, and you can also go gorge swinging there – a stomach-turning variant on the theme. Uganda's Bujagali Falls jump over the Nile is good, too, and Kenya has inched into the arena with a jump over the Tana River. There are other sites in Egypt's Sinai.
- **The Desert Cup (Marathon of the Sands)** An annual exercise in foot-slogging, toe-blistering pain somewhere deep in the Sahara (the location varies). It's not a sissy 42-kilometre affair either, instead involving anything up to 200km and seven days, lugging along your own food and gear. Full details on Ⓦ www.darbaroud.com.
- **Microlighting** Gliding around in an microlight gives you a whole new outlook on life. South Africa has several centres set up for tourists; Victoria Falls aren't to be outdone either.
- **Shark diving (in a cage)** Another one from those barmy South Africans.
- **Sky-diving** One for South Africa.
- **Surfing** Morocco and South Africa are the market leaders here, but for good old-fashioned long boarding, head to chilled out Cape Verde. Ghana and Mozambique can also be good. Ⓦ www.globalsurfers .com covers the lot.
- **White-water rafting** Morocco's Oum er Rbia river is the place in North Africa. South of the Sahara, Victoria Falls is the biggie, and there are good sites in South Africa, on the Nile in Uganda, on the remote Omo River in Ethiopia, in Kenya (the Tana River), and Lesotho.

- **Zorbing** What's Zorbing? Rolling down a hill inside a giant transparent ball, that's what. The Zorb, a Kiwi invention, made its South African debut in 2005.

Tribal Africa

Africa's greatest wealth is its culture. The continent's diversity in terms of beliefs, music and ways of life is staggering, although European colonization, ongoing attempts by missionaries to save the locals from damnation, and other effects of globalization have changed the face of many societies beyond recognition. The most visible traditions, things like dress and architecture, have largely been discarded, but other elements remain; in West Africa especially, musical traditions have morphed effortlessly into contemporary genres, while arts and crafts – of which woodcarving is the most celebrated form – have also adapted to modern tastes.

While tribal encounters feature prominently in tour brochures, relatively few offer genuinely respectful and edifying experiences. If the words "primitive" or "stone age" appear in the blurb, chances are that the experience will be uncomfortably voyeuristic, one where the most visible aspects of culture, such as dances and unusual appearance, are reduced to superficial exoticism.

Much better, often providing a holiday's most memorable highlight, are a small but growing number of community-run tourism initiatives in which locals benefit directly from your payments in return for providing homestays, meals, guided walks around local sights and anything else that might interest. The huge advantage to locals is that they're the ones who determine the limits, so the damaging aspects of cultural voyeurism are greatly lessened, sometimes virtually eliminated. Tanzania's cultural tourism programme (see p.160) is outstanding in this regard, offering well-structured, reliable and massively enjoyable experiences. Uganda has a similar if smaller set-up (see ⓦ www.ucota.or.ug), as does Namibia (ⓦ www.nacobta .com.na). Unfortunately, Africa's cultural tourism trailblazer, namely the village homestays pioneered in Senegal's Casamance region, are quite disorganized these days.

Another great way of experiencing traditional Africa is at a festival, whose themes celebrate everything from successful harvests and heroic ancestors to ceremonial migrations and the passing of the seasons – see "Holidays, festivals and celebrations" in chapter 3.

The Fulani

Pastoralists, for whom nothing on God's earth is more important than their cattle, the Fulani dominate the entire belt of savanna south of the Sahara, almost from coast to coast. Their semi-nomadic lifestyle has kept them apart from much of the modern world, for better and for worse, and as a result they are among the last truly traditional societies on the continent. Among the Fulani (or Peuhl) ethno-linguistic group dominating the Sahel, the most famous tribe are the Wodaabé of Niger, Nigeria and Cameroon, whose eligible young men camp it up in high style during annual get-togethers aimed at capturing the hearts of the girls; see p.130 & p.246.

The Nilotes

In East Africa, most cattle-herders are so-called Nilotes, the name alluding to a probable origin in the Nile Valley. Indeed, there are many compelling cultural clues that connect them with northern Sudan's ancient kingdom of Meroe, which explains some remarkable similarities between what's known of Pharaonic Egypt and certain aspects of Nilotic appearance, such as traditional religion and the braided hairstyles of young warriors. The big stars are the Maasai of Kenya and northern Tanzania. So keen are tourists on Maasai encounters that you'll even meet young Maasai warriors in coastal resorts far from their traditional lands, where a season of dance performances and hawking trinkets can pay for a small herd of cattle – which, for a youth seeking marriage, is enough to cover the bride price. Tanzania's community-run cultural tourism programmes offer many a Maasai adventure, including homestays, long-distance treks, and lessons in ethno-botany. Other visitable pastoralists in East Africa include Kenya's Samburu and Turkana. Even less fazed by the modern world, but virtually impossible to visit, are Sudan's Nuer and Dinka, and Uganda's Karamajong.

The Cushites

Similar in many ways to the Nilotes is the Cushitic ethno-linguistic group in the Horn of Africa's lowlands, including the Gabbra, Borana and Somali, for all of whom camels are God's gift. Although they appear physically to have some Arabian roots, they're very much their own people, with their own calendars and complicated systems of grazing that ensure no area ever gets overgrazed. Given the insecurity that reigns across most of their region, the closest you're likely to get to meeting them is in southern Ethiopia, northern Kenya or in Djibouti.

Saharan nomads

For the people of the Sahara, nomadism is a privileged existence, one that's increasingly at the mercy of the climate – even in a place as apparently desolate as the Sahara, the pernicious effects of global warming have an impact, and the desert's ever-drier fringes mean that many have been forced to settle. Of those that have managed to keep their traditional way of life, the most famous are of course the Tuareg (the "Blue Men" of the travel brochures, their skin tainted blue from the indigo colouring their robes and veils), who are likely to accompany you as guides on desert expeditions in Algeria, Libya and Niger. Elsewhere, for example in Mali, Tuareg encampments can also be visited, but the experience can feel somewhat staged, with the Tuareg sometimes presented as little more than touristic side-shows. And if you meet someone claiming to be Tuareg in Morocco, Tunisia or Mauritania, know that you might be being taken for a ride: none of those countries are traditional Tuareg territory, but locals have learned that pretending to be Tuareg exerts a sirenic charm on visitors, and their wallets...

Hunter-gatherers

Visiting Africa's remaining hunter-gatherers – including the Pygmy groups of the Congo River basin, Tanzania's Hadzabe, and southern Africa's Bushmen (or San) – can be a major thrill for those seeking a touch of exoticism, but ethically the whole thing is a minefield. Only few groups of hunter-gatherers have any say in tourism as it regards them, and the majority benefit little or not at all. Tourist attitudes can be all wrong, too. For some, visiting hunter-gatherers can be a titillating "me and the Stone Age people" kind of lark, but they're depressing and exploitative experiences if you've a modicum of sensitivity. That said, some of the Pygmy tours in Cameroon and Gabon are run ethically, and you're likely to have a Pygmy guide accompany you on walks in Gabon's national parks.

In southern Africa, the Bushmen (also known as San, Khoisan, Basarwa and by various other local names) have had an especially rough time of it since the European landfall – the British even set about exterminating them from Lesotho in the 1870s. Although photos of Bushmen in hunting poses adorn many a brochure and official website, few Bushmen, if any, still follow their ancient way of life. But all is not lost: the recent introduction of community-based tourism in South Africa's Richtersveld, in Namibia, and in Botswana bodes well, even if the Botswanan government is in the Stone Age as regards its forced resettlement of some Bushman communities.

The Dogon

Also unsettling can be trips to Mali's Dogon tribe, who have featured on the tourist agenda for many decades. The Dogon originally sought refuge on the Bandiagara Escarpment to escape the military might of expanding Islamic empires. Their isolation helped preserve much of their culture, including fabulously ornate dance masks, but tourism has managed to change what other invaders failed to touch. Nowadays, most Dogon have abandoned their spectacular cliffside dwellings, and dances are performed whenever tourists stump up sufficient cash. That said, the mass tourism that is so destructive is restricted to just one or two areas, leaving other Dogon largely alone. The escarpment is wonderful hiking territory, so getting to know "real" Dogon in a non-touristic setting is possible.

The Berbers

North Africa's Berbers are the continent's only indigenous "whites", and are related to the Tuareg. Though many Berbers have intermarried with Arabs, "pure" Berbers still live in the mountains and on the desert fringes of Morocco, Algeria and Tunisia. Organized cultural tourism in these areas doesn't really exist, but getting to know people properly is easy enough if you are travelling by bicycle or even on foot. The most visible manifestations of Berber culture are their very colourful festivals (Morocco is especially good for this – see p.117 & p.246).

Rock art

Modern humans had an African genesis, most beautifully shown by an amazing array of rock art left by hunter-gatherers, the oldest of which may be 30,000 years old, and in still older finds of stone fertility dolls, carved ostrich shell jewellery and other artefacts, some of which may even be pushing 100,000 years. The main concentrations of rock art – both paintings and engravings – are in the Tassili N'Ajjer Plateau in the Algerian Sahara, in central Tanzania, and right across southern Africa. The Saharan motifs, which predate Egyptian civilization by many millennia, depict a rich savanna full of wildlife long since gone. South of the Sahara, wildlife is also the main subject, and comparisons with recent rock art left by San, and their religious practices, suggest that much of Africa's rock art may have served shamanistic purposes: the act of painting itself was vital to assure good rains and successful hunts. Shamans frequently achieved this entering trances and "becoming" rain animals such as elands or giraffes – some paintings depict the transformation itself. A selection of recommended books and websites on rock art is included in chapter 5.

Kingdoms and empires

Colonial-era historians would have had you believe that the only history of Africa worth mentioning was that traced by the string of ancient Mediterranean civilizations, and that anything remotely "advanced" south of the Sahara must inevitably have been created or influenced by paler-skinned people from the north, be they Berbers, Egyptians, Arabs, King Solomon and the Queen of Sheba, or even the long-lost tribes of Israel. This was all sheer nonsense, of course, as the following regal and imperial sights on both sides of the Sahara will show.

- **Ancient Egypt** Look for pharaonic treasures not only in Egypt but also in Sudan, which has its own pyramids and monumental temples, and remains from home-grown empires of Nubia and Meroe, whose pharaohs at one time ruled Egypt.
- **Roman Africa and Carthage** Egypt's dynasties came to an end with the death of Cleopatra, after which Rome assumed control. Over time, the whole of North Africa fell under Roman dominion, but not before Rome had vanquished its great rival, Carthage. The ruins of the city can be visited just outside Tunis, while amphitheatres, forums, temples and an array of other remains are littered right across the region; the most impressive are in Libya and Tunisia.
- **West Africa's empires** Until the Moroccan invasion of 1571, the empires of Ghana, Mali and Songhaï dominated much of

central West Africa. They were blessed both by the fecundity of the River Niger and its inland delta, and by gold. When, in 1324, the Emperor of Mali went on pilgrimage to Mecca, his vast caravan dispensed so much gold that the metal's price in Egypt slumped for decades thereafter. The wonderful mosques of Timbuktu, Gao and Djenné, all in present-day Mali, are suitably impressive reminders of that period.

● **Dahomey and the slave-trading kingdoms** The Bantu groups of West Africa, south of the Sahel, have always been hierarchical societies, a fact expressed through the formation of countless kingdoms and chiefdoms, many of which have survived as part of contemporary nations. Their rulers wield some power over local matters, and still appear with all due pomp and circumstance at traditional festivals to receive homage from their subjects. At other times, you might have the honour of being granted an audience, most likely in regions where *toubabs* (non-Africans) are rare.

● **Ethiopia's Christian kingdoms** Before the Portuguese sailed off on their voyages of discovery, the Europeans had heard of an African king named Preste João ("Priest John"), who – it was said – was Christian, and was heroically holding out against Muslim invaders. The name was probably a title, one accorded the rulers of Ethiopia, a country that had embraced Christianity in the fourth century and which was indeed, in medieval times, battling Islamic invaders. Among the country's many wonders are a number of cross-shaped churches that were not so much erected as excavated out of the rock underfoot. A chapel in Aksum, in the north, is said to house the original Ark of the Covenant.

● **Great Zimbabwe** The impressive remains of the turreted capital of the Monomotapa empire gave their name to the country. The empire was all-powerful in medieval times, when it controlled gold mines that may very well have been those of King Solomon. Scattered elsewhere in Zimbabwe are the remains of almost a hundred other related settlements.

● **The Swahili Coast** The tumultuous history of the East African coast is easily read on the faces of its inhabitants: black, white, and every shade in between. Through the monsoon-driven dhow trade, a sophisticated culture arose here, a synthesis of African, Arabian, Indian and Oriental. The Swahili civilization reached its apogee in the fourteenth century, when the rulers of city-states lived in sumptuous coral palaces, prayed in sub-Saharan Africa's largest mosques, and ate off fine Chinese porcelain. The ruins of those towns can be seen all along the coast.

The slave trade

The human capacity for unadulterated evil never ceases to amaze, especially when it's so often mere greed that triggers it. One of the sorriest episodes in human history was the West African slave trade. Although exact figures are impossible to deduce, over the three hundred years that Europe controlled the trade, no fewer than 12 million people were bought and transported into lives in shackles, most of them to the Americas. Countless more perished along the way in the cramped "floating coffins" that were the slave galleys. Before the Europeans got stuck in, the trade was conducted across the Sahara between the empires of northern and western Africa, via Tuareg caravaneers. The wealth of the trade, in which gold and salt also featured, is still visible in the amazing architecture of Gao, Djenné and Timbuktu, all in Mali. In North Africa, slavery's effects linger on in the physical features of many people; in oases, especially, many inhabitants obviously descend from black Africans, and popular North African music owes a lot to West African rhythms and instruments, too.

Less well documented but no less abject was the East African slave trade, the earliest references to which were made in ancient Greek and Egyptian texts. The trade remained small-scale until the seventeenth century, when European demand for cheap labour for their plantation colonies kicked in. In the nineteenth century, the trade, by then controlled by Omanis from Zanzibar, reached its darkest depths; over a million people were traded in Zanzibar's Stone Town alone. The following are the continent's main slave-trade-related sights and experiences.

- **Ouidah, Benin** Formerly the Slave Coast, Benin's shoreline was controlled by a series of European and Brazilian slave-trading fiefdoms, most infamously at Ouidah, the port from where countless captives were sold off and shipped to a life in chains. The point of departure is marked by a monumental "door of no return", and the town's Portuguese fortress is now a museum of slavery, and of Vodun religion.
- **Roots Tours, the Gambia** Alex Haley's bestseller *Roots* kicked off an entire tourist industry based on the theme, and made Juffureh village – Haley's purported ancestral home – a centre of African-American pilgrimage. Don't miss the poignant remains of the slave fort on James Island, in the middle of the River Gambia.
- **Coastal castles, Ghana** Ghana's role in the slave trade is signalled by the many fortresses that pepper its coastline, built by European

powers vying with each for control of the trade. The ones at Cape Coast and Elmina are the most impressive.

- **Lake Malawi** The region around Lake Malawi (also called Niassa or Nyasa) was a major source of slaves for the East African trade. Many lakeshore settlements once acted as slave transit ports, and there's a small slave museum at Karonga in Malawi.

- **Gorée Island, Senegal** This tiny isle just off Dakar is said to have been a major slaving port. Whether or not that's true (it seems too small to have been all that important), it's a popular destination for African-Americans tracing their past. The well-preserved colonial buildings provide an unwittingly ironic contrast to the horrors of the trade, of which you'll be reminded in the museum.

- **Zanzibar, Tanzania** Reminders of the slave trade abound here, whether it's harrowing underground cells beside the market in Stone Town, or a claustrophobic chamber on the northern shore in which slaves were hidden from British Navy patrols after the trade became illegal. Most of Stone Town's majestic palaces and mansions were built with profits from the trade; particularly telling is the house of Tippu Tip, the island's most infamous slave trader.

- **Ujiji and Bagamoyo, Tanzania** On the shore of Lake Tanganyika, the unassuming fishing town of Ujiji was East Africa's busiest slaving port, receiving captives from the upper Congo Basin, who were then forced to march 1200km to the coastal town of Bagamoyo for shipment on to Zanzibar. There are few reminders of the trade in Ujiji other than a plaque and small museum dedicated to Stanley's "Dr Livingstone, I presume?" encounter with the famous missionary, whose tirades against the slave trade were instrumental in convincing the British Government to take action. Bagamoyo has several slavery-related sights, including a fortress through whose tunnels captives were led before embarking for Zanzibar.

A shared experience

Now's the time to think about whether you want to travel independently, or as part of an organized tour, and whether you want to share the experience with a companion, or strike out alone. There are pros and cons to all of these.

Going solo

With the right attitude, travelling alone can be a hugely rewarding experience. You'll be free to change plans at the last minute without recriminations, and follow your nose on the slightest whim. Although there'll be no one to look out for you, you won't have to keep an eye out for anyone, either. With no one to break your mental and physical stride, you'll find that the intensity of the experience is a big part of the pleasure. However, travelling solo is often a very lonely experience, especially if you don't speak the language, and for women there's the additional hassle of having to deal with unwanted attention (see p.315). Male or female, you'll also have to be sociable all by yourself, and with no one to joke with or share your worries, one or two minor setbacks risk reducing the entire experience to a feeling of "this country sucks", which is neither fair nor much reason to go on holiday. Plus, serious mishaps such as getting your credit cards or passport stolen are also harder to deal with when there's no one to help. Still, if you're relaxed, confident and able to shrug off problems, there's a lot going for the solo experience.

Travelling with a companion

East Africa's Makua tribe say that "walking in two is medicine", and they're right – so long as you can find a suitable person to travel with. Like freshly cut flowers, some people just don't travel well, and many a romance has wilted because of a stressful overland trip. Of course, many another romance has blossomed – the shared experience can root your friendship more deeply than ever. Someone with a sense of humour and an easy-going nature is always a good bet, while an impatient hypochondriac who prefers driving to the corner store to walking is, well, best left at home, even if they are your better half.

There are many advantages to travelling with a companion. You'll have someone to share the experience with, talk you up when you're down, and put contretemps into perspective with a joke or a kiss. In practical terms, the big advantage is being able to share costs. Taxi fares and vehicle rental will work out much cheaper per person, and hotel rooms for two, whether with one big bed or two smaller ones, tend to cost less than two single rooms and are often better equipped, too. There are other practical advantages, too: you'll be able to sample more dishes at restaurants (assuming your partner doesn't have a thing for chicken and chips, again), and two sets of eyes are better than one for staying safe, especially when changing or withdrawing money, or keeping tabs on baggage while the other nips off to check out a hotel.

The downside to travelling as a pair is, oddly enough, more hassle. Hustlers assume that there's more money to be made from couples, and have also learned that couples are generally less streetwise than solo travellers – the rationale being that couples are more self-involved, and so have less reason to get to know their environment.

Finding a travelling companion

At home, college and university notice boards and travel magazines are good places to start, both to respond to adverts and advertise yourself. Internet forums, chat groups and newsgroups are also fruitful and have the advantage of eliciting prompt responses, but do exercise caution when gauging the suitability and trustworthiness of potential companions across the wire.

Common sense also means you should arrange your first meeting in a public place, and go with a friend. If you seem to get along, it might be a good idea to try a test trip together, say over a weekend, to be sure. You should also suggest some ground rules, things like who's going to pay for what, what kind of hotels you'll be using, and what each of you wants to see and do.

If you have a particular interest, it could be fruitful to look in that direction. Even the most obscure hobbies have some kind of Internet presence, and the more mainstream interests have national and sometimes international organizations representing them. For example, should "LBJ" mean anything to you ("little brown job", as in birds, to the uninitiated), then get in touch a bird club to ask if anyone's interesting in joining you on a twitching safari to Africa.

Finding a travelling companion after you've arrived in Africa is best done where there are plenty of independent travellers. The usual means of hooking up is via a message left on a travellers' notice board, to be found in hotels, cafés, bars or restaurants that serve as primary focuses for backpackers. The most famous is the one pinned to a thorn tree in Nairobi's *New Stanley Hotel* (hence the name of Lonely Planet's Internet forum). The big advantage of trying to hook up with someone once you're there is that you meet potential companions "in the field", as it were, so their character and adaptability (or lack thereof) should be obvious in how they relate to locals.

Joining an organized tour

A lot of the anxiety and preparation involved in visiting Africa for the first time can be eliminated by joining an organized tour for part or all of your trip. Starting with a package is a gentle way of inching yourself into the mood and feel of the country, and leaves you free to strike off on your own after the packaged part is done. The advantages are manifold: little or no hassle, everything from accommodation and meals to excursions, safaris and activities laid on, and – hopefully – expert guides glad to impart knowledge and passion to their charges. And if you're looking for a mid-range or upmarket experience, package tour rates are rarely more expensive than organizing things yourself. There's also lots of choice: from short breaks in Morocco's imperial cities, to beach-and-bush combos (wildlife safaris followed by quality bonding time with sea and sand), mountaineering expeditions, and specialist tours such as birding or World War I battlefields.

The main disadvantage of package tours is, obviously enough, their packaged nature, unless you'll be splashing out on a really exclusive, customized experience with a personal guide and driver. For the most part, you'll likely be staying in hotels and lodges housing several hundred fellow guests, and day-trips and excursions could be similarly crowded, with travel in minibuses or even convoys of vehicles. Package tours are also disappointing if you're looking for Africa beyond the safari parks, bazaars and beaches. There's also the matter of other clients: do you really want to come to Africa to be surrounded by non-Africans, some of whom could be on the moon for all they cared, with the continent reduced to nothing more than a sanitized backdrop? Upmarket tours will pamper you silly, but may have a neo-colonial feeling about them which can either be charming or morally repugnant, depending on your point of view. On safari, there's also the question of getting on with your peers in close proximity – you might not even like them! Still, the better tour operators are well aware of these potential pitfalls, and, so long as you state your preferences clearly and early on in the game, they should be able to match you up with like-minded clients and establishments.

Recommended tour operators are included in the Directory on pp.414–416.

Getting there

Each of Africa's capital cities has an international airport, and some of the larger countries also have one or two elsewhere. International flights are infrequent by global standards, sometimes only a dozen or two a week. The most useful African hubs are Dakar and Lagos (for West Africa), Rabat and Cairo (northern Africa), Addis Ababa (eastern Africa and the Horn), Nairobi (eastern and central Africa), and Johannesburg (southern Africa).

The main European airports for Africa correspond to the capital of the former colonizing country: London for former English colonies, Paris for Francophone countries, Lisbon for Portuguese-speaking nations, and Brussels for the former Belgian colonies. Most direct flights to Africa from North America are from New York, with a few operating out of other cities. From South America, South African Airways has useful flights from Rio de Janeiro, São Paulo and Buenos Aires. India has direct flights to most countries on Africa's eastern seaboard; coming from elsewhere in Asia, chances are you'll get a one-stop routing via the Persian Gulf. Johannesburg is the main point of arrival for direct flights from Australia and New Zealand.

Overland and sea approaches

The only true overland route to Africa is into Egypt from Israel or the Gaza Strip (usually impassable), or − cheating slightly − by ferry from Aqaba in Jordan to Nuweiba in Sinai. Other ferries connect Spanish, French and Italian ports with Morocco, Algeria and Tunisia. The quickest are from Gibraltar and Algeciras to Tangier (northern Morocco) and Ceuta (a Spanish enclave nearby). Ferries from Saudi Arabia to Egypt and Sudan are most unlikely to be useful, given the impossibility of independent travel in Saudi Arabia.

2

Visas, tickets and insurance

Patience can cook a stone
Fulani proverb

Sorting out the paperwork for your trip can be quite a time-consuming process. You'll need to check your passport's validity, buy tickets and health insurance, perhaps apply for a visa or two, and sort out a number of health matters (for which see chapter 13). So, start early, and be patient.

How do I get a visa?

Africa's infamously burdensome bureaucracy is alive and well (if rather too bloated to be kicking), but presents few hurdles to tourists other than getting a visa. Wherever you're going, you'll need a full, ten-year passport, and have at least six months' validity remaining after the date you plan to return home. It should also have enough blank pages for visas and stamps – roughly one per country. The only "non-standard" thing that may be required is proof of yellow fever inoculation (a health passport), particularly if you're entering an area where yellow fever is endemic, or have been travelling through one; see pp.376–377 for a country-by-country summary of the rules.

Most visitors to Africa will require a visa; likely exceptions are travellers heading to Morocco, Tunisia, The Gambia, Senegal and South Africa. The more popular destinations let you buy visas at land borders and airports. Costs for visas depend on where you buy them (it may be cheaper to get them on arrival than in advance), and your nationality. In general, you won't pay more than $90/£50 for a standard tourist visa, often much less.

As the rules regarding visas can change at any time, get informed beforehand, ideally several weeks before departure. The country's diplomatic mission closest to you will have the latest requirements; some have their own websites, and their contact details can almost always be found on tourist-board websites, but don't rely on visa information posted on the Internet, even if it's from an official site – it can often be woefully out of date.

Getting visas for some countries that are rarely visited by tourists can be awkward, mainly due to Kafkaesque disorganization rather than official policy. In Algeria and Libya, however, the rules require independent travellers (ie those not on organized tours) to provide a letter of introduction from an organization or individual within the country expressing willingness to take you under their wing. Unless you have a local contact, you'll have to get a local tour company to provide the letter (easier if you buy a service from them, say car rental). At the time of writing, the Algerian and Libyan embassies were also able to provide the letter, for a fee.

Another problem with Algeria and Libya, and also Sudan is that travellers whose passports contain Israeli visas or stamps will be refused entry. The solution is to get a new passport before you go, or – if you'll be visiting Israel as part of your African trip – to ask Israeli immigration to stamp a detachable sheet instead of your passport. They're aware of the situation so it's usually a routine matter, as long as your nationality doesn't require you to apply for an Israeli visa in advance, in which case your visa has to be stamped in your passport (at the time of writing, nationals of the European Union, the US, Canada, Australia, New Zealand and South Africa were exempt from visas).

Lastly, Americans will of course be aware that Gaddafi hasn't exactly been their best buddy, in spite of recently renewed diplomatic relations. At the time of writing, Libya still offered no consular services in the US, so visa applications have to be sent to the People's Bureau (as the Libyans term their embassy) in Ottawa, Canada.

Types of visa

The standard "single-entry" visa available to tourists is generally valid for three months of travel, although some smaller countries, for instance The Gambia and Lesotho, may grant just 14 or 28 days. If you'll be leaving and re-entering the country, try to get a multiple-entry visa. A six-month tourist visa is an even rarer beast, as officials will assume that visitors with half a year to spare will be doing something more than just touring around. If you are indeed on business, you'll need a business visa, while volunteers and NGO staff require a special visa.

Visas bought in advance expire three or six months from the date of issue. Obviously, this poses problems if you're planning a long trip through several countries. The only solution in that case is to buy visas from embassies in Africa – which almost always entails visiting capital cities in order to apply.

Getting a visa before you travel

If you're not absolutely sure that you can buy a visa on arrival, apply for one before going via the country's nearest embassy, high commission or consulate. Do this with plenty of time to spare – while embassies for the more popular destinations can deliver a visa the following day (or even on the same day if you're happy paying a small premium), others can take up to two weeks should the application need to be processed elsewhere. Obviously, you'll need to enquire in advance to check the requirements, cost and mode of payment, duration and validity.

Embassy opening hours for visa applications are restricted to weekday mornings. In addition to your passport, a couple of passport photographs and the payment, you may also need some kind of proof that you'll be leaving the country, such as an air ticket, but the oft-cited "proof of funds" (eg a bank statement or a wad of traveller's cheques) is hardly, if ever, required. Applications can be made by post – best done at least a month in advance.

Buying a visa on arrival

If you're sure that you can buy your visa on arrival, it's best to bring hard currency for the payment, preferably US dollars. Airport immigration posts are open whenever there are flights; land borders tend to close at night. Given the queues that can form during the day, especially when buses from nearby towns and cities pull in, arrive with several hours to spare if you want to cross over the same day.

That said, border formalities are increasingly just that: a formality, with one stamp on arrival and another on departure, and the whole process can take as little as twenty minutes. It all depends on the country, its current political situation, and indeed on the mood, efficiency and/or corruptibility of the officer(s) in charge. Whatever you do, don't be rude or unpleasant, no matter how frustrating the charade – border guards have the right to refuse entry, on whatever grounds. Remember too that official regulations aren't always passed on to officials down the line; until recently, for example, semi-autonomous Zanzibar, which is part of Tanzania, insisted that tourists arriving by ferry from the mainland buy a visa, even though they already had one (for Tanzania). The solution for wily travellers was absurdly simple: ignore customs and just stride into town. Needless to say, don't try that with a sovereign state…

Entry cards and stamps

On the plane, you'll likely be given an entry card to fill in: name, date of birth, reason for visiting and so on. At border posts the cards tend to be stacked up in a corner somewhere; make sure you collect one, and the visa application form, before joining the queue. Once you're at the desk, the entry card will either be swallowed up by the country's overburdened bureaucracy, never to appear again, or will be stamped and handed back to you – in which case keep it safe; you'll need to give it up when you leave.

△ Checkpoint on the Sani Pass, on the border between South Africa and Lesotho

Although there are official rules limiting the amount of time particular foreign nationals can spend in the country, exactly how much time you're granted may depend on the official you deal with. It's best to ask for a longer period than you really need, just in case (though three months is almost always the maximum).

As you're handed back your passport, check it immediately for the new stamp. In many cases, the amount of time you've been actually granted, irrespective of what the visa might say, is indicated either on the stamp or in a handwritten note across it. If it's less than you asked for, ask there and then whether there's been a mistake. Chances are that it's policy, so swallow your disappointment and get used to the idea that you'll have to deal with that later on.

Extending your stay

The rules about extending your stay beyond the time specified by your visa or entry stamp vary enormously from country to country. In some countries, getting visa extensions is straightforward, but in others it can be either unfeasible or hugely expensive. In Tanzania, for example, you'll be charged $400/£220 for just one measly extra month, while in neighbouring Kenya, $20/£11 and a painless visit to immigration HQ in Nairobi gives you three more months. Wherever you are, start your enquiries at the nearest immigration office or at a police station.

In most cases, the easiest and cheapest way to extend your stay is to head to a neighbouring country and re-enter on a new visa. Obviously, this looks less suspect if you spend a few days in the neighbouring country rather than just a few hours.

Plane tickets

Wherever you're coming from, there'll probably be several routes to your destination. The widest choice, and greatest variation in fares, is on long-haul flights from Australia, New Zealand and North America, on which you'll be changing planes and probably airlines at least once, probably several times. In general, the busier the airport at your destination, the better your chances are of finding a bargain.

It pays to spend a few hours researching routes and prices, whether on the Internet (see p.413 for recommended websites) or by calling travel agents in your own country. It's admittedly boring and frustrating work, but do persevere as the savings can be substantial. Being flexible in your choice of route also increases the odds of getting a good price. For example, you might find it cheaper to get to Guinea-Bissau by flying into Senegal and overlanding it from there. For the cheapest fares, fly out of season and buy your ticket as soon as possible. The most expensive times to travel are July, August and mid-December onwards, with premiums charged for Christmas, New Year and Easter. Incidentally, if you have special dietary requirements (vegetarian, halal or kosher) or need some kind of special assistance, let the agent or airline know when you book – leaving it to later risks your request being lost in an electronic logjam.

Ticket types

The main drawback with return (round-trip) tickets is that flying in and out of the same airport can restrict your itinerary, perhaps requiring a degree of time-consuming backtracking or else additional expense on internal flights. If there's more than one international airport in the country, or if you'll be visiting other countries, a far better bet – and not all that much more expensive – is an "open-jaw" ticket, flying into one airport and out of another.

A one-way ticket to paradise may have romantic connotations, but countries like to be sure their guests won't outstay their welcome, and a one-way ticket won't convince embassies or immigration officials of this unless you've got a visa for another country down the line. Mile for mile, one-way fares can also be higher than return prices.

Charter flights

Charter flights, operated by package-tour companies, can work out pretty cheap, especially if bundled with a basic package holiday; you'll have an easy and comfortable introduction to the country, and you could always cancel the return part of the flight and head off independently. The disadvantage of charters is that tickets may only be valid for four weeks' stay, and may not be changeable or refundable at all.

The only useful charters for Africa are from western Europe to Morocco, Tunisia and Egypt (all year round), and to The Gambia, Senegal and Kenya (Mombasa) in high season. If you're heading to West Africa, consider catching a charter to the Canary Islands (all year) and flying on by scheduled aircraft to Mauritania or Senegal.

Round-the-world tickets and air passes

If your visit to Africa is part of a multi-continent trip, consider a round-the-world (RTW) ticket. This can either be a special package bought through one of two airline alliances, or individually booked flights strung together by travel agents and RTW specialists. As a general rule, you'll have to select your itinerary and stopovers in advance, travelling either eastbound or westbound with no backtracking. The most popular combination involves flying into Kenya, overlanding it to South Africa under your own initiative, and flying out from there. Most RTW tickets are valid for 6, 12 or 24 months. Prices start at around $2000/£1200 including departure taxes, but can be considerably higher depending on the route taken and the number of stops.

Star Alliance (Ⓦ www.staralliance.com) RTW tickets are useful for routes covered by South African Airways and Lufthansa, and also include Singapore and Thai Airlines flights to Johannesburg. The "Global Explorer" RTW ticket from the competing Oneworld Alliance (Ⓦ www.oneworldalliance.com) is useful for British Airways destinations.

Travel agents specializing in RTW flights can provide more options, and RTW travel is one area where talking to a travel agent over the phone or in person is far better than hacking your way through the Internet. The problem is that there are literally thousands of possible routes, and even though the specialist websites have very detailed online (or downloadable) fare calculators, they're useful only if you have an exact itinerary and dates in mind. Another drawback is that the websites don't show you routes which are similar to, but cheaper than, the one you submit, so it's easy to pay over the odds by choosing the "wrong" airport. Gap Year (Ⓦ www.gapyear.com/rtw/via_africa.html) is one of few specialist travel agents to jump straight in with sample itineraries and prices.

Lastly, there's also the Star Alliance African Airpass, allowing up to ten flights in two months between 25 sub-Saharan airports covered by South African Airways.

Buying your ticket

Air tickets can be bought from airlines, travel agents, and a variety of discount agents, including so-called bucket shops, consolidators and subscription-based discount clubs. They advertise in newspapers (especially weekend editions), travel magazines, weekly lifestyle mags such as *Time Out* and the *Village Voice*, free magazines such as *TNT* (UK and Australia), and may have their own websites.

Before deciding on a particular company, check whether they're members of ATOL (Ⓦwww.atoldata.org.uk) or ABTA (Ⓦwww .abtanet.com) for UK-based companies, or AFTA (Ⓦwww.afta.com .au) in Australia. Membership means that if the company goes belly up before you have your ticket, you'll be refunded. The US lacks similar organizations, but there your credit-card company should cover you. We've cut out your work by reviewing the best ticket agents on pp.413–414.

Shopping online is the easiest and often the cheapest way of buying flights, but a traditional bricks-and-mortar travel agent is convenient, and useful if the person you deal with is knowledge-able about Africa. Even more knowledgeable, and often impartial in recommending airlines and routes, are tour companies specializing in Africa, though if you talk to them it'll be assumed that you'll be buying a holiday or at least a safari from them; see pp.414–416 for recommended outfits.

The following tips will save you money.

- **Shop around**. Fares for the same route can differ radically depending on the exact day or even time you want to fly, and fares for the exact same flight bought from agents can also vary, depending on the agent's mark-up and whatever deals they've arranged with the airlines.
- **Buy early**. In general, the earlier you buy a ticket, the less you'll pay. For long-haul flights, you might want to book six or even twelve months before travelling.
- **Is the ticket flexible?** Find out how easy it will be to change flight dates, how much you'll be charged for doing so, and what refund you'll get if you need to cancel.
- **Do you qualify for youth discounts?** Some agents offer reductions for students and under-26s.

Insurance

Insurance is big business, and not the most transparent one either. Every travel agent, airline and two-bit tour operator will push some kind of policy towards their punters. For Africa, expect to pay around $75/£40 for a month's coverage.

A typical policy covers illness or injury requiring hospitalization, air evacuation or repatriation, and also provides some peace of mind as regards the curtailment or cancellation of your holiday. Tickets and – up to a certain limit – cash and documents are also covered. However, coverage for the loss or theft of valuables is far from adequate, so the first piece of advice is simple: don't take anything with you that you really wouldn't want to lose, things like grandma's earrings and hyper-expensive laptops. The unavoidable exception is photographic equipment.

When buying travel insurance, bear the following in mind:

- **Read the small print.** It's important to understand which eventualities are excluded from cover – you may discover some situations that don't seem that unlikely to happen to you.
- **Can the policy be extended?** Check whether you can extend your policy when you're abroad if you decide to stay longer – this may just require a phone call.
- **Are you already covered?** Some all-risks home insurance policies may cover your possessions when overseas (indeed their cover may surpass that of the typical travel-insurance policy), and many private medical schemes include cover when abroad. Credit-card companies may also provide some coverage.
- **Can you get a refund?** Policies should be refundable in their entirety within a week or two of purchase; check this out beforehand.

What does the policy cover?

Policies can be chopped and changed to exclude things you don't need, which can save you a little money when buying your policy. Conversely, if you want to have specific items or activities covered, ensure they're detailed in the policy. The following areas of the policy deserve particular scrutiny:

- **Medical cover** Check whether benefits are paid as treatment proceeds, or after you return home, and make a note of any 24-hour medical emergency number – most insurers insist that you get their authorization for any prolonged treatment. If you intend to make a claim for medical treatment, keep receipts for medicines and hospital bills. Excluded from cover are injuries caused by obviously dangerous activities, including riding motorbikes over 125cc.
- **Personal effects** For theft or loss, check the per-article limit, the total pay-out limit, and the excess (the fee deducted for each claim).

Note that making a claim might require you to produce the original receipt showing that you owned the lost item, though some insurers will be satisfied with seeing the item's user manual. In general, you'll be lucky to get more than $400/£220 total coverage. Check also whether payment would be for the cost of the item bought new, or is adjusted to account for wear and tear. In the event you have anything stolen, you must obtain an official statement from the police in order to claim on your insurance.

- **Dangerous activities** Policies exclude so-called dangerous sports and activities unless extra premiums are paid. These may include activities such as white-water rafting, bungee jumping, scuba-diving, mountaineering and safaris.

- **Personal liability** Assuming it's included, personal liability insurance – covering you if you're sued because you've inadvertently been implicated in damage to other people's property or in an accident in which someone was injured or killed – excludes many imaginable (and unimaginable) scenarios. Still, if you're renting a motor vehicle, the good news is that the third-party insurance you'll have to buy locally does at least provide cover in the event of an accident.

- **Natural disasters and war** Insurers don't like the hand of god, nor the outbreak of conflict, so don't expect coverage for these.

3

When to go

The toad that wanted to avoid the rain fell in the water

Bayansi proverb

The climate, obviously, is a major factor when deciding when to go. Rainfall and temperature, evidently enough, are important, but don't forget about humidity, especially if you'll be travelling in equatorial climes or along tropical coastlines, where moisture-laden air can make temperatures feel much hotter than they really are. You also need to think about exactly what activities you'll be undertaking. There's little reason in heading for the beach when it'll be raining incessantly, nor in planning extensive travels in remote areas at a time when unsurfaced roads might turn into impassible slurries of mud. But if you'll be tramping around archeological sites, you might well prefer overcast skies to blazing sunshine, while landscape photographers will appreciate the periods immediately after the rains for the colours. For culture, keep an eye on the local calendar; some festivals and celebrations are worth an entire trip in themselves. The profiles of the countries in the "Where to go" section give climate overviews and suggest the best times to visit.

In general, months with the best weather for visitors coincide with high season in the tourist industry, which can be expensive if you'll be staying in upmarket beach hotels or wildlife lodges, whose rates can double compared to those in low or mid-season. Also considered high season, regardless of the weather, are late December and early January, Easter, and July to September. If you're heading to an especially popular destination at any of those times, book well ahead, and don't forget that air tickets – even for high-season travel – are cheaper when bought well in advance.

Africa's climate

Africa's climate changes markedly from north to south. The continent's northern extremes are temperate, with sunshine and temperatures comparable to Europe's Mediterranean region. South of the Mediterranean zone, meaning beyond the Atlas Mountains in the Maghreb and south of the coastal strips of Libya and Egypt, lies the Sahara, a place whose climate requires little introduction. South of that great desert is the Sahel (confusingly also known as the Sudan or Soudan), a semi-arid belt that stretches right across the continent from Senegal and southern Mauritania to the Horn of Africa. The more southerly parts of West Africa, and much of Central Africa, are tropical or equatorial, meaning hot and very humid; without the benefit of air-conditioning, this can be incredibly strength-sapping. South of the equator, the seasons are reversed compared to the northern hemisphere, with high summer coinciding with the depth of European and North American winters.

Lowlands, including coastal areas, are generally hotter than highlands, and often a good deal more humid, too. That said, sea breezes can give coastlines a more pleasant climate than low-lying interiors.

North Africa and the Sahara

North Africa has two distinctive climatic zones: temperate in the north, desert in the south. The weather doesn't have much of an impact on travelling itself, as most roads are surfaced, and where they're not (such as in and around the Sahara), getting over them has far more to do with the condition of your vehicle and driving skills than with the mood of the heavens.

The Mediterranean region, which includes the Atlas Mountains, has four well-defined seasons that correspond to those of Europe and North America. In short, the climate is extremely pleasant: hot summers, warm to hot autumns, none-too-cold winters and short but florid springtimes. The bulk of the rains fall between October and May. At high altitudes, meaning the Rif Mountains in Morocco,

Tropical Africa

Northern and southern Africa have the four temperate seasons you're likely to be familiar with, but in between – meaning most of the continent – it makes more sense to speak of wet and dry seasons. Tropical zones tend to have two of each, though in equatorial regions there may just be one of each, if it even stops raining at all. Periods equating to spring or autumn, where they're discernible at all, may last just a couple of weeks – blink and they're gone.

The dry seasons are almost always the best times for visiting. It's not just clear skies and easy suntans you can look forward to, but good wildlife viewing – animals are easier to see when the vegetation is wilting, and as they tend to congregate around remaining water sources as the dry season progresses, it becomes easy to find a large number of species in a relatively small area. The main disadvantage to dry-season travel is that it's high season for tourists, so you may end up paying a premium for accommodation and other tourist services. Furthermore, landscapes can be uninspiring once everything turns yellow, and the heat can be a trial. The end of the dry season is often hotter and a little more humid, although there is a risk of rain as Africa's climate has become increasingly unpredictable over the last few decades. For culture, the end of the dry season is a great time for catching traditional festivals, given that many are concerned with bringing rain or celebrating harvests.

The rains are a boon to farmers and herders alike, but not travellers. In the more remote corners of West Africa, rural parts of East Africa, and across most of Central Africa (down to southern Angola), unsurfaced roads can become impassable during and shortly after the rains (blocked not by water as such, but by mud and bogged-down lorries), and the mood can be downbeat unless the rains come in spectacular thunderstorms. The bigger hotels, especially on beaches and in wildlife areas, may close during the rains, and some national parks may also be shut at that time, or else inaccessible unless you fly in. There are also many more bugs to contend with. On the other hand, you'll benefit from cheaper rates at hotels that do remain open, and if bird-watching is your thing, the wet seasons are quite spectacular.

Despite lingering mosquitoes, the periods immediately following the rains can be very rewarding times to visit, when savanna and bushland, parched for much of the year, is decked out in a myriad colours and scents. It's also still low season as far as hotels and tour operators are concerned, so you'll benefit from cheaper prices.

the Atlas in Morocco, Algeria and Tunisia, and Libya's isolated coastal massifs, you could be forgiven for thinking you're in central Europe if you're passing through in winter or spring, when even snow can be expected. All things considered, late spring, late summer and all of autumn are the best times to visit. High summer might be too hot for some (needless to say, avoid the Sahara at that time), while winter can bring overcast skies or rain. That said, southern Tunisia (Jerba especially), Egypt and southern Morocco do live up to their reputations as winter sun destinations.

Away from the coast and the mountains, the Sahara dominates. This great desert is one of earth's harshest environments, and becomes bone-meltingly hot in summer, with shade temperatures frequently above 50°C. That said, the fact that the air is absolutely dry makes the temperatures more bearable than they sound. With the exceptions of a few mountainous zones and scattered oases mostly watered by springs or temporary streams, the desert is unremittingly arid, and some parts receive no rain for decades at a stretch. Highland areas are more likely to catch rain, but predicting where and when is impossible.

It's not just the heat and dryness that pushes life in the Sahara to the brink. Strong winds blowing from high-pressure areas over the desert to low-pressure cells outside it are another scourge. Hot, dry and dusty, these winds blow between winter and spring, peaking from February to April when skies are often hazed pink or orange from the dust. The name of the wind differs according to where you are: Sahat in Morocco, Harmattan in Mauritania and West Africa, Simoom or Chichili in Algeria, Chili in Tunisia, Ghibli in Libya, and Khamsin in Egypt and Sudan. The best times to visit desert regions are late autumn and winter, before the winds pick up force.

West and Central Africa

South of the Sahara, the distinctions between the northern hemisphere's four seasons become blurred as they merge with the two-tone dry/wet season system of tropical and equatorial latitudes. For visitors, humidity and rainfall are the main factors to consider. During the rains, although getting around is rarely impossible unless you're heading way off track, the extreme humidity should be reason enough to choose another time. In general, the closer to the coast you are, the wetter and more humid things are likely to be, and Central Africa has rains all year round. In the rest of the region, the northern hemisphere's winter months have the most bearable climate.

Immediately south of the Sahara is the Sahel, a disconsolately dry and hot savanna whose ever-decreasing rainfall is barely sufficient to meet even the meagre requirements of subsistence farmers and herders. Scattered showers occur mainly in July and August, with regions further away from the Sahara also getting rains in June and perhaps in September or October. This makes August to November the best time for travelling along the River Niger by boat. The rest of the year is dry, so temperature is the thing to go by: you'll encounter marginally cooler days from November to February or March, when the Sahara's Harmattan blows in from the north. However, the dust-laden Harmattan also robs the sky of its colour and heralds the start of the "hungry season", when granaries become empty and people get anxious for the rains and harvests to come. Although the wind coincides with times of hardship, the fact that it's dry can be a relief in more tropical climes, where it's nicknamed "the Doctor".

It's a completely different story along the coast and in the more heavily forested parts of Central Africa, where it can rain throughout the year, often in heavy cloudbursts, too. In consequence, coastal zones can be stiflingly hot and humid, which can be difficult to bear. The humidity increases as you approach the equator, where you'll be sweating constantly, even at night. The west coast has the most forgiving climate, with the dry months (April to June and October to December) being the best times to go. Around Africa's bulge, the area from Liberia to Nigeria experiences heavier rains and a shorter dry season, the latter covering February, March, November and December. The rest of the year can be awfully humid and is best avoided. Further east, in Central Africa, it rains all year round, with the heaviest downpours occurring between October and May. The best time to go there, then, is from June to August.

East Africa and the Horn of Africa

East Africa's climate is largely influenced by the rhythms of the Indian Ocean monsoon, and by the region's proximity to the equator. There are essentially four seasons: two dry and two wet.

The historic dhow trading civilizations of the "Swahili coast", from Somalia to northern Mozambique, the Comoros and Madagascar, owed their existence to the western Indian Ocean monsoon, an annual system of switching prevailing winds and ocean currents that causes the alternation of wet and dry seasons. In East Africa, the northerly and very humid Kaskazi blows strongest from November to March, bringing with it stifling heat and humidity, which in turn may be accompanied by cyclones. The drier southerly Kusi wind, strongest from August to October, accompanies the long dry season. The monsoon's effects are most apparent when the winds reverse direction, bringing two rainy seasons – the "short rains", in November or December, and the "long rains" (dubbed "green season" by more lyrical hoteliers), which peak in March and April. The latter tend to fall in afternoon downpours that occasionally flood entire districts. As the rains drag on, the land becomes cooler than the ocean and the winds begin to swing again, eventually sweeping across the Arabian Sea to join another monsoon wind from the Bay of Bengal, to become India's famous summer monsoon.

As such, the best time to visit East Africa is the long dry spell between June and November, which also coincides with high season for tourism. You'll have the advantage of better wildlife viewing, particularly towards the end of the season, and adventurous travellers can get off the beaten track without having to worry about impassable roads. The shorter dry season, generally from January to March but increasingly unpredictable of late, can be very humid. Temperatures are highest on the coast and in deserts inland. As elsewhere in the tropics, it's humidity rather than the level of mercury that really matters: 25°C on the coast will feel much hotter than 35°C in a desert devoid of moisture. Altitude is another factor: much of the region lies at least a thousand metres above sea level. The higher you go, the cooler the temperature and more bearable the experience.

In the Horn of Africa, rainfall is scant so temperatures are a more important factor for visitors. In general November to February are the best times to go, but be aware that in the Horn's hinterland the climate varies greatly depending on altitude: Ethiopia's and Eritrea's highlands can be chilly throughout the year, something that certainly can't be said of Eritrea's and Djibouti's blistering deserts.

Southern Africa

Southern Africa's weather is determined by latitude and by proximity to the coast. In the far south, meaning most of South Africa, Swaziland and Lesotho, the climate is temperate, with four well-defined seasons mirroring those of the northern hemisphere: midwinter falls between July and September, and summer coincides with European winters. Each season has its advantages: November to April for sunny weather, May to September for wildlife, and September to October (springtime) for landscapes.

The northern part of South Africa, and much of Namibia and Botswana, have a semi-arid climate conditioned by the Kalahari and Namib deserts. Neither of these are particularly hot, though they do produce dusty winds at the end of winter, blowing strongest in August. In these areas, winter is the best time to go, especially for wildlife, though bird-watching is best during the summer rains.

Angola, Mozambique, Zambia and Zimbabwe have just two seasons: rains from around November to March, and dry weather along the rest of the year. The Victoria Falls on the Zambezi reach their peak flow in April. Rainfall gets heavier the further east you go, peaking in Mozambique, where often torrential rains can cut off large swaths of the country between January and March.

In the Indian Ocean, the islands of the Comoros and Madagascar are at the tail end of the monsoon system. The Comoros receive heavy rainfall all year round, while Madagascar's rainfall patterns are determined by altitude – the higher up you are, the wetter it will be.

△ A wintry scene in Lesotho

Holidays, festivals and celebrations

The weather aside, the local calendar is the other element that could have a bearing on the best time to go, especially if you're interested in music or other forms of culture. Most countries observe both Christian and Muslim public holidays, even if one of those faiths dominates among the majority of people. We've mentioned the best events throughout the "Where to go" section. Africa's main festivals are covered in more detail in Rough Guides' book *World Party*, while ⓦ www.africinfo.org keeps an excellent cultural diary, from cinema and music to theatre and the visual arts.

Christian holidays

Christian holidays are not normally much of a reason to visit Africa, the big exceptions being events connected to the ancient Orthodox rites of Eritrea and Ethiopia. Elsewhere, some Christian celebrations are notable on account of their incorporation of non-Christian elements.

- **Carnival** On Cape Verde, one of the best times to be around is Carnival (Shrove Tuesday and the days preceding it), which actually has its roots in pre-Christian traditions of Europe. The festival transformed into its sequined incarnation in Brazil, from where it was introduced to Portugal's African colonies. The most vibrant Carnival is probably the one at Mindelo on the island of São Vicente, where the Brazilian influence (colourful parades, giant floats, outlandish costumes and plenty of babes in spangles) is much in evidence, even if the rhythms are different and the ladies not quite so naked. Carnival is also a big day in Bissau (Guinea-Bissau), Quelimane (Mozambique), and Luanda (Angola).

- **Christmas and New Year** In Senegal, the charming coastal town of Saint Louis celebrates Les Fanals, a commemoration of the time of the *signares* – envied half-caste women of colonial times whose elegance and refinement mirrored how the town still likes to see itself. The illuminated paper lanterns (*fanals*) paraded at night give the place a truly magical feel. In Cape Town, South Africa, New Year is so good that they celebrate it twice. Take two, on January 2, is called Tweede Nuwe Jaar ("Second New Year"), and in times past was the only day of the year when slaves were given time off by their Dutch owners. Nowadays, dancing Cape Minstrels from the coloured community give the streets a carnivalesque atmosphere.

- **Corpus Christi** In Tanzania, it's worth making tracks to get to the Sukuma tribe's Bulabo festival, which has become assimilated to the Christian holiday of Corpus Christi. Starting out in the nineteenth century as a contest between two rival healers over which of them had the strongest medicine, the event features competing pairs of dance societies, in which the winner is judged by the size of the crowd they attract. In the spirit of one-upmanship, it's not just the music that matters, but outlandish costumes and props, stilt-dancing, masquerades, all manner of acrobatic prowess, and even messing about with pythons.

- **Orthodox celebrations** Eritrea and Ethiopia were the first countries in Africa to adopt Christianity, way back in the fourth century. The main festivals of interest to visitors are Timket (Epiphany) in January, which sees colourful processions and mass baptisms, and Enkutatash (around September 11), which commemorates the return of the Queen of Sheba.

- **Pilgrimages** The most colourful Christian pilgrimages take place in northern Ethiopia during the Orthodox Christmas (around January 7), when thousands of believers converge on the region's rock-hewn churches to hear sermons and sing praises. Other major pilgrimages take place in Benin (August 15 at Dassa-Zoumé), at Debre Bizen in Eritrea on August 11, and throughout the year among Egypt's Coptic communities.

- **Charlemagne treading the boards** Catholic saints' days are widely celebrated on the islands of São Tomé and Príncipe – religious processions, feasting, music and dance are the order of the day, together with wonderfully eccentric theatrical traditions introduced by the Portuguese. Based on medieval European accounts of Charlemagne, the Auto de Floripes re-enacts the Christian Emperor's semi-mythical battles against Moorish invaders, whilst the Tchiloli play sees Charlemagne's son accused of murder...

Islamic holidays

Islam in Africa displays a good measure of syncreticism – the adoption of, or adaptation to, pre-existing local beliefs. As such, the nature of Islamic celebrations varies considerably from region to region. Africa's main Muslim areas include all of North Africa, substantial parts of West Africa (especially inland, including most of the Sahel), and the East African coast, from Somalia to northern Mozambique, including Zanzibar and the Comoros.

Apart from the pan-Islamic holidays covered below, pilgrimages to the tombs or mausoleums of local saints are also common, especially in North Africa, where they're called moussems, and often coincide with harvests. The biggest and most accessible moussem is the Festival of Sayid Ahmad al-Badawi in Egypt's Nile Delta town of Tanta, every October, which attracts over two million people. Islamic holy days honoured by all Muslims include:

- **Id al-Hajj (Id al-Adha, Id al-Kabir or Tabaski)** Coinciding with the pilgrimage to Mecca (the Hajj), the one-day Feast of the

Sacrifice sees every family with the financial means sacrificing a sheep or goat, to commemorate the willingness of Ibrahim (Abraham) to sacrifice his son Ishaq (Isaac) for the love of God. Far from rivers of blood filling the streets, the event is a very sociable time, akin to the Christian celebration of Easter. In the town of Saint Louis in Senegal, the day is also marked with furious races held in specially-made pirogues (some accommodating up to a hundred rowers).

- **Ramadan** The month-long fast of Ramadan must be observed by all Muslims except for children, the infirm and those travelling. In the hours of daylight throughout that month, people may not eat, drink, smoke or indulge in sex. Ramadan is a hiatus in the normal way of things, one that marks the passage of the old into the new, and the revitalization of one's faith and morality. Ultimately, it performs a spiritual cleansing similar to that provided by Lent for devout Christians. Visiting predominantly Muslim countries or regions at this time might leave a slightly strange impression, as most businesses including restaurants are closed by day, though the evenings are much livelier than usual, and both shops and restaurants stay open late. Public transport and official businesses continue as usual, and you can usually find a discreet restaurant serving food, but you'll offend sensibilities if you're seen eating, drinking or smoking on the street by day.

- **Id al-Fitr (Id al-Fitri, Id al-Sighir, Sikukuu, or Korité)** The first sighting of the sliver-thin new moon marks the end of Ramadan and the beginning of Id al-Fitr, two to four days of merrymaking when the streets resound to the cries of excited children decked out in new clothes, and the explosions of firecrackers and cap guns. It's a time for giving gifts and being charitable, visiting friends and relatives, and dancing. Particularly exuberant celebrations are those at Kano, Zaria and Maiduguri in Nigeria, all of which feature displays of horsemanship.

- **Maulidi (Mouloud, Mawlid al-Nabi or Maulid an-Nabi)** The Prophet Muhammad's birthday is a time for prayer and of giving praise to the founder of Islam, often through poetry or music. Although non-Muslim tourists are generally excluded from activities, at this time you're likely to hear some especially ethereal chanting emanating from mosques and Koranic schools. Mombasa, Malindi and Lamu on the Kenyan coast are good places to catch processions. Elsewhere, for example in Morocco, Maulidi is a popular time for pilgrimages to the tombs of local saints. In eastern Benin, Maulidi is also celebrated, but for a completely different reason: for the local Bariba, it marks their miraculous deliverance from Muslim invaders in the 1700s.

The Islamic calendar is based on lunar cycles, so the year has either 354 or 355 days and dates come forward in relation to the Gregorian calendar by ten or eleven days annually. Precise dates for Islamic festivals in the Gregorian calendar are impossible to give as the start of each month can vary by one day, depending on when the new moon is sighted.

New Year's Day January 10, 2008; December 29, 2008; December 18, 2009; December 7, 2010; November 26, 2011.

Maulidi March 20, 2008; March 9, 2009; February 26, 2010; February 15, 2011.

Start of Ramadan September 13, 2007; September 2, 2008; August 22, 2009; August 11, 2010; August 1, 2011.

Id al-Fitr (end of Ramadan) October 13, 2007; October 2, 2008; September 21, 2009; September 10, 2010; August 30, 2011.

Id al-Hajj December 20, 2007; December 9, 2008; November 28, 2009; November 16, 2010; November 6, 2011.

● **New Year** The Islamic new year is generally an understated affair. A big exception is Niger's Bianou celebration, especially in Agadez, where the Sultan's red-turbaned horse guards compete in devil-may-care cavalcades.

Traditional celebrations

Many traditional festivals celebrate harvests or the regeneration of pastures, and in so doing honour spirit-ancestors who helped bring rain. Others commemorate historical events such as battles or migrations, and the passing of the seasons. On a more local scale, music, dances and drinking celebrate rites of passage, from childbirth and initiation into adulthood, to marriage and death. In short, any one of life's great transitions is cause for celebration. Purification is often a theme, too, as to pass from one life stage to another requires that both body and soul are clean. Ultimately, traditional celebrations are the cement of traditional societies; they are times for people to come together and renew friendships and acquaintances, and put old disputes to rest.

Unfortunately, many of the old ways are long gone. Africa has changed beyond recognition over the last century or so, and very few ethnic groups have managed to keep more than a handful of their traditions intact. Many of the big get-togethers were banned during colonial times, so that much of what remains tends to be very localized. That said, some countries have made conscious efforts to promote their more visible traditions, especially music, masquerades and dance, and you'll find neo-traditional festivals in many countries. Overall, the best area for traditional celebrations is West Africa, particularly Mali, Burkina Faso, Niger, Nigeria, Ghana and Benin. In southern Africa, Zambia is the big party state, with dozens of hugely enjoyable celebrations held throughout the year. Madagascans know how to let their hair down, too, Some selected highlights:

- **Crossing of the Cattle** (Mali, December). When Peul cattle herders return from the Sahel's exhausted pastures to the evergreen world of the Niger's inland delta, the river is swum across by both man and beast. The cattle are garishly painted for the occasion, and once they're over safely, it's time for a major party.
- **Cure Salée** (Niger, September). Towards the end of the rains, Tuareg camel-breeders and Wodaabé cattle-herders converge with their herds on salt flats west of Agadez, whose brine provides their livestock with an annual "salt cure", and the nomads with one big get-together before parting ways. The week-long festivities include camel races, plenty of music and dancing, and beauty contests for men, women and beasts.
- **Egungun** (Nigeria, April). Held throughout western Nigeria, the Yoruba's ancestor festivals sport masquerades, drumming and dancing.
- **Imilchil Wedding Festival** (Morocco, September). The Berbers of the Atlas Mountains have always been a rebellious lot. Their non-conformity is at its most enjoyable at their "Moussem of the Bridegrooms", at which women from all over the mountains come together to find a husband, turning standard Islamic pre-nuptial practice on its head.
- **Ku'omboka** (Zambia, February or March). For half the year, Lozi farmers cultivate the valley of the Upper Zambezi, but at the start of the river's annual floods, they shift to higher ground in a ceremonial migration. Heading the flotilla is the Lozi king and his family, who are paddled across the floodplain in massive war-canoes.
- **Mwaka Kogwa** (Zanzibar, Tanzania, July). Despite being Muslim, the inhabitants of Makunduchi still honour the Zoroastrian New Year inherited from Persian immigrants a millennium ago. The

proceedings include mock fights and the ceremonial burning of a hut, from which elders make theatrical escapes.

- **Swaziland's regal celebrations** The kingdom of Swaziland's best festivals have a royal theme, the most famous of which – Umhlanga, in August or September – sees the king choose a new wife from among 25,000 elaborately-dressed hopefuls.
- **Tuareg celebrations** (Mali and Niger, December or January). The Tuareg masters of the Sahara are largely nomadic, and their annual get-togethers are often the only times when boy can meet girl. The most traditional of these celebrations is Tamadacht in Mali's Gao region in January, where beauty contests (for camels and goats, too), camel and horse races and tons of songs and dances are part of the fun. Other good dates are the Festival of the Desert near Timbuktu (also in January), and the Festival de l'Aïr at Iferouâne in Niger (December).
- **Vodun celebrations** (Benin and Togo). Benin and Togo are the cradles of voodoo, a mixture of traditional and Catholic beliefs. The ritual season peaks in December and January, and Benin even has an official Vodun holiday (January 10) when – apart from the serious business of worshipping – you'll get plenty of chances to stretch your legs and party. In Togo, the big celebration is Epe Ekpe (or Yékéyéké) in mid-September, a sacred, week-long event in which women fall into trances.

Contemporary festivals

Africa's contemporary festivals are often the only chance you'll get to hear traditional music in some countries, and really come into their own for modern music, the visual arts, and cinema. The pick of these events, by genre, are:

- **Music** A couple of Glastonbury/Woodstock-style music festivals well worth coinciding with are the Splashy Fen Music Festival in South Africa's Underberg in April, and the Lake of Stars Festival on Lake Malawi (Malawi) in September. Mauritania's Festival International des Musiques Nomades in April is a celebration of Saharan music, while Morocco's Festival of Sacred Music in Fès (June) showcases an extraordinary roster of bewitching sounds from all around the globe. The Festival sur le Niger at Ségou (early February) boasts Mali's biggest musical stars as well as traditional performers and pirogue races. For jazz lovers, the big event is the Saint Louis Jazz Festival (Senegal) in May. For hip-hop, get to the Festival International de la Culture Hip-Hop at Ouagadougou and Bobo-Dioulasso in Burkina Faso in

October, or the Festival Gabao Hip-Hop in Gabon's Libreville in June. You'll also hear rap and hip-hop at Zanzibar's excellent Festival of the Dhow Countries in July, which features the whole gamut of sounds from the western Indian Ocean, and also doubles as a film festival. There are similar sounds to be heard at the Médina Festival on Nzwani island in the Comoros, every May, June or July.

- **Cinema** The most star-studded film festival is Burkina Faso's FESPACO at Ouagadougou, held in February and March of odd-numbered years. There's also the Quintessence film festival at Ouidah in Benin in January, the Rwanda Film Festival in March, and the Durban International Film Festival in South Africa in June.

- **Visual arts** The main contemporary arts festivals are DAK'ART in Dakar (Senegal, May of even-numbered years), and Dar es Salaam's East Africa Art Biennale (Tanzania, December of odd-numbered years). In Morocco, the Asilah International Arts Festival in August is also a major showcase.

- **Slave-related** The Gambia's International Roots Festival (May/June of even-numbered years) is aimed primarily at African-American "homecomers" wishing to reaffirm their ties with the old continent, and – with luck – invest in the country. In Ghana, the Pan-African Historical Theatre Festival (July/August of odd-numbered years) also has a slavery theme, and features a grand "durbar" of chiefs (to whom mere mortals pay homage), a re-enactment of a slave march, and midnight vigil at Cape Coast Castle.

4

How much will it cost?

Wealth comes in walking but exits running
Ethiopian proverb

Whether you're bumming around as a backpacker or burning hundreds of dollars a night on pampered neo-colonial luxury, Africa has something for all pockets. The total cost of your holiday is obviously related to the amount of time you're travelling, but much more important in determining the dimension of the hole in your pocket is what you'll be doing, and how. Although most African countries are relatively cheap if you stay in lowly guesthouses, eat with the locals and travel by public transport, most tourist activities (things that probably prompted you to consider Africa in the first place) can blow even the most carefully planned budget to smithereens. This is especially true of wildlife safaris, visits to national parks, mountain climbing and scuba-diving, and anything requiring a rental car or flights. If you're more interested in culture than in big thrills like wildlife, you'll find your money stretching much further.

Given that your trip should hopefully be the journey of a lifetime (and, perhaps, the first of many), don't scrimp and save to the extent that you regret not having done things just because they seemed too expensive at the time. The following points should help you plan your budget:

- **Budget flexibly**. Travelling always costs more than you think, so put some money aside for emergencies and treats: you'll definitely appreciate a room with air conditioning and viable plumbing after weeks of bumpy and dusty journeys and bucket showers, and the odd slap-up meal won't hurt either.

- **Count the big expenses before you go**. $400/£220 for a scuba-diving course sounds cheaper before you go than when you're actually there, when you've perhaps become accustomed to spending no more than $20/£11 a day. It's best, then, to make the big decisions, and to put money aside for them, before leaving home.

- **Spend ethically**. Africa is the world's most impoverished continent. Ironically, it can also be the most expensive if you're looking at luxurious or otherwise exclusive experiences. In too many cases, the money goes into the pockets of expatriates or multinationals, from whom the trickle-down effect into the local economy can be scant. Chapter 9, on responsible tourism, contains ideas and suggestions on how you could spread your money more equitably.

- **Keep accounts**. As you travel around, keep a note of what you spend. It's not much fun, but it'll give you an idea of exactly where those pennies are going.

- **Don't scrimp on safety**. Your personal security has no price, so don't cut corners if it increases the risk of being robbed or worse. Common sense is the main thing here: if you're arriving somewhere at night, don't even think about walking to a hotel but catch a taxi instead. Similarly, if the hotel that was glowingly reviewed in your guidebook turns out to be a dodgy-looking dive, go elsewhere, and if the boat looks ready to sink, or the bus driver has crazed red eyes, don't clamber aboard.

Basic costs

For tourists, the basic cost of living and travelling in Africa averages $20–30/£11–17 a day. More expensive places to visit include Libya, Mauritania and Niger (where desert transport bumps up costs), Cape Verde, the Gambia, Senegal and Zanzibar (all four of them popular beach destinations), and – on account of its war-torn infrastructure – Angola. The cheapest countries are Eritrea, Ethiopia, Ghana, Madagascar and Malawi, followed by Benin, Egypt, Burkina Faso, Tanzania, Togo and Uganda. Wherever you are, the main pocket drainers are these:

- **Accommodation** In the most developed countries, you won't find a double room for less than $15/£8 a day, and in cities you could pay double that. Rooms in poorer or more rural areas can be dirt cheap (as little as $2/£1.20 in East Africa), but by and large $5–10/£3–6 is more likely.

- **Airfares** For a return ticket to Africa in low season, count on US$1000–2000 or Can$1500–2500 from North America, Aus$/ NZ$2500–3500 from Australasia, and £400/€600 from Europe. High-season fares can cost considerably more. Internal airfares are comparatively more expensive than long-haul flights – a short twenty-minute hop might cost upwards of $60/£35, while longer domestic flights can top $300/£170.

- **Car rental** Both northern and southern Africa are relatively cheap at around $50/£28 a day for a saloon car, excluding fuel. In East and West Africa, you're likely to need four-wheel-drive and a driver (most companies will insist on providing their own, given the state of the roads), so costs rise to around $100/£55 a day. Renting a car is obviously more affordable if you can share the costs with a group. If you'll be needing a vehicle for a long period, consider buying one secondhand when you get there, and selling it towards the end of your journey.

- **Guides** The cost of hiring a guide depends in part on the country's average per capita income, and also on the level of skill and responsibility required. Overall, $10–20/£5.50–11 a day per guide should suffice.

- **Public transport** Local transport is cheap compared to your home country, but fares do nonetheless add up, and with spiralling oil prices things are steadily becoming more expensive. In general, count on around $2/£1.20 an hour (roughly 50km) for long-distance bus journeys.

- **Safaris** There are three components here: entry fees (which vary according to the popularity of the park or reserve), transport (generally vehicle rental) and accommodation. Southern African safaris are the continent's cheapest, at upwards of $70/£40 a day if you're a happy camper. In East Africa, you won't get anything for under $100/£55 a day. In West Africa, prices are more open to bargaining.

- **Scuba-diving** The basic "Open Water" course averages $350/£200. If you're already qualified, expect to pay $30–50/£17–28 per dive.

- **Tipping** Leaving gratuities is not customary in hotels, bars or restaurants frequented by locals, although it is appreciated. If you're staying in tourist establishments, staff will expect something: a dollar wouldn't be out of place for portering a lot of luggage, but half that would be adequate. In bars, expect to chip in more often than your African drinking friends – which is fair enough, given the comparatively high cost of bottled drinks. Don't forget one for the barman or barmaid, but don't insist they drink it with you (the money will often be more appreciated for buying things like food). On safari, tips are considered part of the pay; expectations vary widely and also depend on group sizes, so get informed about what's right to avoid disappointing – safari companies can provide guidance on this. In general, though, count on spending something in the $20–50/£11–28 range on tips for a three or four day safari.

Saving money

Flights and equipment are the main expenses before you start travelling. Invest time checking out your options and you'll be rewarded by lower costs; the earlier you begin your research, the better your odds on getting a cheap flight or the package you really want. It may be cheaper flying into a neighbouring country, too, and continuing overland to your destination. You'll also save money by avoiding

Teaching English

Teaching English is the way many people finance their travels around the world. Unfortunately, getting work permits for African countries can be awkward, even impossible if you don't have a guaranteed job offer to flaunt, so teaching is only a possibility if you're prepared to commit to working in one place for several months, say half a year or more. There are two ways about it: find or prepare for finding work before you go, or just wing it and see what you come up with when you're out there. Unless a school is really desperate, you'll need one of three qualifications. The basic TEFL certificate (Teaching English as a Foreign Language) is the quickest and cheapest of the courses, and costs around $400/£220. Much more extensive are the TESOL (Teaching English to Speakers of Other Languages) and CELTA (Certificate in English Language Teaching to Adults) certifications, which cost $1500–3700/£800–2000, depending on where you're taught and the exact flavour of the qualification. You don't need a degree to do the course or to teach, but you'll certainly find it easier to get a job with the degree/certificate combination. Teaching experience is also an advantage.

A good starting point is the TEFL website of the UK's *Guardian* newspaper (ⓦeducation.guardian.co.uk/tefl), with useful and unbiased articles, and handy listings of courses worldwide together with their prices (quoted in sterling). For English-teaching vacancies, browse the massive database at ⓦwww.tefl.com.

high season: flights will cost less, and staying in posher hotels in coastal or wildlife areas will be more affordable. And, as there will be fewer tourists around, you'll have a little more leverage when bargaining.

Once you're on the road, apart from camping, the cheapest overnights are in dormitories, meaning youth hostels in North Africa, and church-run places south of the Sahara. Also, if you can live without air-conditioning, room rates will be much cheaper. For more on accommodation, see chapter 11. The cheapest eats are from street food vendors, followed by simple restaurants serving perhaps just one dish. Bringing cooking equipment (at its most basic, a gas-fired camping stove and pan) won't necessarily save you any money, but is definitely useful if you have special dietary requirements; hostels and campsites tend to have kitchen facilities. Supermarkets are expensive; prefer local markets and shops for fresh produce. The cost of bottled water adds up, so consider purifying tap water instead, though using chlorine tablets to do this imparts a truly horrible taste (see p.384).

The various international ID cards available to students and under 26's may get you reductions on flights if booked through a specialist agent, but won't do much for you once you're in Africa other than perhaps getting you the odd discount on museum entry fees. Student rates for national parks are practically non-existent, and neither are accommodation or transport likely to be discounted.

Tourist prices

The fact that you're in Africa at all is proof that you're immensely rich by local standards. Your flight will likely have cost far more than the average annual income, and even the most frugal daily budget is likely to equate to a week's wages locally if not more. So, no matter how poor you think you are, accept the fact that some people will consider you as little more than a cash cow – a fair target for the "special price, my friend!" treatment.

Before you start thinking that you'll be ripped off at every turn, know that "special prices" tend to apply only to tourist goods (infamously, souvenirs) and services. These prices are especially prevalent in beach areas popular with package tourists, where even basic

Once, in Morocco, I met a quack doctor and his stooge, who were staying in the same enjoyably disreputable hotel as I. They travelled the length and breadth of the Rif Mountains hawking spurious panaceas with which they claimed to be able to cure anything from heartburn to heartache. For professional reasons, the "doctor" claimed to be Indian, and his flowing beard and voluminous gold-and-silk turban certainly lent him an air of importance. In each town's busiest square, he would set up an impressive farrago of outlandish remedies, anything from goat hooves for baldness and ground-up ferrets for depression to dried chameleons – not just against snake bite, but a powerful aphrodisiac, too. The doctor then enchanted his audience with particularly florid patter, a piece of theatre that was an absolute wonder to watch. The stooge, for his part, would appear the first day to buy a cure for a sore throat or a bad back, and of course the next day he'd reappear, miraculously cured.

One evening, they invited me to over to their room for supper. Supper over, the good doctor – whose jovial mood had been enhanced by cheap Spanish whisky and ashashin opium juice – produced a wallet with a much rehearsed dramatic flourish. From it he extracted a battered sheet of oft-folded paper, scrawled all over with meaningless characters.

(Continued opposite)

foodstuffs might initially be offered at outrageous sucker prices. Taxis, too, often need quite a bit of haggling to get a decent fare (few are metered), but remember that the drivers rarely own their cars and are not as well off as you might think. Other forms of local transport tend to have fixed fares; if you are charged extra, it won't be all that much more. Where prices are marked, they're generally fixed. Ironically, basic guesthouses, cheap restaurants and markets – businesses that could really benefit from a mark-up – are the ones least likely to try to charge you a premium.

There's also officially-sanctioned tourist pricing to deal with. Mid-range and upmarket hotels are increasingly adopting two-tier systems, one for tourists, the other for locals, and the difference can be considerable. It's standard practice, however, so just accept it. Throughout the continent, too, you may also find that ferries and domestic flights have separate price structures for foreigners. Entrance fees to museums and monuments will often be marked up, with national parks being the most painful example. In Tanzania's Serengeti, for instance, a tourist will pay forty times more than a Tanzanian to gain entrance (\$50/£28 compared to \$1.20/65p). Is this unfair? Not when you consider that the average Tanzanian earns little more than \$50 a month. If you still feel hard done by, try to think of it as positive discrimination rather than the daylight robbery it too often feels like.

Bargaining

Bargaining is an important skill to learn, since every time you pay a "special" price you are not just getting a bad deal, but are making things more difficult for tourists after you, who will find it harder to knock down inflated prices. Once you get into it, you'll rarely end up paying much more than the going rate, and in fact bargaining can be a lot of fun.

North Africa's carpet salesmen are notorious connoisseurs of the art of haggling, and their initial prices may literally be twenty times what they're ultimately prepared to accept. Everything depends on the salesperson's perception of your ability, and willingness, to pay. The bottom line is that if you're happy paying a certain price (say, compared to back home), then it's a good price, irrespective of what locals might have paid.

Remember that bargaining is a game, one that should – if done well – be enjoyable and profitable for both parties. Getting angry will achieve nothing more high blood pressure and ill-will. Charm, politeness, good humour, relaxed chitchat and patience – lots of it – is in order. Remember, too, that it's the seller's prerogative to decide whether to sell to you or not; the customer is definitely not king. The following bargaining techniques should get you started:

- **Know your limit**. Before entering into any negotiation, ask impartial

---

(Continued from previous page)

"A marabout's charm," he explained. "It will bring phenomenally, nay, miraculously good luck."

"But marabouts [Sufi saints] are all dead!" I protested.

"Oh, of course," said the stooge, and apologized for the doctor's drunkenness. "You see, his is a maraboutic family."

"Ah, I see," I said. "So when exactly did this marabout write the charm?" I helped the silence along by suggesting that it must have been a long time ago, even though the charm had been printed on lined paper.

The stooge agreed readily. "It's written in sacred bird blood," added the doctor with a slur, "it is stork. Or perhaps ibis."

Both doctor and stooge knew that I knew the score, but they also knew that humour is the smoothest lubricant of jealously-guarded pockets and purses. The couple's best-selling item was in fact "sacred string", to tie around one's loved ones' wrists, around a bedpost, or to secure the plenitude of one's purse. All for a mere ten dirhams. Everyone knew it was a con; it was the act, the storytelling, the dream-spinning patter, rather than the goods themselves, for which their clientele parted with their money.

I bought the fake charm for the excellent price of 22 dirhams and half a packet of cigarettes and, thus guided, was invited by the quack to divine the names of the winning horses at the next day's meeting in Tangier.

– Jens Finke

locals what they would consider to be a fair price for you, as a tourist, to pay. If buying souvenirs, visit a gift shop in a large hotel beforehand. These have fixed prices; though well over the odds, they'll give you an idea of the absolute maximum you should pay elsewhere.

- **Bargain only for what you want**. Don't start haggling for something you know you won't buy no matter what; it's much better to refuse unwanted offers politely but firmly.
- **Dress and act like a local**. If you've been in the country for a while, you're more likely to have wised up to what's a rip-off and what's not. The less you look and behave like a tourist, the easier it is to get a half-decent price. So, put your camera away, avoid a lobster-red "suntan", pick up a bit more of the local lingo, and get out of those tourist togs (no safari suits or shorts, definitely no swimming trunks or bikinis) – it can be as simple as swapping a T-shirt for a long-sleeved shirt.
- **Feign disinterest**. If the seller knows that you're really hooked on something, it's difficult to work the price down. So, start by bargaining for something else you want, and when the haggling gets slow, casually offer to include the item you really want as part of the deal.
- **Bluff**. The bluffing on both sides is part of the fun; don't be shy of making a big scene. If the bargaining isn't going your way, say it's too much, thank the seller for his time, get up and start to walk away. That's often all that's needed for the seller to drop the price. Of course, if the item is unique or the seller really won't drop any further, you could always return the following day to complete the deal.
- **Buy in bulk**. Striking a good deal is easier if you have more items to play with. This also applies to accommodation, tours and private transport whose marked prices can generally be lowered by a bit if you'll be staying or renting for more than a few days.
- **Show the colour of your money**. Once you're close to finalizing a deal, pull out the cash: the sight of greenbacks may encourage the seller to knock the price down just that little bit more.

Carrying your money

In most of Africa the US dollar reigns supreme, and costly tourist services such entry fees to national parks and upmarket accommodation tend to be priced in dollars. Exchange rates are better for $100 notes than smaller ones, but be aware that $500 bills and old-style notes may be refused, given the risk of forgery. Sterling and euros are also increasingly accepted for direct payment, and you'll find in former English colonies that sterling attracts proportionally better exchange rates than dollars. Be sure to check current rates on the Internet before you go: ⓦ www.oanda.com has the lot.

Don't rely on one source of money alone: take along a mixture of dollars in cash, traveller's cheques and credit cards. The easiest – and cheapest – way to carry money around is as cash, but bear in mind that the payback limit of travel insurance for stolen cash is generally a few hundred dollar tops, and that constantly worrying about your stash doesn't help conjure up the picture of nonchalant cool which can, in turn, help avoid trouble. You're therefore unlikely to want to bring enough cash to last an entire trip, unless you're travelling on a modest budget and just for a week or two. Lastly, try to avoid carrying high-denomination notes in local currency: you'll have trouble getting change from them in out-of-the-way places, and flashing big bills around is also an unwanted advertisement for your wealth.

Traveller's cheques

Traveller's cheques are the safest way to carry money; the inferior exchange rates you'll get for changing them compared to cash are the price you pay for peace of mind. US dollar cheque exchange rates have the smallest differential with cash rates. American Express and Thomas Cook traveller's cheques are widely accepted by banks, at most foreign exchange bureaus, and for payment at the larger and more expensive hotels.

When changing traveller's cheques, you'll need to show your passport and the receipt you received when you bought the cheques (the one that includes the cheques' serial numbers). The importance of keeping your receipt in a safe place and in a legible state cannot be overstated; make photocopies of it and keep it separate from the cheques themselves. In the event that cheques are lost or stolen, the issuing company expects you to report the loss immediately (details are given when you buy the cheques); both American Express and Thomas Cook claim to replace lost or stolen cheques within 24 hours.

Credit and debit cards

The most commonly accepted cards, for both payments and use in ATMs, are Visa and MasterCard; JCB and Diners Club also have wide acceptance. Debit cards carrying the Visa or MasterCard logos are accepted in South Africa, but may not work elsewhere – check with your card issuer. Definitely not welcome is American Express.

Direct payments with plastic are most likely for tourist services such as upmarket accommodation, flights, tours and car rental, but using cards may attract a premium of five to ten percent over the cash price, even more if you're paying with American Express. Always check in advance whether your card will be accepted, and what additional charges may be levied. To avoid abuse, ensure that the voucher specifies the correct currency before you sign, and fill in any empty boxes on the slip with zeroes. Also, be careful not to let the card out of your sight to ensure that only one slip is filled in to ensure that your card details aren't put on to more than one transaction slip.

If for some reason your card doesn't work in the machines, over-the-counter cash advances through banks and credit card agents (often the larger tour companies) are possible, so long as your account has not been blocked. You might need your PIN number, and large transactions may entail an interrogation to screen for fraud.

Exchange rates for withdrawals and payments are determined by your card issuer, and are generally quite fair. What does hike up the cost is the handling charge and the commission on foreign exchange, which can add five percent to the total. Remember also to set up a monthly standing order to cover minimum monthly repayments; failing to do so may get your card blocked just when you need it most.

Should your card be stolen or go missing, you'll need to call the card issuer as soon as possible, so keep a note of the emergency

ATMs

By far the easiest means of getting local currency in Africa's larger towns and cities is through ATM machines, almost all of which accept Visa and Master-Card, so long as you have a Personal Identification Number (PIN). American Express cardholders are limited to South Africa and to a handful of machines in Egypt. To see whether there's a machine in a given location, try Visa's ATM locator at ⓦ visa.via.infonow.net/locator/global, or MasterCard's locator at ⓦ www.mastercard.com/cardholderservices/atm. Some ATMs may also accept bank cards bearing the Cirrus or Maestro logo. A daily withdrawal limit of around $400/£220 is usual; check with your card issuer.

number in a safe place. So long as you report the theft promptly, the card issuer will cover any fraudulent withdrawals.

While it's theoretically possible to access funds using only credit cards while on holiday in Africa, blips in the system – whether local or back home – mean that plastic should definitely not be the primary means of accessing money, especially if you are spending much time away from towns and cities.

Changing money

As a general rule, never change money on the street. There's a real risk of being ripped off, whether through outright theft or elaborate ruses using psychological tricks and sleight of hand (see pp.403–404). That said, in some countries – including much of West Africa (especially Ghana and Nigeria), Sudan, Somalia and Somaliland, and Zimbabwe – black market rates for hard currency can be far better than those offered through official channels. Black markets are of course illegal, so always seek reliable local advice on the safest places for changing cash if you're tempted. Note that it is only cash that you can change on the black market.

Official places for changing hard currencies include banks and foreign exchange bureaus, and (at substantially poorer rates) some large

△ Changing money on the street is seldom a good idea

hotels. Banks pay better rates than foreign exchange bureaus, but the downside is that transactions can be very drawn out – there's a whole lot of paper pushing involved. Long queues are another favourite with banks; be sure you're in the right one. Foreign exchange bureaus are invariably faster, have longer opening hours (often including weekends too) and rarely charge commission or other fees, but this is offset by less favourable rates. Also, not all will change traveller's cheques, and if they do, the rate may be five to ten percent lower than for cash. Once you're done, count your money carefully before leaving the counter.

Except where fixed by the central bank, exchange rates can vary depending on your location. In beach resorts and other tourist areas you'll get far less bang for your buck than in a city, and rates at airports aren't overly generous either. Always ask first what commission and charges will be deducted, as they can vary mysteriously even within branches of the same company. In general, you shouldn't pay more than two percent. In theory you should keep exchange receipts until you leave the country, though they're rarely – if ever – asked for.

Emergency funds

If you really get stuck, having money wired from back home is the solution. The Internet makes this much easier and quicker than once it was (you can even do it yourself if you have a way of paying online), and you can reasonably expect funds to arrive the same day, or even within the hour. The two big players are Western Union (Ⓦwww .westernunion.com) and MoneyGram (Ⓦwww.moneygram.com). Both have thousands of offices throughout the continent, even in small towns, often incorporated into post offices. Both offer time-saving online payment options, so your folks back home won't have to visit an office.

Which of the two companies you choose depends on who has an agent closest to you. Western Union doesn't have agents in Lesotho, Namibia, Somalia, South Africa and Swaziland; MoneyGram's exceptions are Algeria, the Comoros, Djibouti, Sudan and Swaziland. The costs aren't all that high: MoneyGram charges around $31/£17 to send $500/£280 same-day to Cameroon, for example.

5

Guidebooks and other resources

The one who asks questions doesn't lose his way

Akan proverb, Ghana

Once you've got your basic route sketched out, it's time to fill in the details. Guidebooks are the best all-round sources of information; buy one in advance rather than at the airport, as they contain practical advice on preparing for a trip. Having a good guidebook to hand when travelling can be a real comfort, too, especially during the first few days when you're still finding your feet. Some travellers hang on to every word and recommendation they read, but that's not the best way to go: some establishments, having been given the thumbs-up by popular guidebooks, can afford to lower standards and raise their prices. In any case, it's always fun to find things out for yourself.

Choosing a guidebook

While short on practical advice, full-colour guidebooks such as those from Insight Guides (Ⓦwww.insightguides.com) and Eyewitness (Ⓦwww.dk.com) are stuffed with inspirational photography and interesting contextual articles. More useful for actual travel are the series published by Rough Guides (@www.roughguides .com), Lonely Planet (@www.lonelyplanet.com), Bradt (@www .bradt-travelguides.com) and Footprint (@www.footprintbooks .com), which should contain all the info you need: where to sleep and eat (for any budget), how to get by in the local lingo and get around by public transport, plus overviews of history, culture, politics, music and literature.

Obviously, if you'll just be visiting one country it makes sense to get a specialized book, but for trips covering several countries, you can keep the weight of your baggage down by buying a regional guide, even though they can be short on detail. The format and layout of guidebooks isn't too important; all are easy to use (or to get used to), especially if there's a good index at the back. Much more important is breadth, depth and accuracy. Reader reviews on bookseller websites can be useful indicators, but check the dates of the reviews, as some might apply to older editions. If you can, make your mind up in a bookshop or in a library, where you'll be able to compare competing titles directly. Look for the following:

- **Does the book cover your needs?** Accommodation reviews at either end of the scale can be patchy or superficial. If you'll be travelling in the lap of luxury, you'll want a book whose coverage of upmarket hotels and lodges goes beyond merely summarizing what the brochures say, while travellers on a shoestring should be especially concerned about details of public transport, including information on where you'll arrive in each town. Check the index at the back for themes that interest you, things like birding, rock art, music or specific places and ethnic groups, and compare the treatment given to these by each book.
- **Detail and accuracy.** All guidebooks cover the main attractions quite adequately; the differences are in the details. First off, examine their indexes for scope, and compare their hotel reviews: ones that mention unusual details like howling dogs at night or cranky ceiling fans are generally better than those that read like brochures. Bigger selections of hotels, restaurants and bars are a good sign, too. Unfortunately, recent publication dates don't guarantee up-to-date content: you can safely assume that many of the places covered in a guidebook were visited at least six months before the date in the copyright tag. The book might also simply be wrong, especially as regards hotel and restaurant reviews, and transport. Reader reviews

on bookseller websites, and the Internet forums listed on pp.269–270, can contain useful feedback.

- **Opinion and feel.** All guidebooks are opinionated to some degree. This is mostly a good thing, but can ruin a book if taken to extremes, especially if the author quite obviously didn't like the places covered, was too narrowly focused on one aspect of the experience to the detriment of others, or had overly idiosyncratic tastes. Some writers go out of their way to be positive about everything – again, not ideal. Read the book's introduction, and one or two destination introductions, too, to get a feel for the author's attitude and priorities.
- **Cultural coverage.** Even if you're not too interested in tribes and cultures, prefer a guidebook that covers them in as much detail as possible; the more that culture is included, the better the chance that the writer really likes and knows the place.

Other books

Coffee-table books about Africa are not lacking, as the sagging shelves of your local bookshop will testify. Nor are derring-do tales of high adventure in the wilds of a continent that is still largely misunderstood by outsiders. The following are among the better titles for Africa in general. Recommended books – including fiction – pertaining to individual countries are reviewed in the "Where to go" section of this book.

For free downloads of books about Africa, two websites stand out: ⓦ www.gutenberg.org, whose nineteen thousand titles contain many a work connected with Africa, and the French National Library's Voyages en Afrique (ⓦ www.gallica.bnf.fr/VoyagesEnAfrique), which has an amazing collection of scans of dusty old tomes (not all in French, either), covering everything from explorers' accounts to studies in anthropology.

A couple of CD-ROMs also merit a mention here: *Art & Life in Africa*, created by the University of Iowa (ⓦ www.uiowa .edu/~africart), with plenty of cultural information, images and videos, particularly to do with West Africa; and *Encarta Africana*, Microsoft's amazing African encyclopedia (last published in 2001), covering both the continent and its diaspora, particularly in North America, in admirable detail.

History and current affairs

- **Aidan Hartley** *The Zanzibar Chest: A Memoir of Love and War*. An account of the experiences of a war correspondent in Africa's most gruesome recent conflicts. The subject matter is hardly enjoyable, but the superb writing makes it impossible to put down.
- **Alec Russell** *Big Men, Little People: The Leaders Who Defined Africa*. Eye-opening interviews with a mostly motley collection of African leaders (and one or two refreshing exceptions, like Mandela), each symbolizing some aspect of the continent's mostly disastrous twentieth-century history.
- **Christopher Hibbert** *Africa Explored: Europeans in the Dark Continent 1769–1889*. An entertaining read, devoted in large part to the "discovery" of East and Central Africa.
- **John Iliffe** *Africans: the History of a Continent*. Recommended as an overview of Africa's history; also available in abridged form.
- **Karl Maier** *Into the House of the Ancestors: Inside the New Africa*. The best of many books written by non-African journalists about the continent's travails. Maier's anecdotal stories provide respectful vignettes in which ordinary people do make a difference; taken together, they paint a positive picture that goes beyond the usual stereotypes of Africa as a lost cause.
- **Roland Oliver and J.D. Fage** *A Short History of Africa*. Dated, but still the standard paperback introduction.

Africa's regions

- **Carol Beckwith and Angela Fisher** *African Ark*. Sometimes criticized for its *Vogue*-like treatment, this impressive photographic tour de force documents the traditional peoples of the Horn of Africa.
- **Antoine de Saint-Exupéry** *The Little Prince*. Ostensibly a children's book, but capturing perfectly the metaphysical essence of the Sahara.
- **Marcello di Cintio** *Harmattan: Wind Across West Africa*. The Sahara's dusty wind is the metaphoric glue that binds this collection of intimate and often poetic descriptions of West Africa.
- **Martin Dugard** *Into Africa: The Epic Adventures of Stanley and Livingstone*. A compelling, blow-by-blow account of the explorers' travels before and after their famous meeting, that relies heavily on the writings of both men.
- **Jens Finke** *Chasing the Lizard's Tail*. This nutter had his African baptism by cycling across the Sahara when he was 18. The book

blends personal narrative of what was a life-changing experience with a wealth of information on local culture and history. Free at Ⓦ www.bluegecko.org/lizard.

- **Rupert Isaacson** *The Healing Land, The Bushmen and the Kalahari Desert*. Part spiritual travelogue, part ethnography, this documents the ultimately hopeless struggle of southern Africa's hunter-gatherers to retain their culture and identity.

- **Mary Kingsley** *Travels in West Africa*. A quixotic tale by a remarkable Victorian lady traveller who defied convention in travelling alone. If only her compatriots had shared her humane and open-minded vision of the continent and its people, the world might have been a better place. On line at Ⓦ www.gutenberg.org.

- **Peter Matthiessen** *The Tree Where Man Was Born*. The wanderings, and musings, of the Zen-thinking polymath in East Africa. Enthralling for its detail on nature, society, culture and prehistory, and beautifully written, this is a gentle, appetizing introduction to the land and its people.

- **Kazuyoshi Nomachi and Geoffrey Moorhouse** *The Nile*. Stunning doesn't even begin to describe the ineffable beauty of Nomachi's photography, which covers the length of the Nile – and its people – from Alexandria to Sudan, Ethiopia and the Ruwenzori Mountains.

- **Michael Palin** *Sahara*. The comedian's light-hearted description of what was actually a heavy-hearted, looping journey around the western and central Sahara at the time of 9/11.

- **Mungo Park** *Travels in the Interior of Africa*. Still relevant to contemporary travellers is this account of Park's first expedition in West Africa in search of the source of the River Niger, and Timbuktu, in 1795–96. This, and the journal of his second expedition in 1805, are available at Ⓦ www.gutenberg.org.

- **Wilfred Thesiger** *Danakil Diary*. It was in the 1930s that Thesiger began his life as an explorer in Abyssinia (now Ethiopia) – his birthplace – by venturing into the blistering and (then as now) potentially hostile territory of the Afar people. His account is a very readable collection of extracts from journals and letters to his mother.

- **Laurens Van Der Post** *The Lost World of the Kalahari*. A classic of travel literature, erudite and elegant, and necessarily nostalgic too, given that even back in 1957 the end of the Kalahari hunter-gatherers' way of life was in sight.

Literature and traditional stories

The books reviewed here are anthologies; for works by individual authors, see also the reviews in the "Where to go" section.

- **Chinweizu (ed)** *Voices From Twentieth Century Africa: Griots and Towncriers.* A great collection of short stories, traditional tales, riddles and proverbs.
- **C.L. Innes and Chinua Achebe (eds)** *The Heinemann Book of Contemporary African Short Stories.* A nice selection from the big names across the continent.
- **Alice Werner** *Myths and Legends of the Bantu.* Published in 1933, this is a wonderfully jumbled collection of traditional tales from across the sub-Saharan continent. Thankfully, Werner's commentary has little in common with the narrow-minded colonial attitudes of her day. Downloadable from Ⓦ www.sacred-texts.com/afr/mlb.

The arts

- *The Rough Guide to World Music 3rd edition, Vol. 1: Africa, Europe and the Middle East.* We're not indulging in immodesty to recommend this insanely comprehensive work. Arranged by country, it contains thousands of artist biographies and discographies, and detailed introductions to the various genres, from Arabic to zouk.
- **David Coulson and Alex Campbell** *African Rock Art.* If any argument were needed to help preserve Africa's prehistoric rock art (paintings and engravings), this is it – an absolutely fascinating and beautiful work, thanks to lavish photography and intelligent text.
- **Angela Fisher** *Africa Adorned.* A stunning picture book on the dress and jewellery of traditional groups across the continent.
- **Iris Hahner-Herzog** *African Masks: From the Barbier-Mueller Collection.* Eye-candy from the world's most important African art collection, housed in Geneva.
- **David Lewis-Williams and Thomas Dowson** *Images of Power: Understanding San Rock Art.* An academic but accessible overview of rock-painting, with mainly hand-drawn reproductions, and interviews with San recorded in the nineteenth century, supporting the now widely held belief in a connection between rock art and shamanism.
- **Tom Phillips** *Africa: The Art of a Continent.* Among the widest-ranging of African art books, this covers the entire continent and everything from stone tools and rock art to ceremonial sculptures, jewellery and textile, complete with scholarly texts.

Magazines and journals

Travel magazines, even brochures produced by holiday companies and tourist boards, can be useful sources of information about specific places, and may carry general practical information, book and equipment reviews, and travel news. They're also, naturally enough, great visual introductions. Be aware however that only few publications dare to give you the full picture: beautiful photographs and florid prose sell best, so the writing tends to be embedded in dollops of honey, and things like the slums beside the Great Pyramids of Giza, near Cairo, or the herds of tourist-filled minibuses in wildlife parks are unlikely to be depicted. Be aware also that some sorry travel writers live off freebies, so what they recommend may be distinctly biased in favour of their benefactors (hotels, travel agents and tour companies). Among the best for independent travellers are:

- **Africa Confidential** Ⓦ **www.africa-confidential.com** A highly respected weekly journal on African current affairs; it doesn't beat about the bush when covering corruption and other political shenanigans. A few articles are posted on line, together with summaries of the main news.
- **Africa Geographic Magazine** Ⓦ **www.africa-geographic.com** Styled on *National Geographic* and with photography to match, this mainly covers wildlife, with a few features on remote peoples as well.
- **Condé Nast Traveller** Ⓦ **www.cntraveller.com** Holidays for the jet set: glamorous, chic, and far removed from reality.
- **Focus on Africa** Ⓦ **www.bbc.co.uk/worldservice/focuson africa** A quarterly publication from the BBC, the accent being on political, economic and social issues rather than tourism. The website has portions of the current issue.
- **Geographical** Ⓦ **www.geographical.co.uk** Magazine of the Royal Geographical Society, with in-depth features on cultural issues as well as ecology and wildlife.
- **Getaway Magazine** Ⓦ **www.getawaytoafrica.com** Lots of travel-oriented articles, a good selection of which are on line, together with loads of practical information and destination profiles.
- **National Geographic** Ⓦ **www.nationalgeographic.com** This superb publication needs no introduction. There's a mass of resources on line, too.
- **National Geographic Traveler** Ⓦ **www.nationalgeographic .com/traveler** Aimed at upmarket travellers, this spin-off from the famous magazine contains, like its parent, some great photography. Unfortunately, the articles can be somewhat superficial.
- **Outpost** Ⓦ **www.outpostmagazine.com** Canada's glossy mag for adventurous and independent travellers.

- **Travel Africa Magazine** Ⓦ www.travelafricamag.com A beautifully-produced quarterly with articles of a high quality and even better photography, mostly on fairly obvious touristic themes such as safaris and beachside heavens. The online archive is accessible to subscribers.
- **Travel Mag** Ⓦ www.travelmag.co.uk Great stuff, all online too, its articles often dealing with off-beat topics – a pleasant antidote to many of the swisher rags.
- **Wanderlust Magazine** Ⓦ www.wanderlust.co.uk Another visually attractive glossy, published every two months, each issue carrying at least one piece on Africa.

Maps

Although guidebooks will have maps of towns, regions and wildlife parks, the level of detail is limited by the book format, and the maps will not necessarily be accurate either. While they're helpful for general purposes, if you're planning to hike or undertake any kind of travel off the main circuits, then buying a detailed country map is a definite advantage. Plus, big maps that you can spread out on the floor while planning an adventure have the pleasurable habit of helping to conjure up dreams.

For regional maps, Michelin's three-part set is hard to beat: #741 (North and West Africa), #745 (Northeast Africa and Arabia), and #746 (Central, Eastern and Southern Africa). For West Africa, though, the best regional map – so long as you don't mind some Germanized transliterations – is published by Reise Know-How (Ⓦ www.reise-know-how.de), who also have amazingly accurate and detailed country maps: Algeria, Botswana, Cape Verde, Egypt, Kenya, Libya, Madagascar, Morocco, Mozambique, Namibia, Senegal, South Africa, Tanzania and Tunisia. All of these are printed on waterproof and rip-proof plastic "paper", as is the short series of African maps published by Rough Guides (Ⓦ www.roughguides .com), which are pulled from the same high quality sources as Reise Know-How's. At the time of writing, these cover Egypt, Kenya and northern Tanzania, Morocco, South Africa, Lesotho and Swaziland, and Tunisia. Not as accurate nor as detailed, but covering a huge range of African countries including places like Somalia and Sudan, is the series published by International Travel Maps (Ⓦ www.itmb.com).

Maps of national parks and game reserves can invariably be bought on arrival, and most countries have some kind of outlet for official high-resolution topographical maps from geographic or military institutes, useful for hiking way off the beaten track.

Websites

The Internet is an excellent resource, whether for finding information or asking advice, or even finding out what a place looks like (look it up on a photo-sharing website such as Ⓦ www.flickr.com, or try an image search on Google or Yahoo). For websites relating to individual countries, see the "Where to go" section. Portals covering Africa or particular countries are not lacking in number, but only few offer more than the predictable blend of Internet links, weather reports and brief guides decorated with adverts, product placements and more adverts. Far more useful are the following collections of reviewed and categorized links, all of them kept up to date:

- **Columbia University Libraries** Ⓦ **www.columbia.edu/cu/lweb /indiv/africa/cuvl**
- **Stanford University** Ⓦ**www-sul.stanford.edu/depts/ssrg/africa**
- **University of Pennsylvania** Ⓦ **www.africa.upenn.edu/Home _Page/WWW_Links.html**

Advice for travellers

Websites on health matters, and travelling with children, are listed on p.373, p.392 & p.418.

- **The Africa Guide** Ⓦ **www.africaguide.com** A great all-purpose travel site to Africa, this contains everything from country guides and travel journals to links and practical advice.
- **BootsnAll Travel Network** Ⓦ **www.bootsnall.com** A popular online community for independent travellers, with great country profiles and a ton of quirky (and often excellent) articles.
- **Bwana Mitch's Safari Portal** Ⓦ **www.safarilinks.de** This claims to be the most comprehensive directory of safari-related links for Central, Eastern and Southern Africa, as indeed it is.
- **iExplore** Ⓦ **www.iexplore.com/dmap/Africa/Link** A good commercial site teeming with information – country guides, travel diaries and practical info.

- **Fodor's Travel Talk Forums** Ⓦ **www.fodors.com/forums** Suitable for more upmarket wayfarers, this benefits from particularly knowledgeable regulars.
- **Go2Africa** Ⓦ **www.go2africa.com** Another good commercial travel site, dedicated to Southern and Eastern Africa, and aimed at overlanders and wildlife enthusiasts.
- **International Student Travel Confederation** Ⓦ **www.istc.org** Profiles and advice for countries across the globe, taken from Lonely Planet's guidebooks.
- **LexicOrient** Ⓦ **www.lexicorient.com** A brilliant resource for North Africa (and the Middle East), whose detailed coverage about even the most obscure destinations surpasses that of some guidebooks.
- **rec.travel.africa** The best newsgroup for advice from fellow travellers – and from self-appointed experts – about travel practicalities. To access it, you'll either need a Usenet newsfeed and a news client, or you can point your Web browser at Ⓦ groups.google.com
- **Salon** Ⓦ **dir.salon.com/topics/travel** A trendy e-magazine whose content is provided by fellow readers, this contains countless travelogues and articles, from insufferable purple prose and stereotypical puff to unusual treatments of lesser-known topics.
- **Thorn Tree** Ⓦ **thorntree.lonelyplanet.com** A hugely popular travellers' forum, courtesy of Lonely Planet.
- **Travel Talk** Ⓦ **roughguides.atinfopop.com** Rough Guides' travel forum.

News and current affairs

- **Africa News Update** Ⓦ **www.afrika.no** Daily articles and features from Africa's press, a huge archive, and a free email news service.
- **allAfrica.com** Ⓦ **allafrica.com** Comprehensive and up to date, collating articles from both mainstream and not so obvious sources such as UN agencies.
- **BBC News** Ⓦ **news.bbc.co.uk/1/hi/world/africa** Decent if patchy coverage; use this in conjunction with the other resources in this section. Very useful search function though.
- **Pambazuka News** Ⓦ **www.pambazuka.org** Categorized and searchable news features and links to articles covering the continent, with an emphasis on development, human rights, environment and conservation. Their weekly email newsletter is worth signing up for.

History

- **African Timelines** Ⓦ **web.cocc.edu/cagatucci/classes /hum211/timelines/htimelinetoc.htm** Five timelines which, while far from comprehensive, do provide a different way of approaching the subject, and contain a number of interesting links.
- **The Atlantic Slave Trade and Slave Life in the Americas: A Visual Record** Ⓦ **hitchcock.itc.virginia.edu/slavery** Hundreds of archive images, each accompanied by copious notes, concerning the slave trade on either side of the Atlantic.
- **Retelling the Story** Ⓦ **www.pbs.org/wonders/Retell/retlng .htm** A series of scholarly essays inspired by W.E.B. Du Bois' call for the history of Africa to be retold from the African point of view.
- **The Story of Africa** Ⓦ **www.bbc.co.uk/worldservice/africa /features/storyofafrica** An outstanding one-off feature from the BBC World Service, thoughtfully (and accurately) written, and accompanied by numerous photos.
- **World History Archives** Ⓦ **www.hartford–hwp.com/archives** Very good selection of links to documents covering all aspects of African history.

Society, culture and art

Websites on African music are listed overleaf.

- **African Art Museum** Ⓦ **www.zyama.com** A huge gallery of traditional artefacts.
- **African Indigenous Science and Knowledge Systems** Ⓦ **www .africahistory.net** An eclectic potpourri of articles and links, everything from astronomy and philosophy to psychology and mathematics.
- **African Proverbs, Sayings and Stories** Ⓦ **www.africinfo.org** A huge online collection of traditional African wit and wisdom.
- **Art and Life in Africa Project** Ⓦ **www.uiowa.edu/~africart** From the University of Iowa, an impressive collection of scholarly articles, photos, music clips and videos, together with a cultural encyclopedia.
- **Hamill Gallery of African Art** Ⓦ **www.hamillgallery.com** Commercial gallery with thousands of items online.
- **Le sahara néolithique** Ⓦ **ennedi.free.fr** Zillions of photos of Algeria's and Libya's rock paintings, with French text.

- **National Museum of African Art** Ⓦ **www.nmafa.si.edu** A beautiful eye-soother from the Smithsonian Institution.
- **Rand African Art** Ⓦ **www.randafricanart.com** An impressive personal collection of tribal art.
- **Saudi Aramco World** Ⓦ **www.saudiaramcoworld.com** A sumptuous publication (back issues are on line, too) that provides very readable and stylish articles on cultural aspects of the Muslim world, in Africa and elsewhere.
- **Tamarin** Ⓦ **www.tamarin.com** Slick art-gallery website, with interesting thematic exhibitions, including photography.
- **Trust for African Rock Art** Ⓦ **www.africanrockart.org** Headed by photographer David Coulson, the Trust aims to protect Africa's rock art from vandalism and from art collectors. Their website has a small but beautiful gallery, and informative newsletters to download.

Music

Africa's diversity is perhaps no better illustrated than through its musical output, which influenced much of what the Western world now considers its own. Music can also be a great theme for travelling, giving you a fine excuse to delve a little deeper beneath the surface: you'll find a few practical pointers, and some recommended resources, on pp.305–306 in chapter 8. The following are great all-round African music resources; for country-specific websites, see the "Where to go" section.

- **Africanhiphop.com** Ⓦ **www.africanhiphop.com** Rap and hip-hop from across the continent, with news, reviews, details of upcoming events, and audio streams, including two-hour webcasts of fresh talent every two months.
- **Afromix.org** Ⓦ **www.afromix.org** A good portal for African and Caribbean sounds and culture, with plenty of links to performers' websites.
- **Afropop Worldwide** Ⓦ **www.afropop.org** A big mix of mostly modern tracks and radio streams covering the whole continent, together with excellent features articles and gig reviews.
- **BBC Radio 3 On Location** Ⓦ **www.bbc.co.uk/radio3/worldmusic/onlocation** Archive of radio programmes, many on African music.
- **Echoes of Africa** Ⓦ **www.bbc.co.uk/music/features/africa** Another welcome offering from the BBC, this is an encyclopedic

introduction to the continent's multifaceted sounds, with many (albeit short) sound clips.

- **Maghreb Muziek** ⓦ**maghreb-muziek.startkabel.nl** Tons of links to some marvellously obscure North African music sites, well worth exploring despite numerous broken links. Oriental heavy metal, anyone?

- **Music in Our World** ⓦ**trumpet.sdsu.edu/M151/logan_M151 _MOW.html** One of the most accessible introductions to music worldwide, including an excellent African section, but sadly no sound clips.

- **Rhythms of the Continent** ⓦ**www.bbc.co.uk/worldservice /africa/features/rhythms** A short but attractive introduction to African music from the BBC World Service, complete with sound clips.

- **SHOUTcast** ⓦ**www.shoutcast.com/directory** Directory of streaming Internet radio stations worldwide; a good many from Africa.

6

What to take

Blessings are better than possessions

East African saying

The golden rule for any kind of independent travel is to travel light. On public transport, your fellow passengers won't much appreciate your having a mountain of gear, when it ends up crammed between legs, in the aisles or balanced on people's laps. Nor will you appreciate having a bulging backpack, no matter how many goodies you've got stuffed inside it, if you clamber off a bus into the tropical heat only to face an either/or choice of extortionate taxi fare or sweltering yomp to reach a half-decent hotel. You'll also be glad of spare bag room when it comes to buying souvenirs and presents. Some tips on keeping your load light:

- **Pack only the bare necessities.** See the checklist on p.382 for essential items.
- **Bring gear that multitasks.** Keeping things simple doesn't always mean going without, as some items can serve several purposes; Swiss army knives are a great example. If you have a watch or cellphone with an alarm, you won't need an alarm clock.
- **Buy or rent stuff locally.** Items that are widely used in the country you're visiting, such as mosquito nets, are much cheaper in Africa, and everyday necessities such as toiletries are also cheap. New clothes aren't normally a bargain, but good-quality secondhand garments are

available throughout sub-Saharan Africa. Specialist gear – for scuba-diving or mountain climbing, for example – can often be rented in places where tourism is well established.

- **Get rid of excess equipment.** Some travellers send home stuff they've finished with – items like hiking boots and winter gear, that were only useful while they were scaling the Atlas Mountains. Well, you could do the same, but surface mail is potentially unreliable, and can take up to four months, while air mail will cost you an arm and a leg. It can be far better to barter any excess gear for something you do need – there's a ready market for used mountaineering equipment – or even to give it away.

Which bag?

Tourism's ever-growing popularity means there's an embarrassment of choice when it comes to choosing what kind of bag to take. It's a crucial decision, too. For people travelling by public transport, mobility should be the overriding concern, while for trips on which transport will be laid on specially, volume counts for more.

Mobility means as much comfort as possible when lugging bags around, say from a bus station to a hotel. For travelling on public transport, a soft and moreover squashable bag is preferable unless you have something particularly fragile that needs the protection of a hard cover. The smaller, the better, too: if you can squeeze your bag in under your seat or the one in front when you board a crowded bus or minibus, you won't be fretting about the fate of gear up on the roof, and you'll avoid being charged extra for baggage. Having your things with you when you disembark also makes for a quick getaway should you arrive at a place popular with touts and hustlers, who would otherwise have plenty of time to approach you as you wait for bags to be extricated.

As well as a main bag, it's very useful to bring a smaller day pack for carrying stuff like a water bottle, snacks, toiletries, camera and notepad. The kind of bag is really up to your preference, but avoid ladies' handbags as they're far too tempting to steal. Some travellers – this writer included – swear by plastic carrier bags. They're not fashionable, but that's exactly why they might be a good idea if you don't want to draw attention to any expensive gear you're lugging around.

Backpacks (rucksacks)

Backpacks leave your hands free and, as long as the weight is evenly distributed, provide the most mobility when travelling. The various

△ Loading and unloading baggage can be a palaver, so travel light

internal compartments and external pockets make it easy to have quick access to the things you most use, and most models come with various additional attachment loops and straps so you can tie bulky or frequently used gear to the outside. All these features make them a big favourite among ... backpackers!

There are two kinds of backpack. The old-style ones with metal frames are difficult to find nowadays and are in any case only useful for serious expeditions, on which your gear far exceeds airline weight limits. Much more practical and comfortable are backpacks with either a bendy frame or none at all; either style should fit snugly into the contours of your back.

Before buying a backpack, it's vital that you check it fits. Your shoulders will suffer most, so the shoulder straps should adjust comfortably to your back height and girth. The wider and more thickly padded the straps are, the more comfortable carrying a full load will be. One way of lessening the strain on your shoulders is to get a pack with an adjustable waist belt. Assuming it fits snugly, it'll transfer some of the weight onto your hips, making for more bearable long-distance hikes and improving your balance a tad, too. Also important is the backpack's size, or rather its volume. Backpacks tend to accommodate less gear than their appearance would suggest, but don't necessarily jump at the largest one you can find – 40 to 55 litres, or around 2500 to 3500 cubic inches, is about right for most needs. The other thing you should check for is the pack's construction: cheap zippers, weak plastic buckles and badly-sewn straps are always the first to go. Expect to pay $90–140/£50–80 for a good brand-name pack from the likes of Karrimor, Berghaus, Eagle Creek or Lowe-Alpine.

The main disadvantage of backpacks, especially ill-fitting ones, is that they become a very real burden if they're too heavy: even 15kg (just over 30 pounds) rapidly begins to feel like a ton. Another thing to watch for is that, being soft, backpacks are easy targets for bag-slashing thieves (especially once you've checked them in at airports), and are difficult to secure against petty pilfering, too: miniature padlocks connecting the ends of zippers aren't any real protection, but they are a deterrent. Of course, the way to minimize security issues is to avoid taking unnecessary valuables with you in the first place.

Suitcases

Suitcases tend to be unwieldy and, if carried rather than pulled, will quickly tire out your hands or arms, so with a suitcase you can expect to need taxis more frequently than backpackers would. The main advantages of suitcases are that things easier to pack and unpack, and that hard cases are resistant to bag-slashers. Most hard models also come with combination locks, and are thus the safest kind of baggage to leave unattended in hotels. Suitcases with two zippers can be secured – at least against opportunistic thieves – with miniature padlocks.

Wheels built into suitcases can be useful back home and in airports, but outside the more developed parts of North Africa and South Africa, you're unlikely to find many stretches of smooth tarmac or pavements to use them on. It pays to spend more for a decent suitcase: cheap ones have wheels that quite literally melt on a hot surface. An alternative is to buy a normal suitcase and the most robust suitcase trolley – basically a foldable metal frame mounted on wheels – you can find. The larger and wider the wheels and the thicker the frame, the more likely it is to survive Africa's rugged urban terrain.

Travel packs

Travel packs are a versatile combination of backpacks and suitcases. You get wheels and a retractable handle, a set of hand grips, and back straps. All well and good, but if you're planning a lot of hiking, the bulky rectangular shape of the cheaper models should be avoided. You should also check for a waist belt or a harness to distribute the pack's weight more evenly.

Holdalls (sports bags)

Holdalls come in many sizes and sit at the top of the squishability rankings, making them a viable alternative to backpacks if you'll be travelling by public transport. Most makes have both a shoulder strap and two handles. As you'll be carrying the entire weight in just one hand or on one shoulder, ensure that the strap and handles are well padded. Holdalls can also be carried on top of your shoulder should you get tired – an amusing sight for locals, who would actually be in awe if you managed to learn the art of balancing it on your head as Africans do.

Cheap, ultralight bags, like the ones given out free at sporting events, are completely useless as they'll succumb to the very first piece of mangled metal they encounter under a bus seat. So, before buying any holdall, ensure that the fabric is relatively rip-proof. The disadvantage of holdalls, as with all soft bags, is that they're easy to slash open. They're also likely to get very bulky when fully packed, making them awkward to carry (they'll be knocking against your thighs or legs as you walk) – another good reason to travel light.

Clothes and footwear

For most of Africa, including North and Southern Africa in summer, loose-fitting cotton clothes are best, together with comfortable sandals or shoes, a broad-brimmed hat, and a warm sweater or light jacket. Comfortable footwear is essential wherever you are, and should be broken in properly before your trip, as it's far better getting blisters at home than on holiday. If you go for proper shoes, a good grip, comfort and breathable material (suede is a little better than normal leather in this respect) are the important factors. Waterproofing shouldn't be a concern unless you'll be trekking above 3000m in altitude, where temperatures can be bitterly cold. In these places, invest in a good pair of light-weight climbing boots: they provide ankle support, and if they're made of a breathable waterproof material like Gore-Tex, so much the better.

Special walking sandals ("sports sandals" or "reef walkers"; Teva are the best-known brand) are extremely popular among backpackers. They let your feet breathe, provide a sturdy footing, and can be used in many situations, whether you're wading across a river or are on a week-long hike. The disadvantages are that they provide no protection against forest- and bush-dwelling critters like ticks, leeches and snakes (not that you're likely to come across any of the latter). Neither do they don't protect against cold or sunburn, making it easier to understand why one famously rational European nation is known for producing tourists who like to wear socks in their sandals – it may not be pretty, but it's a wise thing to do.

Safari clothes

A whole industry has grown up around the purveyance of specialized safari togs, a business whose rationale is, quite honestly, difficult to understand unless you have a passion for clothes with ten squillion zippered pockets, or have an unusually sensitive backside – in which case special padded trousers might actually be useful. In the main, though, wearing designer safari apparel lends you an air of the ridiculous (at least in local eyes), and also guarantees that you'll be treated as just another tourist. And don't even think about a pith helmet.

Assuming you're adequately dressed for the climate, the only additional consideration for clothing on a wildlife safari is its colour, which should be of an earthy hue, for two reasons. Firstly, it's best to blend in with your surroundings to avoid spooking wildlife. Naturally, that's impossible to do if you're in a shiny white Land Cruiser emblazoned with the colourful logo of a safari company, but nonetheless wearing clothes in earthy colours such as khaki, green and beige is better than decking yourself out in postbox red – unless you're a Maasai warrior wanting to protect your cattle, that is: lions have learned to avoid people dressed in red, a painful lesson taught them from years of experience on the receiving end of spears.

The other reason for choosing subdued colours is to minimize the chance of bites from tsetse flies. Bush lore has it that tsetse flies are attracted to objects whose colour or tone resembles that of their favourite meals, namely buffalo and wildebeest. Tsetse flies don't see colours as we do, so blue, apparently, is the colour that most turns them on, while colours which help avoid getting intimate with them are, according to the general consensus, grey, buff, olive, beige, khaki and brown.

Another safari colour faux-pas is wearing white. With dust or mud being the common denominator linking Africa's wildlife sanctuaries, white clothes are guaranteed to look dirty in very short order. Another no-no is military camouflage, which in many countries is illegal for civilians to wear.

Mountaineering gear

If you'll be attempting one of Africa's classic climbs, such as Kilimanjaro, Mount Kenya or Mount Meru, or Morocco's Mount

Toubkal, it's wise to buy critical equipment at home rather than relying on hiring it locally, especially boots, sleeping bags and specialist clothing. If you'll be going with a hiking company, they'll let you know what you need to bring on top of what they provide.

As regards clothing, the important thing is that several layers of clothing worn on top of one another provide better insulation than fewer, thicker items. As you won't have much chance to dry things out (open fires are rarely permitted in national parks), waterproofs are vital, as is keeping spare clothes dry. Don't wear cotton next to your skin or you'll get soaked with sweat, leaving you cold and miserable. Much better is proper thermal underwear, which draws moisture away from your skin. Tight clothing is to be avoided as it can also make you cold by hampering your circulation. Ordinary clothes to pack include shorts and T-shirts for the lower slopes, a couple of woolly jumpers and two pairs of comfortable trousers. A towel and scarf are also handy.

Essential clothing and equipment for mountaineering include:

- **Footwear** Sturdy, well-broken-in and waterproof hiking boots are vital for the upper sections of the trek. Comfortable shoes with good grip are sufficient on lower slopes (in fact, some porters manage amazingly well with flip-flops). Wear two pairs of socks: a light pair (not cotton) next to the skin, and a thick pair of woollen or synthetic ones for comfort and warmth. Use thermal socks at higher altitudes.
- **Headwear** A brimmed sun hat to avoid sunburn, and a fetching balaclava (or scarf to wrap around your head) – a godsend on summit day.
- **Sunglasses** Essential to avoid snow-blindness; ensure they're screened against UV radiation.
- **Thermal underwear** Long-johns and hiking socks; polypropylene works well but avoid cotton.
- **Fleece** A warm fleece jacket is essential, and a fleece sweater wouldn't go amiss either. You could take two sets – one for hiking, the other for sleeping in.
- **Waterproofs** Jacket and trousers or gaiters; these should be lightweight and made of a windproof, breathable material like Gore-Tex.
- **Gloves or mittens** Ideally down-lined. Mittens are warmer; you can also buy Gore-Tex outer mittens for breathable waterproofing.
- **Sleeping bag and mat** Bring an insulated synthetic sleeping bag ("-10", "five-seasons" or "zero-rated"): night-time temperatures can drop to way below freezing at the top. Insulating foam mats are also essential.

- **Tent** Essential unless there are dedicated refuges. Adventure-tour operators should provide tents, but if you bring your own, make sure it's light and insulated – the collapsible-dome variety is ideal.
- **Walking stick or trekking pole** Saves your knees on the descent.

What to take – a checklist

The bare minimum

Documents and money Stash your passport, health documents, driving licence, insurance policy, plane tickets, money, credit card and traveller's cheques in a money belt; see p.286.

Medicine bag See pp.394–395.

Clothing Apart from ordinary apparel and shoes, consider bringing flip-flops, which come in useful when using bathrooms in cheap hotels. An ultralight waterproof jacket is handy if you're expecting rain, and a sweater is likely to find use for travel at altitude. Don't forget UV-proof sunglasses and a hat.

Toiletries Toothbrush and toothpaste and sun cream. Basic toiletries can be bought in Africa and are cheap, but fancier products are expensive, if you can find them at all.

Guidebook A map is optional.

Swiss army knife Recommended for long journeys or for forays off the beaten track. The most useful components are tweezers, knife, can opener, scissors and, optionally, a spoon or fork. Ensure it really is Swiss – Chinese imitations tend to fall apart.

Towel The smaller and lighter the better; or use a T-shirt.

Camera See p.284.

Notebook and pens

Plastic bags To protect your gear from rain and dust.

Toilet paper Ensure it's kept dry.

Alarm clock Or a watch or mobile phone with an alarm, for catching early morning buses.

Emergency information Make a note of emergency phone numbers for your insurance company, bank, credit card and traveller's cheques, and your country's embassy or consulate wherever you're visiting. Photocopy your passport, driving licence and vaccination certificates (if any), and keep them separate from your original documents.

- **Water bottles** Enough to hold three litres. A thermos flask for soup or something hot is a boon at the top.
- **Thermal blanket** For hikes over 4000m, a reflective metallic "space blanket" can be a life-saver in emergencies.

Optional stuff

Rope A thin but strong nylon cord is handy for hanging clothes and mosquito nets, sealing bags, and replacing broken backpack zippers. Bring at least 40m if travelling independently in the Sahara, where you might need to fill water bottles from wells.

Sanitary towels or tampons These can be bought in African cities though.

Contraceptives Condoms are sold all over Africa but quality isn't guaranteed.

Contact lens solution Or daily disposable contact lenses.

Battery charger

Binoculars

Radio Short wave as well as FM.

Compact umbrella Also useful as a parasol.

Sink plug One that fits several sizes.

Electric plug adaptor

Snorkelling equipment Buying locally can be very expensive, as can renting over several days.

Computer Heavy laptops are a burden, and don't like rough roads. If you'll need a computer, consider a hand-held Pocket PC (PDA) or Palm device together with a foldable keyboard. Pack plenty of spare memory cards for storage and backups, and bring a memory card reader for transferring data in Internet cafés.

Camping equipment

Tent The lighter and smaller when packed, the better. Dome-shaped tents with flexible "poles" are best.

Sleeping bag You won't need a full-on "five seasons" bag unless climbing at high altitude; in most areas "one season" or just a sheet sleeping bag suffices.

Mosquito net See p.375; ensure you have some means of attaching it.

Torch And spare batteries. Useful for wandering out at night in rural areas, when camping, or wherever power cuts are frequent.

Cooking equipment Bring a camping gas stove. Canisters can be bought in major cities.

Photographic equipment

Africa is an immensely photogenic continent, and the temptation is to takes loads of equipment. However, you won't need cumbersome long lenses unless you're spending time in wildlife parks – in which case a 400mm telephoto or better is essential if you want pictures of animals rather than savanna. Whatever camera you take, ensure you have a dust-proof and waterproof gear bag, and spare batteries.

Film is not especially expensive in Africa, but slide and black-and-white film can be difficult to find. Keep film and batteries cool by burying them deep in your luggage. Debates rage about the best film to take: on a two-week holiday, you might just get away with using professional film that would otherwise require refrigeration, but on a longer journey, where exposing undeveloped film to some degree of heat is inevitable, you're better off with standard film unless you can be sure about keeping your stock cool at all times. Processing is best left until you get back home, even though most towns have automatic one-hour-service machines – chemicals may not be changed as frequently as they should be, and slide cutting and mounting can be a disaster.

All in all, digital photography is the way to go. Given the sometimes awkward lighting conditions, a digital camera is particularly handy as you can immediately see when you need to retake a shot because it didn't work the first time. It's worth investing in a few high-capacity memory cards, as well as a memory card reader with a USB connector: having the latter will allow you to go to an Internet café to make back-ups onto a spare card or a CD, or to send the images home by email.

The art of packing

Take everything you'll need for the flight in your hand baggage, plus anything that's breakable or valuable. Everything else should go in your hold luggage.

Having got your gear together, it's a good idea not to shove it in the bag right away, but to test some of it before the trip proper. If you're planning on hiking for more than a day or two, get your boots or shoes worn in well before you go – the last thing you want is blisters appearing on day one of a once-in-a-lifetime trek. Also worth testing, or at least unwrapping, is a mosquito net. Some of the brands sold in Europe are worse than useless – too small to fit over anything other than toddlers' cots, and with holes so large that only birds would feel left out. If you're cycling, do a couple of weekend trips to test out the bike, and your legs.

When packing your main bag, remember the following:

- **Keep to airline baggage weight limits.** These are generally 20kg or 25kg for hold luggage on international flights. On national flights, which might be in light aircraft, the limit tends to be 15kg, although it's rarely strictly applied. Remember that your bags are likely to grow heavier as you travel around picking up souvenirs, books and other stuff, so keep things light to start with.
- **Save space.** Dump any non-essential original packaging, and say hello to bubble wrap, towels and plastic packs – any of which are good for protecting fragile items. Place your medical kit in a small but sturdy box.
- **What goes where?** The heaviest gear should always go at the bottom of a backpack. Things you're more likely to need on a regular basis should go on top. Valuables should ideally go in the centre or at the bottom, where a casual kleptomaniac might not immediately find them. Electronics and films should go in the centre of your bag; you'll get additional thermal protection by wrapping such items in paper, clothes or in a towel. Never put anything valuable in external pockets such as those on backpacks. On public transport, it's best to place valuables in the centre of the heaviest bag, which is least likely to be snatched; on planes, carry all valuables with you if you can.
- **Wrap it up.** Even if your bag is supposedly waterproof, wrapping everything in plastic bags is the only surefire way to avoid getting your gear soaked in sweat or by tropical rain, or caked in dust.

Hand luggage

Rules regarding hand luggage, including exactly what can and can't be carried aboard, vary from airline to airline and from country to country. Until the 2006 UK "liquid bomb" plot, rules regarding the number of items you could take were rarely strictly enforced, meaning that you could also carry a camera or handbag, whatever you bought at duty free, and perhaps also a laptop. For the latest, contact your ticketing agent, airline or the civil aviation authorities. In general, you'll be fine if you keep your hand luggage under 5kg in weight, and smaller than 50cm by 40cm by 20cm. If you have good reason to carry more or bigger bags, check with

Money belts

The safest way of carrying money, passports, tickets and other valuable documents is in a money belt, tied around your waist. Tucked under your trousers or skirt, it becomes practically invisible and thus avoids tempting opportunistic thieves. Be sure that the money belt lies flat against your skin; the voluminous "bum bags" worn back-to-front by many tourists over their clothing invite a mugging (or a deft swipe of a knife from the back to cut the strap), and are only one step short of announcing your stash with flashing neon lights. Equally dumb are pouches hanging around your neck.

The best money belts are cotton or linen – nylon ones can cause skin irritations. Any belt will cause the skin beside it to heat up and sweat, so be sure to wrap your documents in a plastic bag before placing them in the belt. No system of carrying valuables is entirely foolproof, of course, so be sure to keep photocopies of your documents, and cash for emergencies, stashed away in your main bag, perhaps even sewn into the lining.

the airline in advance as to whether this will be allowed. Wherever you're flying to or from, don't put sharp items in your hand baggage (including scissors and Swiss Army knives), or unnecessary liquids or creams – anything that could conceivably (or not) be used as a weapon.

Ultimately, what happens at check-in depends on the rules of the day and perhaps also on the mood of the check-in clerk, so remember that winsome smile. Useful items to pack in your hand luggage might include:

- **Personal medication** Including malaria tablets.
- **Guidebook** Or photocopies of the pages you'll need on your first day, including accommodation reviews and maps.
- **Pen** For filling in immigration forms.
- **Inflatable neck rest** For overnight flights, and – if you have trouble sleeping – eye shades and ear plugs.
- **Basic toiletries** Including a toothbrush, stuff for contact lenses, and moisturizer.
- **Reading** material In-flight magazines are rarely riveting.
- **Music** iPods and CD players can be used on flights except during take-off and landing.
- **Film** If you haven't gone digital, pack your film in hand luggage, as the powerful X-ray machines used to scan hold baggage can fog or discolour film.

- **Chewing gum or sweets** For unblocking your ears after take-off and before landing.
- **Nicotine patches or gum** Smoking is prohibited on all long-haul flights.
- **A fistful of dollars (or euros, or sterling)** Shops in transit lounges price their services in hard currency, and you'll need cash for snacks and other small purchases. Bring low-denomination notes as change may be given in local currency.
- **Clothing** Planes can be chilly, not just at night. They can also be hot and stuffy, so wearing thin layers you can easily peel on and off are good.
- **Toilet paper** If you're flying to an obscure airport and you think you may need to use the toilet there.
- **Valuables and fragile items** Carrying these as hand luggage avoids pilfering and wannabe Rambo baggage handlers (bags literally get chucked around). Having your camera with you is also a good idea, for aerial snaps.

7

Your first night

A long journey begins with one step

Kikuyu proverb, Kenya

Even for hardened travellers well used to dealing with strange and unfamiliar places, the prospect of clambering off a plane at midnight in Nairobi or Dakar, or for that matter at any time of day or night in Lagos or Johannesburg, can be a daunting one, especially if there's no one there to meet you. In truth, though, even in those cities, with their sorry reputations for crime, there's far less reason to be fearful than you might imagine, and if all goes well – as most likely it will – there's every reason to look forward to your first day and night in Africa.

The surest path to serenity on arrival is to have it all planned out beforehand: which hotel you'll be staying at (or at the very least an idea of the general area to head for), and how to get there from the airport. A guidebook is a godsend for this, especially if you're on a tight budget, as Internet coverage of cheap places to stay is patchy and not always reliable. You can save yourself the hassle of digging out the guidebook every time you need to check it by photocopying the book's city plan and hotel reviews, and having them to hand in your pocket.

Good preparation also means reading up on your destination: the attractions and the nitty-gritty practicalities, certainly, but also things like culture, history, literature, music or wildlife – subjects that will give you a good feel for the country you'll be visiting. The books, websites and magazines reviewed in chapter 5 are all useful for this.

The more organized you are, the less you'll have to worry about, and the more likely it is that your first experience will be memorable for all the right reasons. Even the milling confusion at the airport, disorientating though it is, can lend a pleasurable sense of adventure to the proceedings: I'm here, I made it!

The check-in

The check-in desks for long-haul flights generally open three or four hours before departure, and close 30 to 45 minutes before the flight. You can't count on being granted an exception if you arrive late, as there's the whole security procedure to get through first, and in most airports there's a considerable distance between the last of the security checks and the departure gate. So, get there with plenty of time to spare.

Arriving early also means less time spent standing in line and – if you weren't already assigned a seat on the plane when you booked – you'll have a better chance of getting to sit where you want. Window seats have the obvious advantage of amazing views; aisle seats are best if you'll be stretching your legs often, or have long legs or a weak bladder, but also mean being disturbed more frequently by other passengers getting up. Check-in is also the time to ask if any special arrangements you made earlier, such as ordering special meals, were acted on.

Touchdown

Not all that many moons ago, some of Africa's international airports were really little more than glorified sheds, ones in which travellers

---

My first night ... in a mud hut

My first night in a mud hut was wonderful. I had spent the day walking from house to house, meeting with the village chief, elders, mothers, fathers and children, taking tea and chewing on freshly cut pieces of sugar cane. I was happy, yet quite exhausted from both the heat and the jet lag. At that point my bed of dried cow skins was just what I needed for a good night's rest. By putting myself in a situation where I was dependent upon my hosts for not only shelter, but also food and guidance, I was able to see a side of Africa that most tour companies couldn't offer. What I found was a world different from where I had come from, but quite similar when I got right down to it. It did not take long for me to call Africa home.

— Hans Johnson, Ⓦwww .maasaiculture.org

Happy landings

Flying to sub-Saharan Africa from Europe entails crossing the Sahara. This is usually done at night, in which case gas flares are the only thing that can be seen, but if you're a fan of aerial views it is worth trying to catch a daytime flight. The colours – rusty hues of beige, orange, yellow and brown – are absolutely wonderful, and the dark scars left by long-gone rivers are fascinating, as are the jagged contours of Lake Nasser. Flying over Egypt, you'll see the Nile, and perhaps also the pyramids in downtown Cairo. At night over Central Africa, lightning storms are common – and can be an entrancing experience, as the plane weaves among the anvil-headed thunderclouds. In Eastern Africa there's Lake Victoria and mounts Kenya and Kilimanjaro to look forward to. On final approach to Nairobi you should be able to make out the wildlife in the national park adjacent to the airport. Arriving in Lagos or Johannesburg, the plane may circle much of the city, giving you an idea of just how large those sprawling metropolises really are. After touching down at Nouâdhibou "International" airport in Mauritania, the blast of heat that assails you as the doors open is really quite something, as is seeing the plane's wheels already buttressed by miniature sand drifts not five minutes after landing.

Whichever way you're coming, it's always fun to trace your route, and some planes have digital maps on TV screens to help you do exactly that. Some airlines even have a live feed from cameras mounted under the plane and at the front – particularly amazing on take-off, though some spoilsport crews turn them off at that time to minimize the chances of their more delicate guests developing palpitations.

had to negotiate their way past machine-gun-toting soldiers under the watchful gaze of The President, whose likeness adorned every wall. Well, the photos of the *dictateur du jour* remain, but unfortunately for travel writers, most of the rest is long gone. Your destination airport will almost certainly have been modernized, and officials nowadays are far more likely to want to humour your first attempts at mangling the local lingo than go fishing for gifts. In fact, despite the queues and confusion, the whole process is really quite painless, in contrast to the rigmarole faced by some Africans arriving in Europe and America.

That said, the airport will be the place where you'll receive your first (and hopefully only) dose of African bureaucracy. In general, the formalities start with buying a visa if you don't have one already, then passport check, baggage collection, and finally customs, beyond which the outside world awaits. All this is quite a challenge when you've just emerged, bleary-eyed, from a flying cigar case. Patience, a gentle smile, and a sense of humour – even when faced with the most obstructive or obnoxious official – are always better than impatience or an outraged attitude: yes, the queues may stretch almost to the plane's door, and locals may push and shove their way through with impunity, but don't get hot under the collar … you will get through, eventually. And don't forget – you're on holiday!

The first thing to do is join your fellow passengers in the queues for passport check, or else for buying visas. Expect to face lots of seemingly pointless form-filling and queuing (perhaps to find that there's another queue around the corner for the form you missed), but immigration procedures rarely pose problems unless your papers aren't in order.

Be vigilant in the baggage collection area, as unguarded bags can disappear, and check whether anything's gone missing from your luggage. Should the worst have happened, contact the airline representative immediately. Once you've got your all stuff together, it might be a good idea to do a little repacking before you get to customs. The idea is keep your hand baggage light for the journey into town, and to keep valuables safe. Place anything you'd hate to lose, like cameras, in your heaviest bag to guard against bag snatchers (few people are able to sprint far with a heavy suitcase or backpack in tow), and stash your passport, money and other papers safely away in your money belt, keeping just enough cash in your pocket to pay for the ride into town.

Customs can be taken quite seriously by officials, so don't expect to be waved through just because you're a tourist. The main things that excite official curiosity are electronics and photographic equipment, and – in Mauritania – booze. If it's obvious that your stuff is for personal use (it helps if things aren't in their original packaging), you're most unlikely to have any trouble, but if you're carrying heaps of equipment you'll almost certainly have to declare it. There's no hard-and-fast rule about what happens then: some countries will note the details in your passport and will charge you import duty on leaving if you no longer have the items listed. Others will make you pay duty on arrival, to be refunded, in theory, on departure.

Changing money

You may be able to buy some local money back home if it's a major currency such as the South African rand or West African CFA, but don't count on it. In any case, all airports have some exchange facilities, whether banks or hole-in-the-wall exchange bureaus, and possibly ATMs that accept credit and debit cards. Use the first facility you come to as you may not have another chance. Unless you're certain that you're getting a fair exchange rate (not always the case at airports – check the latest rates at Ⓦ www.oanda.com before leaving home), change only what you'll need for the taxi and perhaps a couple of days, and be suspicious of hangers-on if there's no privacy.

Bringing hard currency in cash, especially US dollars, is wise in any case, as greenbacks are widely accepted for tourist services, including taxi rides. Prefer small denominations: this circumvents the old "sorry, no change" trick.

Getting into town

Once you've cleared customs, you'll likely find yourself ducking the attentions of touts for dodgy tour companies while you find a ride into town. You can try to minimize the hassle by biding your time: a lot of hustlers rely on new arrivals' disorientation. So, once you're in the arrivals hall, move off to one side, away from the crowds, and just wait for the hubbub caused by your flight's arrival to subside. Most hustlers target specific flights, and will not bother you while there are still other passengers to try. If you're asked what you're doing, say you're waiting for someone, and the hustlers will leave you alone. Finally, when things have calmed down, you can start asking around for a taxi or bus without being hounded.

Travellers of more modest means will have to rely on taxis or buses. On your first days, being cheap is definitely not best: local transport will likely drop you in the thick of things, and the transport terminals won't necessarily be marked on your map, or be in your guidebook. It's simpler, quicker and safer to catch a taxi, even if it means paying inflated "just arrived" tourist rates. Always settle on a price before getting in (or ask for an approximate idea of the price in the rare event of there being a meter), and don't be afraid to shop around for a better fare.

Finding accommodation

Safety and mental tranquillity should be foremost when choosing where to stay for your first night or two. Even if you're on a shoestring, it's worth spending a little more for a more comfortable hotel than you might otherwise go for – one less thing to worry about while you catch your breath.

Booking ahead buys you peace of mind and, in the most popular destinations (and especially in high season), can also be vital to ensure you get a room in a place that you really want to stay in. Whether you reserve by phone, fax, email or online (direct or through booking agents), get the confirmation in writing or print it off, and bring it with you.

Don't worry if you don't have a hotel reservation, though: cheaper hotels have a habit of losing them anyway, while business-oriented or package-tour-style places may have booking counters or agents at the airport. If you have a guidebook (highly recommended in any case), invest in a phone card or get a pocketful of change and starting ringing around. Alternatively, recommendations from taxi drivers are generally fine, so long as you set out your requirements clearly; otherwise, you'll end up at a place that pays the driver the

△ A backpacker in Zanzibar, en route to accommodation

Travellers from Europe will no doubt wonder what the fuss is all about, but if you're arriving in Africa straight from the Americas, Asia or Australasia, say hello to jet lag. This is caused by your body clock getting confused in a time zone more than a few hours different to your own, and shows up as fatigue, dehydration and sometimes headaches – in short, whatever you'd feel if you hadn't slept a night. Jet lag isn't helped by the tiring experience of flying long-haul.

If you're coming from the Americas, African time is ahead of yours, so you might have trouble falling asleep when you arrive (when it's 10pm in Kenya, it's afternoon in New York). The easiest fix for this is to sleep a few hours less than you normally would the night before leaving. Coming from the east, the opposite is true: you'll feel sleepy by day. The best way to manage this is to try to stay awake until the time you plan to hit the sack in Africa.

The alternative is medication, though this is overkill unless you really can't get your body clock to adjust. Your pharmacist can advise you about sleeping tablets or drugs such as melatonin (not yet licensed in the UK), which can help reset your body clock.

best commission. For more on choosing accommodation in Africa, see chapter 11.

The morning after

Unlike the traditional morning after, this one should be full of promise and free of regrets. Much as you might feel tired or lethargic, do try to get out and about on your first day, at least for a few hours. If you're apprehensive, museums are good places to start, being calm while capable of expanding your horizons. Decamping into a café or a bar is also good, allowing you to watch the world go by without too much involvement on your part. Remember to eat well (easy to forget when your body clock has gone haywire), and don't overdo the booze, at least until you really get a handle on things.

8

Culture and culture shock

If the rhythm of the drum changes, the dancers must adapt

Kossi proverb, Burkina Faso

The sudden switch from familiar to unfamiliar explains why most travellers experience some degree of culture shock during their first trip to Africa. Clothing, language, food, and of course the people, all can seem very strange at first, and the disorderly scenes around markets and transport terminuses, and even *inside* many forms of public transport, can be unpleasant surprises. In touristy areas, you'll also find touts, self-appointed guides, carpet salesmen, beach boys and other wearisome people latching onto you in the hope of prising off some money (see chapter 14 for more).

Jolted by the poverty, perhaps lonesome or homesick, or even frightened to head out on your own, you might find yourself wishing that you hadn't come at all. But don't fret – culture shock is nothing more than a jumble of natural reactions to things that you have yet to adjust to, and you will get over it, probably before you even notice. Here are some tips on riding out the initial experience.

- **Think positively.** Your outlook on life is really the factor that determines how much culture shock, if any, you're likely to experience. To pessimistic souls, a chaotic market is an eminently avoidable place full of pickpockets and hustlers; seen through more positive eyes, the same market becomes a sensual maelstrom that promises to sweep you off your feet. There are no prizes for guessing which approach is better.

- **Travel with an open mind.** The best holidays impart a gift of knowledge, so don't limit yourself to just a safari or decamping to a tropical beach paradise. Africa has a huge amount to teach, and if you travel in a spirit of humility, and ask, listen and observe keenly, you'll enjoy the continent at its richest.

- **Read up, listen up.** Most of the shock can be sailed over quite easily if you've read up on the place and its people. Listening to music from the country you'll be visiting can also be a great way of getting a feel for the place. See chapter 5 for useful books, magazines and websites.

- **Take it slow.** Flights and the stress of preparing for trips aren't kind to bodies, or to minds. You'll likely arrive sleepless and easily overwhelmed, so take it easy at first. If the local imitation *Burger King* appeals for meals, why not? And if you're on an extended trip, consider starting with a prearranged safari or excursion where you won't have to worry about organizing things yourself; it'll give you time to adjust. You might even bring along a comforter along the lines of Linus' blanket in the cartoon *Peanuts*. Small treats are a good idea: sweets, cigars if you smoke, an iPod loaded with your favourite tunes, even a bottle of essential oil that you've grown fond of – whatever turns you on.

- **Take care of your body.** Eat and drink well, get adequate sleep and dress appropriately for the weather. If you're in fine fettle physically, your mental outlook is bound to follow.

- **Learn the lingo.** You can get by with English or schoolbook French in most African countries, but the more you know of the local language, the better you'll be able to understand the country and its people – and folks will be delighted to hear you making an effort, no matter how mangled or comical it sounds.

- **Talk, talk, talk!** While chatting with other tourists is a great way of putting things into perspective, don't limit your exchanges to fellow travellers. Africans are a gregarious bunch, and conversations can be valuable steps on any journey of discovery.

- **Get out and about.** You won't get used to much by only exploring close to your hotel. If you find a few good places to visit, like a museum or a good restaurant on the far side of town, getting there and back will give you a better idea of the place you're in. The more you experience, the quicker you'll get over culture shock.

First impressions

Initial impressions go a long way towards shaping how you're going cope with your new surroundings. Of necessity, perhaps to arrange things like tours, safaris or mountain climbs, many travellers get stuck in a city for their first few days, and find the experience bewildering – whether it's the milling throng outside the airport, or the ride in through overcrowded outskirts, where the poverty can be a real shock. Even in city centres you may encounter mountains of festering garbage in the streets, or open drains whose contents flow nowhere in a hurry. Yet African cities can be disappointingly familiar in other respects: towering blue-glass high-rises in the business districts, advertising hoardings all over the place, and endless traffic jams.

But it doesn't take long to see under the brash veneer of modernity. Sharing the roads with the four-wheel-drive gas-guzzlers of the rich or corrupt, plus missionaries and expats, are battered smoke-belching buses and minibuses literally packed to the rafters with people, and taxis in often comical states of disrepair. At night, private security guards take up positions on street corners and doorways, while in

Having it easy

In parts of Africa less visited by outsiders, people are often baffled by my motives in wanting to travel just for the sake of travelling. Occasionally, they're suspicious. Entering Chad when government forces were still battling Libyan-backed rebels, I was asked by the border guard whether I was a Libyan spy. Not entirely convinced by my answer, he insisted that I take a military escort (two teenage soldiers in flip-flops) 10km on foot to the next village, where I was subjected to a grilling and a thorough search of my bags. The military there were also not convinced that I was a pukka tourist, but they did let me board a pick-up to the next town.

My presence provoked some excitement among local children, who would often come out and wave, shouting whatever the local equivalent is for "White man!" In southern Chad, one little toddler looked especially doubtful. "Go on," said his older sister (not in English, of course), "go and say hello." Bravely but hesitantly, the little lad came towards me, but at the last minute he lost his nerve and ran back crying to the arms of his sibling, who found it all most amusing.

Meanwhile, the police and military continued to be almost as wary as the little boy, and almost every 50km, I had to show my passport, explain my presence and submit to a baggage search. Halfway to Sarh, the next main town, the pick-up broke down and someone had to cycle off to the nearest mechanic, while we passengers bedded down under a mango tree beside the truck.

When we eventually reached Sarh, I'd had enough. Someone had told me it was possible for tourists to hitch a plane ride to the capital, Njamena, with pilots working for the local sugar company, so I went down to the airport to try my luck, and to my amazement, one of the pilots agreed to take me. It just goes to show that, for all the minor hassles, being a foreigner from a rich country allows you to do all sorts of things that are simply impossible for ordinary Africans. We really have it easy.

– Daniel Jacobs

unlit alleyways, the homeless light fires made from garbage collected during the day, lending an eerie brilliance to nocturnal scenes.

Leaving a stronger first impression on visitors is rural Africa, which will show you a side of life that is now all but gone from the "developed" world. Life in the countryside is tough – there are few surfaced roads, basic facilities we take for granted, things like running water and health care, are rare or non-existent, and of course the constant work of sowing, tilling and reaping (without the aid of machines), or braving days or even months away from home tending the herds, is exhausting. African villages also look very different to towns: houses are very simple, often of sunbaked mud bricks or else breeze block, and topped by thatch or corrugated roofs. Yet despite the poverty, and the obvious hardships and uncertainties faced by farmers and herders, the thing that will likely leave the strongest impression on you is the genuinely warm welcome.

Village life revolves around closely knit communities in which mutual help is the surest way to survive disasters such as droughts, floods, and the devastation wrought by AIDS. The cornerstone of society is respect: for one's elders (male and female), who are often the arbiters of disputes and the makers of communal decisions; and for deceased ancestors (who may, in the form of spirits, continue playing a role in the affairs of the living).

Harsh realities

There is no place where extreme poverty is more evident than sub-Saharan Africa, robbed blind by generations of colonists and kleptocrats. According to the United Nations Development Programme, in 2005 Africa accounted for 37 of the world's 40 least developed nations. Other statistics are similarly depressing. Urban unemployment frequently tops fifty percent; infant mortality remains high; and life expectancy is the world's lowest, and falling as the AIDS pandemic continues to spread – sixty percent of people living with HIV are in Africa.

With the main exception of the drought-prone Sahelian region immediately south of the Sahara, the really poor parts of Africa tend to be its towns and cities. Urban drift has led to truly shocking unemployment levels, and often fewer than one in five urban dwellers has a steady job. The areas in which most people live, dubbed "unplanned" by governments to avoid having to call them slums, are generally bereft of running water, electricity, sewerage, garbage collection and other services that the developed world takes for granted.

Yet the figures can be misleading, and for visitors, it's too easy to take things out of context. Accustomed to equating decent housing with bricks and mortar, you may find the use of clay and mud, straw, reeds, even cow dung as building material comes as a shock. But you can be sure that Africans are as houseproud as any, and in fact traditional building materials are often far better suited to local environments than concrete and steel. Farmers and herders may well be destitute in monetary terms, but few official figures tally the value of subsistence farming and cattle herds, for example. Rural economies are often partially based on barter, too, again something that doesn't figure in the numbers. Unless you visit remote parts of countries immediately south of the Sahara during a particularly harsh famine, you won't see people dying of starvation, either.

Even in the worst shanty towns, you're likely to be made welcome – and will be the object of much attention and amazement given that few tourists venture into those parts. Be generous wherever you're travelling, and don't begrudge someone a few extra coins when it's obvious that they could make all the difference.

Beggars

You'd think that so poor a continent as Africa would be crawling with beggars. It's not. In rural areas, beggars are virtually non-existent – the support of extended families, friends and neighbours sees to that. At worst, you may be greeted by the local madman or madwoman, an experience that might give you a fright but nothing more; locals will eventually come to your rescue after having milked the spectacle for its full comic potential.

The beggars you will see, mainly in the cities, are quite often visibly destitute. Some are cripples, lepers or blind, others are homeless mothers with children. The most shocking are people living with the effects of polio. The disease, which has yet to be completely eradicated, wastes one or more limbs, which can eventually wither away into little more than skin and bone. In cases where legs are affected, the lucky few have tricycles powered by hand-cranked chains, but most have to push and pull themselves around on low trolleys or even on pieces of cardboard using whichever limbs they have left. It's a devastating sight that you'll never forget.

More commonly seen are women with young children, who may or may not be professional beggars, and street children. Some may be AIDS orphans or may have escaped physical abuse; others may be begging on an adult's behalf; some are lost to the world on glue; all are persistent. Western sensibilities make them hard to ignore, especially when they trail you around murmuring pitifully until you cough up.

How much to give, if anything, is up to you. For many Africans, the giving of alms is a habitual thing. Some people argue that giving street children money encourages a culture of dependency. If you want to help, it's probably best to give food, or else contact an organization that provides shelter and education for homeless or otherwise at-risk kids. For a deliberately topsy-turvy insight into the unlikely importance of beggars in Senegalese society, read *The Beggars' Strike*, a brilliant novel by Miriam Ba.

Religion

Christianity, Islam and the continent's many traditional religions all embody a measure of fatalism: poverty and other misfortunes are more easily borne if it was God or some other supernatural force that had a hand in them. The majority of

Africans are either Christian or Muslim, if sometimes only in name. Traditional beliefs are not so much religions as holistic concepts of the universe and of man's place within it; almost all acknowledge the existence of just one God, although the common belief in spirits has long been misunderstood by outsiders to mean polytheism, or even devil worship. With the exceptions of northern Nigeria and southern Sudan, which have active Christian–Muslim conflicts, religion is not a divisive issue.

For all travellers, what can be genuinely surprising is the profundity of people's faith. God, the afterlife, and the existence of spirits are all considered just as real as anything else. If you're an atheist, you'll find that people have great difficulty in understanding your lack of faith, and may either try to convince you otherwise, or take pity on you. So, if you're a non-believer, keep your godless status to yourself, or at least come across as agnostic.

Islam

Islam is the dominant religion in North Africa, in coastal areas of East Africa and the Horn, and across much of West Africa. Before reading on, do please forget any "Islam equals terrorism" nonsense you might have been fed by the media over recent years; if you need convincing, remember that during the Inquisition not all Europeans were heretic-burning fanatics.

African Islam has generally found room to accommodate pre-existing popular beliefs in, for example, the existence of ancestral spirits, spirit possession (and exorcism through music and dance) and various forms of magic, including sorcery and divination, all of which would be guaranteed to offend in more orthodox corners of the Islamic world. That said, the last two decades have witnessed an upsurge in fundamentalist beliefs, as lamentably expressed through a number of terrorist attacks in North Africa, Kenya and Tanzania. The underlying causes of the resurgence of fundamentalism include deeply ingrained poverty, estrangement from mainstream society (and power), and a lack of faith in democracy thanks to too many decades under self-serving dictators, most of them propped up by two-faced Western governments or the former Soviet Union.

For travellers, the main areas in which Islamic sensibilities may have an impact are:

Islamic fundamentals

The religion of Islam – an Arabic word meaning "surrender" (to the will of God, Allah) – was founded in the year 622 of the Christian calendar, year 1 for Muslims, when the Prophet Muhammad arrived in Medina, having been chased out of Mecca by unbelievers, and began his conversion of the citizens. For Muslims, their holy book, the Koran, is the literal word of God, having been revealed to Muhammad over a period of 22 years by the Archangel Gabriel. Muhammad, far from being divine, was merely the messenger, although the respect paid him by Muslims means that his face is never depicted in images.

Stemming from the Middle Eastern monotheistic tradition, Muslim cosmology and the Islamic conception of a person's role within it is not very different to that of Judaism or Christianity: behave and do good to others, and you'll go to heaven; if not, the fires of hell await. That said, the Koran is a far more legalistic guide to life than is the Bible. It provides the foundation for *sharia* (Islamic law), and as such is read as God's writ. Each of the main branches or sects of Islam has its own interpretation of the Koran, and its preferred collections of sayings (*hadiths*) attributed to Muhammad, which complement the Koran. Christians, Zoroastrians and Jews are considered to "share the book", and Islam recognizes their prophets.

The Koran spells out five duties that each Muslim must fulfil, the so-called Pillars of Islam. These are: the heart-felt profession of faith (the *shahadah*: "There is no God but Allah and Muhammad is his Prophet"); recitation of five daily prayers; almsgiving (*zakat*); fasting from sunrise to sunset during the month of Ramadan; and – as long as the devout can afford it – a pilgrimage to Mecca. For information on Islamic festivals, see p.243.

Sufism

In many Muslim areas of Africa, the dominant form of Islam is Sufism, a broad catch-all term that encompasses all sorts of unorthodox sects and beliefs. What they have in common is the belief that personal communion or experience of God is possible. For some Sufi sects, this is achieved through nothing more than prayer, but for others, all sorts of tricks can be used: repetitively hypnotic chanting (*dhikr*), dizzying spinning dances (there are "whirling dervishes" in Sudan), even "howling dervishes" who slash themselves and use the pain to achieve detachment. Central to each Sufi sect is the saint (*marabout*) who founded the sect or otherwise inspired it. Annual pilgrimages to the saints' tombs are popular blends of sacred and secular elements, and are worth trying to coincide with.

● **Modest dress.** For men, this means long trousers or knee-length shorts, and not going bare-chested. In really conservative areas, your arms should be covered down to your elbows. For women, dressing decently is of greater importance. You'll never be expected to wear Islamic clothes (and the wearing of veils by locals is in any case rare, as opposed to headscarves), and leaving your hair uncovered won't cause offence, but you will need to cover your legs and shoulders. The easiest and most elegant way of doing this is to buy a sarong-like cloth wrap when you get there. Often beautifully decorated, these also make great souvenirs (or bed covers). Alternatively, loose trousers are generally okay, though they just might elicit unwanted attention from men unaccustomed to seeing the form of female legs, no matter how baggily they're covered. On the beach, women should be okay in bikinis if the area is frequented by tourists, even if you'll be sharing the water with fully dressed local women.

- **Alcohol.** For all the opprobrium attached to drinking (being seen drunk in public is none too wise), bars do exist in Muslim countries, though winkling them out in Mauritania and parts of Sudan can be a challenge. Where they're in public places, the entrances and windows tend to be covered with a sheet or screen to shield passers by from the depravity inside. Needless to say there's isn't much of a drinking tradition, so locals boozing away are likely to be assuaging a bout of alcoholism rather than drinking for pleasure. If female, they'll generally be of the looser variety.

- **Visiting mosques.** In African countries with Muslim majorities, Egypt being a notable exception, most mosques cannot be entered by non-Muslims unless permission is given explicitly. If you do enter, always take off your shoes at the entrance and, naturally enough, dress decently.

- **Displaying affection.** Overt public displays of affection between a man and a woman, such as kissing or hugging, are bound to cause offence. Holding hands is fine, though unusual among locals. However, men holding hands is quite normal – you're likely to be led that way if being shown around.

- **Ramadan.** The month-long fast is not the best time to be around; peoples' moods aren't at their cheeriest, and a lot of shops and businesses – including places selling food – are closed by day. See pp.244–245 for more information and dates.

Christianity

In most of the continent, Christianity was a religion imported (and often imposed) by Europeans, and their churches played important roles in the process of colonization, destroying countless cultures and societies in the process. Not so in Ethiopia and Eritrea, both of which had established Christian states by the fourth century

AD. The name of one Ethiopian king, Prester John ("Priest John") became known to Europeans, and encouraged a train of explorers and missionaries in search of him. Distantly related to Ethiopia's and Eritrea's brand of Orthodox Christianity is Egypt's Coptic Christianity, which may be even older.

Some African countries have over a thousand denominations. Many of them are based around the teachings of local preacher-prophets who may or not claim supernatural powers. Radical evangelical churches that actively try to convert people are common, too. A blend of Christianity and traditional beliefs is common in West Africa, most spectacularly in the form of Vodun.

Traditional beliefs

Traditional African religious beliefs, and for that matter the cultures with which they are intricately bound up, are an ever more scarce species. Traditional beliefs survive strongest in mountainous or otherwise remote areas, particularly among the pastoralist peoples of the Sahel, East Africa and the upper Nile Valley.

With the exception of West African Vodun (voodoo), which is properly polytheistic, indigenous religious beliefs are almost always based around the idea of a supreme God who created the world and the first people. Where traditional beliefs differ from Christianity and Islam is in the notion that this God has very human foibles and weaknesses. Several Nilotic groups in the upper Nile Valley say that when rains fail to come, it's because God simply forgot. The solution is animal sacrifice: the smoke from the roasting meat spirals up to heaven, where its sweet, delicious aroma reminds God that the folks down below are going without.

In most cultures, however, God tends to be distant from the living (too far away, certainly, to smell what's cooking), and is not normally prayed to or given offerings. Instead, the spirits of deceased ancestors act as intermediaries between God and the living. It's to them that people address their prayers and make offerings in times of need, in the hope that the spirits can convince God to bring rain, call off floods, or heal diseases.

In general, the habits of the spirit ancestors follow, in exaggerated form, those they had when they were physically alive. Thus, a kind-hearted person will become a similarly public-minded and benevolent spirit. On the other hand, the spirit of a murderer will predictably have bad effects on the living unless frequently placated with offerings. Bad luck, such as accidents, illness or sudden death, may be caused by spirits irked at having been neglected. Good or bad, no one likes to be forgotten.

Music: the pulse of a continent

Music is likely to be a constant companion in Africa, whether it's underground rap or R&B blaring out of the speakers of mini-buses, or the often ethereally delicate calls to prayer from mosque minarets, or even the rhythmical chanting and shaking of seed rattles of street hawkers. Africa is the world's musical powerhouse, and has influenced many a popular "western" genre. Music serves as a great theme for wanderings, and the hunt for the best venues and musicians can be the perfect excuse to go AWOL from the usual traveller's circuits.

Clubbing is best way to get a feel for the latest sounds: virtually all capital cities have great nightlife, but to get the best out of your nocturnal explorations, avoid the more touristy nightclubs (where Bob Marley and disco sounds can dominate, together with a zillion hopeful hookers) and head instead into the suburbs – ideally with a local companion – to hear the real deal. Music of course goes hand in hand with dancing, and even if you have two left feet, give it a go: locals will admire your efforts, if not your style (though most Africans will be far too polite to let you know).

Recordings can be bought all over the place, including from hawkers at bus terminals. Tapes are still the primary medium, although the more popular bands also produce CDs. For compila-tions and traditional music, you'll often find that you have more choice when buying outside Africa. Traditional genres are sometimes considered passé in their home countries, although there is a gradual cultural renaissance afoot.

At home, there's a wealth of African music out on CD, from the most traditional sounds to international stars such as Youssou Ndour, Miriam Makeba and Cesaria Evora. You should find recordings from the big-name stars in most of the big retailers, and of course on the Internet: good online stores include ⓦwww.calabashmusic.com, ⓦwww.sternsmusic.com and ⓦwww.cdbaby.com. Rough Guides' own series of world music CDs, published in association with the

World Music Network (⊛ www.worldmusic.net), comprises compilations of many different genres and styles, and are always worth listening to. For traditional sounds, the best labels – where virtually every release is a gem – are UNESCO/Auvidis and Ocora Radio France. For a great sampler of traditional sounds, get hold of the Africa Folk Music Atlas, which includes an excellent CD-ROM, three audio CDs, and a book: see ⊛ www.silab.it/eng/fr_catal.htm.

The best all-round book on African music is our own *The Rough Guide to World Music 1: Africa, Europe and the Middle East*, which contains more artist biographies, CD reviews and essays than you can shake a drumstick at.

Food and drink

So long as you're not overly picky and don't have special dietary requirements, eating and drinking in Africa doesn't offer much sustenance for culture shock. African cooking is generally quite gentle to conservative tastes; the intriguing delicacies mentioned in the box on pp.308–309 are very much the exceptions. In fact, familiar foods like pizza (or at least attempts at pizza), burgers, fried chicken and chips are widely available in towns, and Chinese and Indian restaurants are common enough, too. In touristy areas bistro-style cafés stock all sorts of treats, from fresh juices and real coffee to freshly baked croissants, pancakes and hash browns. Major cities will also have other immigrant cuisines – West Africa has a considerable Lebanese presence, for example.

Traditional African food is always based around one or more stodgy staples: cassava, yam or other kinds of tubers; rice, often sticky; maize, either grilled as cobs or as flour cooked into a stiff porridge similar to grits or polenta; and all manner of bananas and plantains, which can be prepared any way you imagine. Couscous – steamed pellets made from the flour of many kinds of grain, especially wheat, millet or sorghum, is the big thing in northwestern Africa. South of the Sahara, millet and sorghum are becoming rare as preparing the grains takes more effort and water than, say, rice, despite the fact that those plants are much better at surviving inclement weather.

Accompanying the staples are all kinds of stews. Meat doesn't feature all that frequently, but you will find chicken on virtually every menu on the continent, and sometimes guinea-fowl.

Africa's great cuisines

Africa's finest gastronomic traditions are Moroccan, Ethiopian and Swahili. Morocco offers tajines, couscous (possibly inherited from West Africa, where it's traditionally steamed in baobab leaves), excellent soups and scrumptious sweets. Along the East African coast, Swahili cooking makes loving use of herbs and spices introduced long ago from Arabia, India and the Far East, with seafood being especially good. Ethiopian cuisine is in a class of its own: the staple is a large pancake called *injera*, from which diners tear off pieces with which to scoop up dollops of highly spiced stews.

Many places have their own special way of preparing seafood, whether it's Zanzibar-style – spicy, in coconut sauce – or stuffed with vegetables and cooked in tomato, as in Senegal's *chep-bu-jen*. In South Africa, Brits can feel right at home with fish and chips, minus the newspaper. Inland, it's best to eat fish close to where they're caught. For carnivores, South Africa, Namibia and Botswana are the places to be: popular here are *braais*, barbecues featuring all kinds of meat and Boerwurst sausages, all washed down with good beer. Those countries, and Kenya, are also good for trying game: specialist restaurants dish up all kinds of antelope steaks, crocodile burgers and ostrich to a discerning clientele. In rural Malawi, smoked wild birds are a popular street food snack.

Where's the vegetarian option?

In North Africa, vegetarians have a reasonable choice. For a start, there are all kinds of soups to sample (though you might want to ask if meat stock was used in the cooking), from spicy Moroccan *harira* (with chickpeas and pasta) and *baisa* (fava beans seasoned with cumin, chilli and olive oil) to Egypt's *mouloukhia* (a delicious if slimy green leaf soup). Main courses are frequently vegetarian, too: all manner of beans and pulses, especially lentils, chickpeas and – in Egypt – earthy brown beans called *ful*. Marvellously fresh salads are also characteristic of North African cuisine, and snacks make for excellent picnics: there's fresh cheese, amazing olives, capers and great bread, falafel (or *taamiya*) made from chickpeas, and all manner of nuts and dried fruit.

South of the Sahara, vegetarians have a harder time of it, not because vegetarian foods are lacking, but because restaurants are

Mystery meats

You may be relieved to hear that none of the following dishes are in any way commonplace (indeed, some of the ingredients are endangered), and you're most unlikely to have them dished up for you at someone's home unless you specifically ask for them.

Snails West Africa's giant, fist-sized snails put French cuisine in its proper place.

Snakes Rarely eaten, and then only mainly in Central Africa, the Gaboon Viper is apparently very tasty.

Rodents One of West Africa's tastiest dishes is *agouti*, also called *akrante* or "grasscutter", a large guinea-piggish creature. Its meat is particularly fine, but it's the sauces and stews, which may well contain bits of fur, that make the dish really memorable. Further south, mice are a countryside favourite, particularly when they reach plague-like numbers (population explosions can be responsible for famine among humans, as they lay waste to field after field). In Malawi, Mozambique and Lesotho, they're crunchy barbecued treats on a skewer.

Mopane worms These giant grubs, also called *macimbe*, are a Southern African treat, especially in Zimbabwe. Deep fried or roasted, they go best with tomato sauce.

Monkeys Not that you'll ever want to try, but eating your distant cousins isn't a good idea, either ecologically or for your health: dead primates may be one of the vectors for transmitting Ebola or Marburg. Still, if you don't

places locals go to for a rare treat, which usually means meat. Apart from the ubiquitous and boring omelette solution and, in places more accustomed to tourists, pizza, local restaurants can be relied upon to supply beans and vegetables, and the better ones may be able to rustle up a fresh salad. Tourist-class hotels always have vegetarian options, and you can also eat remarkably well at Indian and Chinese restaurants in larger towns throughout the continent.

Dairy products

Most tourists steer well clear of dairy products for fear of catching something, but nowadays yoghurts and cheeses sold in towns and cities are almost always made from pasteurized milk (often on an industrial scale), so you can indulge safely. Tastier though are the cheeses found in rural areas: Tanzania's Usambara Mountains, Morocco's Atlas Mountains and many parts of South Africa produce care, why not sample monkey brain in Guinea-Bissau? Quite what you're supposed to do with the dried monkeys sold in Cameroon's markets, though, is anyone's guess.

Cats and dogs You don't really want to try these, do you? You do? Then Ghana's Volta Region is the place for stewed pussy (tastes like chicken), while Calabar in Nigeria has a thing about dogs – quite palatable, they say, if roasted in the manner of beef.

Termites In some parts of Africa, colonies of termites are so numerous that their combined weight outstrips that of all other animals in a given area. Termites are highly nutritious, so in Cameroon, Rwanda, Malawi and Uganda you'll find them being eaten pan-fried, deep-fried, mashed, or live. They're best sampled with a dash of chilli and a bottle of beer (possibly quite a few to begin with).

Locusts and grasshoppers Think terrestrial prawns, and the thought of eating locusts isn't all that bad. In fact they can be rather tasty, particularly when fried in butter. They're a popular bar snack in Uganda, Malawi and Cameroon, and egg-laden females are a delicacy in the Sahara.

Other creepy-crawlies Tuck into deep-fried beetles in Zimbabwe, similarly cooked grubs and giant grilled rhinoceros beetles in Congo, butterfly larvae in Burkina Faso, and millipedes in Namibia (hard on the outside, gooey within). The latter are mainly eaten at funerals, the taste apparently matching the experience of having lost someone dear.

truly excellent cheeses. For a traditional take on dairy produce, Saharans have a thing for fermented milk (fermented in a goatskin bag called a *guerba*), while East Africa's cattle-herding tribes, such as the Maasai, are famous for subsisting on little more than a mixture of milk and fresh cow's blood: the blood is drawn from a wound inflicted by an arrow in the cow's neck, after which the wound is closed and the cows potters off to live another day.

Fruit

It's always worth trying local fruits. Mangoes are the big thing all over sub-Saharan Africa, as are papayas, bananas, (smelly) jackfruit and coconuts. North Africa is Mediterranean: pomegranates, cactus fruits ("Barbary figs" or prickly pears), guavas, apricots and peaches, and quite likely the best citrus fruits you've ever tasted. The Sahara works its wonders on desert melons and oasis fruits such as figs and dates.

Liquid inspiration

Traditional non-alcoholic drinks are comparatively rare, so if there's a local fruit juice, give it a whirl: juices made from tamarind or baobab fruits are especially refreshing. Crates of Coke, Fanta and other sodas get to the unlikeliest places, as do bottled beers – most countries produce perfectly decent brands of lager similar to anything you might find at home. One bottled beer that's worth trying at least once, for the shock, is Guinness. Although Africa's take on Ireland's most famous brew is licensed by the Guinness company, it has almost nothing in common with the real thing. In fact, it tastes more like fizzy soya sauce, and has an ever so mean kick to boot (locals wisely tend to mix it with soda to mask the taste).

Even more eclectic is a mind-thumping array of home brews, based on virtually anything that can ferment. Palm wine is a big favourite, even in Muslim North Africa, where drinking sessions are strictly hush-hush. South of the Sahara, popular traditional concoctions might be made from honey, millet, sorghum or corn, bananas, papayas or cashew fruit. These brews, loosely termed beers, were originally the preserve of elders, whether men or women, and would often be drunk from a communal calabash at times when major decisions had to be made. Beer was also sprinkled on graves as a libation, and still features as such in Vodun ceremonies.

Traditional spirits are quite another thing. The problem is that some unscrupulous producers bypass the bothersome process of distillation by adding surgical alcohol or even worse. Sorry tales of mass poisonings are common enough south of the Sahara, and as a result home-made spirits are almost always illegal, though they're often sold quite openly.

Wine is, as you might expect, a big thing in South Africa, and the country's output can be found in upmarket restaurants throughout Southern and East Africa. North Africa also produces some wines, though the quality is variable, while Tanzania's output can be challenging to drink to say the least.

Being a good guest

The days of villagers launching ululating celebrations in honour of a guest are largely gone, but Africans are still incredibly welcoming (humblingly so, in fact), particularly in rural areas. It's important to act accordingly (ie honourably), and never forget that you're a guest, no matter how much you might have paid for the privilege of holidaying in Africa. And it really is a privilege to be able to travel without having to worry much about the cost. So, while you don't have to do exactly as the Romans do, you'd do well to pay due respect to local customs, cultural and religious beliefs, in areas such as the following.

- **Vices and virtues.** The main solecisms are public displays of anger or impatience, physically showing affection towards someone of the opposite sex (though holding hands is fine), and immodesty, be it verbal or material (flaunting your wealth). Patience and good humour are virtues, and will ease your way around.
- **Respect and deference.** Many African societies were and still are hierarchical, so much so that the pecking order continues up past elders to the spirits of ancestors. Cultivate a healthy deference for elders, and go out of your way to be civil to bureaucrats. Don't be shy about piling on honorific titles and greetings, and while stooping to obsequiousness is not normally required, it can work wonders if you're up against an especially stubborn official.
- **Taboos.** Other than immodest dress in Islamic areas, the only other taboo that's likely to have an impact on you is using your left hand for greeting, eating or receiving anything, as that hand is considered to be unclean due to its use in ablutions. If someone's hands are wet or dirty when you meet, they'll offer a wrist instead.
- **Gestures.** You're most unlikely to offend anyone with an unintended gesture, as everyone knows you're not from thereabouts. In general, though, pointing a finger at someone isn't too cool, nor is waving with the palm of your hand.
- **Dress well.** The simple rule is to wear comfortable, decent clothes, which should be as clean as they can be considering prevailing levels of dust or mud. No one will understand why a tourist would wear tattered garb – only the very poorest people are seen with holes in their clothes.

Greetings

Lengthy greetings – preferably in the local language – are extremely important, and people will value an effort to master them. Elderly men and women are invariably treated with great deference, and are often addressed via honorific titles. In East Africa, being called grandmother, even if you're 35 and childless, is a compliment and certainly not a comment on your appearance. Similarly, calling someone a teacher shows that you appreciate their intelligence. Well-behaved children (in other words, those not used to seeing tourists) will tend to greet and treat you as they would an elder. Try to respond with the requisite reply, although if you're stumped, pulling a silly face goes down a storm, too.

Greetings can go on and on, eventually coming round to the same questions: How are you? And your health? And your family? And your wife/husband? And the journey? … The longer you can spin it out, the more impressed will be your interlocutor. Incidentally, no one expects you to answer the questions properly. It's the same as in the Anglo-Saxon world, where a litany of medical conditions in answer to "how are you?" is inappropriate.

As well as offering a verbal greeting, younger women do a slight curtsy when greeting elders, while men invariably shake hands when meeting and parting. Among younger people there are a number of elaborate handshakes which anyone will be happy to teach you, and which vary according to the location and the person's age. It's a fashion thing rather than anything structured.

Being invited home

If you're invited into someone's home, do accept – it's something of an honour both for you and for the people whose home you visit. Be sure you leave a big hole in your stomach before coming: your hosts will probably make a huge play out of the fact that you're not eating enough, even if you've just gobbled up twice what anyone else has. It's good manners to succumb to their goading; it means you appreciate the hospitality, and indeed what's in the bowl or bowls in front of you – home-cooked food is likely to be much, much better than what you'll find in an average restaurant.

Food is traditionally eaten by hand from a communal bowl or plate. Although you may be presented with a plate and cutlery, it's best to try to eat with your hand: the gesture will be valued, even if you make a mess. Before eating commences, one of the girls or women of the house will appear with a bowl, soap and a jug of hot water to wash your hands with.

Paying for hospitality can be awkward, and insisting on it may even cause offence, no matter that they cooked their last chicken for you. So, instead of money, bring presents. Always appreciated are practical items that help keep down household expenses, things like soap, sugar, tea or a few loaves of bread, and – for more than a fleeting visit – more elaborate gifts like cloth wraps or blankets. You could also bring something fancy for the table: sweets make great gifts in North Africa. Elderly men often appreciate tobacco, whether in traditional form (often a thick and very pungent coil) or as cigarettes. Ballpoint pens and writing pads will always find a use, and kids will be fascinated by books. Most African bookshops are poorly stocked but will likely sell illustrated children's books in the local language. For other gift ideas, ask your host before coming.

The polite shutterbug

Africa and Africans are immensely photogenic, but few people like to have their picture taken by complete strangers. The golden rule is always to ask for and obtain permission before taking someone's photograph. Don't be offended should they refuse, and don't quibble if you're asked for a small fee in return – it's fair enough given the few opportunities that rural people have of earning ready cash. And, after all, they have the monopoly: only a Tuareg is a Tuareg, only a Maasai can be a Maasai (well, excepting the pretenders you might see in Kenyan beach resorts).

△ It's usually fine to take pictures, but ask permission first

In some areas, notably the Atlas Mountains, you may be refused point-blank. It's not out of spite but rather a lingering superstition that having your likeness taken is akin to losing a little bit of your soul. Elsewhere in the Islamic world you may be refused permission by particularly pious people as, theoretically at least, the Koran forbids the representation of Allah's living creations – hence Islamic art's amazing feats of geometric abstraction, such as arabesques.

Lugging along a Polaroid camera has the advantage of returning a favour instantly, as few tourists keep their word about sending copies of photos to the subject once they get back home. Digital cameras also have the advantage of instant feedback; if there's an Internet café nearby, you can get at least half-decent prints done to give away.

General crowd shots should be fine unless there are policemen, soldiers or politicians within your angle of vision. Few events are ever completely off-limits to cameras; some Vodun ceremonies in Benin and Togo count among these. Lastly, don't take pictures of border posts, police stations and military installations, nor of policemen, soldiers or airports – in short, anything that might trigger a fit of official paranoia. The same applies for snapping the President, not that you're ever likely to meet him.

Sexual attitudes

African sexual mores cover both ends of the scale: repressed or secretive in Muslim areas, hedonistic and unfettered elsewhere. The downside of sexual openness of course is that sexually transmitted diseases are rife. Despite this, female prostitution flourishes quite openly in urban areas south of the Sahara, and male gigolos ply their (mostly subtle) trade in beach resorts right across the continent.

In most regions, women travelling alone may find their motives uncomfortably open to debate. In short, men will likely consider you to be free and available, and you'll need to be confident with yourself and in your dealings with others to ride the fairly constant attention. You may occasionally come across overly persistent hasslers, but seldom much worse. If you suspect ulterior motives, turn down all offers and stonily refuse to converse, though you needn't fear expressing your anger if that's how you feel. Asking other locals for help in ridding yourself of a leech also works. A useful trick if you're unmarried and travelling alone is to wear a modest "wedding" ring, though for this to work it would be helpful to take along a picture of a male friend with a suitably husband-like message written on the back as "proof".

On the other hand, enough female tourists arrive expecting sexual adventures that flirtatious pestering – irritating or amusing as it strikes you – is a fairly constant part of the scene, though machismo is rare. If you're a woman looking for a holiday affair, be aware that your lover more likely than not does this for a living.

Surprisingly perhaps, male homosexuality is an accepted undercurrent in Muslim areas such as North Africa and along the coast of

We don't have homosexuals here

On a bush taxi very far off the beaten track in the west of Burkina Faso, I got talking to a local resident who had lived for a time in France. Thinking that it must be some contrast to arrive in Paris after being born and brought up in rural Burkina, I asked him what most surprised him about the city when he got there, expecting him to say something like the amount of traffic or the size of the buildings. Instead he said that the thing which most surprised him was the number of homosexuals.

Thinking that Paris has no significantly higher rate of homosexuality than any other big city, I said, "So are there more gay people in France than here in Burkina?"

My companion was quite shocked. "We don't have homosexuals here," he said. It wasn't that he had any strong ill-feeling towards gay people, simply that he didn't believe they existed in Africa, and nothing would convince him otherwise.

– Daniel Jacobs

East Africa, although it's officially illegal and can – in theory – get you time in the slammer. Attitudes elsewhere can be even more unenlightened, and many people don't even believe in the existence of homosexuality. The big exception is South Africa, where same-sex couples have the same rights as heterosexual couples under law. Obviously, if you're out in the sticks in South Africa you might encounter some less tolerant attitudes, but in places like Cape Town you'll find a thriving gay nightlife. Elsewhere on the continent gay nightlife tends to be far more secretive and even seedy.

Finding cheap accommodation can be a problem for two men wanting to share a room, as few guesthouses outside North Africa will allow this. It's usually fine for women to share a room.

9

Responsible tourism

Money makes ugly things look beautiful

Sudanese proverb

Tourism is one of the world's largest industries, and its growth in Africa has been spectacular. It provides an invaluable source of revenue for many countries, and – if conducted in a sensible and sensitive manner – can support local economies, help preserve indigenous cultures, and protect wildlife and natural habitats. Unfortunately, the mantra that tourism equals development is far too simplistic to be universally true, as there are many potentially detrimental and irreversible consequences of ill-thought-out tourism.

As someone who's probably arriving from one of the world's richest countries, your spending power – modest though it may seem to you – can have a huge impact locally. Being a responsible tourist, then, is a combination of respectful personal behaviour, minimizing the environmental impact of your trip, and making ethical and equitable choices in how and where you spend your money. It's not as restrictive as it may sound, and knowing that your trip is ethically and ecologically sound actually adds to the enjoyment.

Among the most active organizations concerned with responsible tourism are Tourism Concern (Ⓦwww.tourismconcern.org.uk) and Transitions Abroad (Ⓦwww.transitionsabroad.com). Their websites

contain heaps of practical advice, lists of recommended tour operators and more. Transitions Abroad also offers free downloads of its
annual *Responsible Travel Handbook*, and Tourism Concern publishes
the recommended *Ethical Travel Guide*, which reviews a selection
of community-based tourism initiatives and holidays in twenty
African countries, and elsewhere around the globe. While you're on
the net, have a look at *The Rough Guide To A Better World* (Ⓦ www
.roughguide-betterworld.com), which has useful links and free
downloads of the UK-government sponsored book of the same
name. A selection of responsible tour operators and travel agents is
included in the Directory at the end of this book.

Spending wisely

Seeking unspoiled landscapes and equally wild wildlife, many
tourists are happy spending fortunes in return for a few weeks
of adventurous hedonism. At the height of colonial power in the
1920s and 1930s, the perceived danger (and romance) of "darkest
Africa" was still thick in the air, and suffused many a Western
dream. What Karen Blixen did not dwell on in *Out of Africa*,
however, was the cruel injustice and frequent brutality of the
colonial situation. Things are much better now, you might think,
and politically speaking you might just be right, but economically
there's no question that little has changed.

One of the many problems with poverty is that virtually everything can have a price, so long as there's a buyer. For unscrupulous
art collectors and museums that think it's best to "protect" material
heritage by removing it from Africa, for multinationals heedless of
their environmental impact, and even for paedophiles – Africa offers
fabulously rich pickings. No matter that there may be laws restrict-
ing what can and can't be done: too many politicians, policemen
and other decision-makers will turn a blind eye in return for "a
little something". And the promise of eco-tourism is sometimes far
from reality.

Africa's economic divide is nowhere more obvious than in the tourist
industry: most of the continent's luxury wildlife lodges and camps,
upmarket hotels, safari companies, local airlines, even some game
reserves, are owned and managed by a tiny minority, a good many of
which aren't even African. How and where you spend your money is
vital in ensuring that your holiday benefits local communities rather

than serving to widen the gulf between rich and poor. The following are simple ways in which you can make a positive difference:

- **Buy locally.** If you have a choice, prefer locally run services and locally made goods (which will tend to be cheaper, too). For example, buy the bulk of your food and provisions from markets rather than supermarkets, and prefer modest guesthouses to big hotels that are part of a chain – the big resorts will survive quite nicely without you, but for a local hotel your contribution may well help keep them afloat. Buying locally doesn't mean making do with lower quality, either: some of Africa's most luxurious wildlife lodges are community-run initiatives, and for that matter some of the best meals are to be had in smoky, collapsing lean-tos in which chickens peck around your feet.
- **Give to charity.** The charities listed on pp.417–418 all do sterling work in Africa, and are among the more responsible and truly ethical of their kind. While you're travelling around, though, try to resist the temptation of giving out coins, sweets or pens to children: it encourages begging, as you'll notice in the chorus of "give me money/pen/sweet" that accompanies you anywhere tourists have given hand-outs in the past. If you really want to give something, hand it to an adult for sharing out, or – even better – make a donation to the local school.
- **Don't quibble over peanuts.** Honing half-decent bargaining skills is vital for avoiding the biggest rip-offs, but don't take it so far that you end up arguing the toss over the price of a handful of tomatoes, even if the price has been bumped up for you – the mark-up can make a big difference for the trader.

Eco-tourism: myth and reality

It wasn't so long ago that the words "savage" and "darkest" were off-the-peg adjectives for writing about Africa. Nowadays, the words "wild", "unspoiled" and "paradise" are preferred. Not that you'll need any reminder of the extraordinary riches of Africa's wild side: there are probably more wildlife documentaries shot annually in Africa than in any other continent. The upshot of this is the passion, even obsession, of tourists to see Africa's animals first hand.

Eco-tourism is big business, and most of Africa's wildlife lodges and tented camps claim to be eco-friendly. In some cases this rings true, but for the majority things are never quite as green as the brochures and websites would have you believe, and the eco–tourism tag guarantees neither environmental soundness, nor ethical propriety. For instance, privately owned wildlife conservancies can perform miracles in preserving endangered species, but few documentaries and no brochures will ever tell you that the land might have been expropriated from local people. If a truly ecologically sound holiday is important to you, take the time to research your options thoroughly, and don't believe the hype.

Environmental matters

The lingering problem with wildlife tourism, even when well managed, is that it's difficult to maintain the supposedly pristine state of Eden when there are tens of thousands of tourists passing through each year. Roads, airstrips, park gates and headquarters need to be built, and materials for hotels, camps and lodges have to be sourced, often locally. Then there are the daily environmental costs, in which

Air travel and climate change

It's beyond doubt that the world's climate is changing, and that air travel is a major contributor to the problem. As well as CO_2 – the main cause of human-induced climate change – planes also generate climate-warming contrails and emit oxides of nitrogen, which create ozone (another greenhouse gas). The figures are frightening: a flight from London to Cape Town and back produces the equivalent of 2.8 tonnes of CO_2 – similar to the yearly output of an average family car.

For now, there are really just two options for concerned travellers: to reduce the amount we travel by air (take fewer trips – stay for longer), and to make the trips we do take "carbon neutral". Rough Guides, together with Lonely Planet and other partners in the travel industry, support a carbon-offset scheme run by Ⓦ www.climatecare.org (see also Ⓦ www.roughguides .com/climatechange). This, and similar schemes such as Ⓦ www .carbonneutral.com.au, allow you to compensate for some or all of the greenhouse gases that you are responsible for releasing. To do this, they provide "carbon calculators" for working out the global-warming contribution of a specific flight (or even your entire existence), and then let you contribute an appropriate amount of money to fund offsetting measures. These include reforestation and initiatives to reduce future energy demand, and are often run in conjunction with schemes for sustainable development.

An alternative to paying a carbon-offsmet schee is to donate directly to a tree-planting organization. A good one for Africa is Nobel prize-winner Wangari Maathai's Green Belt Movement (Ⓦ www.greenbeltmovement.org).

your needs play a part: food and drink needs to be trucked in, as does fuel for vehicles; water may need to be supplied (few are the lodges whose water needs are covered by rainfall), and sewage needs treatment. There might also be fences, electric or otherwise, for keeping a safe distance between humans and animals. Fences, like farms, cut migratory wildlife routes, so the more responsible parks and reserves need to consider how to provide alternative routes for animals. In short, every aspect of human presence in wildlife areas can have an impact, for better or for worse.

The following points will help minimize the negative effects of your presence on the environment; for more on treading lightly while on safari, see p.360.

- **You are what you eat.** You're unlikely to be offered elephant steak these days, but you will find various, admittedly very succulent, cuts from antelope in upmarket lodges and restaurants. Some bush meat can be legal but the trade is so badly regulated that it's best to steer clear.

- **Energy and water are precious.** Poorer African countries undergo regular power cuts – it's increasingly difficult to keep adequate water levels at hydroelectric dams, so save power by only using ceiling fans and air-conditioning when you really need to, and turn off the lights when you go out. Prefer short showers to baths, and in hotels that clean guest rooms on a daily basis, let the housekeeper know that you don't need a fresh towel and crisp bed sheets every day.

- **Recycle.** Even though Africans are inventive when it comes to finding new uses for discarded items (elaborate toys made from soft-drink cans are a great example), it's best to keep your rubbish to a minimum, and to dispose of it carefully. Buy a shopping bag made of reeds or straw, or else paper, to avoid adding to the millions of plastic bags littering Africa's beauty spots, and re-use bags until they fall apart. You might also prefer purifying tap water for drinking to buying bottled water; that said, plastic bottles are valued in rural areas for storing liquids, so give them away instead of chucking them. Lastly, prefer products made from renewable resources: a novelty that has made a big splash in Fair Trade circles is paper made from elephant dung – much more beautiful than it sounds!

- **Use ecologically sound hotels.** The best eco-lodges have all sorts of useful tricks up their sleeves to minimize their impact: natural waste-disposal systems using reed beds, biogas plants to generate energy from organic waste, solar power and solar-heated water, even cleverly designed roofs to catch breezes and so do away with the need for air conditioning. All great stuff: if a hotel has gone to great lengths to adapt, you can be sure that eco-tourism is more than just a label.

- **Don't buy products made from endangered species.**
  Internationally banned but often freely hawked to tourists are products made from any number of endangered species. High up on the list of stuff to avoid is ivory, "elephant hair", rhino horn, crocodile and snake skins, and pretty much any kind of marine life: large seashells, corals, turtle shell (often called tortoiseshell), and sea horses. Plant products to stay away from include carvings made from ebony or blackwood, or anything taken straight from the wild – such as orchids and African violets.

- **No hunting.** Trophy hunting – an upmarket tourist activity in many countries – is so badly regulated and prone to corruption regarding animal quotas that there's no telling the damage you'd be doing to the ecosystem by going hunting. There's also a moral question regarding local populations: the best hunting grounds were formerly village lands, whose inhabitants will likely have been deprived of their traditional hunting areas.

- **Respect the rules.** Fragile environments such as grasslands, savannas and coral reefs can easily be damaged through ignorance. Most national parks ban off-road driving (wheel tracks trigger erosional chain reactions in semi-arid areas) and open fires are generally also prohibited. The general rule is only to leave with memories and photographs, never any flowers or other things you might find.

On the beach

Potentially the most damaging aspect of "Third World" tourism is a beach holiday. For various reasons – corruption, and arm-twisting from the IMF's implacable economists among them – African governments have been happy selling prime beachside (and animal-side) real estate to foreigners, without necessarily seeking the opinion of affected communities, or regulating the environmental impact. In some areas, virtually all the infrastructure is foreign-owned, everything from restaurants and hotels to scuba-diving schools, gift shops and even supermarkets. In places where locals are particularly badly affected, the result can be resentment. The good news is that you *can* enjoy Africa's marvellous beaches with a clean conscience if you bear the following in mind:

- **Avoid all-inclusive resorts.** There are a few exceptions, but by and large the biggest ethical and environmental offenders are prepaid "all-inclusive" holiday resorts. In return for a flat fee, you get pretty much unlimited food, booze and activities, with the result that there's little room left for local businesses such as restaurants, bars or even souvenir shops. The sheer scale of such places can also be a problem, especially for delicate marine environments. Inevitably, perhaps, many are fenced off from the outside world, their exclusivity protected by barbed wire, electric fences, and armed guards.

- **Smaller is beautiful.** Much better for the environment and locals, and for you if you value intimacy, are smaller-scale beach hotels. Often in the form of bungalow resorts, these range from hyper-luxurious bijou-style places to little more than basic flophouses. The chances are that they have bars or restaurants open to locals, too, so there's less sense of exclusion.

- **Be gentle with coral.** When scuba-diving or snorkelling, don't touch corals with any part of your body, and be careful with your flippers – one careless swipe can easily suffocate a patch of coral with sand.

- **Game fishing is no game.** Tall tales of blue marlin "this big" and wahoo "that big" attract sizeable numbers of thrill-seeking fishermen to Africa's shores. Unfortunately, the effect of picking off the ocean's largest natural predators can kick off devastating chain reactions further down the food chain: with fewer big predators, populations of the next species down increase, in turn putting abnormally high pressure on their prey, an effect that trickles right down to crustaceans and even algae.

- **Don't buy or collect marine souvenirs.** Even the collection of seashells that are uninhabited can be damaging, as it deprives a hermit crab or – with larger shells – an octopus of a potential home. Many species of shellfish are endangered in any case; knowing which of them aren't is only a decision that an expert should make. Sea horses are endangered all around the globe; they're indisputably attractive, and also have a ready market in the Far East as aphrodisiacs (as if China doesn't have enough endangered species in its traditional pharmacopoeia already).

Community-based tourism

For all the scintillating wildlife and awe-inspiring views, gorgeous beaches and unbeatable sense of adventure, the best thing about Africa is its people. The sense of community, solidarity and hospitality that still thrives across most of the continent, in rural areas especially, provides a huge and refreshing contrast to what little communal life survives in the "First World", and certainly puts monetary concepts of development into a different light.

△ A visitor being shown round a village in northern Kenya

Many tour companies and package holidays feature optional excursions to visit whichever tribe is locally the most famous – Zulu, Ndebele, Nama, Maasai, Hadzabe, Tuareg, Bedouin, various Bushman and Pygmy tribes – but only few tour operators are really serious about their responsibilities. As a result, many so-called cultural trips can be disturbingly Disneylandesque escapades into voyeurism, in which "exoticism" as touted by allusions to primitive Stone Age people (sometimes using those very words) appears to be all that matters, with little real interaction beyond the obligatory tribal welcoming dance and selling of trinkets.

To really get to know indigenous Africa, either take part in genuinely community-based tourism initiatives (see "Tribal Africa" on p.211), or just take your time – it's a breeze to get to know "real" people if you're travelling around on foot or by bicycle, and you'll find it easier to get off the beaten track, too.

Campaigning and volunteering

Apart from travelling responsibly, supporting a charity or becoming involved in a campaign is a good way of making a positive difference, and of prolonging your involvement with Africa. NGOs working towards wildlife conservation are two to a penny, and not all of them are as respectable as they sound. Find out about their achievements and, if you're making a donation, check up on their official status as charities or non-profit organizations.

Major environmental organizations working in Africa, and which pay more than lip service to community involvement, are listed on pp.417–418, together with influential and effective campaigning organizations for indigenous rights and poverty alleviation.

Volunteer programmes

A great way of getting to know a country and its people is mucking in with voluntary work. In exchange for your time and perhaps specialist skills, you gain work experience, pleasure at being able to help out, and – just as importantly – an intimate and rewarding experience with locals that few other travellers can hope to taste. Volunteering generally requires a commitment of several months, although some set-ups – especially those accepting paying volunteers or offering sponsored holidays (for which you raise a certain amount of money for the NGO, the reward being the trip) – are happy receiving volunteers for only a week a two.

The usual way of arranging voluntary work is through a specialist organization or agency in your home country. Some accept anyone,

Getting involved

I had gone to Africa in part because I felt a desire for adventure – something exotic. I returned with a realistic picture of the people and the place. I've witnessed many foreigners – not just tourists – treat the people as just another part of the scenery. Instead of passing through, buying handmade crafts and taking a few pictures to show friends back home, I decided I was going to get to know the people on their level.

I happened to go during a time of a massive drought. The UN warned that eleven million people in Kenya were at risk of starvation. Like most people, I would have read the numbers in the newspapers, forgetting most of it as I went about my day. This time it was inescapable. "We are all dying!" one woman replied to my greeting. During our conversation she told me that she and her children had no food or water. Like so many others I met, she was exhausted and frustrated. No one, no organization, not even the government had come to help. They lived in an area with no roads and little communication with the rest of the country.

I began calling international aid organizations as soon as I returned home, asking if any of them was planning a relief effort in the neglected areas I had visited. I made a website, contacted the press and wrote my friends, sharing what I had witnessed. There was no way I could not do anything after what I experienced. Joined by concerned friends and strangers, we were able to convince an international relief organization to deliver food and water to that area and open up a special account for funds to go directly towards the effort.

– Hans Johnson,
Ⓦ www.maasaiculture.org.

but most require skilled volunteers: teachers, healthcare professionals, wildlife experts, people with knowledge of agriculture or livestock, IT technicians, and so on. Salaried employment is a possibility (just don't expect to get rich), but usually you'll have to pay for your own upkeep. If you're expected to pay a substantial amount for the privilege of helping out, take care as the voluntary sector isn't without its scams. So, do a little Internet research on the NGO before signing up. In particular, try to find out whether their ideals and projects as espoused in their brochures and websites actually translate into concrete action. Also watch out for religious NGOs bent on converting the locals using an unpleasantly combative approach towards what they perceive as "spiritual warfare."

Travel magazines often have jobs sections that include placements or ads from volunteer agencies. The websites Ⓦwww.studyabroad.com and Ⓦwww.worldvolunteerweb.org have useful listings and links to study and work programmes worldwide, plus information on grants and sponsorship. Major organizations for volunteering in Africa are listed on pp.417–418.

10

Getting around

It is the traveller who knows what happened on the way

Dangme proverb, Ghana

There are two parts to any journey: the travelling itself, and the destinations – the sights and attractions that doubtlessly tempted you to consider Africa in the first place. The most memorable holidays are a blend of both, even if the physical discomfort inflicted by some countries' transport systems may leave you with rather different impressions at the time.

Africans themselves are forever on the move. For the vast majority, despite the impression you might get from gridlocked city centres at rush hour, public transport is the only way around other than walking. Few people have the means to own a car or a scooter, and in places even bicycles are a luxury. Not that that's a hindrance to some geniuses: wooden bikes can still be seen here and there, amazing contraptions in which the only non-wooden bits are bent nails for cog teeth, a strap of sturdy fabric for the chain, and perhaps bits of old truck tyres nailed onto the wheels for a modicum of comfort.

Given the public need, you'll find that even places in the back of beyond are likely to have some kind of transport service, even if it's just a supply lorry running once a week. Other than the low cost, the great advantage of public transport is that it's an easy way for you to get to know people, and perhaps share something of their lives. Friendships struck up on long, bumpy bus journeys may well prompt invitations into someone's home, something that's well worth accepting.

There are also, inevitably, some inconveniences. For a start, terminals, stations and boat docks can be very chaotic and bewildering for people not used to them, and you should keep an especially wary eye on your bags and belongings. In much of the continent, too, you might also find that public transport is far from being a comfortable experience. Most countries have a huge number of rickety buses that get packed to the rafters with squashed up passengers, together with their luggage; rural roads, too, can be in a pitiful state. This isn't always the case – public transport is likely to be better in North Africa, Botswana, Namibia, South Africa and along main routes in East Africa – but by and large it's best to expect a bit of discomfort as part and parcel of the experience. If you're at all claustrophobic or don't fancy spending hours cramped up in a confined place, it's best to steer clear of public transport altogether unless there are options which will give you the comfort and space you need (eg first- or second-class rail travel).

Except on roads where there's no public transport at all (a rarity), hitching is not recommended as a means of getting around, especially for lone females. If you do find yourself having to hitch, beckon the driver to stop with your whole arm. A modest thumb is more likely to be interpreted as a friendly, or perhaps even rude, gesture than a request for a lift. Also, don't think you'll save money by hitching: you'll almost always be expected to pay for the ride.

As you travel around, it's worth remembering these general points:

- **Don't underestimate the time you'll spend on the road.** If a map indicates anything other than asphalt, count on no more than 40kph in the dry season if travelling by public transport, and expect the road to be impassable during the rains or after a particularly heavy downpour.
- **Don't rely heavily on published schedules.** Departure days and times for trains and ferries change constantly, while buses rarely operate to much of a timetable other than leaving at dawn. Flight schedules are more reliable; their timetables are often seasonal, so ensure that the dates and times you're consulting apply for the period when you'll be travelling.
- **Take things easy if travelling with your kids.** Children, especially infants, tire easily during long journeys. Allow for plenty of stops and chilling-out time during the day, keep excursions short, and leave evenings free, too.

- **Be prepared.** You'll appreciate packing some snacks and drinks, but you don't have to lug along mountains of victuals. Trains and ferries should have basic catering, buses and other vehicles will stop briefly for meals at roadside restaurants, and there's plenty available from hawkers at bus stations and roadside villages. Toilets are less convenient: in ferries and trains, they're rarely pleasant to use once you're underway, and few buses have toilets in any case. Instead, they'll stop every few hours for passengers to scurry into the bushes to relieve themselves, men heading off in one direction, women in another – bring some toilet paper.

Buses, minibuses and shared taxis

For most Africans – and foreigners on a budget – buses, minibuses and shared taxis (also called "bush taxis", often marvellously battered station wagons) are the usual means of getting about. Though they can be slow, uncomfortable and driven with breathtaking lack of road sense, they can get you close to almost anywhere you might want to go. To reach more remote destinations, you might find yourself using a more informal means of transport – anything from being squished inside a dilapidated Land Rover or perched on the back of a pick-up truck, to clinging to the roof of a lorry or getting intimate with a cargo of onions.

Although buses tend to have impressively souped-up suspensions, on particularly rough, unsurfaced roads you will be tossed around. On some rides, painful really is the right word for the experience,

Enjoying the wait

If you fancy a flawless holiday where everything runs smoothly, with no surprises, don't go to Africa. The same goes for people who are impatient and can't live without that watch around their wrist. Whether you're at a border or checkpoints, or on public transport, there will always be time to read and relax, and there's no point in getting stressed.

My longest experience of waiting was in Guinea. My partner and I rode our motorcycles from Guinea-Bissau over to Guinea and had planned to stay in the country for about seven days. In the end, we were there for a whole month.

There was a slight problem that we had never experienced before: the country ran out of fuel. The fuel tanker that was due to arrive in Conakry was late. Our only options were either to buy black-market fuel at extortionate prices, or wait it out. We even spent an entire day waiting at a service station because the attendant kept assuring us that fuel would arrive "in a few hours". After what seemed like an endless wait, we met some expats who worked at a nearby gold mine. They took us in and spoiled us, feeding and sheltering us for a couple of weeks. Then they gave us the perfect leaving present: forty litres of free fuel!

–Tyler Keys

to the extent that you might begin to envy those passengers who arrived too late to get a seat: standing is a far better way of riding out the rodeo. That said, there is a certain camaraderie that forms between passengers whose heads smack the ceiling every time the bus careers over a bump or thumps in and out of a pothole.

Overcrowding is the other demon as regards (lack of) comfort. You might find yourself taking part in what appears to be an attempt on the Guinness World Record for packing as many people as possible into a confined place. It seems to be a matter of pride for bus and minibus owners to keep the manufacturer's "so many seated passengers only" signs intact and visible, just so you can marvel at the audacity and skill involved in doubling the limit. Getting a seat-numbered ticket is no guarantee of comfort, either, at least in most Africa south of the Sahara. Sure, you'll get the seat, but before long you might be sharing it with one or two other pairs of buttocks, and may well find your legs trapped by bags and boxes and sacks, trussed-up chickens, bewildered goats, and other peoples' legs ... It's not always so extreme, but bus companies that maintain parity between passenger and seat numbers are still relatively few.

When choosing your seat (assuming you have a choice), consider which side of the vehicle will be shadier, remembering that in the southern hemisphere the sun travels in the northern half of the sky, and vice versa. Seats in the middle or front of the bus, away from the axles, avoid the worst of the bumps.

Playing it safe

Physical discomfort is a pain, if you'll pardon the pun, but of far greater concern is safety. Africa has an appalling road safety record, especially regarding public transport on fast asphalt; head-on collisions while overtaking on blind corners, catastrophic rolls, and vehicles swerving off bridges into rivers are so common in some countries that all but the most gruesome crashes are relegated to the inside pages of newspapers. Suicidal driving is in fact the single biggest risk for travellers in Africa.

Given all this, always seek local advice about the best company or vehicle to take before you buy a ticket – but be aware that for some people, "the best bus" means the fastest, not necessarily the safest. A lot depends on the company, as speeding and reckless driving may be encouraged by a company's unrealistic timetables.

You'd also do well to check out the vehicle yourself before boarding it. New tyres or ones with well-defined tread are no guarantee of safe driving, but may be indicative that the company is a little more respectful of road safety than its competitors. Conversely, an ancient and very battered bus apparently held together by rust may also be a good choice, if only because its top speed may be limited. Another tip is to catch a glimpse of the driver before clambering aboard. Bloodshot eyes or vacant stares don't bode well, and are not as unlikely as you might think. None of this is an exact science, however – as mentioned above, seeking local advice is definitely your best guide. If you're really worried, you could try to minimize the damage in the event of an accident by sitting in the middle of the vehicle and away from the windows.

If you're lucky, though, your route may be covered by one of a small but growing number of bus companies that offer more than just lip service to road safety and passenger comfort, and for which you'll gladly pay the premium asked. These companies don't generally allow standing passengers, and should benefit from saner

The devil in the driver's seat

There's a pious Swahili proverb that says: "In this world we are all passengers, and God is the driver." All would be well and good were it not for the rather too literal interpretation of that proverb by East Africa's bus and minibus drivers, some of whom appear to have dispensed with even the most basic driving skills, and common sense, placing in their stead a quasi-religious belief that any crash or accident is caused by God's will. As it may be impossible to have faith in the driver, even atheists will find themselves praying to a greater being to ensure a safe journey.

I was in Moshi, at the foot of Mount Kilimanjaro, and had to catch a minibus back to Arusha, along a fast but narrow eighty-kilometre ribbon of a road that's easily the most dangerous stretch of tarmac in Tanzania. I arrived early at the bus station, intent on checking vehicles tyres for tread, and the drivers' eyes for red – the telltale sign of one too many joints or bottles of hooch. After giving the thumbs down to the first three vehicles, I settled on the fourth, whose driver was a very gentle – and genteel – old man, with an especially charming smile; other passengers, too, seemed to choose this vehicle on account of the driver's promising demeanour. Our collective smugness lasted precisely 50m, when we stopped at the rope barrier that marked the bus station exit. The elderly driver climbed out, flashed us another winning smile, and was promptly replaced by a teenage lunatic with glazed, bloodshot eyes and a selective deafness – to our increasingly panicky entreaties to drive more slowly, and to the whining alarm of the vehicle's obligatory speed limiter. The alarm began to warble at 100kph, and finally shut up completely after the third or fourth time we topped 140kph.

Two bribed traffic cops and a handful of near-misses later, we arrived in Arusha, thankfully still in one piece. Perhaps it was God in the driver's seat.

– Jens Finke

△ Getting around in Africa often means making do

drivers. Their vehicles should also be in better condition, and may even be fitted with speed limiters, although the effectiveness of these is debatable.

Journey times

Throughout the continent, public road transport tends to head off very early if the journey is long. The crack of dawn, maybe even earlier, is normal, so heavy sleepers should pack an alarm clock. For places closer in, you could find transport until mid-afternoon, but for longer journeys you might find the bus station empty of vehicles as early as 10am. In any case, it's always best to leave early: breakdowns and delays are to be expected (which is why many vehicles carry their own mechanics), and you'll want to minimize your chances of arriving anywhere after dark.

On routes taking more than a day to complete, you may find that your transport stops somewhere for the night – a security precaution against accidents (and bandits) that is a legal obligation in many countries. Overnight arrangements on such trips vary. It may be worth seeking out a local guesthouse for a bit of shut-eye, but most passengers just sleep on or even under the bus.

Tickets and fares

With buses commonly taking twice as many passengers as they have seats, it's always best to buy tickets in advance – the earlier, the better. Buying the day before your journey is fine on most routes, but on others – especially with the safer companies – you may find it impossible to find a seat even three days before departure.

Fares are low, often just a couple of dollars an hour. Baggage charges aren't normally levied unless you're transporting unusually bulky items, though plenty of touts will try and convince you otherwise. For shared taxis, bush taxis and minibuses, passengers pay some time after the journey has begun. This isn't a question of being ripped off, but too often the first departure is just a cruise around town rounding up passengers and buying petrol (with your money) and then back to square one – a rigmarole which could go on for hours.

Most transport departs from a central bus terminal, generally an open patch of ground enclosed by ramshackle ticket offices and perhaps market stalls. The better companies may have their own terminals. Few bus stations have labelled parking bays (South Africa is a pleasant exception), so to avoid being given the runaround by touts, either come with a local or find the correct bay the day before.

The Sahara's loneliest tree

The Sahara Desert, you might think, is the least likely place for a road accident, not to mention a head-on collision. It's not as though traffic is confined to narrow and congested lanes – most of the Sahara's "roads" are in fact nothing more than a welter of tyre tracks spreading over several kilometres in breadth. Choosing which set to follow boils down to hunches, and whichever tracks appear to be more recent.

Such generous driving conditions make the sorry tale of northeastern Niger's Tree of the Ténéré even more hard to believe. This solitary acacia, the only tree for 400km around, was the sole survivor of forests that had once covered this corner of the desert. Having braved an almost impossible climate, and the loss of its main branch in the 1950s when a lorry reversed into it, it finally came to blows with fate in 1973, when it was toppled by a speeding truck. Just how the Libyan driver managed this amazing feat remains a mystery to this day; rumour has it that he was drunk. A plaque now marks the spot where the famous tree stood, and you can see some of the tree's remains at the museum in Niamey.

Trains

Most of Africa's railways are colonial legacies that were instrumental in the conquest (or, in colonial speak, the "pacification") of many

Great African train rides

The Benguela Railway Stretching from Angola's Atlantic coastline to Zambia's Copper Belt, the Benguela Railway was a real humdinger until Angola's wars put a stop to it. Work is now underway to re-establish the full extent of the line. For now, you can catch a steam train between Benguela and Huambo, both in Angola.

The Blue Train South Africa's Rovos Rail company (ⓦwww.rovos.co.za) offers hyper-luxurious trips lasting up to two weeks throughout Southern Africa, occasionally venturing up to the Victoria Falls on the Zambia–Zimbabwe border, or even to Dar es Salaam in Tanzania. Believe every word of their spiel about comfort: their trains, including lovingly-restored, wood-panelled nineteenth-century classics, are rolling five-star hotels.

The Copper Express The 1860-kilometre Tanzania–Zambia Railway was built in the 1960s with Chinese funding and engineers to provide access to the ocean for Zambia's copper exports, at a time when other routes were either politically incorrect (because of apartheid regimes) or impassable due to war. Delays are notoriously frequent, but with luck, there's a good deal of wildlife to be seen from the carriages, especially along the edge of Tanzania's Selous Game Reserve. A recent development has been the introduction of luxury tourist trains from Dar es Salaam to Selous – a fine way of kicking off upmarket safaris.

Egypt's trains British ambitions to colonize the entire eastern flank of Africa and connect their possessions by rail made a good start in Egypt, whose rail network will get you from the Mediterranean to Aswan, close to Sudan. The problem is the authorities' insistence that tourists use the snazzier (and more expensive) services, not as interesting as local trains.

The Fianarantsoa–Manakara Railway Madagascar's only railroad is the continent's slowest, taking eight hours to cover a modest 163km. This ponderousness is no bad thing: you'll have plenty of time to savour the wonderful scenery as you descend to the coast.

The Imperial Railway An overnight, 780-kilometre journey from Ethiopia's capital to Djibouti, stopping at every two-bit settlement along the way. The terrain is spectacular, and the company agreeable – it's a good time to chew the fat, or in fact *qat* (also called *qhat*, *chat* or *miraa*), a herbal stimulant that keeps its users wide awake.

Le Lézard Rouge Southern Tunisia's "Red Lizard", built at the end of the nineteenth century, is a great way of experiencing the Saharan fringes. The regions. The French planned (but never began) a trans–Saharan railway, but Cecil Rhodes' dream of connecting Cape Town to Cairo with a steel ribbon did make considerable headway. With a bit of cheating (meaning catching buses and planes), a lot of patience, and

original carriages have been restored and provide a regal setting for a two-hour round trip, ducking in and out of tunnels and along spectacular desert gorges.

The Marrakesh Express It might well only be the song that propelled this journey – any route from Tangier to Marrakesh – to fame, but Morocco's rail network is part of the European InterRail scheme, so grab a ticket, and sixty hours after leaving London you could find yourself hunting for souvenirs in one of Africa's most enchanting cities.

Mauritania's desert train Far from luxurious but ineffably romantic is Mauritania's iron-ore railway, from the haematite-rich mountains at F'Dérik and Zouîrat, deep in the Sahara, to the port town of Nouâdhibou. The trains are among the world's longest, hauling several kilometres of ore-carrying wagons through the sand and dust, and returning with shipments of gas canisters and other mining equipment. You can ride for free on top of the freight wagons or cough up for a seat in a carriage.

The Mombasa Express This Kenyan railroad's colonial moniker, The Lunatic Express, derived from the enormous cost – in money and lives – spent building the line from the Indian Ocean to Lake Victoria, and eventually into Uganda. Overnight passenger trains operate between Mombasa and Nairobi.

Océan–Niger Only two West African railway networks cross borders: the Abidjan–Ouagadougou route from Ivory Coast to Burkina Faso, which is currently prone to closure because of the upheavals in Ivory Coast, and the Océan–Niger train from Senegal's capital, Dakar, to Bamako in Mali, on the banks of the River Niger. Officially taking 36 hours, the gruelling ride can be considerably longer.

Sudan's trains Sudan's extraordinarily overcrowded trains, which rattle along tracks laid by the British, offer many an epic if uncomfortable adventure. Woe betide passengers sleeping on the roof: delays caused by searches for punters who rolled off in their slumber are common enough.

Tanzania's Central Line Laid out by German engineers just before World War I, this 1254-kilometre ribbon of steel follows almost exactly the path of the old slave caravans between Lake Tanganyika and the Indian Ocean. The mango trees you'll see along the way sprouted from seeds discarded by slaves on their forced march. The branch line from Lake Victoria was added by the British, and also follows an old slave route. Total journey time from the lakes to the coast is around forty hours.

the stout ability to endure discomfort, you can in fact travel much of the continent from north to south by train. The rhythmical rattle and shake of the carriages, the whistles, the colourful scenes at colonial stations and the subtly changing landscapes can all make for memorable rides.

One thing you shouldn't expect of Africa's railways is speed (don't be fooled by the word "express"). The continent's trains are almost always slower than travelling by road, but have the big advantage of safety. While big train crashes do make headlines, the risk of finding yourself embroiled in an accident is minimal compared to road transport.

Ticket classes should be familiar: on overnight journeys, first class will get you a bunk in a compartment for two or four people, perhaps with a wash basin (but no guarantee of water). Second class is similar, the main difference being that you'll be sharing a compartment for six or eight people. In both first and second class, you should be provided with bed linen and blankets for overnight journeys, and breakfast or dinner may be included in the fare.

Lowly third class is a place where dreams of creature comforts are quickly banished in the face of incredible overcrowding, even on services where every ticket has an assigned seat. Given the crowds, security on overnight journeys while travelling third class is a concern: it helps if you're in a group, so one person can stay awake to keep an eye on your possessions.

Most long-distance trains have a dining car (which can see more use as a dissolute bar), and food might be available from a roving waiter. On long journeys outside of North Africa's and Southern Africa's networks, trains might make meal-time stops at track-side villages, whose enterprising inhabitants set up trestle tables to sell often exquisitely good food. Tickets are always best bought in advance; on popular routes, it would be wise to do this a week or more before travelling.

Flights

Air travel can be an option if you're in a hurry, and is often an attraction in itself, especially if you'll be flying over rainforests, mountains, deserts, sandbanks, creeks or coral reefs – any of which are well worth seeing from above at least once. Keep your camera to hand.

All African countries have domestic airlines, linking cities to one another, and with the main national parks wherever wildlife tourism is a big deal. You'll also find planes flying to mining towns, generally in very remote areas; such flights can save days compared to tackling the same journeys overland. Most companies operate modest fleets of light aircraft such as propeller-driven Cessnas. Don't expect cabin service; there's hardly room to stand up in or even stretch your legs. It can be a lot of fun, though, as there's no screen between the cockpit and cabin, so you can see exactly what the pilot's seeing, and doing. Baggage limits for light aircraft are usually 15kg, but additional weight can sometimes be carried at the pilot's discretion, possibly at extra cost.

Safety standards vary widely. In South Africa and North Africa you should have little to worry about, and planes covering major destinations in East Africa should be fine, too. But take care elsewhere, where maintenance isn't always what it should be, and some of the planes in use really ought to have been gracing museums of aviation history by now.

If you're lucky you'll have a number of airlines to choose from: ask around locally as to which is the most reliable, and – if you're worried about flying in planes with only one engine – find out which companies fly what. National carriers are also a good bet for domestic flights, but their services are limited to the main destinations. In general, fares on scheduled flights average $100–300 per person depending on the distance covered – quite reasonable once you consider that there are few economies of scale with which to cushion the impact of spiralling fuel costs.

An alternative to scheduled flights is to charter a plane, not necessarily bank-breaking if you can find enough people to fill the seats. Charters are particularly useful for accessing wildlife parks in very remote areas. Upmarket wildlife lodges and tented camps in those places may even have their own planes, and will certainly be able to find you a seat on a charter; the cost of such flights may be included in the price of the safari.

Ferries

Despite their undeniable romance, Africa's ferries are beset by safety concerns, as there's little guarantee that vessels are truly seaworthy. The last decade has seen a number of high-profile African ferry disasters, the most deadly being the sinking of the *Joola* off southern Senegal in 2002, in which over 1800 people died. It's impossible to say with certainty which ferry routes are safer than others. All ferries can be very crowded, if more comfortable than road transport or travelling third-class in a train. Nonetheless, it's worth paying more for a cabin if the journey is overnight. Given that it's often just one or two vessels that operate on any given route, delays and cancellations can be expected.

Classic ferry journeys include the Egyptian and Sudanese stretches of the Nile; East Africa's Great Lakes (Tanganyika, Victoria and Malawi/Nyasa); and along the River Niger's Saharan loop in Mali.

Driving

Renting a car has obvious advantages, not least the fact that most of Africa's wildlife parks are open to rented vehicles. If you're travelling with young children, a car affords you the flexibility and privacy you need for changing nappies, toilet stops and shouting at each other.

There are plenty of car rental companies in major cities and tourist areas, but the main international franchises are pricey and capable of rolling out some real clunkers, particularly in less developed countries. In countries with awful roads, rental companies may insist that you hire a driver as well – no bad thing, as they tend to double as excellent safari guides with the unerring ability to spot a leopard's tail dangling from a tree half a mile away. When arranging car rental, you may have to leave a hefty deposit, roughly equivalent to the anticipated bill; credit cards are useful for this.

If you're going to be in Africa for some time, consider buying a secondhand vehicle rather than renting. As an example, a used Land Rover 110 TDI in good condition can cost up to $5000/£2600 in Africa, but you can offset some of the cost by selling the vehicle when you're done. You will need time to arrange things, though, including the paperwork when buying and selling. On the other hand, if you just need an ordinary saloon for a day or two, it's much easier to negotiate a daily rate with a taxi driver.

Costs

In East and West Africa, where four-wheel drive may be essential, car rental costs can be extortionate: around $120/£65 per day is actually pretty good going for a vehicle including a company driver and 100km a day mileage. Self-drive isn't necessarily any cheaper: the saving on not paying for a driver is offset by having to pay insurance premiums. In North Africa and Southern Africa costs are far more reasonable, especially as a saloon car may be all you need: costs start at around $50 a day. Rates are always cheaper by the week, and many firms are prepared to negotiate a little as well, especially off-season.

When given a quote, allow for taxes if not included, and read every word of the small print. Check whether the driver's daily allowance is included, or if self-driving, check – especially – the insurance arrangements. It's a good idea to pay for the optional waivers for collision damage and theft, although some companies are distinctly cagey about setting these terms out in black-and-white. Even with the waivers included, you may still be liable for a substantial excess if you total the car or it gets stolen. As a rule of thumb, high excess liability is the trademark of dodgy companies hoping for misfortunes to befall their punters so they can earn some quick cash.

Fuel is available everywhere except in the very smallest villages, but it's worth filling up before heading out on a long drive. The further inland or away from a major town you get, the more expensive fuel becomes. If you're intending to do a lot of driving in remote areas, carry spare fuel in cans.

Choosing a vehicle

Off tarred roads, high clearance is useful, thanks to the dire state of many roads, even in dry weather. A four-wheel drive (4WD) is essential for wildlife parks, mountainous areas and on minor roads during rains. Land Rovers and Toyota Land Cruisers are the most widely available 4WDs; try to avoid posher, gas-guzzling alternatives, not just because they're more expensive to run, but also because they're more lucrative targets for car thieves. Diesel engines are best: they're more economical than petrol engines, and bush mechanics are very much at ease with them.

One or two rental companies still have diminutive Suzuki jeeps, which are light, rugged and capable of amazing feats. Don't expect them to top more than 80kph, however, and beware of their notorious tendency to fall over on bends or on the sloping gravel hard shoulders that line many roads.

Don't automatically assume your rental vehicle is roadworthy: check it out yourself before signing anything, and insist on a test drive – it's amazing how many vehicles "fresh from the mechanic" have weak brakes, dodgy clutches, leaky radiators or wobbly wheels (in one car I took, a wheel actually fell off). Things to check include tyre treads, that the car has the full complement of wheel nuts, and the gearbox and engine mounts (you'll have to get under the car to check for cracks). The vehicle should have at least one spare tyre, preferably two, a spanner that fits all the wheel nuts, and a jack.

If you're planning to spend any time off surfaced roads in dusty or muddy areas, the carburettor intake has to be close to roof height to avoid getting clogged; most safari vehicles are customized with a "snorkel" for this purpose. A working mileometer is also useful, even if you're not paying by the kilometre, as navigating using map distances is often the only way to avoid missing turnings.

Other items you should carry, certainly for longer drives, are a shovel for digging your way out of mud or sand, engine oil and brake fluid (which can also be used as clutch fluid), a spare fan belt and possibly brake pads, tow rope, spare fuel and plenty of drinking water. Finally, try for the first day and night to stay close to the place from which you rented the car, as the first day's drive will give you a chance to spot any mechanical problems without the hassle of being miles from anywhere.

Paperwork

Documentation required for car rental varies a little between countries. In general, though, tourist drivers must be between 25 and 70 years old, and have held a driving licence for at least two years. Some countries require an international driving licence, available from motoring organizations in your home country. If you don't have an international licence, temporary permits may be available on production of your national licence and a small fee, but shouldn't be counted on.

If you're arriving in your own vehicle, a carnet de passage is highly recommended to avoid a potentially time-consuming paper chase on leaving each of the countries you visit. With a carnet, you may still have to pay modest taxes, permits and insurance on arrival, but nothing major. The carnet is valid for a year, and is available from motoring organizations in your home country: you pay a deposit of several thousand pounds, euros or dollars, plus an annual fee in the hundreds. Without a carnet, you may have to leave a deposit in the country you're visiting, equivalent to the tax payable on new cars (this can be several thousand dollars) – retrieving the deposit is a hassle and worry you don't want to have. Motorbikes may be eligible for temporary import permits, possibly free of charge.

Driving hazards and etiquette

When driving, expect the unexpected: rocks, ditches, potholes, animals and people on the road, as well as lunatic drivers. Irrespective of what side of the road traffic officially drives on (left in Eastern and Southern Africa, right elsewhere), you'll find people driving on whichever side has fewer potholes or pools or mud. It's accepted practice to honk your horn stridently to warn pedestrians and cyclists of your approach. Be especially wary of buses – which seldom slow down for anything – and also be careful when overtaking heavy vehicles, even more so when passing lorries groaning uphill: sometimes a line of them churning out diesel fumes can cut off your visibility without warning – extremely dangerous on a narrow mountain road. Avoid driving after dark, but if you must, be alert for stopped vehicles without lights or hazard warnings, and also for "one-eyed" vehicles: what looks like a motorbike can suddenly turn into a truck at full speed.

Driving on unsurfaced roads can be a challenge. Negotiating loose sand requires constant play on your steering; the same technique is used to get through mud and across black cotton soil, which becomes treacherously slippery during the rains. Don't be worried about getting bogged down: locals or other drivers will help out, and getting covered in mud is all part of the fun.

The use of indicators and flashed headlights can be different to what you're used to. In East Africa, a right signal doesn't necessarily mean that the vehicle is about to turn right, but is more likely meant to deter drivers behind from overtaking. Similarly, left-hand signals are used to say "Please overtake" – but don't assume that a driver in front who signals you to overtake can really see whether the road ahead is clear. Throughout the continent, it's common practice to flash oncoming vehicles if they're leaving you little room or their headlights are blinding you.

If you break down or have an accident, the first thing to do is pile bundles of sticks or foliage at fifty-metre intervals behind and in front of your car. These are the red warning triangles of Africa, and their placing is always scrupulously observed (as is the wedging of a stone behind at least one wheel, even when you're on a perfectly level road). When you have a puncture, get it mended straight away so that you're never without a spare tyre – it's very cheap and can be done almost anywhere. Spare parts, tools and proper equipment are rare off the main routes, though local mechanics can work miracles with minimal tools. Always settle on a price before work begins.

Cycling

Second to walking, cycling – riding a bicycle, not a motorbike – is the best way to get around if you want to really get to know people. The sight of pedalling tourists remains novel enough to warrant special attention, and in places unaccustomed to foreigners, get ready to be the star attraction. For the most part, this is a whole lot of fun. Brave kids may muster the courage to give your legs a tweak, and adults will find it both amusing, and impressive, to see a visitor exerting so much effort. A bicycle can give you access to corners of the continent that would be next to impossible to see by any other means except on foot, though the climate, varied terrain and reckless drivers make Africa challenging cycling country.

You can avoid the most dangerous driving by staying off major asphalted roads. If you must take one of these roads, bolting a mirror on to your handlebars is a recommended precaution, and do as local cyclists do: scatter like chickens at the approach of a bus, even if it means performing somersaults into the bushes. Cycling at night is definitely not recommended, but just in case you get caught out, fit dynamo-powered lights, reflectors to the wheels, pedals, and front and rear of the bike, and bring fluorescent safety straps with you.

Consider the climate carefully before deciding when or where to go: you won't make much progress on dirt roads during the rains when chain sets and brakes become jammed with mud. The prevailing wind is another factor that makes a huge difference: the western Saharan crossing, for example, is far easier to attempt from north to south than from south to north.

Lastly, no matter how fit you are, there will be times when you're feeling dog tired, teetering on the brink of defeat by the headwind, or tired of the jibes (or even the encouragement) hurled from passing vehicles. Swallow your pride and consider the unmention-able: cheating. Buses in most countries will carry bicycles (you may be charged extra for the privilege), and truckers may also be amenable to giving lifts, for a fee. Long-distance trains will also take bicycles, usually as paid luggage in the baggage compartment; be sure that your bike will be travelling on the same train as you, as it risks disappearing otherwise.

Equipment

The days when the only bicycles to be found in Africa were Indian or Chinese three-speed, cast-iron roadsters have gone: nowadays you're just as likely to find basic mountain bikes for sale. The cost can be high compared to what you might pay at home, but on the other hand bicycles find ready buyers, so you can easily recoup part of the outlay at the end of your trip. Bringing a bicycle with you from home is fairly straightforward, but check with the airline for additional charges, and whether they have special packing require-ments. Carry any easily detachable items, like the pump, in your hand baggage. Remember that the weight of your bicycle counts towards your total baggage limit, usually 20kg or 25kg.

Whatever you take, it will need low gears and strong wheels. Mountain bikes are best off-road, both for their suspension and thicker tyres, but if you'll be travelling mainly on asphalt, a bike with thinner wheels and no suspension is better as there's less friction. Fit a pair of toe clips to the pedals: being able to pull as well as push will reduce the overall effort.

In general, the less fancy your bike is, the easier it should be to find spares and get it fixed. At the very least, bring a puncture kit, an adjustable spanner to fit all the nuts on your bike (ensure that you can reach them all, too), and a spoke key. You'll also need two tyre levers to prise off the tyres; the spanner handle can serve as one of them. The most useful spares to bring are spokes, axles, brake cables, brake pads, an inner tube, and – if your bike has non-standard wheels – a spare tyre.

For your belongings, you'll need a set of panniers (you can spread the weight by fitting them front and rear) – the lower they hang, the more stable your bike will be. Wearing a rucksack while cycling is a bad idea: you risk backache. Water bottles are essential: most bicycle frames have room for bolting on at least three, and you can attach two more to the handlebars. In arid or semi-arid areas, carry extra bottles in your panniers, and consider wearing a Tuareg-style muffler to cover your nose and mouth.

You don't need special cycling clothes, but your shorts should be either well padded or made of a material that won't wear out too quickly. Very well-padded cycling gloves are essential for absorbing some of the shocks. As for shoes, they should be comfortable to walk in (you may begin to understand why some people call bicycles push bikes), but not have soles so soft that pedalling becomes more difficult.

Walking

With the heart of an adventurer, and a sturdy pair of shoes, walking can be a fantastic way to get around. You'll frequently find yourself being invited to stay in people's homes, and will of course be the centre of attention wherever you go – local admiration for your strength and endurance will doubtlessly also be blended with a dose of pity, as it can be hard to understand why a rich person would choose to travel in such an exhausting manner. The disadvantages to footing it are that you'll have to carry all your gear with you (including a lightweight tent and, optionally, cooking equipment), and put up with blisters, muscle ache and the rest of it. You'll also need a dose of good humour, and to be able to put up with being trailed by kids for hours.

Good countries for long-distance walks, combining inspiring scenery with bearable climates and comparatively few fences, include Morocco, Kenya, Uganda, Tanzania, Malawi, Madagascar and Lesotho. See also "Trekking, hiking and mountaineering" on p.208, and "Walking Safaris" on p.368, for some recommended hiking areas.

Security, at least for men and couples, should not be much to worry about so long as you avoid obviously dangerous regions, and the outskirts of big bad cities like Lagos and Johannesburg. Even so, few thieves will mark you out as a target, given that you're apparently so poor that you have to walk.

Urban transport

Getting around Africa's larger towns and cities is both simple and cheap. It's easiest just to use taxis, which are especially recommended for nocturnal meanderings in cities where crime is a hazard. Most lack meters, so settle on a fare before getting in. Given that you're a tourist, drivers will invariably try for more – haggle hard, but bear in mind that drivers rarely own their cars and have to pay a hefty slice of the day's takings to the owner.

Locals get around on buses or minibuses, the latter often toting garish paint jobs and outlandish names to fit: in Nairobi, you might prefer to catch "The Survivor" rather than brave "The Undertaker" or "Doctor Stupidity". The scenes at the terminuses can be chaotic (watch out for pickpockets), but the popularity of public transport means that you're unlikely to have to wait long for a ride, and you should also be able to get to

Overload

One of the more entertaining things in Africa is to see just what "overloaded" means. In West Africa, vehicles routinely carry twice their height in baggage lashed on to their roofs. Outside of Dakar, I saw two mopeds completely covered in live chickens, tied by their feet in the front, on both sides and all over the back. All I could see of the moped were the handlebars that the guy was holding onto, and the lower half of the tires. There was also a dude carrying a mattress on his back … while riding a bicycle.

But the most memorable sight was in Ouagadougou, Burkina Faso, where I noticed a loaded-up lorry getting ready to leave. What caught my eye was the guy getting up on top of the cab of the lorry with a long bamboo pole. I went up and asked him why he was up there with that stick. He told me matter-of-factly that he would push up all the low-hanging power lines in the city as they drove under them.

– Tyler Keys

any corner of the city in just one or two hops. However, you may well have to put up with a distinct lack of comfort – vehicles can be just as packed as those running longer distances between towns. Although you might find yourself dreaming up evil destinies for the "turn boys" (touts-cum-conductors), for whom the concept "no room" simply does not exist, they do provide entertainment by hanging on to the vehicle's exterior while the vehicle careers along at full speed.

When boarding a vehicle at a terminus, choose one that looks full and about to leave, or you'll have to wait inside until they're ready to go. Competition is intense and people will lie unashamedly to persuade you the vehicle is going "just now". This extends to populating empty vehicles with touts pretending to be passengers, in order to attract real ones.

11

Accommodation

A visitor is a guest for two days. On the third day, give him a hoe
Swahili proverb, East Africa

Africa has a wide range of accommodation, from cheap, very basic guesthouses used by locals that charge a few dollars a night, to exclusive wildlife lodges and luxurious semi-permanent "tented camps" pitched out in the middle of the bush. A destination's popularity doesn't guarantee value for money in terms of places to stay: while competition can lower rates and raise standards, it can also – if demand outstrips supply – result in mediocrity at outrageous prices.

Hotel terminology varies from one country to another, but the basics are much the same. Single rooms have one bed and are generally intended for one person only, even if the bed is big enough for two. Some cheap hotels may let couples use a single room for the same price as a solo traveller, but it's not to be relied on. A double room has a large bed suitable for couples, or two smaller beds, which might be called a twin. An en-suite or self-contained room has a private bathroom.

Reserving rooms in budget or mid-range establishments is only really necessary if they're special in some way, if you're visiting a booming destination during peak season or if there's a big festival on in town. Bear in mind that reservations may be mislaid or even ignored in budget places. If you're going upmarket, reservations are always a good idea (you may be able to do this through the hotel's website), and can be essential – the best places can be fully booked months in advance. Any specialist travel agent or safari outfitter should be able to match you up with suitable establishments. National tourist boards have (not always up-to-date) lists of mid-range and upmarket hotels, but coverage of budget places varies considerably. In Tunisia, for example, the official line is that budget hotels don't even exist (a big fat lie, that one).

Choosing a place to stay

You'll rarely be completely at a loss for a place to stay, but to be sure of finding something really worthwhile calls for a little bit of planning and some careful consideration. And while accommodation is a major expense, it's not worth saving a few dollars here and there if, for little more, you can stay in a far better establishment. It's also good to splash out from time to time. Emerging battered and bruised from a bumpy bus ride, you'll appreciate creature comforts and facilities like proper showers,

The sacred scarab beetle

Crossing the Sahara was my first experience of Africa, so when I visited Tunisia a few years later on another trip, I was up for a bit of nostalgia. I packed my bicycle and headed south, off road, into the desert close to Libya. One day the heat seemed a little more intense than usual – something that seemed to please a lot of black scarab beetles the size and shape of walnuts. They were all over the place. At first I made an effort to avoid crushing them with my wheels, but on one occasion I felt too tired to bother swerving into deeper sand, so I just rode over one. I still remember the cracking sound it made, and I instantly felt guilty. I still do. Anyway, I rode on until mid-afternoon, once again avoiding jay-walking beetles, until I came across an abandoned village of *ghorfas* – traditional honeycomb-like granaries that Saharan Berbers used to build to store what little they could eke out of the unforgiving sands. I settled on one particularly comfortable-looking *ghorfa*, where a sand drift had engulfed half the interior, making for a comfortable bed – a perfect place to spend the night.

It was still dark when I awoke, thinking how wonderful it was to be back in the Sahara. But something didn't make sense – the stars. It was then I realized that part of the roof had caved in while I slept, and had landed less than a metre away from my head. Somehow, I didn't think to leave, but fell asleep again, thankful to be alive.

When I rolled up my sheet the following morning, I saw that a scarab beetle had spent the night with me, burrowing between the sheet and the sand. I recalled the beetle I'd crushed the day before. It felt as though the soul of the dead beetle had taken pity on me, and had somehow saved me from being similarly crushed at night. And I felt I understood, at least in my way, the ancient Egyptians' well-known reverence for the scarab.

– Jens Finke

air-conditioning instead of fans, satellite TV, or perhaps a restaurant or a bar in the same building.

On the other hand, you might also find that a hotel's charm or character outweighs the inconveniences of its blocked drains and rattling ceiling fans. Good views are another reason to forego fittings and trimmings: even a bird's-eye view of the goings-on at bus stations and markets can provide many a fascinating moment.

Whichever area you're arriving in, it's worth getting there early so that you have plenty of time to orient yourself, and to track down another hotel if your first choice doesn't work out. Check-out time is generally late morning, so turning up around then gives you the best chance of finding a spare room. Making contact beforehand by phone or email is a good idea, too, saving you the trouble of going there in person. Bear the following additional points in mind when choosing where to stay:

- **Where in town do you want to be?** Budget travellers should prefer areas with several hotels within walking distance of each other, in case option number one has closed or dropped its standards since the guidebook was written, or if the guidebook got it wildly wrong. If you want to be out and about early the next day, or like the bustle of being in the thick of things, it's worth being in a central location, even if this means sacrificing a little comfort and perhaps putting up with more noise. If you'll be moving on directly, stay close to the bus terminal, train station or airport.
- **Get recommendations from other travellers.** Guidebooks are very useful when it comes to choosing a hotel, but remember that despite the eagle-eyed attentions of their editors, the authors can be partial in their choices and with their descriptions, and their personal preferences may not match yours. Guidebooks also get out of date – prices rise, hotels close down, and conditions and facilities can nose dive or in fact improve. The best approach is to select a handful of suitable places from a guidebook, then crosscheck them with feedback on the websites reviewed on pp.269–270. Once you're on the road, the travellers' grapevine is the best source of unbiased recommendations.
- **Try the place next door.** No guidebook or website is ever comprehensive: the hotel next door to the one that's glowingly reviewed may be twice as nice at half the price. It's always worth visiting several establishments before choosing.
- **Don't be star-struck.** Not all countries have hotel grading systems, and where they exist the criteria for awarding stars may differ;

furthermore, all schemes are open to abuse. While hotels claiming five-star status are generally of a very high standard, other stars aren't always a reflection of quality; in some countries, the awarding of the stars depends on things like the width of elevator shafts or the number of rooms, or whether there's parking. No amount of stars necessarily translates into value for money.

- **Trust your instincts.** If something about the hotel you've just walked into gives you bad vibes, look elsewhere. Surly staff, unfriendly stares from guests, or idle men hanging around entrances are none too promising signs. For actual things to look for before parting with any cash, read "Checking out a room" on p.354.

Hostels

Other than camping (see p.351), Africa's cheapest overnights – especially for lone travellers – are the dormitories in hostels (and in some of the cheaper guesthouses). In these, you'll be sharing a room with several other men or women (dorms are segregated by sex). Some hostels additionally have more expensive family rooms or rooms for couples. The better hostels also have cooking facilities, restaurants or bars, and all can be good places for meeting local young people.

Youth hostels are rare except in North Africa. For their locations, and details of the youth hostelling movement (including how to get membership cards), see the International Youth Hostel Federation's website Ⓦ www.hihostels.com. The disadvantage of hostels is that they're likely to impose night-time curfews, so night owls will have to stay out the whole night, or else hope that the security guard or whoever's on night duty is willing to bend the rules and let you in at the wee hours.

In East Africa, church-run hostels – for which you don't need membership, or even faith in a greater being – are common. As with youth hostels, curfews are enforced, and some places can feel rather staid and and lifeless.

South Africa's backpackers' hostels are the liveliest of the lot, and many have become part of established backpackers' circuits, in which a string of hostels and the attractions along the way are connected to each other by the door-to-door Baz Bus service (Ⓦ www.bazbus .com). As well as offering the country's most affordable accommodation (normal rooms, plus bunks in dorms), these hostels are the best places for meeting fellow travellers. They're also likely to have

Internet access, and boast cafés and bars stocked with treats you might have been missing.

Guesthouses and cheap hotels

Nearly every town and city in Africa has at least one clean and comfortable guesthouse (sometimes styling itself a hotel), providing adequate accommodation for tourists on a tight budget, and for better-off locals. In the best ones, often aimed at backpackers, you might benefit from a bar or a restaurant or even a rooftop terrace, but by and large they're purely functional places with little more than bedrooms and bathrooms. Average costs can vary quite considerably between countries, but you're most unlikely to pay more than $20/£11 a night for a double room (rates are often half that).

Few countries have schemes to monitor guesthouses for quality, so their condition varies greatly, from mildewed dumps with bathrooms colonized by cockroaches, to stylishly restored former palaces stuffed with antiques. The cheapest guesthouses can be very basic indeed, with shared bathrooms and toilets, and bedroom furniture not stretching much beyond a bed and perhaps a chair. Still, most guesthouses will have some more expensive rooms with attached bathrooms (whether or not that's an advantage depends on how well kept the place is), and the very best can be fabulously friendly family-run affairs.

As you might expect, establishments located close to transport terminals are likely to maximize their potential by admitting couples on "short time", though not all are tawdry and the passing trade tends to be discreet. In East Africa, the more puritanical guesthouses display belligerent signs stating that "women of immoral turpitude" are not welcome …

Mid-range and upmarket hotels

Mid-range hotels charge anything from $30/£16 to $100/£55 a night for a double room, and are popular with businesspeople, lower-end package tours and some families. Facilities usually include an attached bathroom with Western-style flush toilet, hot water (most of the time), breakfast (included in the price), air conditioning and, often enough, satellite or cable TV. But as with guesthouses, standards are far from uniform: you'll come across bristlingly smart and efficient establishments as well as a few bland and boozy places.

Africa's five-star hotels – many of which belong to international chains – are well up to global standards, and can come with a bewildering array of mod-cons and amenities, including several bars and restaurants, gymnasiums and swimming pools. For all their comforts, the urban variety are often completely lacking in charm, and have little that's really African about them (the same could be said of most mid-range places, too).

Camping

Africa has enough campsites to make carrying a tent worthwhile, and camping is cheap, at around $5/£3 per person for a pitch on a public campsite. It's also the cheapest way of overnighting in wildlife parks or reserves, and doesn't usually require prebooking, although you may need a vehicle to reach the campsite in the first place, as walking in parks and reserves is rarely allowed.

In rural areas, hotels may let you camp discreetly in their grounds. When camping rough in populated areas or on someone's farmland, always ask before pitching a tent – otherwise, worried locals may send an armed delegation to see who you are. In any case, it's always polite to call on the headman, chief or another authority figure (such as a teacher) to explain your presence – the mere act of which is likely to prompt an invitation to spend the night at someone's house.

Camping is generally pretty safe, but there are some places you should avoid. Don't camp right by the road (to avoid casual theft), in dried-out river-beds (prone to flash floods), or on trails used by animals going to water, and avoid areas where cattle-rustling or local disputes are prevalent. In addition, sleeping out on any but the most deserted beaches is an open invitation to robbers. On the subject of animals, if you're way out in the bush, lions and hyenas are very occasionally curious about fires, but will rarely attack unless provoked. Nonetheless, listen seriously to local advice about lions and other dangers.

Lugging camping gear around is thankfully not much of a hassle these days, with modern lightweight tents having little in common with their bulky ancestors: for $55/£30, you can get a two-person tent that weighs under 3kg and takes up less than 15cm by 60cm of bag space. When buying a tent, get one bigger than you strictly need – a two-person tent if you're travelling solo, or a three-person tent for a couple – to guard against too much of a squeeze once you and your gear are inside. To avoid sleepless nights spent swatting bugs, choose a model with a mosquito net incorporated into the tent's entrance.

In tropical or equatorial parts of Africa, you don't need a full-on sleeping bag. In fact, a sheet sleeping bag (or a normal bedsheet folded and sewn up) is quite sufficient. Wherever you're going, you will also need a foam mattress; it's not heavy but it is bulky, although it can easily be strapped on to a backpack.

Cooking equipment isn't necessary unless you'll be spending days or weeks away from civilization. There are cheap restaurants pretty much everywhere, and eating out is in any case part of the fun of travelling in Africa. Collecting firewood is rarely permitted in protected wildlife areas; some parks and reserves provide firewood for a small fee, but most insist that you use gas stoves. Camping gas cartridges are available in the supermarkets of big cities but rarely elsewhere.

Wildlife lodges and tented camps

Staying overnight in national parks and game reserves is rarely very cheap unless you're happy camping. Wildlife lodges are the mainstay of mid-range safaris, and are often large if ageing four-star-style hotels, the better ones complete with swimming pools, transported into beautiful corners of the bush. Most wildlife lodges are far from intimate, however – this is package-tour territory, where you can forget any "alone in the wilderness" dreams you might have been entertaining. Much better, but top of the price range, are smaller eco-lodges and elegant "boutique hotels", which can be extremely luxurious. They're likely to have many a designer touch, too: unusual takes on traditional architecture (including tree-house accommodation), antiques and fine nicknacks like blown glass baubles in the bedrooms, and cast-iron bathtubs. These are the places that feature in lifestyle rags such as *Vogue* and *Condé Nast Traveller,* and as such can charge pretty much what they please. In one or two areas, $300/£160 a night could be considered a screaming bargain, and some establishments don't even smile when quoting rates in excess

△ Accommodation in wildlife parks can be plush, and sometimes very unusual

of $1000/£550 a night – in which case the price might include game drives, the services of expert guides for bush walks, and all meals. You can't simply turn up expecting to find a room, however: they're often booked months in advance.

Similarly priced, and often with a similar range of facilities and designer appeal, are tented lodges or tented camps – which aren't exactly camping as you might have known it. Their accommodation is in large, walk-in tents (some big enough to be called marquees) pitched on concrete or wooden platforms, and offering a proper bed, perhaps some antique furniture, a bathroom plumbed in at the back, and possibly solar-powered electric light. At the very best tented camps, you'll be able to observe wildlife from the comfort of your veranda, a scintillating experience that can easily justify the expense. Other than the price, the downside to such places can be a rather neo-colonial atmosphere, especially as many camps are owned and run by non-Africans. Also, be aware that not all "eco-lodges" are quite as eco-friendly as their patter makes out; see p.319.

Beach accommodation

A sizeable chunk of African tourism revolves around life on the beach, and it's along coastlines that you're likely to find the widest choice of accommodation, and the highest standards. It's always worth spending a little more for a sea view, if there is one – lounging in a hammock or deckchair on a private veranda while watching the sunrise is all part of that holiday magic. Do be sure you're paying for a proper view, though, and not just a distant glimpse through trees, and remember that "garden view" is a polite way of saying there's no sea view.

North Africa's beach hotels are a mix of high-rise resorts – along the lines of those in Spain's Costa del Sol – and more recent open-plan designs that make a less negative impact on the skyline. South of the Sahara, touristic beach developments tend to be low-rise, and at their best are quiet, laid-back and enjoyably personal in feel. Some are bungalow resorts, featuring a number of thatch-roofed, whitewashed cottages, generally containing two or four guest rooms apiece, all set back from the beach in manicured gardens. The resort's main building is often an impressive foray into neo-traditional architecture, with vast thatched roofs and plenty of woodcarvings. Many resorts also have swimming pools and separate buildings, perhaps overlooking the beach, for more romantic wining and dining.

A completely different kettle of fish are the large package-holiday resorts that have mushroomed along many of the continent's most popular beaches. To call them brash would be an understatement for many. They tend to pay fleeting homage to local style in their architecture and decoration, but otherwise have little that's recognizably African about them, including their clientele. On the positive side, they do come with fancy swimming pools, lots of bars and restaurants, perhaps a disco, and often a whole raft of activities. If booked in Africa, such places can be extremely expensive: it's usually much cheaper to stay in one as part of a package tour bought at home.

Checking out a room

Rooms vary in size and quality, and some hotels will try their best to offload their least attractive or most expensive room onto you, so ask to see a selection before checking in. If you're on your own, ask to see some doubles or twins, too. They'll be more expensive than singles but may not be as poky, and may also be in better condition. If a hotel is awkward about letting you inspect the goods, look elsewhere. Bear in mind the following:

- **Silence is golden.** Street noise and the proximity of mosques might wake you up earlier than you want, and a bar or disco nearby (or inside the hotel itself) may keep you from sleeping until well after midnight. If you can't sleep with noise, bringing ear plugs would be a deft move.
- **Follow your nose.** Smell can be a good indicator of comfort. Rank bathrooms, mouldy air conditioning, and too liberal applications of bug spray are all good reasons to leave.
- **Test the power.** Flick switches to find out what works, or what doesn't. If you need a socket, see whether it's actually hooked up to anything. And in countries blighted by power cuts, ask about whether they have a back-up generator, and when it gets fired up.
- **Mod-cons.** Do you really need a hair dryer (probably not) or a personal safe (maybe)? If there's a TV, check whether it only receives local channels, or is hooked up to some cable or satellite network.
- **Ceiling fans and air conditioning.** These can be essential in tropical and equatorial climes, but you don't want to cohabit with, say, a fan that sounds like a chicken being strangled.
- **Mosquitoes and nets.** Squished mosquitoes on the wall are an indication that mozzies will be a problem. In mosquito-infested areas, it's essential that mosquito nets be free of holes unless you fancy repairing them yourself, either with thread, sticky tape or even a stapler. Nets should also fit *all* of the bed, ideally leaving you ample room to move about in your sleep; rectangular ones are better than circular ones for this reason. In upmarket places the nets may have an entrance flap; ensure that both sides overlap completely when drawn. If a hotel relies on window screens (definitely not as good as using nets), check them too. Lastly, peek through the window for puddles, open-topped tanks or even banana plants, all of which are breeding grounds for mosquitoes.
- **The state of the beds.** Few hotels, even the poshest ones, bother cleaning under the beds more than once or twice a year, but basic cleanliness is vital. Bathrooms, obviously, and bed sheets should be spotless: small, rust-coloured spots suggest fleas. There's nothing wrong with lumpy pillows *per se*, but they can suggest that rooms aren't as cared for as perhaps they could be. Bed springs are another bane; worst of all are saggy mattresses, guaranteed to give you back ache. Sheets should ideally be linen or cotton, as one-hundred-percent-synthetic sheets have a nasty tendency to stick to sweaty bodies. You can tell if sheets are synthetic by creasing them with your fingers and then flattening them with your hand; if the crease all but disappears, they are. Incidentally, the creaseless quality of nylon is prized by some lazy hoteliers who don't want to have to wash and iron sheets for every new guest ... bits of hair are telltale signs.

- **Is the room secure?** As you're being shown around, catch a glimpse of the keys being used to open the rooms. If they're skeleton keys (those with long cylindrical shafts) rather than standard house keys (ones with jagged teeth along most of their length), you shouldn't rely on the lock to keep out thieves, especially in hotels with attached bars or night clubs. Splintered door frames aren't promising either. In really basic guesthouses, door locks may amount to a hoop on the door and another on the frame, or an external deadbolt, for either of which you'll be supplied with a padlock. If you want to be extra safe, bring your own small padlock. Inside the room, check whether windows are accessible from the outside, and if so whether they can be locked. If you're driving, ask about enclosed parking.

The plumbing

A favoured subject for traveller's horror stories, not just in Africa, are bathroom escapades. After all, we tend to grow fond of our thrones, and end up looking down on other, perhaps rather less royal

Cleansing body and soul – hammams

In North Africa, one of the pleasures in life is visiting a hammam. Bearing an obvious similarity to Roman baths, hammams (also called Turkish baths) can be full-blown cultural experiences that combine an exhaustive scrub-down, a massage and a soak in a steam bath with plenty of chitchat. The best ones are architectural masterpieces, and even the most humdrum ones, perhaps a little worse for wear, can still resemble fairytale grottoes. For local women, hammams also perform a social function: being segregated by sex, they're places where they can talk frankly about issues that would be taboo in the company of men, or even out on the street. Female travellers can benefit from this: hammams are a great way of getting to know local women.

The actual process of washing in a hammam is similar to that of a sauna, but a good deal more humid. You start off by sitting in a hot, dry room, where you'll work up a good sweat. Moving along, you can either brave an even hotter room, or dunk yourself in a cold pool. Then comes the serious business of dealing with all that dirt: if you've been on the road for a while you'll probably need a full-body scrub, for which the masseur will duly oblige with a fetching pair of abrasive gloves. Scraped, gouged and pummelled, you'll emerge refreshed and smelling of roses.

The cleaning of the body traditionally went hand in hand with spiritual cleansing, so hammams are often attached to mosques (these bathhouses are unlikely to admit tourists). Hammam visiting hours are different for men and women if there's only one set of baths.

arrangements. Of course, there is a chance of seeing cockroaches *this big*, or of having to brave dozens of pesky flies or clouds of mosquitoes as you tend to your needs (a good reason to like the harmless fly-gobbling geckos that cling to many an African bathroom wall), but for most travellers Africa's bathrooms and toilets provide thankfully uneventful experiences.

In a continent known for a lack of water, it's no surprise that showers are the norm, and bathtubs are seldom encountered other than in old colonial hotels or in upmarket places heedful of their clients' expectations. In more humble places, running water isn't always guaranteed, even in cities – where power cuts can knock out water pumps – which is why you'll find a bucket of water taking pride of place in many a bathroom. In warm areas, you're unlikely to find hot water in cheap or even some mid-range hotels unless you specifically ask for it, in which case it'll come in a bucket.

Where water supplies are unreliable, or have to be trucked in and stored in tanks, showering can mean scooping and sloshing from a bucket. There's actually an art to bucket showers – once you become an adept, you won't need even half a pail to wash your entire body with. The better hotels, even cheap ones, will provide you with a fresh bar of soap and clean towel, and a pair of plastic sandals, but in less salubrious places it's best to bring your own: you never know what fungus will take a liking to you.

Toilets

Except in South Africa where they're the norm, Western-style toilets are only frequently encountered in tourist hotels (in all price ranges), and in restaurants serving a similar clientele. In the cheapest places, these toilets can look rather sorry for themselves, having lost their seats long ago.

Everywhere else, you're likely to have to use loos over which you squat. The best are hygienic wonders of shiny white porcelain with pedestals for your feet, placed over properly plumbed-in pipes, and with effective flush mechanisms. The worst variety are dirty wooden planks placed over festering pits or even more horrid buckets. Luckily, you're far more likely to come across the former kind. Silly though it may sound, the following is good advice if you'll be staying in local hotels: be sure that you're able to squat and get back up. If you can't, it might be worth practising a bit before you leave, to tune up those thighs.

Unless the toilet is in a place that deals frequently with tourists, budget travellers are unlikely to be given toilet paper, so you might want to bring your own. Locals get by with the time-honoured wash-and-go method, which usually means filling a small tub or other container with water (most squat toilets have a tap on the left-hand side), and using that to rinse your bottom with your left hand (which explains the widespread taboo on using your left hand for eating or shaking hands). Always check whether there is in fact water in the tap or the bucket before getting down to business.

Lastly, if there's a bin for used toilet paper, sanitary towels or tampons, do use it even if the thought repels you: African plumbing and sewerage systems don't cope well with paper and objects, so the bin is a much friendlier proposition than having to deal with consequences of blocked pipes.

12

On safari

No matter how long a log stays in the water,
it doesn't become a crocodile

Bamana proverb, Mali

For many visitors, Africa *is* wildlife, and the prospect of going on safari – a Swahili word that means "journey" – is a major factor in choosing Africa as the setting for the holiday of a lifetime. Virtually all countries south of the Sahara have at least one wildlife park in which you'll be able to see a good range of species, including the celebrated "Big Five" (see the box on p.361). For some visitors, ticking off species from a checklist can be all safaris are about; for others, a specialized trip, say focused on bird-watching (many of Africa's parks and reserves boast species counts several hundred strong), bug-spotting or even running after butterflies, does the trick.

Serving as centre stage for safaris are Africa's savannas, not just on account of animal numbers but also because the open landscapes make them easy to see. Rainforests, as you might expect, are much more challenging locations for wildlife-spotting, but the forests are in fact far richer than savannas in ecological terms, whether it's monkeys, birds or bugs that inflame your passions. Apart from what you want to see, and where, bear the following in mind when planning or choosing a safari:

● **The cost.** Safaris don't come cheap, though the best, in all price ranges, can offer excellent value for money. In West and Southern

Africa — the most affordable areas for safaris — the most basic minibus-and-camping foray starts at $70/£40 a day, including everything from meals and overnight accommodation to transport and entrance fees. In East Africa's most famous parks, though, you'll be hard pressed to find anything under $100/£55 a day.

● **The duration.** In general, four to seven days is recommended. While one-day excursions are possible if the park or reserve is close enough to where you're starting from, the distances involved and the wealth of things to see mean that longer safaris are far better. Bear in mind also that a safari advertised as "three-day" actually means two nights, with sizeable chunks of the first and last day spent driving to and from the wildlife areas. You can avoid this by flying to and from wildlife parks in light aircraft (safari companies can arrange this), which also dispenses with the dusty discomfort of road travel.

● **Local involvement.** With the focus squarely on seeing animals, it's easy to ignore locals, some of whom may have been excluded from their ancestral homelands when the park or reserve was created. If you can, prefer safaris that have some kind of local involvement. In both Eastern and West Africa, you can take safaris on village-owned land and stay in lodges that pay part of their profits to local communities. Alternatively, combine the safari experience with some kind of cultural tourism; doing this will give you a more balanced view of the country and its wildlife, and an insight into the thorny question of local peoples' needs versus the views of more radical conservationists, who advocate the elimination of all human activity in wildlife areas with the exception of research and tourism.

What to see, and where

All but two of the major countries for wildlife safaris are in East Africa (Kenya, Tanzania, Uganda and Rwanda) or Southern Africa (Malawi, Zambia, Zimbabwe, Botswana, Namibia and South Africa). Also shining bright among Africa's wildlife stars are the Central African state of Gabon, and the island of Madagascar — famed for its tree-dwelling lemurs and for all sorts of unique bugs and amphibians. The following is a rundown of the main species, and where to see them.

Predators

Lions and leopards are prevalent in many parts of sub-Saharan Africa. Lions are the more easily seen, and many are the morbid tales of

The Big Five ... and the Little Five

For most safari-goers, it's the "Big Five" – lions, elephants, cheetahs or leopards, rhinos and buffaloes – that exert the keenest attraction. Those biggies sure are the crowd-pullers, but spare a thought for those species excluded from the list. It can be just as rewarding to observe a herd of antelopes or a family of warthogs go about their daily business as it is to ogle a pride of fly-covered lions sleeping off their last meal. If you really need a list to go for, might we suggest our own "Little Five" to look out for – lion ants, elephant shrews, leopard tortoises, rhino beetles and buffalo weavers. Buffalo weavers are enterprising birds that like to hitch rides on the backs of said buffaloes, waiting for bugs disturbed by their vehicle's passing. The other "Little Five" can be quite a challenge to find. Some clues for you: lion ants make funnels with which to catch their prey; leopard tortoises, sometimes seen on asphalt roads, have carapaces whose blotches account for their name; rhino beetles are nocturnal but might be given away by their hissing squeaks as they ward off rivals; and elephant shrews look like hobbling mice with tiny elephant's trunks for snouts.

"kills" you'll hear across Africa's wildlife lodges in the evenings. However, spotting leopards (apologies for the pun), which are mainly nocturnal creatures that prefer woodland to plains, is not guaranteed. If you do track one down, it's likely to be lounging most memorably on a branch high up in a tree, with or without the remains of an antelope that it'll have dragged up there with it. Elegant cheetahs like flat open ground, where they can use their incredible bursts of speed to snag a meal. Botswana's Okavango Delta is a great place for seeing them, as is Nairobi National Park, on the doorstep of Kenya's capital – photos of cheetahs here with skyscrapers in the background are a classic image.

Hyenas, those limping, much-maligned dog-like creatures, are commonly seen, especially in the mornings. The rarest of the predators – in many areas, in fact, on the brink of extinction – is the African hunting dog or wild dog. Your best chance of seeing them is in Moremi Game Reserve in Botswana's Okavango Delta, or at the remote Liuwa Plains National Park in Zambia.

All these are just the most famous predators. Others, mostly nocturnal, include civet and serval cats, genets and caracals, various species of foxes and jackals, and honey badgers (also called ratels).

△ Cheetahs have a habit of turning up in unexpected places

Plains game

Featuring on the main courses of many a predators' menu are all manner of antelopes, which can be seen right across sub-Saharan Africa, from the Sahel and the Nile Valley to the southern tip of the continent. Antelopes are at their most impressive in East Africa's Serengeti, where more than 1.5 million wildebeests – together with almost a million zebras – take part in an annual, cyclical migration between Tanzania's Serengeti grasslands and the rainy-season pastures of Kenya's Maasai Mara. Giraffes and buffaloes are also commonly seen throughout the continent: giraffes wherever there are trees tall enough for browsing on, and buffaloes wherever there's mud to wallow in, or thick bush or forest to lie out in.

Primates

Africa's best places for primates are the dense and often mountainous forests along the Equator, though you'll find vervet monkeys and baboons all over; both of these are frequently pests, as neither get fazed by humans.

Chimpanzees used to populate much of Africa's equatorial belt, but pressure from logging and hunting has greatly reduced their numbers, and four sub-species are now officially endangered. You can go chimpanzee tracking at various locations in Gabon and Nigeria, and in Rwanda, Uganda and Tanzania in East Africa.

Even rarer than chimps are gorillas, who provide the highlight of many a trip to Uganda's Bwindi Impenetrable Forest National Park and Rwanda's Parc National des Volcans. They can also be seen in several Gabonese parks, in Cameroon's Dja Faunal Reserve, and at Cross River National Park in Nigeria. Most of these places also contain an abundance of other primates. Other good locations for primates include Cameroon's Korup National Park, Kakum National Park in Ghana, much of Madagascar for dozens of unique species of tree-dwelling, saucer-eyed lemurs, and Tanzania's disjointed East African Arc mountain range, especially Udzungwa and Kitulo national parks, the latter being home to the recently discovered Kipunji monkey, which may be a genus unto itself.

At night, you might hear the haunting cries of bush babies, and with a bit of luck (and a flashlight) might see one, too. These cute, saucer-eyed creatures have come to appreciate gifts of bananas and other fruits, so you might spot them at wildlife lodges or outside rural homes.

Elephants

Having come close to extinction in many areas in the 1980s, elephant populations have rebounded quite spectacularly. Pachyderms can easily be seen in most sub-Saharan countries, but the long-time favourite sites are in South Africa (Addo Elephant and Kruger National Parks) and Tanzania (Tarangire National Park). Kenya's Amboseli National Park – a flat basin in the shadow of Kilimanjaro – is the most scenic area for elephants. For rarer forest elephants, head to Rwanda or Uganda, Ghana, Cameroon or Gabon.

Rhinos

Africa's most endangered big mammals can be found in isolated locations throughout East and Southern Africa. The continent has two main species of rhino, black and the more common white. The difference has nothing to do with colour (they're both grey); "white" came from the mistranslated Afrikaans word for "wide", referring to the shape of the animals' mouth – ideally suited for grazing. The narrower, hooked lips of black rhinos are much better for browsing.

They're most easily seen in privately run game reserves, often set up for the specific goal of increasing their populations. In Southern Africa, sightings are guaranteed at either Mokolodi Nature Reserve or Khama Rhino Sanctuary, both in Botswana; at Mokolodi, you can see them from horseback or even from on top of an elephant. Other good places include a string of Zimbabwean national parks; Zambia's Mosi-Oa-Tunya National Park (where you can get around by elephant); Namibia's Waterberg Plateau; and Hlane Royal National Park and Mkhaya Game Reserve, both in Swaziland. For sheer numbers, however, nothing beats South Africa's Hluhluwe-Imfolozi Park, which is home to over two thousand white rhinos.

In East Africa – where rhino poaching was at its worst – Tanzania's celebrated Ngorongoro Crater is probably the finest place, though you're also likely to see rhinos at Murchison Falls National Park in Uganda, and perhaps at Kenya's Aberdares National Park, if you stay overnight at one of the lodges overlooking floodlit water holes.

Hippos

Hippos can be seen in many lakes south of the Sahara; special places for seeing them are Tanzania's Katavi National Park and Malawi's Liwonde National Park, in both of which they can form pods several thousand strong.

Everyone's favourite blubbery things are in fact Africa's nastiest mammals, killing more people than all the predators combined. The reason is that they're extremely possessive of their watery homes; without a river or mud pool to wallow in, they'd quickly

Desert wildlife

Life in the desert can be tenuous in the extreme, and large animals are rare. The best place overall for Saharan wildlife is the Aïr Mountains of northern Niger, where you might chance upon gazelles or ostriches, antelopes, or even giraffes, leopards or lions. Oryx antelopes and bat-eared foxes (fennecs) are rare, however. The Kalahari fares better, mainly because it's not as arid – antelopes and lions abound. The Namib, for its part, promises the unusual sight of elephants, perhaps even along the Skeleton Coast, and flocks of flamingoes congregating around salt pans amid the dunes.

dehydrate as their skin is far more delicate and sensitive to sunlight than it appears.

Crocodiles

Nile crocodiles – the world's biggest – are not confined to the Nile, but are also found in Kenya's Lake Turkana (once, a very long time ago, one of the river's sources) and elsewhere in East Africa. Taking river trips along the Zambezi or River Niger, you're bound to see crocs, too, doing very good impressions of floating logs. In West Africa, crocodiles can be sacred creatures, and villagers keep them in special pools: you can visit these at Kachikally in The Gambia, at Paga in Ghana, at Sabou near Ouagadougou in Burkina Faso, and at Amani in Mali's Dogon country.

The least likely place for crocodiles, you might think, is the Sahara, but with patience and a good bit of luck, you may well come across one or two dwarf crocs in the pools of Ayoun el-Atrous oasis in Mauritania, or in southern Algeria's oases (where, having long been believed to be extinct, a few examples have cropped up over the last few years).

Birds

Africa is absolutely amazing for birds, whether you're on the Atlantic shores of the Sahara, in the mountains of Lesotho, or even in downtown Tunis, where enormous wheeling flocks of starlings provide evening entertainment. A somewhat arbitrary selection of Africa's top ten birding sites is included on pp.207–208.

Types of safari

For most safari-goers, the experience boils down to being driven around one or more national parks or game reserves in search of animals, pausing here and there to admire and take photographs of the denizens. In fact driving – and remaining within the metallic confines of a vehicle – is often obligatory in national parks, primarily to keep you from becoming some critter's meal. Still, a growing trend is for parks and reserves to allow walking in the company of armed rangers or experienced guides. Horseback safaris are also possible, and you might even get to see things from the back of an elephant.

A typical safari day starts at dawn, in time for an early morning drive or bush walk on which you have a good chance of seeing species that are primarily nocturnal. Returning to base after a few hours, you'll have time to rest, take breakfast or lunch, and maybe spend some quality time with a pair of binoculars scanning the plains or nearby waterholes, before setting off mid-afternoon for another game drive or walk, which will generally last until nightfall. On a shorter safari, where you're likely to be shifting location every night, the game drive can take up the whole day, which sounds enticing but can be exhausting, and you risk missing species that are particular to one area or another if you've only got little time in each.

Few national parks permit driving after dark, a fact that privately managed game reserves have capitalized on by offering night-time driving safaris. Assisted by a powerful searchlight, you cruise around at walking pace (indeed, some places let you loose on foot), catching all manner of startled eyes in the glare. The animals never seem too bothered by the intrusion; they may well freeze in the spotlight, but as soon as the beam shifts away, they resume whatever they were up to before you barged in. Night-time safaris are often the only way of seeing otherwise elusive species such as leopards, civet cats, caracals, hares and porcupines.

Driving safaris

Driving safaris can be as simple or as plush as you like. Virtually every safari company on the continent offers them, and you might consider self-drive if you're confident about your skills behind the wheel.

On the most basic "camping safaris", you'll be sleeping in simple tents, may well have to share cleaning-up duties, and – on shorter trips – can expect a mad dash to spot as many species as possible before being driven back. Be prepared for a degree of discomfort: thin mattresses and patchy sleeping bags, not having a shower every night, and basic food. Mid-range packages let you stay in more comfortable wildlife lodges. Going more upmarket still brings lodges with facilities such as swimming pools, several restaurants and bars, or "luxury tented camps" (or "tented lodges"), which feature bedrooms in spacious tents pitched on permanent platforms, often with balconies and bathrooms.

The type of vehicle that will be used is an important consideration. On the cheapest trips, you can expect to be driven around in a minibus, on which there's not necessarily any guarantee of getting a window seat. Land Rovers and Land Cruisers fare better in this respect, and of course also feel right in the context of a safari: you'll have seen plenty of such vehicles on documentaries, but probably not one minibus. Whatever the vehicle, it's a bonus if it has a roof hatch that can be opened fully for taking photographs, and perhaps a small fridge for keeping drinks cool. Other than the possibility of your driver being a speed freak on tarmac, safety is not really a concern, though a vehicle fitted with HF radio for emergencies gives additional peace of mind.

Mobile safaris

An odd name, this, given that all safaris are mobile, but in safari-speak a mobile safari is the height of bush luxury – a throwback to colonial days, when animal-bagging expeditions were led by pith-helmeted explorer-types. Of course you'll only be shooting through a camera, but the rest of experience can be quite a period piece, one positively oozing nostalgia. Accompanied by expert expatriate guides, many of whom seem to model themselves on the white hunter chaps from *Out of Africa*, you'll be treated to intimate wildlife experiences in remote or otherwise exclusive areas, often on foot, too (albeit with vehicle backup never far behind).

The real treat, though, is the accommodation. If you thought the walk-in tents used in "standard" tented camps were spacious, you'll

Balloon safaris

Four hundred dollars, more or less, is what you'll part with for the pleasure of a "balloon safari" – a short jaunt lasting an hour or two that will give you a bird's eye view of the comings and goings in safari land, and hopefully plenty of amazing photo opportunities. Tanzania's Serengeti National Park, Kenya's Maasai Mara, Moremi Game Reserve in Botswana's Okavango Delta, and several locations in Namibia and South Africa are the main places. If you time things right in Kenya or Tanzania, you might catch sight of the Serengeti's annual wildlife migration – which, seen from the air, resembles a tangle of dark ribbons.

Lift-off is at dawn, and the landing is traditionally followed by a sumptuous breakfast out in the bush, before the ground crew catches up to drive you back.

be astounded not just at the marquees used on mobile safaris. Even more amazing is that the tents, and the eating and lounge areas, are likely to have been pitched that very same day, by a largely invisible retinue of staff. The pampering is also evident in the details: luxurious touches like champagne breakfasts, fresh flowers in your tent, a personal butler, exquisite cooking, and a tribal "warrior" ostensibly ensuring your security, but whose real purpose is to lend a touch of exoticism to the proceedings. Such Hemingwayesque capers have a price, of course: expect to pay no less than $600/£320 per person per day.

Walking safaris

Walking safaris, or bush walks, are the most exciting ways to see wildlife. You won't see as much as on a driving safari, but any big animals you do see are likely to provide heart-stopping moments as they emerge suddenly from the bush. You'll also catch all the little details that are impossible to see from a vehicle: the sticky secretions of dik-diks and other small antelopes left on grass stems to mark out territory, the broken twigs left by leopards, bones from recent kills, weird and wonderful bugs and butterflies galore, and − with luck − chameleons, of which there are some real beauties (the horned Jackson's chameleon, for one, and tiny little critters half the length of your little finger). And of course, being outside the confines of a vehicle imparts a sense of freedom that's impossible to get any other way.

Most game walks last just a few hours, but longer trips are possible, making long-distance hiking safaris very exciting possibilities. Hiking is most likely to be allowed in mountainous or heavily forested parks, where in fact "footing" (as they say in East Africa) is often the only way around. The following are just some of Africa's great places for walking safaris:

- **The Crater Highlands (Tanzania)** Grab a guide and escape the crowds by walking from the lush Ngorongoro Crater to the desert Lake Natron, seeing all sorts of wildlife (and clambering up an active volcano) along the way.
- **Dja Faunal Reserve (Cameroon)** A huge tract of virgin rainforest, best explored in the company of a Pygmy guide.
- **The Eastern Arc Mountains (Tanzania)** Eyeball-to-eyeball encounters with primates, bugs and butterflies in Tanzania's ancient rainforests.

- **The Ethiopian highlands** Perfect for walking are the Simien Mountains, and Bale Mountains National Park. Apart from birds, look for Gelada baboons, Simien foxes and the Walia ibex.
- **Fish River Canyon (Namibia)** A mostly dry, 161-kilometre-long cleft near the South African border, with surreal desert landscapes (and flora), and an outside chance of seeing leopards and mountain zebras.
- **Mana Pools National Park (Zimbabwe)** Abutting the Zambezi River, the waterholes here attract a ton of plains game, including elephants and rhinos.
- **Mokolodi Nature Reserve (Botswana)** A privately run reserve stocked with all the "Big Five", plus lots of antelopes.
- **Mosi-Oa-Tunya National Park (Zambia)** A good selection of wildlife beside the Zambezi, including rhinos.
- **Namib-Naukluft Park (Namibia)** Explore the Namib Desert and meet its inhabitants: springboks, zebras and ostriches are common enough, and flamingoes are a special treat.
- **Nyika Plateau (Malawi)** A botanical paradise 2500m above sea level, of particular interest to orchid-lovers and with unusually good odds on seeing leopards.
- **Parc National des Volcans (Rwanda)** Seeing gorillas is the big thing here, but Virunga's primeval rainforest will also drown your senses in sights and sounds.

Riding safaris

If you use a horse or an elephant as a vehicle, you'll be able to approach other species much more closely than you would if you were on foot or in a car. Neither horseback nor elephant-back safaris are particularly widespread, however; in general horses don't have too good a time of it in Africa thanks to sleeping sickness and other parasitic diseases. Good places for horseback safaris include Botswana's elephant-packed Tuli and Mashatu Game Reserves, Northern Malawi's inspiring Nyika Plateau, Zimbabwe's Lake Mutirikwe National Park (where you can get close to white rhinos), the alpine highlands of Ethiopia's Bale Mountains National Park, and Swaziland's Mlilwane Wildlife Sanctuary.

Unlike their Asian cousins, Africa's pachyderms have never been too partial to the idea of having to lug people around on their backs, so the recent introduction of elephant-back safaris in Zambia (Mosi-Oa-Tunya National Park), South Africa (Pilanesburg National Park and near Addo Elephant National Park), and in Botswana's diminutive Mokolodi Nature Reserve, owes unwitting thanks to the days of ivory poaching. Orphaned elephants rescued by sanctuaries, and their offspring, have grown up to be trusting of humans.

Lastly, don't forget camels. In Niger's Aïr Mountains, where small populations of savanna animals still survive, you can spend days on camelback exploring the edges of the Ténéré sand dunes. Actually, "days" isn't quite true: after a few hours in the saddle, you'll probably find walking a rather more comfortable experience.

Canoeing and boating safaris

Paddling up creeks, gliding across placid lakes and pushing through reeds while dodging crocodiles is an exciting way of seeing wildlife, not so much for the glimpses of crocs, or hippos (which may just be showing their nostrils), but for the animals that come to drink on the shore. Approaching them if you were on land would be difficult, but water-borne humans have the big advantage of being far less likely to spook animals, so you can get much closer. Canoeing or boating safaris are most rewarding in semi-arid areas, whose rivers and lakes are obviously of paramount importance to local wildlife.

In West Africa, drifting along in a canoe on the River Niger is a major thrill, especially on the edge of Niger's portion of the Parc National du "W", where elephants and buffaloes, lions, hyenas and jackals can be seen. Guinea's Parc National du Haut Niger is more wooded, and gives you a chance of spotting chimpanzees. Gabon is excellent for pirogue trips, with boats available in the coastal Akanda National Park, and inland at Minkébé Lopé national parks. In East Africa, Tanzania's Selous Game Reserve is the main place for boating, which can be combined with bush walks.

You're spoilt for choice in Southern Africa. Boating safaris in Zambia's South Luangwa National Park are very popular, and the country also allows canoeing safaris in the swampy Kafue National Park (great for water-loving antelopes), and along the Zambezi. In the latter, you can extend your trip over several days, spending nights under canvas. Neighbouring Zimbabwe also offers Zambezi canoeing expeditions, as part of trips to Mana Pools National Park. To the north, Malawi's Liwonde National Park is an exceptional place for seeing elephants, hippos, crocs and birds from a boat, while boats are also the best way to get around the swampy wildlife sanctuaries of Namibia's Caprivi Strip.

Organizing a safari

There are three ways to arrange a safari: buy a package, customize a trip with a safari company, or arrange everything yourself. Each has its advantages.

Prearranged safaris make the most of precious holiday time, as you won't waste hours and days finding and booking reliable transport and accommodation. Be very careful when choosing a safari company, however, particularly if they're expecting you to pay in advance (standard practice these days, alas); given the rich pickings to be had, scams and dodgy outfits abound, and you certainly don't want to make a down payment only to find when you arrive that the company doesn't even exist. Any guidebook should have reviews of decent companies, but asking fellow travellers − either once you're in Africa, or using Internet forums and newsgroups (see pp.269–270) − is helpful for double checking. In fact some guidebooks are lamentably sloppy when it comes to sifting the wheat from the chaff. That said, the safari companies reviewed in the "Directory" at the end of this book should make excellent choices.

Group size is the main factor to bear in mind when booking. For some tourists this doesn't seem to matter, and indeed many of the larger operators catering mainly for package tours commonly shunt their clients around in convoys of vehicles − not exactly the wildest way of experiencing wild Africa. You'll also find that group relations can assume surprising significance, for better or worse, in a very short time.

Lastly, don't take too passive an attitude on a shared safari. Although some of the itinerary may be fixed, it's not all set in stone, and as long as you can get your fellow safari-goers to agree to changes, most staff will go out of their way to oblige.

Arranging things yourself

It's perfectly feasible to organize your own safari, either by renting a vehicle, or − for a limited number of parks − getting there by public transport. If you're thinking of self-driving, do seriously consider the option of hiring an experienced local driver for the safari. Road conditions inside wildlife areas can be absolutely terrible, especially during and just after the rains, and will require uncommonly assured off-road driving skills in addition to four-wheel drive. In fact, in most countries you'll be hard-pressed to find a car rental company willing to let you loose in one of their vehicles without a driver included in the bargain, if they know you'll be going on safari.

Arranging your own trip has the advantage of flexibility in planning your route, but isn't necessarily cheaper than going through a safari company unless you form a group. This shares out the cost of vehicle rental, but won't give you much of a reduction on accommodation – especially in mid-range or upscale places, where you'll likely have to pay full-whack "walk-in" or "rack rates", unlike the safari companies, who get discounts.

Other than transport and accommodation, you'll also have to arrange food and drink, buy or rent camping equipment, perhaps hire an expert wildlife guide (handy for spotting tails dangling out of trees half a kilometre away; you might be able to hire a guide at the park gate), and buy a specialized guidebook and map. You may also need to pay entrance fees in advance.

13

Staying healthy

Disease and disasters come and go like rain, but health is like the
sun that illuminates the entire village

Luo proverb, Lake Victoria

For Africans, poverty is the biggest health threat:
contaminated water supplies, inadequate medication
and insufficient healthcare facilities are among the
more obvious repercussions. For travellers, though,
Africa is not about fending off diseases and critters
(the most common affliction affecting visitors is nothing more
serious than an upset stomach), and health isn't something that
should worry you unduly so long as you're sensible and have
prepared well. There are vaccinations for many of the most dangerous diseases, such as yellow fever and hepatitis, and, with common
sense, the rest can be almost completely avoided, too. As a traveller,
you're one of the lucky few that can afford effective preventative
measures and medications, and treatment should you need it.

Take care when looking up health information on the Internet, as
misinformation, dodgy drug peddling and alarmism are all stock-in-
trade on line; trustworthy travel-health websites (and travel clinics)
are listed on pp.418–419. The *Rough Guide to Travel Health* offers
comprehensive treatment of the potential health problems facing
travellers worldwide. A good place to ask fellow travellers for tips
and advice is the rec.travel.africa newsgroup.

Incidentally, if you do get sick in the year following your journey,
it's worth telling a doctor exactly where you travelled: malaria can

take a month to show itself, and other diseases such as amoebic dysentery can have longer incubation periods. The pointers below should help you prepare for the trip itself:

- **Keep things in perspective.** Headline-grabbing diseases such as Ebola are so rare that you stand a much bigger chance of meeting your maker through a bolt of lightning.
- **See a doctor before you go.** Your family doctor or a travel clinic will provide inoculations and destination-specific health advice. If you're planning anything physically testing, such as climbing Kilimanjaro or travelling in the Sahara in summer, get a health check done too. Do all this at least two months before travelling, as you may need time to stagger vaccinations.
- **Get insured.** Ensure that you're adequately covered; see p.231.
- **Get a dental check-up.** Do this before you go, and take extra care of your ivories while travelling – Africa does have good dentists, but they're few and far between.
- **Take more care than usual over cuts and scrapes.** In the tropics, the most trivial scratch can quickly become a throbbing infection if you ignore it.

Vaccinations

Many of Africa's most serious diseases can be avoided entirely by getting yourself vaccinated. Family doctors are often well informed about routine injections and are likely to charge you a relatively low fee for these. For yellow fever and other exotic shots you'll normally have to visit a specialist clinic (see p.419). You'll receive an International Vaccination Certificate detailing the jabs, the dates you had them, and how long they'll remain effective. Bring this document with you, as you may need to show it at passport control on arrival, especially for yellow fever; see the table on pp.376–377.

Vaccinations don't offer lifelong immunity, and the effectiveness of those you probably had as a child may have lapsed, so enquire about boosters. Inoculations or boosters against the following diseases are commonly offered to travellers heading to Africa:

- **Diarrhoea** The new Dukoral vaccine, not a jab but a fizzy drink, guards against some forms of travellers' diarrhoea, including that caused by *E. coli*, and cholera.
- **Diphtheria** You should already have been vaccinated (the childhood DTP jab).

- **Hepatitis A** Gamma-globulin is effective for up to five months. More expensive, but offering ten years of immunity if you have a booster, is Havrix.
- **Polio** Get a booster if your last jab was over ten years ago.
- **Rabies** Unnecessary for most people; optional if you'll frequently be handling animals, or cycling or walking extensively. The three jabs are taken over a month.
- **Tetanus** Get a booster if your last jab was over ten years ago.
- **Tuberculosis (TB)** Mainly recommended for children.
- **Typhoid** Not completely effective but still useful; may lay you low for a couple of days.
- **Yellow fever** The vaccine offers immunity for ten years and becomes effective ten days after the jab.

Insect-borne diseases

Forget about lions and crocodiles: humble mosquitoes are Africa's biggest killers, thanks to their nefarious blood-sucking habits which provide the vehicle for a host of specially adapted parasites, especially *Plasmodium*, which causes malaria. Tsetse flies are another unwelcome dinner guest, though the chances of contracting sleeping sickness from them are thankfully slim. Both are endemic to the tropics. For travellers, flies are really just a pest rather than a health threat.

Avoiding bites is the surest way to minimize the odds of catching malaria and sleeping sickness. The problem is that unless you have the patience of Job and unusually keen hand-eye coordination, swatting mozzies before they get to chew on your arm can be a thankless task as some varieties have developed the irkingly successful survival technique of preferring to fly against dark surfaces, like wooden cupboards, rather than across light surfaces where they're more easily spotted and swatted. And no matter how many you swipe, there's always one more ...

Sleeping safely

Sleeping under a mosquito net, which even the most humble guesthouses in mosquito-prone areas should provide, is essential. Conical nets hung from single points are most common, but can be too small to cover the bed properly. Much better are rectangular nets draped across a frame or bed posts, giving you more room to move about

Potential health risks by country

	Malaria	Sleeping sickness	HIV/AIDS incidence ages 15–46	Yellow fever Prevalence	Yellow fever Inoculation required ?
Algeria			0.2%		no
Angola	**	**	4	**	†
Benin	**	*	2%	**	yes
Botswana	** (north)	*	37%		†
Burkina Faso	*	*	4%	**	yes
Burundi	**	*	6%	*	yes
Cape Verde	*		0.1%	*	yes
Cameroon	**	**	7%	**	yes
Central African Republic	**	**	14%	*	yes
Chad	* (south and east)	**	5%	* (south and east)	no
Comoros	**				no
Congo, Democratic Republic	**	**	4%	**	yes
Congo, Republic	**		5%	**	yes
Côte d'Ivoire	**	**	7%	**	yes
Djibouti	*		3%		†
Egypt	* (El Fayoum)		0.2%		†
Equatorial Guinea	**	*	4%	*	†
Eritrea	**		3%		†
Ethiopia	* (under 2000m)	*	5%	*	†
Gabon	**	*	8%	**	yes
Gambia	**	*	1%	**	†
Ghana	**		3%	**	yes
Guinea-	**		10%	**	† Bissau
Guinea (Conakry)	**	**	3%	**	†
Kenya	** (except Nairobi and north)	*	7%	*	†
Lesotho			29%		†

	Malaria	Sleeping sickness	HIV/AIDS incidence ages 15–46	Yellow fever Prevalence	Inoculation required ?
Liberia	**	*	6%	**	yes
Libya			0.3%		†
Madagascar	**		2%		†
Malawi	**		14%		†
Mali	**	*	2%	*	yes
Mauritania	** (south)		0.6%	*	yes
Morocco			0.2%		no
Mozambique	**	**	12%		†
Namibia	** (north)	*	21%		†
Niger	**		1%	*	yes
Nigeria	**	*	6%	**	†
Rwanda	**	*	5%	*	yes
São Tomé and Príncipe	**		4%	*	yes
Senegal	**	*	0.8%	*	yes
Sierra Leone	**	*	7%	**	†
Somalia	*		1%	*	†
South Africa	** (north east)		22%		†
Sudan	**	**	2%	** (south)	†
Swaziland	** (lowlands)		39%		†
Tanzania	** (under 1800m)	**	9%	*	†
Togo	**	*	4%	*	yes
Tunisia			0.2%		†
Uganda	*	**	4%	*	†
Zambia	**	*	17%		no
Zimbabwe	** (except Harare and Bulawayo)		25%		†

* denotes a low, but not negligible, risk

** denotes a more serious risk that may, however, be localized

† denotes that a certificate of vaccination is required only if travelling from an endemic zone

in your sleep. However, the nets in even the poshest hotels are often full of holes: you'll appreciate bringing a needle and thread, or some packing tape. If you'll be travelling a lot in malarial zones, it's worth bring your own (rectangular) net – just be sure that it's possible to hang it from a single point.

Some places to stay prefer to rely on window screens or bug-spray, but neither is an adequate substitute for a good net. Air conditioning gets closer, but there's always one bug that seems strangely immune to the cold. Before you turn in for the night, you might want to burn mosquito coils, which are readily available locally.

Clothing, repellents and insecticides

In the evening and after dark, cover limbs, and consider using insect repellent, especially for your ankles, neck, and any other uncovered bits. Repellents don't actually repel, but mask the carbon dioxide from your skin so the critters can't find you. Sprays and deodorant-style roll-ons are the handiest products. Whatever you choose, test it out before you travel to be sure it doesn't irritate your skin. If you're bringing a mosquito net, consider buying one that's impregnated with insecticide, but be aware that the most common product, synthetic permethrin, is potentially carcinogenic. Much better would be to apply natural pyrethrum flower extract, available in pharmacies and at stores selling camping supplies.

Most repellents contain one of the following ingredients:

- **Picaridin (KBR3023)** Highly effective, non-greasy and odourless, and it's too new to have gathered much of a list of side-effects.
- **DEET (diethyl-meta-toluamide)** Just as effective and more widely available, this is a nasty oily substance that corrodes plastic. Side-effects such as rashes are occasionally reported, especially on children under 10 or if using products containing over 30 percent DEET, but it's generally considered safe so long as you apply it properly.
- **Oil of lemon eucalyptus** Plant-based protection comparable to products containing low concentrations of DEET or Picaridin. Not tested against malaria-carrying mosquitoes however, and unsuitable for children under 3.
- **Citronella oil** Extracted from lemon grass. Not widely tested, but its effectiveness appears to match that of low-concentration DEET and Picaridin products.

- **Geranium and cedar oil** Neither of these have been scientifically tested, so use them at your own risk.

Malaria

Malaria is endemic in tropical Africa (see the table on pp.376–377), accounting for at least one in seven deaths among children under 5. It's also the biggest cause of death among adults after HIV/AIDS, though it should be reassuring to know that fewer than one in a hundred infected people die from it.

The disease is caused by a parasite carried in the saliva of female *Anopheles* mosquitoes, which tend to bite in the evening and at night. Common symptoms include waves of flu-like fever, shivering and headaches. Joint pain is also characteristic, and some people have diarrhoea after the first week. The destruction of red blood cells caused by the *Plasmodium falciparum* strain of malaria, which is most prevalent in Africa, can lead to cerebral malaria (blocking of the brain capillaries by blood clots) and is also the cause of blackwater fever, in which urine is stained by excreted blood cells.

Malaria is most common in low-lying areas and around bodies of still water, meaning along the coast, around lakes, and in areas of heavy banana cultivation (the plants hold pools of stagnant water). The risk of contracting the disease increases during rains and for two months thereafter, but decreases as you gain altitude (where there are fewer mosquitoes), becoming minimal over 1400m and non-existent over 1800m. The disease has a variable incubation period of a few days to several weeks, so it's possible for it to show itself up to a month after you've returned home.

Malaria can be avoided by taking prophylactics, although no method offers one-hundred-percent protection; the best way to avoid contracting malaria is to avoid getting bitten. Pregnant women are not advised to visit malarial areas; both the disease and the prophylactics can damage the foetus.

If you think you've caught malaria, get to a doctor as soon as possible to have a blood test. Cures are readily available, which will leave you feeling thoroughly wiped out for about a week.

Anti-malarial prophylactics

Anti-malarial drugs can be bought in sub-Saharan Africa, but you won't necessarily have much choice there, and there's no real guarantee of quality (fake drugs are a problem), so it's best to buy a course before you leave home. You'll probably need a prescription. Most regimens need to be started a week before entering a malarial zone, and the drugs should never be taken on an empty stomach, lest headaches, nausea and stomach cramps follow. Test your reaction to any prophylactic by starting the course earlier than necessary, to give you time to switch to another if you react badly. Unless you're spending an extended period at high altitude, don't break your course of prophylactics, as it's vital to keep your parasite-fighting level as high as possible. The main drugs are:

- **Malarone** A combination of atovaquone and proguanil, with few if any serious side-effects. Tablets are taken daily, starting just one day before entering a malarial zone. Unsuitable for breast-feeding women.
- **Mefloquine (Lariam)** Effective and cheap, this only needs to be taken once a week, but side-effects affect a significant minority of travellers. Sleep disturbances, rashes anor trips over a month, for children weighing under 11kg, and for pregnant d dizziness are among the milder symptoms; more serious are anxiety, depression, paranoia and even hallucinations. Unsuitable for pregnant women, scuba-divers, people with liver or kidney problems, epileptics, or infants under 3. The low cost makes it worth considering for longer trips, but test your reaction to it before leaving.
- **Doxycycline** The cheapest option, doxycycline is an antibiotic, taken daily. The major drawback is that it can cause an exaggerated sensitivity to sunlight in both skin and eyes, so be sure to protect yourself. It can also cause thrush in women, reduce the effectiveness of contraceptive pills, and is unsuitable for children under 8 and pregnant women.
- **Chloroquine and proguanil** If you can't or won't take any of the above, this combination (chloroquine taken weekly, proguanil daily) provides a lower but nonetheless useful level of protection.

Sleeping sickness

Potentially fatal sleeping sickness, or trypanosomiasis, is transmitted by the blood-sucking tsetse fly in parts of sub-Saharan Africa. The flies are extremely persistent and come in swarms, but you'll be relieved to know they're only found out in the bush wherever there's big game, so you won't get bitten in towns or on the beach. Furthermore, they only bite by day. Curiously, tsetse flies don't try to fly away if you attempt to swat them, but they have evolved amazing resilience – you'll need to put quite some gumption into your swipes. One trick worth trying is to wear light-coloured clothes: the flies are attracted by dark hues (especially blue, but not red), which to their eyes resembles the colour of their favourite meals, wildebeest and buffalo. Though being bitten is painful, the bites don't linger and aren't venomous.

One or two bites are most unlikely to give you sleeping sickness, but if you get feasted on, seek local advice about presence of the disease, and see a doctor immediately should your neck lymph nodes swell up or an irregular fever develop; the quicker the disease is diagnosed, the better the chances of success in treating it.

Yellow fever

Yellow fever, a haemorrhagic disease endemic to parts of tropical Africa and South America, is passed from wild monkeys to humans by *Aedes aegypti* mosquitoes. The initial symptoms – yellowish skin and eyes – develop three to six days after infection. The mortality rate is around five percent. You can eliminate any risk by getting inoculated, which is in any case an entry requirement for many countries (see the table on pp.376–377).

Dengue fever, West Nile virus and Rift Valley fever

This trio of viral diseases are, like yellow fever, transmitted through mosquito bites. Gauging the risk in any given country is next to impossible given the lack of data for Africa, but all three diseases are rare, and not usually fatal. Unlike with malaria, there's no drug you can take to reduce the risk of infection, making avoiding mosquito bites all the more important.

Dengue occurs in sporadic epidemics. Fever, headache, muscle and joint pain, a rash and some kind of haemorrhaging (which can also show itself as bruising) are the classic symptoms. It can also feel like a bad flu. The related West Nile virus, which also gives flu-like symptoms, hit the headlines in 1999 when the disease appeared in New York, and there have since been thousands of cases across much of the USA. Africa's last major outbreak was in Congo in 1998. Rift Valley fever is prevalent along the entire eastern flank of the continent and in low-lying parts of West Africa. It primarily affects livestock and is relatively benign for humans, though around one in ten victims suffer visual impairment due to inflammation of the retina. Most cases occur as isolated epidemics.

Parasites

Malaria and sleeping sickness apart, there are a few other parasites you might encounter in Africa. One creature you might play host to is a jigger, the pupa of a fly that likes to burrow into your toes. More horrible than it sounds, this is easily dealt with by physically removing the bug with a sterilized needle or tweezers, then repeatedly dousing the cavity with iodine or another disinfectant. The cavity will heal within a few days. Unless you're planning a *National Geographic*-style expedition though swamps and jungles, you can forget about leeches (though yes, burning them off with a cigarette is the recommended way of getting rid of them).

Much more serious is bilharzia (schistosomiasis), a dangerous, common but curable disease which comes from tiny flukes (schistosomes) that live in freshwater snails and which, as part of their life cycle, leave their hosts and burrow into animal (or human) skin to multiply in the bloodstream. The symptoms are difficult to diagnose: a rash or itchy skin appears a few days after infection, and you may also feel severe fatigue and pass blood. After that you won't experience any further symptoms until a month or two later, when fever, chills, coughs and muscle aches may kick in. If it's left untreated, internal organs can be permanently damaged, and paralysis is also known, although all these effects are thankfully rare. The snails favour stagnant water, so the usual recommendation is never to swim in, wash with, or even touch lake water that can't be vouched for. Salt water is fine, as are well-maintained swimming pools.

Contagious diseases

The following contagious diseases include some the most frightening causes of death known to man. With the exception of tuberculosis, they're thankfully extremely rare.

Tuberculosis

The bacillus causing tuberculosis affects the lungs, and was on the decline until the appearance of HIV/AIDS in the 1980s – people with depressed immune systems are more likely to catch it. Roughly one in two hundred Africans are infected, not all of whom are contagious. Children can be inoculated with the BCG vaccine; adults have to rely on treatment, via antibiotics.

Transmission is through inhaling minute particles coughed out by an infected person whose company you have shared over an extended period, or by consuming unpasteurized dairy products infected with the bovine form of the disease. If you think you might have contracted TB (you shouldn't be – travellers are at low risk), get a tuberculin skin test.

Ebola and Marburg

The world's ghastliest disease, publicized to the hilt by sensationalist media and Hollywood, is Ebola, a viral haemorrhagic fever that kills at least sixty percent of its victims. Yet its global death toll since 1976, when it was first identified in northern Zaïre (now DR Congo) and Sudan, is under 1500. Subsequent epidemics have occurred in both Congos, Gabon and Uganda, with minor outbreaks reported in Ivory Coast and Liberia. Ebola tends to kill so quickly that it has no time to propagate, so outbreaks remain extremely localized. Monkeys are the infectious vector; subsequent transmission between humans is by physical contact. The symptoms appear four to ten days after exposure.

The related and equally deadly Marburg virus was recognized in 1967 when simultaneous outbreaks occurred in Germany and Yugoslavia. The victims were laboratory workers testing polio vaccines on Ugandan green monkeys. Infected humans are contagious. Serious epidemics have occurred in northeastern DR Congo (1998–2000) and in northern Angola (2004–2005), with isolated cases reported from western Kenya, Uganda and Zimbabwe.

Leprosy

Deformed lepers begging on street corners are a common sight in African cities. Leprosy, also called Hansen's Disease, is not particularly contagious, with most cases being passed from parent to child rather than to strangers. It's also very rare (Africa's highest infection rate, in Mozambique, is less than one in three thousand). Skin lesions and sensory loss in skin are the first signs of infection, at which stage leprosy is treatable.

Food and water

The shortest path to falling ill is not taking care with what you eat or drink. Dirty drinking water especially can wreak all sorts of havoc on your digestive system, and is also the vector for more serious maladies such as cholera. African sewage systems, where they exist, were mostly constructed in colonial times and are now well past their prime, and contamination of drinking water supplies in parts of sub-Saharan Africa is common enough. If you're only staying a short time, it pays to be scrupulous.

Water filters and purification

Most tourists choose to give tap water – and ice – a wide berth. Bottled purified water is sold everywhere. A much cheaper alternative is to purify water yourself. If you'll be travelling extensively in out-of-the-way areas, a portable filter is best, which you can buy in any travel supply store or travel clinic. Alternatively, filtering water through a fine muslin cloth and then boiling it for ten minutes should also dispense with bugs, but means carrying a camping stove and gas canisters. Much more practical is to purify water chemically. After filtering it though a muslin cloth, use two-percent-iodine tincture (four drops per litre), or – for an especially vile taste – chlorine tablets, and wait twenty minutes.

Food

For longer stays, re-educate your stomach rather than fortifying it; it's impossible to travel around Africa without exposing yourself to strange bugs. Take it easy at first, wash and peel fruit, and be wary of ice creams and salads served in cheap or empty restaurants, as well as the pre-cooked contents of their ubiquitous display cabinets.

What you eat is also important. Fruit and vegetables in season are invariably tastier and safer, as are ingredients grown or raised locally. Meat, fish and shellfish should always be thoroughly cooked. While milk is a crucial component of the diet of cattle-herding societies, dairy products are rarely sold, and then only in urban centres. Packaged pasteurized cheese, milk and yoghurt is usually fine, but be careful – heat can spoil everything quite magnificently.

To be sure of safe food, it's best to eat what locals eat, and in the busiest restaurant you can find. Remember too that food quality is rarely related to cost. In fact, you're much less likely to catch a bug in a dirt-cheap lean-to that only serves two kinds of stew than in a place trying to catch passing tourists with ambitious menus.

Travellers' diarrhoea

Travellers' diarrhoea is the catch-all for anything that turns your stomach or twists your tubes, and can usually be traced back to a badly prepared meal, or having drunk something you shouldn't have. E. coli is the habitual offender. As travellers have little resistance, getting the runs is something you should expect (or feel justifiably smug about should you give it the slip). If you're really concerned, consider having a Dukoral injection before you go.

Diarrhoea, and vomiting, are your body's methods of expelling toxins – and though effective, make a daunting prospect out of having to travel long distances if you're having to run to the toilet every half hour. Effective anti-diarrhoeal remedies include codeine phosphate and loperamide (trade name Imodium), both available locally. These work by stalling your digestive system rather than dealing with the source of the problem, but are useful if you must travel. If diarrhoea or other symptoms persist, see a doctor. Avoid jumping for antibiotics at the first sign of trouble: they don't work on viruses, and risk annihilating your gut flora, which may result in long-term disequilibrium in your digestive system.

Dysentery and giardia

If you get diarrhoea with traces of blood, there's a good chance you've caught dysentery, especially if you're also suffering from intestinal inflammation, abdominal pain or stomach cramps, or pain when defecating. Vomiting and fever may also occur. Get a stool test done as soon as you can to determine the strain, as the treatment varies. As with travellers' diarrhoea, it's important to keep your body hydrated, no matter how rough you feel.

Giardia is something you'll know you've got if you catch it. Apart from making you feel generally ill and drowsy, it makes you pass wind – from both ends of your body – that smells worse than a sewer. The bug generally works itself out after two or three days, but may recur after a few weeks. Both giardia and dysentery are easily treatable.

Cholera

You're most unlikely to catch cholera, although outbreaks are a regular occurrence throughout Africa, usually coinciding with heavy rains. Areas lacking basic sanitation and sewerage systems are most at risk. The Dukoral vaccine offers two years of immunity.

Cholera symptoms are fever and chronic diarrhoea; most attacks are relatively mild and clear up naturally after a few days, but if untreated, the sudden and severe dehydration they cause can be fatal. Treatment is simple: lots of oral rehydration therapy (see p.395) or, in severe cases, rehydration fluid administered through a drip. Antibiotics can help but aren't essential.

Heat, sun and humidity

Sunshine, lots of it, is likely to be one of the reasons why you're considering Africa, but too much is also one of the reasons travellers fall ill, especially when coming from sun-challenged climes. Apart from the specific advice below, get enough rest wherever you are: running around all day in the heat tires unaccustomed bodies, and will make you more susceptible to other maladies.

Sunburn

Once you arrive, it's important not to overdose on sunshine, even if you *are* an Englishman or a crazy canine – the powerful heat and bright light can really mess up your system. Just twenty minutes of sunbathing a day, either in the morning or in the evening, over a week is quite enough for a tan you can show off back home, and will minimize the chances of sunburn, heat stroke or skin cancer. Cover exposed skin with high factor sunblock (SPF 30 or there-abouts), and wear a wide-brimmed hat and UV-shielded sunglasses. You might even consider pretending you're German and wear socks in your sandals, though a more glamorous solution would be to carry an umbrella; you can buy one locally. When swimming or snorkelling, it's very easy to burn your back, shoulders and calves as you won't feel the heat, and most sunblocks will wash off no matter how waterproof they claim to be. If you don't want to wear sunblock around reefs (a kind thought, as coral polyps are unlikely to appreciate it), don a T-shirt and light trousers. To alleviate sunburn, aloe vera cream, calamine lotion, yoghurt, or a mixture of olive oil and lemon juice helps. Remember also that it's easy to burn at high altitude where the sun is more powerful.

Drinking, heat stroke and heat rashes

Sunburn is one half of the equation; keeping cool and hydrated are vital to staying healthy. Apart from covering yourself up (think of Saharan nomads), drink plenty of water, juice or soft drinks throughout the day. Alcohol and caffeine-packed drinks like coffee are no substitutes. If you urinate less frequently than usual, or your urine is dark, then you're dehydrated.

While cold drinks provide immediate relief, don't shirk on hot ones either. Saharan nomads drink tiny glasses of piping hot tea throughout the day; though it sounds unlikely, the effect is strangely cooling. Eating well is also important: prefer balanced meals to big ones, and be sure to have breakfast. Missing it makes you more likely to overheat as the sun gets higher, and you'll have trouble stemming the tide of sweat if the day's first meal is

When in the Sahara, do as the Saharans do

When I started my bicycle ride across the desert, I was spectacularly unprepared. The journey, in fact, was an unplanned diversion from my original plan to cycle around Europe. By the time I'd crossed the Atlas Mountains, reducing the weight of my gear was the primary concern. Two heavy padlocks and a sturdy frying pan were first to go, exchanged for a couple of fake silver and turquoise necklaces, and a *chèche* – what Moroccans call the *litham* turban made famous by the Tuareg.

I admit to having enjoyed a fleeting and very vain flush of pleasure at picturing myself as a latter-day Lawrence of Arabia, though for the most part I felt rather silly wearing my *chèche*, at first. Three thousand kilometres later, beyond the Senegal River, the *chèche* had become my most treasured possession. Not only had it given me that mad-Englishman-in-the-desert look, but it also worked miracles in protecting me from the Saharan summer. Sure, completely wrapping my head and face made me feel hotter at first (I also wore a long sleeved shirt and trousers), but in less than an hour after setting off each day, the magic got to work. By completely covering my skin, and just as importantly my mouth and nose, the *chèche* hugely reduced my water intake. In fact, just four or five litres of water sufficed for a full day's cycling (or pushing) the bike though sand.

Back home, when I read that the British Army was recommending twelve litres as the minimum daily water intake, my *chèche* and I, how we scoffed!

– Jens Finke

a weighty lunch. If you tend to sweat heavily, sprinkle extra salt on your food.

Heat stroke, or hyperthermia, begins when you stop sweating but are still hot. The initial symptoms are exhaustion and hot skin, followed by fever, cramps, rapid pulse and vomiting. Subsequently, a victim can suffer mental confusion and even hallucinations. It's a dangerous condition that needs immediate attention: the victim should be removed to as cool a place as possible, covered in wet towels or have their clothes soaked regularly with water, and be given a rehydration mix to sip. Victims may not necessarily feel thirsty, so you may need to force them to drink.

Many people get occasional heat rashes, especially at first on the coast where your skin feels the heat more keenly thanks to the humid air. Cotton clothes, and a warm shower to open the pores, should help.

Fungal infections

Fungal infections such as ringworm thrive in humid, tropical regions, and can be avoided by not using used soap in cheap hotels, or towels if badly washed or still damp – better to bring your own. An excess of alcohol, or generally feeling out of sorts, makes you more susceptible to infections. Don't go wandering around barefoot, wash frequently and dry yourself well. Treatment is with zinc oxide powder or a commercial fungicidal cream.

Animal hazards

The fact that each and every case of a tourist being mauled, trampled or eaten by African wildlife gets splashed all over the world's tabloids reflects the fact that such occurrences are extremely rare, and that – certainly for visitors – Africa's celebrated wildlife isn't half as bad as you might fear. You won't have any trouble if you heed the rules of the park or reserve you're in, which usually means never leaving the safety of your vehicle except at specially designated places such as picnic sites, or else being accompanied by an armed ranger. Outside the parks, heed local advice about camping spots, take a guide when hiking, and resist the temptation to swim in lakes and rivers if they're likely to be inhabited by hippos and crocodiles.

You can also forget about rabies unless you go around petting every stray dog or are cycling (dogs hate bikes for some reason). Strays tend to be sorry, skulking creatures only too wary of past mistreatment.

Mammals

First off, rest assured that most of Africa's most hazardous species tend to be safely tucked away in national parks and reserves. Predators such as lions and leopards are quite obviously dangerous, but fellow predators such as humans are not normally part of their diet, so whenever they get too close for comfort – most infamously at the Serengeti's campsites – they're more motivated by curiosity than by hunger. The sheer bulk of elephants also makes them a threat, especially in areas that were devastated by poachers. Elephants do indeed have long memories, but will not charge before giving due warning: flapping their ears, stomping their feet and perhaps trumpeting, all of which will instantly turn your legs into jelly.

Far more dangerous are buffaloes, whose unpredictable temper and bad eyesight encourages them to charge at things they can't see too well; they also like to take siestas in bushes, so always take a guide with you whenever walking in areas likely to be inhabited by them. In terms of deaths caused, Africa's most dangerous mammals are hippos. Don't be misled by the lugubrious appearance of these blubbery beasts: they're quite capable of capsizing small boats, and on land can out-run humans. The golden rule is to never get yourself between a hippo and water, lest it feel threatened.

Scorpions, spiders and snakes

Scorpions and spiders abound but are hardly ever seen unless you deliberately turn over rocks and logs. Scorpion stings are painful but almost never fatal (clean the wound and pack with ice to slow down the spread of the venom, then see a doctor), while spiders are mostly quite harmless. Although the "scorpion in a shoe" nightmare is more of an Asian thing, it would be wise to knock out your footwear and check your clothes each morning just in case.

Snakes are common, but again, the vast majority are harmless, and to see a snake at all, you'd need to search stealthily; walk heavily and most species obligingly disappear. Still, if you plan on doing much walking, wear boots, socks and long trousers, and be wary of caves, wood piles and of turning over large rocks. The most dangerous species are the puff adder (on account of its lazy disposition and camouflage, which makes it more likely to be trodden on), East and Southern Africa's black mamba, the North African carpet viper, and Southern Africa's yellow or Cape cobra. The Gaboon viper and boomslang hardly ever attack humans.

Reported cases of snake bite are uncommon, antivenin is not usually necessary, and deaths resulting from snake bites are extremely rare. The biggest danger is in fact shock, which could lead to a heart attack. If you do get bitten, don't try to suck out the venom (a thoroughly discredited technique), but instead apply a tourniquet, release it briefly every fifteen minutes and seek immediate medical attention.

Other bugs and creepy-crawlies aren't worth worrying about: African spiders are far more benign than their American and Australian cousins, even if the size of some of them may rattle arachnophobes.

Marine stings

Apart from the slim possibility of shark attack when surfing, snorkelling or diving in South Africa and Mozambique, and the problem of getting cut on jagged coral rocks (wear sandals or flip-flops), the only other hazards are stings. Ones from sponges, corals and jellyfish are generally easily treated with vinegar; stings from sea urchins, crown of thorns starfish, stingrays and surgeonfish are treated by applying scalding water to the wound. The only really serious stings are from cone shells (you shouldn't be handling marine life in any case), for which immediate medical attention is needed.

Sexually-transmitted diseases

An estimated 26 million Africans live with HIV. The prevalence of minor ulcers from other sexual diseases is thought to account for the high incidence of heterosexually-transmitted HIV. Infection rates vary greatly from country to country, and are included in the table on pp.376–377. Particularly high-risk areas are towns and cities, settlements along major highways, and – increasingly because of sex tourism – beach resorts. The highest infection rates are in Southern Africa (with Botswana and Swaziland most badly hit; incredibly, almost two-fifths of their adult populations are infected).

Obviously, rates of infection among prostitutes are much higher, rarely under fifty percent, and in places over ninety percent. Needless to say, unprotected sex is a deadly gamble you should never accept. Female visitors should also be aware that "beach boy" lovers often romance for a living, no matter the blandishments lavished on that week's flame. Standard advice is to avoid sexual contact or to use condoms. Locally-produced brands can be reliable, but as there's no guaranteed quality control, if you're hoping for a fling you'd do well to bring some from home. HIV is not transmissible through mosquito bites.

Children's health

Get fully informed about the health risks to children before deciding where, and just as importantly when, to go. Rural healthcare facilities are few and far between in Africa, so think long and hard about taking the kids off the beaten track for longer than a day or two, particularly if they won't settle easily or don't enjoy robust health. Sunglasses are essential for children as their eyes are more susceptible to UV radiation than those of adults. Be especially careful in avoiding sunburn and sunstroke; ensure to take broad-brimmed hats and clothing offering adequate protection, and remember that children are particularly susceptible to the effects of dehydration. For tiny tots, perfect bug protection when in a cot or a pram is a freestanding mosquito net (it looks like a tea cosy), available in travel stores. Recommendations for vaccinations and anti-malarial medicines vary according to a child's age and weight, and remember that under-7s may not have completed their DTP vaccinations (which may need to be accelerated), so seek advice from a qualified medical practitioner or travel clinic well in advance.

For sensible and practical health advice on travelling with children, get hold of *Take the Kids Travelling* by Helen Truszkowski (Lonely Planet), or *Your Child's Health Abroad* by Dr Jane Wilson-Howarth and Dr Matthew Ellis (Bradt Publications). Lonely Planet's Thorn Tree website (Ⓦthorntree.lonelyplanet.com) is a good place to seek the advice of fellow mums and dads; jump to the "Kids To Go" section.

Healthcare in Africa

Should you be unlucky enough to need medical attention on your travels, first port of call for everything but major emergencies should be a clinic or doctor's surgery. This will be especially helpful for diagnostic tests, malaria treatments, heat-related conditions and gastric infections. Most towns with sizeable expatriate populations will have at least one recommendable clinic, and perhaps even a reliable dentist. Even out in the sticks, you may be pleasantly surprised at the medical facilities that religious missions have managed to drum up, but if you can seek treatment in a town, your chances of getting adequate attention are better. Try to resist the temptation of letting things linger until you get home: local doctors are well attuned to local maladies, and much more likely to diagnose them correctly than would a doctor outside Africa.

Some drugs that require prescriptions back home are sold openly in pharmacies, so if you're absolutely sure of what you need, you could save yourself a consultation fee by going direct to the nearest pharmacy. Generic drugs are commonplace. Pharmacies in cities and major towns are well stocked, but elsewhere the choice of drugs can be limited to the barest essentials, the not-so-curious exception

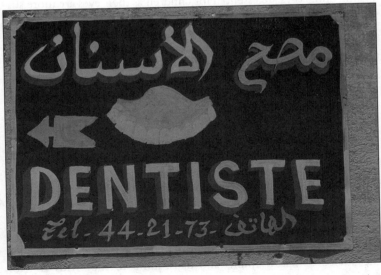

△ A dental surgery in Marrakesh advertises its services

being fungicidal creams. Pills are often sold individually, which facilitates the distribution of fake or sub-standard medicines. So, if you need expensive drugs worth faking, seek out a local clinic's advice about where to buy the genuine thing.

Most African countries lack state-run ambulances, and even when such a service exists, don't expect them to come in a hurry. Much more efficient are the ambulance services provided (for a fee) by private security services, the same ones whose signs are posted outside every fenced-in expatriate residence in town. Pre-hospital paramedic care is poor to non-existent, however, so if you really need to get treatment in a hurry and aren't too messed up, simply catching a taxi to the nearest hospital is the quickest way.

The main hospitals are state-run affairs which, with the exception of those in South Africa and, to a lesser degree, North Africa, suffer from the perennial curses of underfunding, inadequate supplies and low pay. If you're warded, you may be expected to pay on a daily basis for the treatment, and "gifts" are always welcome, and sometimes expected: hospital staff are poorly paid by any standards, and for that matter may not have been paid for months. More reliable are private hospitals, the best of which are little different to those you might find back home.

Lastly, obtain receipts for everything you pay, so you can claim something back on your insurance policy.

Traditional medicine

Given the high cost of drugs, and the perceived inefficacy of some "Western-style" treatments (particularly against AIDS), it's no surprise that traditional medicine has kept a big following in Africa. In contrast to Western medicine, the African approach is holistic, combining credible ethno-botanical knowledge and skills with social and cultural elements.

Crucial to the concept of traditional African medicine is that a disease, or its symptoms, are considered to be merely outward signs of a deeper malaise. As such, treatment involves not just the medicine itself, but environmental precautions (sweeping out houses, fumigation), changing diets, and a good measure of psychology. The practice of conjuring up ancestral spirits and obliging the patient to undergo strange and often incomprehensible rituals, rooted in local beliefs and superstitions, bolsters the

Assembling a first-aid kit

Commercially packaged first-aid kits for travellers err on the site of caution: you'll save money and bag space by only buying items you might actually need. The most common medicines are available locally, so there's no need to take a mass of drugs and remedies unless you'll be spending extended periods way off the beaten track, say in the Sahara. If you get tubes of cream or salve, ensure that the tube is plastic (or empty the contents into a small jar), as metal tubes invariably spring leaks. The following items might be worth buying in advance.

Anti-diarrhoeal tablets. See p.365.

Antiseptic cream

Cold remedy If leaving home in winter, when you might catch a cold on the plane.

Disinfectant Alcohol or alcohol swabs, iodine tincture or tea tree oil.

Equipment Tweezers and scissors (both found in Swiss Army knives). Needles and syringes are unlikely to find use, but may give you peace of mind.

Fungicide See p.388.

Insect bite cream Antihistamine cream, calamine lotion, or just toothpaste – all can reduce swelling and itching when rubbed on bites.

Insect repellent See p.378.

Lip-salve

Mosquito net Even the cheapest guesthouses should have bed nets, but bring one if you'll be camping, or travelling rough south of the Sahara; see p.375.

---

patient's expectation of being cured, and with the mind pointing the right way, it's easier for the body to follow. Music, as part of healing rituals, can also play a role. It's well known that certain rhythms and pitches have a modulating effect on brain waves, and some believe this hastens the healing process. Particularly hypnotic sounds may also be associated with summoning up the spirits of the dead who, it's believed, can act as intermediaries between God and the living to bring cures or relief. Some spiteful spirits may even have caused illness, or may be possessing the victim; bringing them out into the open using music or magic gives the doctor a better chance of confronting them.

It's not all in the mind, of course. In all cities and towns, villages and markets, you'll see men or women sitting beside impressive spreads of glass bottles containing bewildering arrays of natural cures: dried herbs, peeled bark, gnarled roots, powders, ointments,

Pain relief Aspirin or paracetamol. A natural remedy for headaches is any menthol-and-camphor-based essential oil (eg. Olbas Oil): rub drops on your temples, under your ears and on the nape of your neck.

Plasters Fabric, not synthetic. If you'll be doing things like mountaineering or rafting, pack gauze dressing, surgical tape and wound-closure strips.

Rehydration mix Basically one part salt to eight parts of sugar; to use, add nine teaspoons per litre of water.

Skin care Avoid taking a mountain of cosmetics. See p.386 for advice on sun cream.

Vitamin tablets Only needed in deserts and semi-arid areas.

Water purifier See p.384.

Prescription drugs

Allergy medication

Antibiotics Given the often disease-specific usage of the dozens of antibiotics out there, buying a course beforehand isn't recommended unless you're allergic to penicillin. If you start a course of antibiotics, see it through – abandoning it increases the odds of bacteria becoming resistant.

Diamox For altitude sickness; useful above 3000m.

Emergency malaria treatment If you'll be spending weeks away from civilization.

rocks and stones, even bugs and lizards. All have their uses in treating specific diseases, even without the mental tribulations of a visit to a traditional healer.

To find a healer, just ask around: everyone will have their favourite. For more serious treatment, some ethnic groups are renowned for their healing prowess, so much so that people from other regions will often be prepared to travel vast distances for extra–powerful treatment.

14

Staying out of trouble

No one knows caution as regrets
Embu proverb, Kenya

Other than avoiding the countries and regions mentioned on p.188, heeding common sense is the most useful piece of advice we can give for staying safe and sound while travelling around Africa. In fact, the main hassle is really just that: hassle. First-timers fresh off a plane are a tempting and visible target for hustlers and touts, especially in tourist areas, where they'll try to sell you anything from tours or hotel bedrooms to drugs or even their company. With clean clothes, new luggage, a little awkwardness, and – if you're white – perhaps rather pasty skin, you'll stick out a mile. Dressing down might help a bit, as might a few sessions on a sunbed before leaving home, but by and large there's nothing much you can do to avoid looking wet behind the ears early on. So, for your first few days, be especially wary of propositions from perfect strangers: you want to minimize the chances of getting conned or talked into buying things you might neither want nor need.

Once you've got a feel for the place, though, you'll find yourself relaxing and behaving more normally, and that in itself will remove a lot of the potential pitfalls. And, by following the advice in this chapter, you should hopefully be wondering what on earth all the fuss about safety was about when it's time to leave.

Robbery and theft

Rural Africa tends to be extremely safe, with robbery and theft often unheard of. Urban Africa is a completely different story, especially in big cities, which are magnets for rural Africans looking for a better life. Unfortunately, the majority wind up trying to eke out a living by any means possible. It should be comforting to know though that even in cities with the worst reputations for crime, namely Lagos, Nairobi and Johannesburg, only a handful of travellers run into real problems.

Still, walking unaccompanied in big towns and cities at night can be asking for trouble, and even by day there are parts of town where you shouldn't be walking around, at least not with valuables on you. Areas to be particularly wary of are crowded suburbs, the streets around ferry ports and docks, bus stations and train stations – especially when arriving – and anywhere with inadequate or nonexistent street lighting. Note also that there are always more pickpockets about at the end of the month, when people are

△ Tourist police on duty in Egypt

carrying the salaries they've just been paid. Good guidebooks will mention specific areas to avoid, but seeking local advice is always wise; the fact that you're a tourist means that such advice will tend to err on the side of caution.

Although your chances of being robbed are slim, you should nonetheless be conscious of your belongings and never leave anything unguarded. The easiest way around all this is not to take valuables with you unnecessarily, and to travel around a city by taxi whenever you're carrying your bags or have no idea of your bearings. It should go without saying that you shouldn't wear anything that looks expensive, whether jewellery, sunglasses or watches; even certain brands of sports shoes (sneakers) can be tempting. Similarly, try to avoid carrying valuables in those handy off-the-shoulder day bags or even small rucksacks, as these provide visible temptation. Old plastic bags are a much less conspicuous way of carrying cameras. It's best to carry money, passports and other documents in a money belt hidden under your clothes (see p.286).

Most of Africa's ATMs tend to be either inside the banks, or in individual cubicles that, often enough, are watched over by a security guard. If the machine is on the street, get a friend to look out for you while your back is turned. Avoid withdrawing money at night, too, and don't linger once you've collected your cash. It can be worth investing in a taxi to the ATM and back. After changing money, be sure to stash it all away in a money belt or somewhere else that's out of sight before heading back out on to the street. The more surreptitiously you can do this, the less chance there is that someone will finger you as a potential target for robbery – one more reason for not changing money on the street.

If you do get mugged, don't resist, since the crook may have a knife or a gun. It will be over in an instant and you're unlikely to be hurt. You'll have to go to the nearest police station for a statement to show your insurance company, though you may well be expected to pay for it. You can usually forget about enlisting the police to try and get your stuff back – lack of resources, corruption, and perhaps other more pressing matters will see to that.

As angry as you may feel about being robbed, it's worth trying to understand the desperation that drives men and boys to risk their lives for your things. Thieves caught red-handed are usually mobbed – and occasionally killed – so if you shout "Thief!", be ready to intercede once you've retrieved your belongings.

Keeping things secure in hotels

Losing your belongings from a locked hotel bedroom can be a devastating experience, especially if it means cutting short your holiday, but thankfully this is most unlikely to occur. In all my time in Africa, mostly staying in dirt-cheap guesthouses, the only thing I ever lost from a bedroom was a couple of oranges to a hungry maid.

Obviously, the more an establishment relies on a bar for its income, the less secure its rooms might be. Room keys, too, are often so simple that they'd open every other door in the country; you could bring your own padlock, but it won't fit all doors, assuming there's even something the padlock could fasten onto.

If you decide to leave things with the management, get an itemized receipt, and ensure that it's the manager, not just the receptionist, that you're leaving your stuff with. Otherwise, the best way to avoid pilfering or outright theft is not to leave things lying about openly. Having a sturdy suitcase with a proper lock is obviously ideal, but burying stuff in the bottom of your rucksack and closing all bags will at least serve to deter temptation. Hiding stuff between a mattress and bed frame is also usually safe, at least judging by the amount of accumulated grime under most hotel mattresses.

Safe travels

When renting a car, you might feel a little safer choosing one of the lowlier models, especially if it's a four-wheel drive you need; the latest gas-guzzlers are more tempting targets, having a far greater resale value on the black market. On public transport, be alert to pickpockets and bag-slashers and -snatchers, especially at crowded transport terminals, and on overnight trains, and always keep your bags close and within view (standing over them while waiting is a good deterrent). Travelling in a group is an advantage, as someone can always be tasked to keep an eye on things.

If you're in a compartment of an overnight train or ferry, keep the door and window locked when you're asleep or outside. Be especially careful when the train pulls in at main stations, or when the ferry docks at major ports. You should also be wary of people looking for a spare seat in first- or second-class (genuine passengers always have numbered tickets corresponding to a particular compartment) and of passengers without bags – they may walk off with yours. If you really get suspicious, stay awake until the ticket inspector comes round. In third-class you'll probably have to stay awake all night or else stash your valuables out of reach (in a bag under your seat hemmed in by other people's bags, for example). All this is not to say that you should be paranoid, but just that you shouldn't drop your guard.

The cops, and other big potatoes

"Big potato" is the rather magnificent Tanzanian nickname for powerful men, and sometimes women: politicians, policemen, and officials all the way along the line, from petty clerks to director-generals and even presidents. All can succumb to the temptation of bending or ignoring rules in order to return favours, or may put up obstacles in the hope of eliciting a bribe. This is nowhere more obvious than in West and Central Africa where, if you need a permit for something, or to extend your visa, you can expect a good number of requests for "gifts" along the way. In Egypt there's a longstanding tradition of baksheesh, which at its most innocuous is simply giving a tip, but has a more glorified form in which you grease someone's palm to bend the rules or do you a favour.

Bribes are actually rarely solicited as such. In most situations requiring the oiling of palms, the "little something" will be hinted at. You might also be spun a sorry yarn concerning the official's lamentable family situation or ruined finances in the hope that you'll understand. Luckily, corruption and bribery as regards travellers is mostly a petty matter, and neither expensive nor anything to worry about.

The police, though rarely out to solicit bribes from tourists, are well worth steering clear of. Though you might sometimes hear stories of extraordinary kindness and of occasional bursts of efficiency that would do credit to any police force, in general African cops are notoriously corrupt. Drivers, for instance – even the minority who diligently respect speed limits – may well get pulled over at roadblocks manned by officers quite capable of finding something, anything, wrong with the car or with the driver's papers. The deal there is for the driver to have the option of paying a smaller "fine", so long as they're happy forgoing an official receipt.

If you need to deal with officialdom, patience, politeness, smiles and handshakes will smooth your dealings with even the most brazenly corrupt official. If you know you've done something wrong and are expected to cough up a bribe, wait for it to be hinted at and haggle over it as you would any payment. The equivalent of a few dollars should suffice to oil small wheels, so long as the infraction wasn't serious. Be aware that bribery is illegal, not that you'd ever guess. If you've done nothing wrong and are not in a rush, refusing a bribe will only cost a short delay until the official gives up on you and tries another potential source of income. If you're really getting nowhere, you can always kick up a loud fuss.

Drugs

In tourist areas popular with backpackers, you may be offered drugs at some point, usually by hustlers also offering souvenirs, dodgy tours and currency exchange. Hashish (cannabis resin) isn't all that common except in parts of North Africa, but grass (cannabis leaves or marijuana) is widely smoked and remarkably cheap. However, cannabis is almost always illegal, and authorities do make some effort to keep it under control. If you're caught in possession of it, you'll be hit with a heavy fine, and possibly imprisoned or even deported. Anything harder than cannabis is rarely sold and will obviously get you in much worse trouble if found on you.

The use of, and attitudes to, cannabis vary considerably, but you should be very discreet if you're going to indulge, and watch out who you get high with. Never buy cannabis on the street – you're almost guaranteed to be ripped off or else shopped to the police, and your embassy is unlikely to display much sympathy for drug-related offences. There are also a number of scams associated with buying drugs, the most common one being approached by fake (or real) policemen shortly after buying, who will shake you down for everything you have.

Touts and hustlers

In areas much frequented by tourists, such as beach resorts and towns serving as starting points for tours and excursions, and also at transport terminals (airports included), you'll come up against touts or hustlers. These are generally young men who latch on to tourists and become a complete nuisance by trying to flog any and every type of service or product that you might conceivably want: tours and safaris, drugs, guides, loose women (or men, or boys), recommendations for hotels and restaurants, cut-price carpets, favourable deals on ferry fares or for changing money, batiks or wood carvings, even secondhand books and newspapers. In Morocco, one guy's line of business seemed to consist entirely of boring his victims into submission: after a few hours of being trailed by the most tedious man in the kingdom, I coughed up just to get him to go away.

The Zanzibari name for this adorable species of creature is most appropriate: papasi, meaning tick. A royal pain they are, that's for sure, and they're not that easy to get rid of either ("no, thank you" too often doesn't feature in their vocabulary), but their attentions are perhaps understandable given the chasm between your wealth and their comparative poverty. It's worth remembering that local communities, even in the most touristic areas, are often completely marginalized from the tourist trade and from the profits to be made from it.

Some touts, though, can be genuinely helpful and even fun to have around (what they claim to be the town's best budget hotel may well turn out to be just that, and they can also introduce you to the exuberant local nightlife that eludes many a guidebook), but the rich pickings to be made from tourists make it far more likely that they're just looking to make a quick buck, no matter how. Some might even be thieves.

The best approach is to politely but firmly turn down unwanted offers and self-appointed helpers early on in the game. If you can't or won't pay, say so, even if you risk offending the minority who are genuinely trying to be helpful.

Scams

Most scams are confidence tricks, and though there's no reason to be paranoid (indeed, one or two scams play on a tourist's paranoia), a healthy sense of cynicism is always helpful. If you're on the sharp end of a scam, you probably won't appreciate the fact that the process of ripping you off may have been impressively elaborate, and might even have required days of work on the part of the scammer to get you to fall for the bait. Some of the world's best-known confidence tricks are African – the infamous "419" email scams, named after the section of Nigerian criminal law dealing with fraud, aim at convincing the victims (contacted via mass mailings) that they'll be paid handsomely in return for helping transfer an immense sum of money. The victim coughs up a succession of advance fees to move the transaction along (which mysteriously enough is endlessly delayed), before finally coming to his or her senses.

Of course, these email scams require unbelievable greed and stupidity on the part of the victim to work, but they can be instructive when it comes to understanding some of the scams you might encounter while travelling around. First off, remember that if something sounds too good to be true, then it almost certainly isn't true, especially if you didn't ask for it in the first place. So, if someone offers you cut-price ferry tickets, a half-price safari, or a bag of shiny stones and claims that they're diamonds, you'll know that you're about to be taken for a ride. Many products and services you'll be offered by hucksters don't even exist: some night-time ferries, trips into areas that are actually out of bounds, gold that's merely pyrites or even painted gravel...

As a traveller, you have the advantage as you're unlikely to be spending all that long in one place, so the trickster has to work quickly to spin a credible web of deception. Some scammers ultimately looking to steal your bags may ask you to mind their own bag for a while. The desired outcome is for you to think: "Well, he placed his trust in me, so why shouldn't I should trust him?" The answer is because you would never have left your valuables in the care of a complete stranger, so if anyone trusts you in a similar way, there may well be a catch.

A long-time favourite across much of Africa is men offering to change money for you at favourable rates, often at border crossings or in city centres, even where there's isn't a black market in currency. At its simplest, the scammer merely runs off with your money, but more usual is sleight of hand. You want to change, say, $100. The scammer offers you an enticing rate, and proceeds to count out the correct amount in local currency, rolls up the bills and wraps them with a string or an elastic band. Convinced that you're about to make a good deal, you hand over your cash. The scammer gives you the bundle of local currency, helpfully suggests that you not flaunt such a large amount of cash in public, and you part ways. Of course, when you open the bundle in a non-public place, you'll find that the bundle was switched for another containing only low-denomination notes, or even pieces of newspaper.

One scam that's been around for years is completely obvious, and its popularity across the continent really shows up what a greedy bunch of animals we humans can be. If a guy who has just picked up a wad of money in the street seems oddly willing to share it with you down a convenient nearby alley, you'll know you're about to be robbed.

Instability and terrorism

Despite the impression you might have formed from media coverage of Africa, only few areas are really no-go zones for tourists (these are mentioned on p.188). So long as you avoid them, you'd be extremely unlucky to unwittingly stumble into a war zone. Obviously, local advice is a good guide as to where is safe and where's not; also very useful are the travel-advisory websites listed in the Directory.

In West Africa, there is a very slight chance that your visit will coincide with a coup d'état. Though nowhere near as frequent as they once were, coups do happen from time to time, whether they're genuine attempts at grabbing power, or – very much a West African speciality – a coup monté (a "mounted coup"), which is a sham coup attempt staged by the incumbent ruler and his cronies with the aim of seeing who's loyal and who's not. Either way, coups aren't necessarily anything to worry about: civilians are rarely involved, any fighting tends to be limited to skirmishes around barracks and airports.

Inevitably, given the media barrage of post-9/11 scare-mongering, terrorism is a worry for some people, and there have been a handful of suicide bomb attacks targeting tourists in Africa, including in Egypt's Sinai Peninsula's beach resorts (and, in the 1990s, along the Nile), in Morocco (Casablanca), Tunisia (a synagogue in Jerba), Kenya (the US embassy and an Israeli-owned beach resort) and in Tanzania (also the US embassy). Shocking and horrific though those outrages were, try to keep things in perspective: tens of millions of people visit Africa each year without incident, and if you tally the number of victims, it turns out the very rare Ebola virus is a much more deadly scourge than terrorism.

15

Keeping in touch

We should talk while we are still alive
Kalenjin proverb, Kenya

Once up a time, keeping in touch from Africa was an adventure in itself. With post taking months to arrive (in parts of the continent it still does), and telephone networks so ill-equipped that you sometimes had to wait days for a connection, going to Africa was akin to vanishing, at least as far as the folks back home were concerned. It's not like that any more. The advent of mobile phones and the Internet has revolutionized African communications, and international courier services now offer fast and reliable alternatives to the continent's patchy postal services.

Getting on line

Email is by far the quickest and cheapest way of keeping in touch (and sharing digital photographs). If you don't have an email address already, get one before you go. Given that the majority of Africans are unable to afford their own computers, there are Internet cafés all over the place, particularly in urban areas. If you want to use your own laptop, PDA or Pocket PC, you'll find WiFi access in many upmarket hotels.

Curiously, Internet connectivity can be best in countries that have the worst terrestrial telephone systems, which has prompted the fast-track adoption of the very latest technologies: optical fibre networks in Rwanda, for example. Of course, it depends on where you are; in rural areas, you're most unlikely to find any kind of connection.

If you'll need to access online banking or other sensitive services, be aware that computers in Internet cafés can be riddled with malware. It may be wise to bring a CD, memory card or pen drive containing an anti virus program (Grisoft's AVG is free), a spyware sweeper such as Ad-Aware, and an alternative browser such as Opera or Firefox.

Telephones

Other than in South Africa, and throughout North Africa, the continent's fixed-line phone networks have long suffered from underfunding, congestion, power cuts and even the theft of copper wires. Given the sorry state of many such networks, Africans have embraced mobile phones with gusto: you'll see cellular masts in the unlikeliest of places, and "Crazy Frog" ring tones are sadly all the rage.

You can phone abroad from the offices of telecom companies, often found in or close to main post offices. The "traditional" method involves placing a call request with a clerk: you'll give the phone number to dial, and specify (and pay for) the amount of time you think you'll require. Then, depending on the country, you sit and wait. And wait. And perhaps wait some more. Tough luck if it's an answerphone you eventually connect to: you'll still have to cough up for it.

You can avoid this rigmarole by using coin- or card-operated phones, if they exist. You'll find them outside post offices, at bus stations, and in some bars and hotels. Some work with prepaid cards, others need to be fed coins (lots of them, if you'll be calling abroad). More convenient are private telephone bureaus, known in Anglophone countries as "assisted call centres". Sometimes they're proper businesses, other times they're just a desk outdoors with a handset. Rates are rarely much higher than in telecom offices, and can sometimes be significantly lower.

One thing to be very careful of is using phones in hotels: the rates can be stratospheric, sometimes twenty times the cost of calling from a phone office. If you must call from a hotel, check the price very carefully beforehand, and get your folks to call you back.

Internet-based phone services using VoIP technology are not yet widespread, but in Internet cafés that offer the service, you can expect to pay considerably less for an international call than were you to go through a standard phone company. You'll either get a headset, or a proper phone.

Mobile phones

If your cellular phone is GSM900/1800 (North American phones need to be triband), you should be able to use it in Africa, though don't expect to have a signal in the sticks. Phoning apart, cellphones are useful for text messages – a simple and cheap way of staying in touch. Roaming charges, however, can amount to a small fortune, so check them out beforehand with your provider at home. Invariably cheaper is changing the SIM card on your phone to a local one, easily and quickly done in most African towns: a replacement card costs a few dollars, and the skills of a "phone mechanic" for unlocking your phone (if required) come cheaply, too. Phone usage is prepaid using scratch cards bearing PIN numbers; the cards should be available wherever there's a signal. Ⓦ www.kropla.com has useful advice on using mobiles while abroad.

Mail and couriers

Snail mail is slow and unreliable in Africa, so it's only really useful for sending or receiving things other than letters. Even then, parcels can take months to arrive at their destinations, and may not arrive at all. Far safer, if more expensive, is to use an international courier such as DHL or Federal Express; couriers have offices in most African towns.

If you're planning on receiving mail via poste restante (general delivery), usually available in major towns at the main post office, ensure that people writing to you mark your surname clearly. When you go to the post office to pick things up, ask the clerk to also look under your first name (and sometimes other names), as filing can be somewhat random. You'll have to show your passport to collect your mail, and pay a small fee.

The media

Staying in touch with friends is one thing, but on a longer trip you might also want to stay abreast of news stories back home and internationally. Global editions of US and UK newspapers such as the *Herald Tribune*, *The Guardian* and various tabloids, together with magazines such as *Time*, *Newsweek* and *The Economist*, can generally be found on sale in city centres and in towns close to airports, often enough being hawked on the streets. You'll also find French and Portuguese publications for sale in, unsurprisingly, former French and Portuguese colonies.

Wherever you go, it's certainly worth sampling the local papers. Press freedom in Africa, though still far from perfect, has improved markedly since the end of the Cold War. In 2006 the pro-press-freedom organization Reporters Sans Frontières ranked several African countries, including Benin, Namibia, Ghana, Mali, South Africa and Cape Verde, ahead of Japan in terms of freedom of speech. The worst-ranked countries for press freedom included Eritrea, Ethiopia, Sudan, Libya, The Gambia, Tunisia, Somalia, DR Congo, Zimbabwe and Equatorial Guinea.

At its best, coverage of both national and international affairs in the African media can be lively and boast hard-hitting investigative journalism. The very best newspapers have their own international staff, and carry syndicated articles from well-known and respected international papers. Noteworthy here are some Kenyan publications, notably the weekly *The East African* (also published in Tanzania and Uganda).

Even the most slavishly pro-government rag can provide illuminating insights into local issues and affairs, and may even come up with a gem or two. Kenya's *Daily Nation* once carried the sorry tale of a farmer who tried to milk an elephant: amazingly, he'd managed to extract five litres before the pachyderm's mood darkened, with painful but thankfully not fatal consequences.

TV, radio and cinema

For rural Africans, radio is the most important source of information. Bringing a radio with you (be sure it receives shortwave, AM and FM) can also be a great way of getting a broad sample of a country's musical tastes (and perhaps an earful of the latest global fad you hoped you'd left behind). Some local stations carry feeds from the BBC World Service (Ⓦ www.bbc.co.uk/worldservice) or the Voice of America (Ⓦ www.voa.gov), both of which also broadcast independently on shortwave.

Satellite or cable TV is widespread in urban areas and in mid-range or upmarket hotels, where you'll find anything from the Discovery Channel to (in East Africa) interminable sermons given by Iranian clerics. Local stations can be strange and often marvellous, blending eye-opening programmes (from soap operas and other dramas to documentaries, festival reports, and sound advice on both human and animal hygiene) with international sitcoms, CNN and BBC World newsfeeds, and some sheer oddities: the only time this author ever saw professional women's wrestling was on Moroccan TV. In East Africa, Bollywood's song-and-dance dramas are always a hit, while in North Africa Egypt's home-grown soap operas have something of a cult following.

The cost of a TV set still lies beyond the purchasing power of many, so if you want to watch the box somewhere else than in your hotel bedroom, head to a bar – the wiliest of which pack in the punters with a video or DVD player. Watching a US block-buster movie dubbed into Arabic and with Chinese subtitles while sitting in a bar in, say, Timbuktu is one of those things you'll remember fondly.

Unfortunately, cinemas are a dying breed, though Nigeria and Egypt retain prolific film industries whose output you'll find screened on TV and sold on video throughout the continent. If you find a cinema open, it's always worth going: the supporting film, perhaps a video of a local music star, may be why most people coughed up the coins for a ticket – so don't be surprised if the audience suddenly gets up to dance.

First-Time Africa

Directory

Discount flight agents

Note that fares for the exact same flight can vary greatly between agents, so shop around. It's also worth noting that many online ticket agents accept bookings from any country.

eBookers UK ☎0800/082 3000, ⓦwww.ebookers.com; Republic of Ireland ☎01/241 5689, ⓦwww.ebookers.ie.

Expedia UK ☎0871/226 0808, ⓦwww.expedia.co.uk; US & Canada ☎1-800/397-3342, ⓦwww.expedia.com and www.expedia.ca; Australia ⓦwww.expedia.com.au.

Flight Centre Australia ☎133 133, ⓦwww.flightcentre.com.au; Canada ☎1-877/967 5302, ⓦwww.flightcentre.ca; New Zealand ☎0800/243 544, ⓦwww.flightcentre.co.nz; South Africa ☎0860/400 727, ⓦwww.flightcentre.co.za; UK ☎0870/499 0040, ⓦwww.flightcentre.co.uk; US ☎1-866/967 5351, ⓦwww.flightcentre.us.

Go Holidays New Zealand ☎0800/468 332, ⓦwww.goholidays.co.nz.

Harvey World Travel Australia ☎132 757, ⓦwww.harveyworld.com.au; New Zealand ☎09/968 2422, ⓦwww.harveyworld.co.nz; South Africa ☎011/452 6394, ⓦwww.harveyworld.co.za.

North South Travel UK ☎01245/608 291, ⓦwww.northsouthtravel.co.uk.

Opodo UK ☎0871/277 0090, ⓦwww.opodo.co.uk.

Orbitz US ☎1-888/656-4546, ⓦwww.orbitz.com.

Travel Cuts US ☎1-800/592-2887, Canada ☎1-888/246-9762, ⓦwww.travelcuts.com.

travel.com.au Australia ☎1300/130 483, ⓦwww.travel.com.au.

Travelocity UK ☎0870/273 3273, ⓦwww.travelocity.co.uk; US 1-888/872-8356, ⓦwww.travelocity.com; Canada 1-877-282-2925, ⓦwww.travelocity.ca.

Travelosophy US ☎1-800/332-2687, ⓦwww.itravelosophy.com.

World Travel Centre Republic of Ireland ☎01/416 7007, ⓦwww.worldtravel.ie.

Youth travel specialists

SAYIT Travel Republic of Ireland ☎1850/487 283, ⓦwww.sayit.ie.

STA Travel Australia ☎134 STA, ⓦwww.statravel.com.au; New Zealand ☎0800/474 400, ⓦwww.statravel.co.nz; South Africa ☎0861/781 781, ⓦwww.statravel.co.za; UK ☎0871/230 0040, ⓦwww.statravel.co.uk; US ☎1-800/781-4040, ⓦwww.statravel.com.

USIT Republic of Ireland ☎01/602 1904, Northern Ireland ☎028/9032 7111, ⓦwww.usit.ie.

Round-the-world (RTW) air tickets

The following RTW specialists have online fare calculators, but given the many permutations possible on such tickets, it's best to speak to someone in person when buying. The youth travel specialists listed on p.412 also can be great for this. For advice from fellow travellers on RTW tickets and itineraries, there's no place quite like ⓦwww .bootsnall.com.

Air Brokers International US ☎1-800-883-3273, ⓦwww .airbrokers.com.

Airtreks.com US and Canada ☎1-877/AIRTREKS, ⓦwww.airtreks .com.

Circle the Planet US ☎1-800/799-8888, ⓦwww.circletheplanet.com.

JustFares.com US ☎1-800/766-3601, ⓦwww.justfares.com.

Tour operators and travel agents

A good place to start searching for an environmentally sound holiday is ⓦwww.responsible travel.com, which presents holiday options from almost three hundred companies worldwide, together with information detailing the benefits to locals for each option. There's a lot of good stuff there, and the holidays are supposedly vetted, but don't assume that everything is one-hundred-percent kosher. Though pretty much all tour companies these days claim to operate responsibly, in some cases it's just talk, and "eco-tourism" doesn't necessarily equate to being ethical. Another handy site is ⓦwww .atta.co.uk, belonging to the African Travel and Tourism Association, whose members – mostly high-quality tour companies and lodges operating in East, West and Southern

Africa – can be found through a search engine.

In the listings below, firms whose ethical and ecological credentials have particularly impressed us are marked with an asterisk. Note that most operators will accept bookings worldwide, so don't limit yourself to companies located in your home country.

* African Initiatives UK ☎0117/915 0001, ⓦwww.african-initiatives.org .uk. A registered charity working to bolster the rights of pastoralists and hunter-gathering communities in Tanzania and Ghana; they offer excellent sponsored holidays.

Africa Travel Resource UK ☎01306/880770, US ☎866/672 3274 or 831/338 2383, ⓦwww .africatravelresource.com. A leading mid-range and upmarket "outfitter" for tailor-made tours of Tanzania, Botswana and Namibia. Their website is a superb resource for all travellers.

African Offroad Tours US
☎800/816 2693 or 954/646-4395,
Ⓦwww.africanoffroadtours.com.
Dirt-bike adventures in South Africa
and Lesotho.

African Portfolio US ☎800/700-
3677 or 203/637-2977, Ⓦwww
.onsafari.com. Highly-regarded
US/Zimbabwean outfit offering
customizable packages in East and
Southern Africa.

Alken Tours US ☎800/327-9974 or
718/856-9100, Ⓦwww.alkentours
.com. Offers a wide variety of cultural, heritage, wildlife adventure
tours and educational programmes;
particularly strong on West Africa.

* Ashanti African Tours UK
☎0870/766 2283, Ⓦwww
.ashantiafricantours.com. Culture,
wildlife and history tours, including
boating and walking, in West Africa,
mainly Ghana.

Backroads US ☎800/462-2848 or
510/527-1555, Ⓦwww.backroads
.com. Cycling, hiking and safari
holidays in Kenya, Morocco, South
Africa and Botswana.

* Baobab Travel UK ☎0870/382
5003 or 01902/558 316, Ⓦwww
.baobabtravel.com. Tailor-made
packages all over Africa, with plenty
of cultural tourism.

Batafon Arts UK ☎01273/605791,
Ⓦwww.batafonarts.co.uk. Drum
and dance holidays (including workshops) in The Gambia and Guinea.

* Birding Africa South Africa
☎021/685 4081 or 082/545 8000
Ⓦwww.birdingafrica.com. The
African twitchers' leading holiday
company, covering a wide range of
sub-Saharan nations.

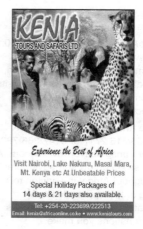
* Exodus UK ☎020/8675 5550,
Ⓦwww.exodus.co.uk. Overland truck
tours and a wide range of hiking and
cultural experiences.

Expert Africa UK ☎020/8232 9777,
Ⓦwww.expertafrica.com. Intimate
upmarket jaunts in Eastern and
Southern Africa, including a variety
of special-interest tours, that use
only the very best accommodation.

* Gane & Marshall UK ☎020/8445
6000, Ⓦwww.ganeandmarshall.co
.uk. Small-group tours with plenty of
culture, in the main safari destinations, and in Ethiopia and Morocco.

* Hands Up Holidays UK
☎07765/013 631 or 0800 783 3554,
Ⓦwww.handsupholidays.com. A
simple but effective blend of ingredients: two measures of luxurious
pampering to one measure of
volunteering (building, planting or
teaching). Covers South Africa,
Uganda, Morocco, Botswana,
Namibia, Mozambique, Kenya, Libya
and Rwanda.

* Ibike (Bicycle Africa) US
☎206/767-0848, Ⓦwww.ibike.org

/ibike. No-frills, pedal-powered jaunts around Africa.

* **IntoAfrica** UK ℡0114/255 5610, ⓦwww.intoafrica.co.uk. Safaris and mountain treks in East Africa, including cultural tourism and visits to community-run development projects.

* **The Imaginative Traveller** UK ℡0800/316 2717 or 0147/366 7337, ⓦwww.imaginative-traveller.com. A wide selection of "soft adventures" throughout Africa; in addition to using only responsible local operators, the company matches any donations you make.

* **Intrepid Travel/Guerba** Australia ℡1300/360 887 or 03/9473 2626, New Zealand ℡09/520 0972, ⓦwww.intrepidtravel.com; UK (Guerba) ℡01373/826611, ⓦwww.guerba.co.uk. Adventurous small-group tours right across the continent, and overland truck tours.

* **Kuvona Cultural Tours** South Africa ℡015/556 3512, ⓦwww.kuvona.com. Tours in South Africa, Namibia and Botswana, combining wildlife and history with plenty of cultural immersion.

Mountain Madness US ℡800/328-5925 or 206/937-8389, ⓦwww.mountainmadness.com. Safety-conscious specialist in ascents of Mounts Kenya and Kilimanjaro.

* **Naturetrek** UK ℡01962/733 051, ⓦwww.naturetrek.co.uk. Natural-history holidays led by experts.

* **North South Travel** UK ℡01245/608 291, ⓦwww.northsouthtravel.co.uk. Friendly and competitive all-purpose travel agency, with one very big trump card: its profits support projects in the developing world.

Ornitholidays UK ℡01794/519445, ⓦwww.ornitholidays.co.uk. Not just birding but also primate-spotting; particularly good offerings for Gabon and South Africa.

* **Premier Tours** US ℡800/545-1910, ⓦwww.premiertours.com. Environmentally sound upmarket safaris in Eastern and Southern Africa.

Regaldive Worldwide UK ℡0870/220 1777, ⓦwww.regal-diving.co.uk. Scuba-diving breaks in all of the main Red Sea and Indian Ocean destinations.

Sahara Overland UK ⓦwww.sahara-overland.com. Highly adventurous self-drive tours by 4WD or motorbike into the heart of the Sahara, especially Algeria, Niger and Libya.

* **Tribes** UK ℡01728/685 971, ⓦwww.tribes.co.uk. A true fair-trade travel company, offering luxurious yet adventurous tours in Botswana, Egypt, Gambia, Morocco, Namibia, South Africa, Tanzania and Zambia.

* **Turtle Tours** US ℡888/299-1439 or 480/488-3688, ⓦwww.turtletours.com. Great cultural tours in the Sahara and throughout West Africa's Sahel.

Wilderness Travel US ℡800/368-2794 or 510/558-2488, ⓦwww.wildernesstravel.com. An impressive array of upmarket holidays in less well trodden destinations, including Libya, Ethiopia, Ghana, Madagascar and Niger's corner of the Sahara.

Volunteering

AFS Worldwide ⓦ www.afs.org. One of the world's oldest and largest volunteering organizations for both adults and students, its philosophy being one of intercultural exchange. Its African projects are in Ghana and South Africa.

Australian Volunteers International Australia ⓦ www.australianvolunteers .com. Placements of up to two years for teachers, health professionals and other skilled hands.

Earthwatch Institute Australia, UK & US ⓦ www.earthwatch.org. Not-for-profit organization offering environmental and archeological research projects, primarily for paying volunteers.

Frontier UK ⓦ www.frontier.ac.uk. Active in Madagascar and Tanzania, Frontier places paying volunteers in schools, development projects or marine conservation work. One month upwards.

Peace Corps US ⓦ www .peacecorps.gov. Places Americans with specialist qualifications or skills in one- or two-year postings.

Raleigh International UK ⓦ www .raleighinternational.org. Paying participants aged 17–24 join four-to-ten-week expeditions combining hands-on environmental and community work with a dash of adventure. Older volunteers get to look after the participants, and manage projects locally.

Teaching & Projects Abroad UK ⓦ www.teaching-abroad.co.uk; US & Canada ⓦ www.projects-abroad .org. Placements from two weeks to a year for teachers, healthcare workers, journalists, conservationists, vets and students, in Morocco, Senegal, Ethiopia, Ghana, Swaziland and South Africa.

Volunteers for Peace US ⓦ www.vfp.org. A not-for-profit organization with links to a huge international network of volunteer work camps.

Voluntary Service Overseas (VSO) UK ⓦ www.vso.org.uk. A government-funded organization that places skilled volunteers on various projects around the world.

Voluntary Service Overseas Canada Canada ⓦ www.vsocanada .org. Affiliated to the British VSO.

Charities and NGOs

ActionAid International ⓦ www .actionaid.org. Effective poverty alleviation on all fronts, from the provision of education and healthcare to disaster relief.

The Dian Fossey Gorilla Fund ⓦ www.gorillafund.org. Works to preserve gorillas and their habitats.

Friends of Conservation ⓦ www .foc-uk.com. Supports wildlife conservation and community development projects in Southern and East Africa.

The Jane Goodall Institute Ⓦwww .janegoodall.org. Primate conservation worldwide, working particularly to save Africa's chimpanzees.

Oxfam Ⓦwww.oxfam.org. Founded in 1942, Oxfam has much more to it than emergency relief operations, its primary objective being sustainable development through the establishment of equitable economic and social conditions.

Survival International Ⓦwww .survival-international.org. Militant campaigners for the rights of indigenous people worldwide, including Africa's San (Bushmen) and Pygmies, Maasai, Nuba and others.

Tourism Concern Ⓦwww .tourismconcern.org.uk. Campaigns for ethical and fairly traded tourism; its website is a gold mine of information for travellers.

WWF International Ⓦwww.panda .org. Funds over 2000 environmental projects worldwide; founded in 1961.

Official advice on international trouble spots

Australia Department of Foreign Affairs Ⓦwww.smartraveller.gov.au.

Canada Department of Foreign Affairs Ⓦwww.voyage.gc.ca.

Ireland Department of Foreign Affairs Ⓦwww.foreignaffairs.gov.ie.

New Zealand Ministry of Foreign Affairs Ⓦwww.safetravel.govt.nz.

UK Foreign & Commonwealth Office Ⓦwww.fco.gov.uk/travel.

US State Department Ⓦtravel.state .gov.

Medical resources for travellers

Online resources

Ⓦwww.cdc.gov/travel Diseases and preventive measures by region, from the US government's Centers for Disease Control and Prevention.

Ⓦwww.fitfortravel.scot.nhs.uk Travellers' health advice from the Scottish NHS; contains extensive country lists of diseases and how to avoid them.

Ⓦwww.travelvax.net Everything you probably didn't want to know about diseases and vaccines, with potted country-specific recommendations.

Ⓦwww.who.int/mediacentre /factsheets Detailed disease facts and figures from the World Health Organization.

Travel clinics

Travel clinics offer vaccinations, medication, equipment and general travel health advice. Your family doctor may also be useful in this regard.

UK and Ireland

The Hospital for Tropical Diseases Travel Clinic London ☎0207/388 9600, Ⓦwww.thehtd.org.

Liverpool School of Tropical Medicine UK ☎0151/708 9393, Ⓦwww.liv.ac.uk/lstm.

MASTA (Medical Advisory Services for Travellers Abroad) ☎0113/238 7575, Ⓦwww.masta-travel-health.com. Dozens of clinics across the UK.

Nomad Travel Clinics Ⓦwww.nomadtravel.co.uk. Inside Nomad Travel stores in Bristol, Southampton and London.

The Travel Clinic UK ☎028/9031 5220 in Belfast.

Tropical Medical Bureau Republic of Ireland ☎1850/487 674, Ⓦwww.tmb.ie. Sixteen clinics.

US and Canada

Canadian Society for International Health Ⓦwww.csih.org. Extensive list of travel health centres.

International Society for Travel Medicine ☎1-770-736-7060, Ⓦwww.istm.org. Has a full list of travel health clinics.

Australia, New Zealand and South Africa

Travel Doctor Australia ☎1300/658 844, Australia and New Zealand Ⓦwww.tmvc.com.au, South Africa ☎011/214 9030, Ⓦwww.traveldoctor.co.za.

Travel store

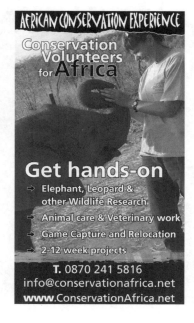

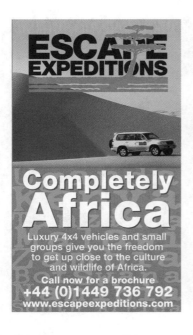

Avoid Guilt Trips

Buy fair trade coffee + bananas ✓

Save energy – use low energy bulbs ✓
– don't leave tv on standby ✓

Offset carbon emissions from flight to Madrid ✓

Send goat to Africa ✓

Join Tourism Concern today ✓

Slowly, the world is changing.
Together we can, and will, make a difference.

Tourism Concern is the only UK registered charity fighting exploitation in one of the largest industries on earth: people forced from their homes in order that holiday resorts can be built, sweatshop labour conditions in hotels and destruction of the environment are just some of the issues that we tackle.

Sending people on a guilt trip is not something we do. We know as well as anyone that holidays are precious. But you can help us to ensure that tourism always benefits the local communities involved.

Call 020 7133 3330
or visit **tourismconcern.org.uk** to find out how.

A year's membership of Tourism Concern costs just £20 (£12 unwaged) – that's 38 pence a week, less than the cost of a pint of milk, organic of course.

Fighting Exploitation in Tourism

TourismConcern

ROUGH GUIDES Complete Listing

D: Rough Guide
DIRECTIONS for
short breaks

Available from all good bookstores